DEBUTANTE

Gioia Diliberto

POCKET BOOKS

New York   London   Toronto   Sydney   Tokyo

POCKET BOOKS, a division of Simon & Schuster Inc.
1230 Avenue of the Americas, New York, NY 10020

Published by arrangement with Alfred A. Knopf
Library of Congress Catalog Card Number: 86-46006

ISBN: 0-671-66022-5

First Pocket Books printing December 1988

10 9 8 7 6 5 4 3 2 1

POCKET and colophon are trademarks of
Simon & Schuster Inc.

Printed in the U.S.A.

for Dick,
who made it possible

CONTENTS

One   CHILD   5

Two   DEBUTANTE   77

Three   SYMBOL   123

Four   WIFE   159

Five   SHADOW   189

Notes   289

Selected Bibliography   321

Acknowledgments   325

Index   327

ON A WARM spring day in 1976 a brown Mercedes with a distinctive monogram—back-to-back B's—painted in white on the sides drove through the leafy suburban streets of Lexington, Massachusetts. The car glided to a halt outside the Ida Krebs School, a colonial-style brick building nestled back from the road on Concord Avenue. A chauffeur opened the door and out stepped a frail middle-aged woman wearing a green linen dress and white high heels. Forty years earlier she had had the most famous face in America. Her translucent white skin, deep red lips, and dark hair with the prominent widow's peak had defined glamour. At the time her photograph was published everywhere; hardly a day went by without her name appearing in the newspapers. She had been the goddess of Café Society at a time when Café Society was the only society that mattered, when the world of celebrity was stuffed into a few gaudy Manhattan nightclubs and reported in a handful of purplish gossip columns.

Her spectacular debut at New York's Ritz-Carlton Hotel had attracted 1,400 aristocrats and generated as much press as a coronation. *Life* had put her on its cover. For a few years her romances, her appearances at nightclubs, her comments about the social whirl, had been reported daily in the newspapers. The public couldn't seem to get enough of her. She never held a job, never acted in the movies, never said or wrote anything significant. She could barely manage her own affairs.

Brenda Diana Duff Frazier was unofficially crowned the world's "Glamour Girl No. 1."

When she visited the Ida Krebs School, her youth and her beauty were far behind her. She was living as a recluse in a back room of a cluttered Boston apartment. She was addicted to alcohol and drugs, and surrounded by servants. The years had caricatured all the features of her youthful beauty. Her once lustrous dark hair was thin and dull. She had taken to drawing over her widow's peak with eyebrow pencil to form a large, heavy triangle in the middle of her forehead. Her milky-white skin was now a hard, powdered mask. Her once graceful curves had given way to a feeble, emaciated body.

Even leaving her apartment was a monumental task for her. Except for visits to her psychiatrist, who had been trying for almost twenty years to unravel the mysteries of her psyche, Brenda rarely left her bed. In a nightgown and bed jacket, she would lie propped up against lacy pillows, drinking steadily and swallowing pills. In the background, the television was a constant buzz of voices. A table next to her bed was littered with jars of cosmetics, Sherman cigarettes, and pill bottles. Her bed was strewn with stuffed animals, letters, and books, including the *Physician's Desk Reference,* an encyclopedia of drugs. Because she was afflicted with so many physical problems—liver disease, nausea, cramps, water retention, psoriasis, dental problems, to name only a few of her chronic ailments—doctors routinely wrote prescriptions for her. Over the years Brenda became a deft manipulator of her doctors, and her address book contained the names of dozens of them. If she couldn't get the pills she wanted from one, she went to another.

Although she rarely did anything but read, talk on the phone, and watch television, Brenda employed an army of servants. Each day they would wander in and out of her bedroom—to dust her cosmetic jars, snuffboxes, and porcelain figures; to refill her vodka glass; to write down the menu for dinner. This was a court, and she was the queen. The servants had replaced the photographers and reporters, and, like the press corps of 1938, they gave her a sense of who she was.

She would never leave the house without putting on her glamour-girl mask. So elaborate was her toilette that she was frequently two and sometimes four hours late to her appointments, even to her own parties. The contrast of dark hair and stark white face had been her trademark, and now she worked for hours to achieve the look that had made her famous. Before venturing out to the Ida Krebs School, she sat on a pink-cushioned chair in front of her dressing table, applying foundation, powder, false eyelashes, liver-red lipstick, and a black velvet stick-on beauty mark, which she glued under her right eye. Brenda's requirements for whiteness went beyond what ordinary makeup could provide, so she usually finished off her face with several powderpufffuls of rice powder mixed with cornstarch, which gave her the patina of a Kabuki dancer. As Brenda's life grew darker, the mask grew whiter.

If she was traveling at midnight from her summer home on Cape Cod back to Boston, Brenda would follow a complicated beauty routine. She would take a bath (drawn, usually, by a maid), apply a full array of cosmetics, put on her "stop and go" pearls—two strands of genuine South Sea pearls, one with a fake ruby clasp, the other with a fake emerald clasp—and pin a corsage of three pink carnations on her sable coat. If the car should break down on the highway and a strange policeman see her, she was still Glamour Girl No. 1, and she had an image to protect.

Although celebrity had ruined her life, the memory of fame consoled Brenda in her last years. She was always delighted to find a reference to herself in a book she was reading. She was thrilled when she got a call from Bette Davis or some other acquaintance from her glamour-girl days. She was also flattered to be asked, as one of Boston's more notable personalities, to grant an interview, judge a beauty contest, or give a speech.

When she spoke before the parent-teacher meeting at the Ida Krebs School, a private institution founded in 1963 for children with learning disabilities, Brenda arrived promptly at nine in the morning. Dozens of parents were seated on steps and folding chairs in the auditorium. They were shocked at first by Brenda's appearance—her Kabuki-like mask, her emaciated body, her prancing invalid's walk. But gradually they were mesmerized by the drama and poignancy of her story. She told them about the emptiness of her childhood and her family's failure to teach her proper values. She described her victimization by two powerful, selfish women—her mother and grandmother—who had used her to further their own social ambitions. She spoke of her debut, which had been torture for her, of her two failed marriages, and of the hollowness of her fame. She knew that celebrity had stolen her privacy, and her health, and even, in some ways, her identity. Brenda was scheduled to speak for only an hour, yet she talked for three. As she spoke, frail and ravaged, her voice a whiskey-and-cigarette rasp, she evoked, like Miss Havisham in *Great Expectations,* ''the phantom air of something that had been and was changed.''

A faint beauty was still with her, the hint of an earlier, glorious time.

PART ONE

CHILD

CHAPTER ONE

B RENDA'S STORY begins with her grandmother Jane Fayrer Henshaw, an adventurous and formidable woman who grew up in St.-Hyacinthe, Quebec, near Montreal.

Jane was the daughter of a prosperous lumber dealer and his English wife. Her father, Joshua Henshaw, was descended from British Loyalists who had fled the United States and settled in Canada after the American Revolution. Her mother's brother, Sir Joseph Fayrer, was a noted British scientist and tutor of the Prince of Wales. These English ties gave the family a certain prestige and no doubt kindled Jane's social ambition, a consuming passion that cast a shadow over several succeeding generations of her family.

Jane was tall, blond, and slim, with a striking face that was too strong to be truly beautiful. She seemed "born sophisticated," as one acquaintance put it, and also born wild. In an age when women of her class chatted about the weather, worked needlepoint, and played the piano, Jane told dirty jokes and wrote fiction. People whispered that she sunbathed in the nude.

One morning, on an errand at the Bank of Montreal, Jane met a handsome, well-dressed teller named Frederick Williams-Taylor. Fred was the son of a Canadian shipbuilder and had been reared in the rugged river town of Moncton, New Brunswick. He had quit school at fifteen to work as a clerk in one of the bank's country outposts, where he quickly gained a reputation as a tireless worker and outstanding athlete. In bank-sponsored competitions he routinely won medals for a panoply of sports: snowshoeing, rowing, skating, squash, tennis, and even bowling. Within a few years the tall young man with the Vandyke beard and the elegant clothes had been promoted to teller and transferred to Montreal.

In Fred's good looks and quiet elegance Jane must have sensed the perfect complement to her ambition. They began to date and were married in June 1888, in a traditional ceremony at Montreal's Christ Church Cathedral. Less than a year later, on April 30, 1889, Brenda's mother, Brenda Germaine, was born. A son, Travers, followed.

Over the next ten years Fred's career was an "unbroken run of successes," as one journalist described it. The family moved from one Canadian town to another as he rose through the ranks at the Bank of Montreal. Soon he became known as a financial wizard. His newspaper articles and speeches on the Canadian economy began to draw attention and earned for him a silver medal from Canada's prestigious Royal Society of Arts.

Jane was eager for social success, but it would be wrong to think this was her sole motivation. Her ambitions were far greater than that, her interests far wider. She was devoted to the arts, and her salons at the family's large formal estate on Montreal's Mountain Street regularly attracted painters, composers, and writers. She herself did some writing, turning out a few stories and articles on Canadian history in prose that was rhetorical and arch.

Throughout her marriage she spent long periods away from home, traveling all over Europe, America, and the West Indies, collecting a string of adoring lovers. One admirer, an American industrialist, bought a mansion in Nassau for her; another, a mysterious European millionaire, gave her a pear-shaped diamond ring, now worth a half-million dollars.

Although he did not have lovers of his own, Fred tolerated Jane's affairs with aplomb. He and his wife lived separate lives. In the cosmopolitan circles in which the Williams-Taylors moved, marital fidelity was not particularly prized, and such arrangements were not uncommon. Divorce would, in any event, have been out of the question—a social catastrophe for the Williams-Taylors and a professional disaster for Fred. The two were often apart, even on holidays. The Reverend

John Morden, a nephew of Jane's, remembers spending several Christmases and Easters at the Williams-Taylors' house. Invariably, the guests would arrive to find Fred alone with the servants.

Fred was actually proud of his wife and her accomplishments, and he drew rich satisfaction from his work. Some of Jane's relatives believe that she slept with her husband's colleagues and that her talents in bed aided his career. In any case, her intelligence and charm undoubtedly did. "Jane was brilliant," wrote her niece, Margaret Morden, in a letter to Brenda. "But no one ever showed her how this brilliance could be put into a home and country. Her ambition was different. She was determined that Uncle Fred would climb to the top."

Within Jane's household, this ambition took its toll. A maid, Alice Armstrong, once described her as "loud and vulgar." Jane's treatment of Fred, Alice claimed, was often cruel. Once when he came into her bedroom, she turned him away, saying, "You annoy me." "She was fearsome," recalls Jane's stepgrandson, James Watriss. "She liked to think that she made Sir Frederick, and she didn't let him forget it."

Jane was also a domineering mother. "To my grandmother, my mother was never a real individual with a life of her own to lead, but merely an embellishment to the family's glory," Brenda wrote years later. "I doubt that my mother saw much of my grandmother as a child, or that, in later life, my mother was ever permitted to make an important decision of her own. She grew up without a personality . . . and was forced to cling to Grandmother Williams-Taylor's skirts, childlike and insecure, even after she herself was supposed to fill the roles of wife and mother."

Under Jane's autocratic ways, Brenda had grown up plain, overweight, and dull. Nevertheless, Jane was determined that her daughter be a social success, and to this end she enrolled Brenda in a fashionable finishing school in Paris.

After a two-year stint at the Bank of Montreal's Chicago branch, the Williams-Taylors were tranferred to London in 1905. They moved into a flat at Hans Court and filled it with paintings, tapestries, and Jacobean furniture. In the summer they lived in an estate near the Ascot racetrack. The house, which sat amid a fragrant rose garden, was surrounded by deep woods where Henry VIII and Anne Boleyn had once hunted.

Growing up in a prominent Montreal family, Jane had always known that the real proving ground of social worth was three thousand miles away in England. Now she had a chance to play out her ambitions. It was relatively easy to hobnob with the English aristocracy, as long as one had some connections, dressed appropriately, and was adept at conversation. Money was relatively unimportant. The English upper crust had little reason to be xenophobic, because it was impossible, except through marriage, for even the most ambitious outsider to join their ranks.

Jane took well to her new country. While many Canadians found her vulgarity offensive, the English loved it. She was a master of the gossipy, bitchy chatter and ribald remarks that dominated social conversation in the early twentieth century. One of her favorite dinner-party jokes was to point to a male guest's crotch and say, "Oh, my, isn't he attractive." Soon she was a fixture at fashionable London parties. She met Theodore Roosevelt at a dinner party and became good friends with the writer G. K. Chesterton, who often lunched with her at her London flat.

One year Jane was a guest a Chesterton's birthday party in his apartment overlooking Battersea Park. As Jane later recalled, the party was the occasion for an unusual glimpse of Chesterton's relationship with his wife. Mrs. Chesterton had given him a miniature model theater, and Chesterton had written a play, which he staged for the guests with doll actors. During the performance, a candle that illuminated the little stage started a fire, and within minutes the entire theater was in flames. Panicking, Chesterton "seized his wife's greatest treasure, a large vase, and, regardless of her roses, dashed it frantically on his burning toy," Jane said. "She screamed. He then seized her best green silk drapery, and mopped up the horrid mess!"

Jane's social ambitions ruled her family's life. Every summer the Williams-Taylors entertained at their country estate. In London they took a box for the opera at Covent Garden, bought a subscription to the ballet, and gave luncheons at the Ritz. In the spring they joined hundreds of aristocrats on the emerald lawns of Windsor Palace for the King's garden party.

At least twice a year the family went abroad. One summer they rented a cottage in Tours and motored through the Loire château district. Some winters Jane went to Sicily. Once Robert Smythe Hichens, author of *The Green Carnation,* a gossipy portrait of his friend Oscar Wilde, visited her at Taormina, where she had taken a suite at the San Domenico. Hichens finished his novel *The Fruitful Vine* in her sitting room, while Jane was confined to bed with pneumonia. In Rome, the entire Williams-Taylor family had a private audience with Pope Pius X. Jane described him as "a great pearl of a man. . . . One look at that saint's face and we all sank reverently to our knees."

The audience that Jane coveted most, however, was with King Edward and Queen Alexandra. Presentation before the English court, a custom designed mainly for young, unmarried girls, was an expensive, exhausting ordeal. Dress requirements were rigid. A manual for the occasion dictated that the women wear on the sides of their heads "three small white feathers mounted as a Prince of Wales Plume, the centre feather being a little higher than the two side ones . . . with the tulle veil of similar color attached to the base of the feathers. . . . " But for socially ambitious mothers that ordeal was well worth it; once a girl had been presented to the King and Queen of England, invitations to all the big balls in the great houses of London followed as a matter of course.

Foreigners, in particular, clamored to "bend the knee" in the hope of edging into English Society. Americans "are everywhere," Ambassador Walter Hines Page wrote to President Woodrow Wilson, describing a presentation ball in 1914. "Americans of all sorts from 24 karat to tinsel." The tinsel seemed to predominate. As Edith Wharton wrote, "The Americans who forced their way into good society in Europe were said to be those who were shut out from it at home. . . . And as for the American women who had themselves presented at the English court—well, one had only to see with whom they associated at home!"

Still, the presentations were dominated by Englishwomen, and the competition among foreigners was keen. Jane, however, had no trouble getting past the screening committees.

At 7 P.M. on June 6, 1907, she escorted her pudgy, eighteen-year-old daughter to Buckingham Palace. Dozens of nervous women, all dressed identically in floor-length white satin, were gathered in the state library. Some passed the time by knitting or reading; others played bridge on portable card tables. At exactly nine-thirty the orchestra began playing "God Save the King," and King Edward and Queen Alexandra took their places on huge thrones under a gold-embroidered red velvet canopy. For the next two hours the jittery girls, tripping occasionally on one another's trains, paraded before the royal couple. Finally, it was Brenda's turn to stand before Queen Alexandra. She curtsied clumsily. Her Majesty smiled.

The Canadian newspapers eagerly reported the Williams-Taylors' social progress. When Jane and Brenda visited Montreal in 1912, they were fêted like international celebrities at a round of teas, parties, and balls. Photographs of them in presentation gowns were published in the society pages, and they were interviewed endlessly about England, which Jane described as that "delectable land."

She boasted that she was great friends "with all the best people in Europe," and in later life regaled American friends with tales of her social triumphs. "She was so proud of her friendship with [British royalty]," says Winston Thomas, a retired New York antique importer. "She'd always say, 'Oh, I just heard from Her Majesty.' " At a bridge party once she opened her purse and pulled out an envelope emblazoned with the Buckingham Palace seal. When she dropped it, the other guests noticed it was dated years before—and in fact it contained only a form letter thanking her for a charitable contribution. The truth was that, despite their feverish successes, the Williams-Taylors were never embraced by the English aristocracy's innermost set, people like Lady Sackville and Lady Cunard. Not that it really mattered to Jane. "She got as far as she wanted to go," says her great-granddaughter, Victoria Kelly.

The ultimate cachet was conferred in February 1913, when Frederick Williams-Taylor was knighted for his contributions to Anglo-Canadian trade. Jane suddenly became Lady Jane. In a country chockablock with princesses, duchesses, and countesses, there was nothing awe-inspiring about a lady; but in New York and Nassau, social worlds Jane was soon to conquer, the title certified her membership in that gloriously remote elite—the English upper crust.

In November of that year, Sir Frederick was appointed general manager of the Bank of Montreal, one of the most important financial posts in Canada. The English celebrated his achievement by honoring him at several lavish dinners. He was toasted at a formal stag banquet for two hundred at London's Canada Club. Another party in his honor at the Savoy Restaurant featured a nine-course meal starting with caviar and ending with forty-year-old champagne. On his last day at the London bank, before the doors were locked for the day, the staff gathered around him with farewell presents: a pair of antique silver snuffers, a silver tray, and a pair of George III candlesticks.

The family sailed triumphantly to their homeland on the *Olympic,* one of Britain's great White Star liners. Nine hundred feet long and eleven decks high, the ship featured a Louis XVI dining hall, Turkish baths, Tudor fireplaces, and an enormous swimming pool. Sir Frederick, who had eaten some bad fish before leaving London, spent the entire crossing in bed. But Lady Jane and Brenda had a gay time, strolling the decks, chatting with the other travelers, and dining in rooms that were exquisite replicas of the great halls in European castles.

The Montreal papers treated the family's arrival as a celebration. "He left us a plain gentleman and returns a knight," announced the Montreal *Sunday Herald* in a front-page story. Wearing her pearl-and-topaz-studded cream satin presentation gown, Lady Jane looked down on all Montreal from a photograph on the society pages. To chart her social progress, she meticulously clipped the newspaper accounts of the family's achievements and pasted them in giant scrapbooks, an obsessive practice passed down to her daughter and granddaughter.

While Sir Frederick settled in at the bank, Lady Jane plunged into a whirl of social functions. She christened ships, gave lectures on Canadian history, and threw parties. She'd trained her pet parrot to say "God save the King" and "Yes, my dear," and he was often trundled out to amuse her guests. Lady Jane's new title and position had not dulled her bohemian tastes. She continued to cultivate artists, writers, and actors. "Only by intimate and sympathetic association with the brains of this world can one overcome its stupid conventions, and attain the tolerance, mental independence [and] originality that lighten life's burdens and inevitable gloom," Lady Jane once told a group of Canadian creative-writing students.

She invited struggling artists to display their paintings in her home and introduced aspiring writers to her editor friends at literary magazines. Her energy and intelligence attracted those who were already famous. Once she tried to arrange an interview for the writer Cleveland Moffett with Sarah Bernhardt, with whom Lady Jane was friendly. After trailing the actress's car around Montreal for several days with no luck, Moffett showed up at the Williams-Taylors' front door one night at ten. "Sarah wants you, she's in a good humor; for heaven's sake, come. She'll be pleased with me if I bring you," Moffett said. Lady Jane put on a fur coat over her nightgown and rushed to the theater with Moffett. The writer and Lady Jane talked for a while with Madame Bernhardt in her dressing room. But Lady Jane never learned whether the interview resulted in a published story.

The one member of the family who was not part of this social whirlwind was Travers, the Williams-Taylors' son. He had gone from boarding school in England to the army. When World War I broke out in 1914, Travers, whose nickname was Felix, was sent with the Canadian troops to England. Lady Jane and Brenda soon followed, trailing him from camp to camp. Though they were obviously concerned about Travers, it is likely that the two women were also eager to return to the country of their social success. At one point they took a cottage in Combe Bissett, Wiltshire. Brenda pasted a picture of her brother in his uniform in her scrapbook. Underneath she wrote: "We had as much fun and as good a time as was possible with the cloud of Felix, whom we adored, and the others, whom we were fond of, going to fight."

In 1915 Lady Jane and Brenda visited Palm Beach on a trip that would change both their lives. There Lady Jane met the industrialist George Stevens, with whom she would carry on an eccentric and passionate affair for the remaining five years of his life. Brenda met Clara Duff and Franklin Pierce Frazier, who soon became her in-laws.

The Fraziers were an overeager but well-meaning family of Midwesterners who lacked the Williams-Taylors' social clout but had much more money. Franklin Frazier had left his family's Massachusetts farm around 1880 and moved to Chicago, where he became an enormously successful grain broker. As president of the Bartlett-Frazier Company, he cornered the wheat market, as later newspaper accounts put it, and reportedly made $4 million. Fortified by his financial success, Frazier moved his family East in 1908. Their Fifth Avenue apartment, Palm Beach palace, and New England estate became the scenes of many fashionable parties.

Still, "Skip" Frazier and his quiet, intelligent wife remained unacceptable to Old Guard eastern society. The family's hopes for social success rested on the skinny shoulders of their only child, Franklin Duff, born in 1882. Frail, taciturn, and moody, Frank was an unlikely candidate for such achievement. As one acquaintance described him, he was "so quiet, so inconspicuous that one never noticed him." After he dropped out of Yale in 1904, his chief interests in life were fishing and womanizing. He never held a job, and he was virtually incapable of doing anything for himself. As a grown man he employed a nurse, a valet, a cook, a maid, a chauffeur, and a secretary.

He was also a legendary alcoholic. During one winter in Nassau, he hired a taxi and driver to follow him around town in case he got too drunk to walk home. Once during Prohibition he paid $1,000 to have fifteen wood cases of whiskey delivered to his apartment. Within two weeks they were gone. To accompany his drinking, Frank pursued a series of women, including at one point two mistresses whom he saw in alternating shifts. Short and thin, with a high forehead and delicate features, Frank had a penchant for models, actresses, and tarts—but only "nice tarts, ones who aren't lewd at all," he once explained. After one such lady chased him aboard an ocean liner and then threw a violent tantrum in his stateroom, he hired two bodyguards to stay with him through a summer in France.

That spring in Palm Beach the Fraziers, who were visiting without Frank Jr., apparently saw the Williams-Taylors as a vehicle for social advancement. Clara Duff was "very anxious to meet me," Lady Jane later said. Mr. Frazier sent Jane orchids, and Mrs. Frazier gave a dinner in Jane's honor. One of the guests at the dinner was George Stevens, head of the Chesapeake and Ohio Railway Company and a social leader in Richmond, Virginia, and White Sulphur Springs, West Virginia. Lady Jane, who was always impressed by big titles, big houses, and big bank accounts, was immediately attracted to the generous executive.

Over the next few months their romance blossomed. Finally Jane went to White Sulphur Springs, where she shocked proper society by staying alone with Stevens at his house. It was the first of many such visits. She also visited him in Richmond and traveled with him to Palm Beach on his private railroad car, the ultimate symbol of wealth and status in the early twentieth century. Jane called Stevens, who was barrel-chested and round-faced, with blue eyes and blond hair, "the greatest gentleman who ever lived." Their affair, however, greatly embarrassed his colleagues and his daughter, Helen. Once when Helen arrived at her father's doorstep in White Sulphur Springs, Jane turned her away, announcing, "There's no more room." Helen had to stay with a friend.

Sir Frederick, for his part, not only accepted the situation but became friendly with Stevens. Sometimes the three of them stayed together in Stevens's house. Both men openly acknowledged the affair, although, out of a sense of delicacy, they always referred to it as a platonic relationship. In 1918, Stevens gave Jane a six-bedroom stone mansion called "The Hermitage" in Nassau, and Sir Frederick, far from objecting, offered to contribute to the mansion's upkeep. But Stevens wouldn't hear of it. "My dear Sir Frederick," he wrote,

referring to the Hermitage matter, who else could so grace that establishment as your wonderful and accomplished wife and to whom am I more indebted for a companionship such as has not previously come to me. Any man who has had a mental intimacy with Lady Jane is one to be congratulated and he is a much better man in a business as well as a social way by reason of this contact. The expense attached to this enterprise is trifling compared with the great pleasure it has given her and I rejoice that I am able to make this small contribution to her future happiness.

On one visit to Stevens in White Sulphur Springs, Jane was walking with Brenda when she again ran into Clara Duff Frazier. The Fraziers, it turned out, had taken a cottage in town, and they invited Brenda and Lady Jane to dinner. "When my son, Frank, meets you, my dear," Clara Duff told Brenda, "he won't leave tonight as he says he will."

In 1915, at age twenty-six, Brenda Williams-Taylor seemed to have little chance of making a good match. She was heavy and ordinary-looking; she had her mother's vulgarity but none of her flair. Once at a fashionable Manhattan dinner party, as a striking young footman was about to serve the soup, Brenda glanced up and exclaimed, "My God, I think you're about the best-looking thing I've ever seen!" Brenda had already lost one chance to marry when her engagement to a British captain, Denzil Cope, had been broken. But the plain young woman was taken with the frail, alcoholic heir to the Frazier fortune.

At thirty-three, Frank Frazier had already divorced one wife, Rachel Peabody. Sir Frederick warned his daughter about Frank's reputation and begged her not to marry him. But the engagement was announced, anyway. There is no doubt Brenda felt some affection for Frank, yet it seems unlikely that she would have defied her father, whom she adored, if Frank's family had not been worth $4 million.

Brenda and Frank were married on December 14, 1916, at the Williams-Taylors' Montreal home. Dozens of guests from New York, London, and Canada filled the drawing room, which was softly lit by candles. The couple took their vows under a twelfth-century tapestry. The bride wore a white silk faille gown, with a floor-length tulle veil held in place by a wreath of orange blossoms. Her only jewelry was a single-strand pearl necklace, a gift from the Fraziers. The bridesmaids, in pale pink georgette trimmed with sable, carried dense bouquets of roses and wore diamond bar pins, gifts from the bridegroom.

Following a short trip to Ottawa, the newlyweds spent the rest of the winter on an extended honeymoon at the Breakers Hotel in Palm Beach. Afterward they lived with Frank's parents, moving among the Frazier houses in Manhattan, Palm Beach, and Manchester, Massachusetts, as the social seasons changed.

The marriage was miserable from the start. Frank complained that Brenda continually nagged him, that she criticized his parents and dragged him to large, loathsome parties. "Our tastes differed so entirely," he said later. "I didn't like any of the people or very few of the people that she had at the house or wished me to go to their houses." Brenda also demanded huge sums of money, although Frank's income from two trust funds was only $30,000 a year.

Brenda complained that Frank "was almost always totally drunk," that he often didn't show up for dinner, and that he would disappear for days at a time. In all of Brenda's copious scrapbooks, there are only two pictures of her with her husband. The single indication that they ever had any fun is an entry under a picture of a beach party in Palm Beach in 1917. "We certainly had a good time," wrote Brenda in her large, looping handwriting. "A very amusing lot of people."

What little romance remained in their marriage was wrung out in the summer of 1917, when Frank volunteered for the army. On November 20, 1917, he was commissioned a first lieutenant in the infantry. He served in the 153d Depot Brigade until December 15, when he was transferred to the aviation service. For a while Brenda was the dutiful soldier's wife, following Frank from one camp to another. In April 1918 she accompanied him to Montgomery, Alabama, where a young infantryman named F. Scott Fitzgerald was also stationed. Thousands of soldiers and aviators were training at Camps Sheridan and Taylor, just outside of Montgomery. Sometimes the men were invited to dances at the local country club. At one of them Fitzgerald met Zelda Sayre. Zelda observed that the men came from all strata of society—"men who were better dressed in their uniforms than ever before in their lives . . . men from Princeton and Yale who smelled of Russian leather and seemed very used to being alive."

Unlike Zelda, however, Brenda did not find the atmosphere romantic or exciting. The Fraziers set up housekeeping in a simple boardinghouse that Brenda complained "was hotter than hell." She got up at 6 A.M. to cook breakfast, and when Frank returned in the evening they look long walks or played cards. In October, Frank was transferred to Langley Field, Virginia, and Brenda went back to New York.

Brenda moved in with her in-laws on Fifth Avenue. Every

day she had at least three social engagements, for lunch, tea, and dinner. Several times a week she went to bridge parties, plays, or nightclubs. When the war ended in 1918, Frank returned, he said, to find "no home life at all." He spent most days drinking at the St. Nicholas Hotel at Broadway and Spring Street. Typically, before leaving the house he'd promise his wife to be home for cocktails; later a hotel valet would call to say he wouldn't be coming home.

Frank was a mean drunk. He fought publicly with his wife; he was rude to her friends; he sniped at the servants. One Friday night in the spring of 1920, Brenda went to dinner at Bishop Herbert Shipman's home. Frank went to a poker game. While Brenda and the Shipmans were eating, a friend called to say that Frank was drunk at a nearby bar. Brenda arrived to find her husband slumped over a table "with one of the most awful looking women I ever saw." She went back to the Shipmans'; Frank stayed out for three days.

In September 1920, Brenda discovered she was pregnant. In a rare burst of domesticity, Frank decided the couple should have their own apartment. Brenda's friend Ethel Jones described the Fraziers' first home of their own, at 15 West Fifty-fifth Street, as "one little dark cubby hole, black as ink," at the back of the building. Frank's mood was as dark as the decor. "He was very inconsiderate," recalled Ethel. "Brenda would be left all alone not knowing where he was. She would call me up and say, 'I'm all alone, can't you come down?' Her maid even spoke to me about the crying spells she had when she was alone in that dark apartment."

That winter they went to Nassau, where things got worse. At a dinner party at a Mrs. Ward's house, Frank got so drunk he couldn't get up from the table. A chauffeur he hired by the week for just such emergencies was waiting outside. During the day, the couple rarely spent any time together. Frank passed his afternoons with a woman drinking at a hotel, and Brenda lunched with her mother at the fashionable Porcupine Club.

One night, when his cab wasn't available, Frank walked home after a formal dinner at the Colonial Hotel and fell into a ditch. Brenda dragged him out, and her friend Marian Aubert, who was following a few steps behind, helped her get him home and upstairs to his room. He was too drunk to undress himself, and they left him sprawled on the bed in his tuxedo and shoes. Brenda, pregnant and weeping, went to bed in another room.

As the time approached for her to give birth, Brenda went to Montreal to be with her parents. On June 9, 1921, at 10 P.M., a daughter was born at Montreal Maternity Hospital, after a long and painful labor. Her parents named her Brenda Diana Duff. Frank Frazier, who'd arrived the evening before, spent the day getting drunk downtown. The next morning he left for his parents' farm in Manchester, Massachusetts, and didn't see his wife and daughter again for months.

When the couple were together, their fighting grew violent. On New Year's Eve 1921, Frank's parents had a big party in their Fifth Avenue apartment. Many of Frank's and Brenda's friends were there, and the young people had taken up the rug in the living room so they could dance to the gramophone. After most of the guests had left, Brenda asked Frank to help her put the living room back in order. Frank refused. "Go to hell," he told his wife, before stumbling upstairs.

Soon afterward Brenda went up to her room. She took off her party gown, put on a nightdress, and got into bed. Before she fell asleep, she heard her husband, whose bedroom was down the hall, at her door. He tried to climb into bed with her. She fought him off. When Brenda came down to attend the Fraziers' New Year's luncheon the next day, one guest noticed that her neck and arms were bruised. According to the guest, the bruises formed the imprint of a hand closing around her throat.

A few weeks later, Frank's father sent him to China in the futile hope that the trip would help him dry out. Brenda and her in-laws went to Sea Gull Cottage in Palm Beach. To cheer up their daughter-in-law, the Fraziers gave her a "baby" party at the Everglades Hotel. Everyone dressed up as toddlers in bonnets or sailor suits. In the childlike, naïve style that characterizes all her writings, Brenda wrote under a photograph of the party pasted in her scrapbook:

It was and still is quoted as one of the best parties ever given in Palm Beach. It was divine. Hundreds of people—

*Champagne flowing. Music divine. We all had a glorious
and gay time and arrived home about 5:30. . . .*

Soon afterward, Frank Frazier's father became seriously
ill. The family moved back to New York to be near his doctor, and Frank was recalled from China. Skip Frazier died
on May 7.

Immediately Frank Frazier checked into a suite at the Ritz
Hotel and started drinking. One night, very late, the second-
floor night maid at the Ritz was sitting in her office when
Frank ran out of his room. His vest was open, his collar and
shirt were torn, and his hair was in tangles. "Come quick,"
he said to her. He led her inside and then slammed the door
shut and barricaded it with his body. He told the maid that
he had killed a man and a woman and they were someplace
in the suite. "You can't leave until you find them," he insisted. The maid remembered the pretty young woman who
had visited Frank every day, and figured that she was one of
the victims. When the maid's search turned up nothing, Frank
told her to call the desk downstairs. "Tell them to get the
best detective in the city," he ordered. Instead, the desk sent
up a bell captain who arrived to find Frank running wildly
about the suite and darting in and out of a closet. He had
caught his reflection in the mirrors and imagined that someone was chasing him. The bell captain searched the four
rooms, but could find no evidence of a dead woman. Finally
he thought he saw a man's feet sticking out from under one
of the beds. "Oh, my God, there he is!" the bell captain
shouted. Frank was hysterical. "I told you he was there!" he
screamed. "I knew he would be there!" Filled with dread,
the bell captain got down on his knees and lifted the bed-
spread. There was no body. Lying propped up on their heels
was a pair of Frank Frazier's shiny black shoes.

With alcohol and socializing dominating their lives, Frank
and Brenda hardly had time to devote to their baby daughter.
Left exclusively to the care of governesses and nurses, Brenda
Diana was shuttled around the houses of both sets of grandparents. Meanwhile, Frank and Brenda were on the road,
following the social seasons from one fashionable locale to
another. Every summer Brenda spent three or four months

abroad. On the rare occasions when the couple were in the same house in the same city with their daughter, they would visit her in her nursery for only a few minutes every day—in the morning and in the evening, on their way out.

Still, the child was a major source of contention, something that was apparent in the most basic ways. Until the little girl was five, most people called her "Diana," to avoid confusion with her mother. Her mother nevertheless insisted on calling her "Brenda." Around the house, the mother became known as "Big Brenda." Frank Frazier, however, always called his daughter "Diana." In later life Brenda saw this confusion as a major schizophrenia of her childhood. Her parents couldn't even agree on her name.

CHAPTER TWO

At three, Brenda was plump and pretty, with straight dark hair, white skin, and large brown eyes. Usually she was extremely shy. But on a boat to Nassau in the winter of 1924, she suddenly ran up to a strange child who was playing on deck with his governess. "You are a dear little boy and I love you!" shouted Brenda. The boy was Jimmy Watriss, youngest son of Frederic Watriss, a once widowed and once divorced New York lawyer with five children and stepchildren. Watriss was from Chicago and was a Harvard graduate; at the time he was vice-president and legal counsel to the Mexican Seaboard Oil Company. Although not rich, he made a good living—approximately $75,000 a year.

Jimmy and Brenda were the same age—born just a week apart—and they immediately became friends. The children played together throughout the voyage, and later their parents were introduced. Big Brenda quickly saw Watriss as a potential beau. Tall and husky, with gray hair and a cheerful disposition, Watriss was the physical and emotional opposite of Frank Frazier.

By this time, her marriage to Frank was effectively over. They were no longer sleeping together, and they hardly ever saw each other. In the summer of 1924, their small daughter stayed in Manchester, Massachusetts, with her father and grandmother Frazier, while Big Brenda went to London. There she met Watriss, and they subsequently sailed home together.

23

Back in New York, Big Brenda moved into a rented house on East Seventy-ninth Street. While Frank was traveling, she continued her romance with Watriss. Currie, the Frazier chauffeur, spent much of his time driving Big Brenda back and forth between East Seventy-ninth Street and Watriss's house in Westbury, Long Island. Sometimes Watriss would meet Big Brenda for lunch in the city, and then they would spend the afternoon driving around Central Park. Once, when Big Brenda went on a short trip to Washington, D.C., she left Brenda in Westbury for three days. Frank Frazier knew about the friendship and seemed to accept it, in much the same way Sir Frederick had accepted Lady Jane's dalliances. Frank and Big Brenda even vacationed together that fall, taking a short holiday to Hot Springs, West Virginia. The night before they left, they had been to Watriss's house for dinner.

Later that fall, on the evening of November 16, Frank and Brenda were hosts to Watriss for dinner at the Seventy-ninth Street house. The next day Frank joined 76,000 fans who endured a driving rain and rivers of mud to watch Yale beat Harvard 19 to 6 at the Yale Bowl in New Haven. After the game Frank sent a telegram to Big Brenda from the stadium telegraph office. The message: I'm not coming home.

In the summer of 1925, Big Brenda went to Montreal and then Europe with Watriss. By this time, however, Frank Frazier, no doubt believing that a dossier on his wife's activities would be valuable in any divorce or custody suit, had hired detectives to spy on her. On June 29, Big Brenda, Watriss, and their children took night train No. 65 to Montreal. Frazier's private detective, Harry Brissette, followed the lovers, boarding the train in a New York suburb and riding it all the way to Montreal. He later filed a report with Frazier.

After a short stay with the Williams-Taylors, Watriss sailed for France, where he deposited his children and their nannies at a villa in Houlgate. Big Brenda, her parents, Brenda, and the child's nanny, Mabel Bishop, sailed on July 22. Big Brenda and the Williams-Taylors traveled first class. Nanny Bishop and Brenda slept in steerage several decks below, in a bargain room that doubled as a luggage closet. Years later, Nanny Bishop remembered how they were jolted awake all night long by other people's luggage shifting about.

As soon as the boat landed at Cherbourg, Brenda and

Nanny joined the Watriss children at Houlgate, where they stayed the rest of the summer. The Williams-Taylors and Big Brenda took a train to Paris and checked into the Hôtel La Pérouse. Watriss was already in Paris, at the Majestic.The group spent the week dining at fancy restaurants and visiting Lady Jane's friends at magnificent châteaux in the countryside. Frank Frazier was also in Paris at the time, and he sent a note to Big Brenda at the Pérouse asking if he could have custody of Brenda for the month of August. Big Brenda refused. "Dear Frank," she wrote on August 3. "Thanks for your nice note. Unfortunately, Diana is not with me as I did not consider Paris a proper place for a child in the month of August. She is in the country and shortly going to England and shortly after that again [she'll] return with me to Canada."

On August 6 Big Brenda and Lady Jane, accompanied by a lady's maid, met Watriss at the Hôtel Mirabeau in Aix-les-Bains. Big Brenda and Lady Jane were assigned rooms 114 and 115. Watriss was in 107. Room 112 was occupied by another of Frank Frazier's private detectives, Hippolyte Duchemin.

Duchemin took his work seriously. He hid in a telephone booth by the elevator and spied on Watriss as he sneaked out of Big Brenda's room late at night. Other times he crouched on the balcony outside and peered in through the windows. For eight days Duchemin watched the lovers follow an unerring routine. After dinner Watriss and Big Brenda would chat awhile in Lady Jane's room. Then the two lovers would go to Big Brenda's room. At about two-thirty or three in the morning Big Brenda would open her door and look right and left down the corridor. If the hall was empty, Watriss would creep back to his own room.

From the Mirabeau, Duchemin and his brother Marcel followed Big Brenda and Watriss to the Hôtel du Grand Cerf at Évreux. There the Duchemins were joined by two other detectives. Big Brenda took room 9; Watriss, who registered as "David Ferguson," was next door in 10. From their position on a nearby balcony, the detectives could see into both rooms, but all the action was in 9. They saw Big Brenda put on a dressing gown before Watriss shut the curtains. Later Brenda and Watriss dined downstairs and took a short walk, returning at 9:30 P.M. The detectives noticed that room 9 was lit for a short while, but that 10 remained in darkness. No longer happy with their view from the balcony, the detectives climbed down and spent the rest of the night kneeling on the corridor carpet, peeping through Big Brenda's keyhole.

The next day Big Brenda and Watriss returned to Paris and cavorted for eight days at the Hôtel San Regis. By this time, however, they suspected they were being watched by detectives, and sailed home on separate boats.

After her return to New York, Big Brenda conferred with her lawyers, and on December 24, 1925, she filed for divorce. She had hoped to avoid a trial. But on January 13, 1926, Frank Frazier filed a counterclaim, seeking custody of Brenda on the grounds that the little girl was already spending most of her time with him and his mother.

The trial was to be held in Palm Beach. As the date approached, Big Brenda went to Florida and checked into a hotel. Frank, Clara Duff Frazier, and Brenda stayed together at Sea Gull Cottage, the Frazier mansion in Palm Beach. After all the anger and spying, the divorce trial lasted just one day. Only three witnesses were called: Big Brenda, Frank, and his mother.

Frank and Big Brenda had by now come to hate each other, but they showed remarkable restraint on the witness stand. Big Brenda did not accuse her husband of drunkenness or infidelity. She merely asked Palm Beach Circuit Judge Curtis E. Chillingworth to award her $20,000 a year in alimony and child support. "Can you live comfortably on less than $20,000 a year?" Frank's attorney, Frank Wideman, asked her.

A. It is a little bit doubtful after being accustomed to what I have been.

Q. Don't you think you could live on $10,000 a year?

A. Certainly not, impossible.

Q. Quite sure you couldn't live on $15,000?

A. I don't know, it is hard to judge, because for the past year, what I could live on, if I have to establish a home for my child, I can't live on less and bring her up as she is accustomed to being brought up.

Frank Frazier listened to Big Brenda's testimony, then took the stand himself. When Wideman asked him why he left his wife, Frank mentioned nothing about Watriss:

A. I found it impossible to live at home any longer. I found I had no home with my wife, constant trouble, irritation. I just found it impossible to stay there any longer.
Q. Was your wife inclined to stay at home and make a home for you and your child?
A. It didn't seem so to me.
Q. Well, you just had domestic bickerings, is that the idea?
A. Well, we had a great deal of trouble, more than unpleasant.

The last witness was Clara Duff Frazier. She so loathed Big Brenda that she would not speak to her to say hello. But on the witness stand, she was a model of civility. "Are you a home-loving person?" Wideman asked her.

A. My home has always been my first consideration.

The lawyer asked her if she thought she could create a better home environment than her daughter-in-law. "I want to be fair in every way," Clara Frazier said. "I naturally think my way is better than the way of others. One always thinks that. I think I would bring up the child well because I would give it a great deal of thought. I haven't so many things to distract me as a younger woman. I am more at home than younger women are. That perhaps answers it, more or less."

That afternoon, Frank and Big Brenda privately agreed to share custody of their daughter. According to an agreement drawn up by their lawyers and signed by Judge Chillingworth, Clara Duff and Frank would have Brenda every year from October 15 to May 15. Big Brenda would have custody of the girl the remaining five months. In the event of Clara Duff's death, custody was to be equally divided between Big Brenda and her ex-husband. Each parent had unlimited visiting privileges while the child was in the other's custody, although neither parent could take her abroad without the other's consent. In addition, Frank agreed to pay Big Brenda $15,000 a year in alimony and child support.

Later, Big Brenda insisted that she had agreed to joint custody only because Clara Duff had threatened to cut Brenda off. Frank Frazier flatly denied this. But even if no actual threat had been made, Big Brenda greatly feared that Brenda would be disinherited.

The divorce agreement was filed in January 1926. Brenda was four. In theory she now had two homes. In fact she had none. She never believed that either of her parents wanted her, except as an emblem of victory. "I felt rejected on all sides, unloved, alone in a frightening world," she wrote years later. "To add to my young confusion, I learned in my father's home that his family would not even speak to my mother; and in my mother's home I was told that my father was a cad who got drunk when I was born and disappeared for two days, even though my mother nearly died in childbirth."

Less than three months later, on March 29, 1926, Big Brenda and Fred Watriss were married at the American Presbyterian Church in Montreal in a simple ceremony witnessed by just five relatives. Her divorce from Frank Frazier had shocked society, and it caused Big Brenda to be shunned by many fashionable hostesses in New York and Palm Beach. Her marriage to Watriss restored her respectability.

Brenda was at the wedding, but her memories of it were "vague but terrible." Just before leaving New York for Montreal, Big Brenda had dismissed Nanny Bishop in a fit of jealousy. In her devotion to social life, Big Brenda didn't have time to spend with her daughter, but then she was annoyed when Brenda developed a closer attachment to Nanny than to her mother. Since Brenda was getting too old for a baby nurse, Mabel would probably have left within a year anyway. But Brenda, who would one day dismiss her own daughter's beloved governess for similar reasons, loved Nanny more than anyone.

That summer Brenda moved with her mother's new family to a seven-story townhouse at 7 East Seventy-fifth Street. The children, Brenda, Jimmy, and his older brother, Freddie, lived on the top two floors with their governesses. Brenda and Jimmy were friends "right from the start," recalls Jimmy. They used to play together every day after school. "As a child Brenda was not at all as attractive as she became," says

28

Jimmy. "But she always had a great sense of humor. She was a lot of fun and very intelligent."

Brenda's new nanny was a stern Russian woman named Beta Kara, whom Brenda hated on sight. "I had never seen this woman before. I was so miserable that I cried myself to sleep for months afterward," she wrote later.

While Brenda was in New York, she attended Miss Hewitt's Classes at 68 East Seventy-ninth Street. The school was founded by Caroline Danella Hewitt, an English-born spinster who came to America in 1892 to be the tutor for the children of a family in Tuxedo Park, New York. Eventually she went to Manhattan, where she taught small groups of children with family names such as Whitney, Astor, Vanderbilt, and Pulitzer. Their grateful parents lent her the money to start her own school in 1920.

"Misshew," as she was affectionately known, was more mother than teacher to her charges. She remained close to her girls throughout their lives, attending their weddings and children's christenings, and writing them long, chatty letters. Caroline Hewitt was hopelessly stage-struck, but was considered too ugly for a theatrical career herself—one friend said "she looked like Churchill and, when she got mad, Queen Mary." She enjoyed a vicarious celebrity through her students. Brenda's classmates included Enrico Caruso's daughter, Gloria, and John Barrymore's daughter, Diana.

Brenda was a good student. On one report card in 1932 she received twelve A's and three B+'s. Her lowest grade was a C+, in geography/history. She won the English composition prize and honorable mentions in poetry and art. She also got a perfect score in arithmetic and a 99 in French.

During the winters with her father in Florida, Brenda attended the Palm Beach School for Girls. A teacher there described her as "one of the most well adjusted little pupils." Still, Brenda didn't have any close friends. One schoolmate remembers seeing her alone on the beach a lot, playing by herself.

The situation was different in New York, where Brenda became good friends with Diana Barrymore and Cobina Wright, junior, the daughter of a New York singer and socialite, Cobina Wright, senior. Brenda, Diana, and Cobina used to whisper together about where babies came from. One day, after watching a pregnant woman walk down the street, Diana asked Cobina to get the facts from Mrs. Wright. The next morning in the girls' room, Cobina reported back to her friends that she had taken her mother into the bathroom, locked the door, and demanded, " 'Mommy, Brenda Frazier and Diana Blythe said that when a woman has a big stomach it means that she's going to have a baby. Is that true?' 'Yes, that's right,' her mother said. 'God planted a seed that grew like a lovely flower into a beautiful little baby.' " That may have satisfied Brenda and Cobina, but not the precocious Diana. "But how does the seed get there?" Diana asked.

Brenda certainly didn't know. Gertrude Bennet Folmsbee, the family's longtime factotum, remembers Brenda as shy, innocent, sweet-tempered, and caring: "She was content just to be herself and she was as nice to the kitchen maid as she was to the Prince of Wales. She was a very loving little girl." Folmsbee, however, was troubled by Brenda's childhood docility. "When I first knew Brenda, she couldn't let herself go," says Folmsbee. "She'd start to tell me something, and then she'd pull back. She wasn't sure she could trust anyone. She thought she had to keep everything to herself." Eventually Brenda opened up. One day, when Brenda was about seven, she visited Gertie in her office in the family's library. Dressed in party clothes, white kid gloves, and a feathered hat, Brenda walked up to the desk and folded her hands on top. "Gertie," she said angrily, "I don't see why I had to get all dressed up to visit some friend of my grandmother's. I don't want to go."

Meanwhile, Big Brenda maintained her social schedule. The Watrisses went out several times a week, and on the other days they entertained at home, at small dinners, luncheons, and card parties. Big Brenda loved cards and games, particularly Mah-Jongg. Frank Frazier's first wife was an occasional guest at her parties. Her married name was Rachel Douglas, but everyone called her "The First Mrs. Frazier," the title of a play on Broadway at the time. "I remember those card parties well," says Winston Thomas, who was a frequent guest. "The maid would wheel in a table and we'd play Mah-Jongg for about two and a half cents a point. It was just background for conversation. It wasn't serious like bridge." Big Brenda took her winnings seriously, though.

Under the heading "Gambling of all kinds," she neatly recorded her gains in a diary. In one four-year period she won $7,459.

When her mother had guests, Brenda would often be brought in to say hello. This was a special treat, like lunches alone with her mother in the Japanese Garden at the Ritz. Usually Brenda saw her mother for only about an hour a day. The governesses would send her and the boys into "Mummie" and Daddy's bedroom for twenty minutes before school. Then, after they'd washed their hands for lunch, the children would visit Big Brenda in the parlor, if she was home. They would get one more visit, from six-thirty to seven in the evening, before their parents went out. Brenda's mother would shake hands with her child in a rigid, formal way and say, "Oh, hello, how are you?" Sometimes she would kiss little Brenda on the cheek, says Gertie, "But not with the vehemence you or I would. Brenda was such a cutie. Yet, usually, the mother's attitude was 'Bring her in so I can look at her when she's all dressed up.' "

Although it seems strange today, Big Brenda's coolness was in line with the era's prevailing child-rearing philosophy. In a book dedicated to "the first mother who brings up a happy child," Dr. John B. Watson, a Dr. Spock of the thirties, wrote: "Never hug and kiss [your children], never let them sit in your lap. Shake hands with them in the morning. Try it out. In a week's time you will find how easy it is to be perfectly objective with your child and at the same time kindly." Watson's prescription fit nicely with the habits of the upper classes. Many wealthy society women abandoned their babies to governesses. These nanny-raised children were status symbols who stamped their mothers as glamorous ladies free from pecuniary concern.

European society raised its children in a similar way—so of course Lady Jane believed in the distant parent. Whenever Jane was in New York, Brenda's meetings with her family took on the formality of a royal audience. Instead of shaking hands, little Brenda curtsied. Sometimes Lady Jane would offer the back of her hand for Brenda to kiss. Big Brenda also had troubles with Lady Jane. Folmsbee remembers Big Brenda sighing heavily and saying, "Oh, Mother is in town. Now I can't live my life. I have to live hers." Decades later,

Brenda's psychiatrist saw his most difficult task as closing the wounds opened by Brenda's "self-centered, infantile, obsessively mother-devoted mother. Brenda had no mother."

She was brought up by a chain of outsiders, abandoned by her parents even on holidays. "Christmases were the worst," Brenda recalled. "My mother always seemed to be visiting friends at Christmastime, often in places as far away as Europe, and I was left to open my presents alone, except for the company of a maid or the butler."

By age seven she had had six different nannies. In 1927 Big Brenda hired Mademoiselle Ducolomb, a proper French governess whom Brenda called "Mam'selle." Rigid and tyrannical, Ducolomb terrorized Brenda with an unbending, militarylike routine. She made Brenda get up every morning at six to practice the piano for an hour and a half before going to school. In the evening Ducolomb forced her to practice another two and a half hours. "Unless I placed first in my classes, or at the worst, second, Mademoiselle hardly spoke to me for days at a time," Brenda recalled later. "Yet with my music and my riding lessons and all the rest of the regimen that was imposed upon me, I had no time to study before lights-out, which came as promptly and rigidly as in a prison. Sometimes, I studied in bed by flashlight under my blankets. Once Mademoiselle walked into my bedroom and nearly caught me. I tried to hide my guilty face by drinking a glass of water, but was so nervous that I drank from the thermos, forgetting to pour the water into a glass."

Ducolomb would not even allow Brenda time out for illness. "If I felt the urge to cough, I had to swallow it, for Mademoiselle considered a cough to be a sign of malingering. Once I had a cough that lasted two months—and never dared give way to it except when I was out of the house, or in bed with the covers over my head."

Mademoiselle Ducolomb left when Brenda was, at twelve, presumably too mature to need a governess. It was a measure of Brenda's profound loneliness that she greatly missed this unpleasant woman.

Brenda's unhappiness was aggravated by the household's general turbulence. Big Brenda was incompetent at domestic management. During one year alone she fired three cooks, three butlers, two footmen, and two parlormaids. One maid,

Isabel Armstrong, said Mrs. Watriss was well liked by the servants, but that she was ineffectual in settling their many disputes. The maids said they left because the food they were given was bad. Mrs. Watriss, they said, started scrimping after Mr. Watriss complained about household expenses. Armstrong said the children ate mostly tough meat and canned vegetables. In the evening, she said, the children would often have nothing more for dinner than salad and an egg. Dr. Alton Goldbloom, who examined Brenda for boils in 1926, attributed Brenda's condition to a poor diet.

Dr. Goldbloom also thought that Brenda was a victim of too much "mental stimulation." The servants grumbled that Big Brenda told "risqué, dirty" stories, sometimes in French, in front of her daughter; she also kept pornography in her bedroom.

Later, although Big Brenda denied it vehemently, the servants insisted she was having an affair during the late twenties with a British naval officer she had met in Europe in 1924. When the captain was in town, they saw each other twice a week at the home of a Mrs. Porter, ostensibly to play bridge. According to Mrs. Porter's servants, the meetings always followed the same schedule: Big Brenda arrived at 5 P.M., and the butler directed her to the second-floor library, where the captain, in full military garb, was waiting. Then Mrs. Porter left the house. She'd be gone for two hours. Once, while the captain and Big Brenda were alone in the library, Fred Watriss called. A parlormaid overheard Big Brenda lie to her husband and tell him that she was with Mrs. Porter. The captain also visited Big Brenda on Seventy-fifth Street. One time when she had a cold, he went up to her bedroom. When the butler, Lewis Jones, brought Brenda a whiskey, he noticed that her bedclothes were turned down, and that her breasts, thinly draped in a nightgown, were exposed.

Throughout this time Brenda was going back and forth between the Watriss household and the Frazier homes. Brenda's departures from Seventh-fifth Street were always painful. Brenda and Jimmy Watriss were devoted to each other. Jimmy remembers heartbreaking scenes with both children wailing uncontrollably as a nanny dragged Brenda out the door with her toys and luggage. Sometimes, after Brenda left, Jimmy cried all day long.

Once she was with her father, however, Brenda adjusted well. At the time of the divorce, Frank Frazier had not seen his daughter for an entire year. During this time, says Brenda's psychiatrist, ''he had nothing to do but play poker with his gang . . . and go off to a sporting event. . . . He [lived] like a Yale student. He never got beyond that.'' Now that she was around more, Frank discovered he was greatly fond of Brenda. As Katherine Reilly, one of Frazier's housekeepers, said, the only time Frank smiled was ''when Diana is around.''

Frank Frazier was an empty, failed man, but he truly loved Brenda in a way that Big Brenda probably could not. She loved her daughter, but she saw Brenda as a vehicle to fulfill her own dreams for social success. Frazier's love was uncluttered. In fact, it was probably the only good thing in his life. Brenda felt the purity of her father's love, and although he remained a somewhat distant figure, she was secure and happy in his company.

In Palm Beach, where Brenda spent most of each winter, Frank took her swimming and fishing, and every Sunday they would go on picnics together. After dinner, before Frank went out for the evening, Brenda would run up and kiss him. She would climb in his lap with her pad and crayons and draw pictures for him. When it was time for bed, he would carry her to the stair landing and put her down on an upper step. From there she'd leap into his arms and kiss him good night. The servants at Sea Gull Cottage, her father's mansion, adored her. If one of them got sick, Brenda would make a get-well card in her nursery and have her nanny send it down on a silver tray. Once she arranged a party for the servants and sent out little invitations emblazoned with pictures of them that she had drawn herself.

Frank was respectful of his daughter's innocence. She never saw him drunk. In New York, he kept a one-bedroom penthouse at 383 Park Avenue to entertain his mistresses. Whenever Brenda was in his custody, he slept there every night so she wouldn't see him with a strange woman. Brenda sometimes went to the penthouse for lunch, but she always slept at the Frazier house on Fifth Avenue. Despite his love for his daughter, Frank's restlessness was unabated, and he was frequently away. In one year-and-a-half period from February

1926 to September 1927, Frank crossed the Atlantic six times, flitting from New York to Paris and back to New York. During several of those trips Brenda was in his custody, and she was left with servants.

In New York, Frank typically rose at ten in the morning. His valet, Frederick J. Christmas, would serve him breakfast—often a mixture of raw egg, milk, and whiskey. Then Frank would spend the rest of the morning in his pajamas, reading the papers and drinking champagne. The cook would prepare lunch for Frank and whichever of his mistresses had spent the night. Occasionally Frank would go to his club in the afternoon, but often he didn't get dressed until 5 P.M. Christmas would draw his bath, lay out his clothes, and help him get ready for the evening. During the summers in France he completely reversed night and day. Once, while staying in a luxury hotel at Fontainebleau he threw an all-night party in his suite for a group of art and music students from the local conservatory. All the guests, who were dressed in exotic costumes, were drunk. One young woman showed up in a grass skirt with the picture of a sailor painted on her back. On her knee were tattooed male and female sex organs that simulated intercourse when she moved.

Several times a month a barber and a manicurist would visit the New York apartment. Frank was especially fond of the manicurist, a teenager named Agnes. Having done his nails in the morning, she would sometimes return in the evening for dinner and the night. Frank's other mistresses included a socialite named Antoinette Boynton and a fashion designer named Ruth Donnelly. There was also a Miss MacGonigle, a Ziegfeld chorus girl, who enlivened Frank's trip to France in 1926. That summer, Frank was standing on the steamship deck with Christmas when he saw Miss MacGonigle running toward him. Apparently, she was upset because Frank had ended their relationship. Naturally, Frank was alarmed, but Christmas told him, "Take no notice, just carry on in the ordinary way." Although Miss MacGonigle invited herself to take drinks and dine with Frazier, she didn't cause any real trouble until the last day of the voyage. Then she started banging frantically on Frank's stateroom door, demanding to be let in. He rang for Christmas, who was in the next room. Frank told him to open the door and wait outside, but not to go too far away. Christmas waited outside while the argument raged. Miss MacGonigle hurled a water bottle, glasses, even the sides from the bed. Eventually the ship's purser took her back to her own cabin and Frank and Christmas were moved to a suite on the opposite side of the ship. At five the next morning they were escorted to land and put on a baggage train for Paris. Once settled at the Hôtel Mirabeau, Frank hired two bodyguards who followed him wherever and whenever he ventured outside.

Late in life, Brenda told her psychiatrist that her father was kinder to her than her mother. Nonetheless, her life with him had its cruel moments. One Thanksgiving, Brenda was staying with her father at his Fifth Avenue apartment. Brenda was unhappy. She wanted to be down the street with her mother and Jimmy. A lively family party would certainly be more fun than eating alone with Daddy. There were tears. But Frank refused to let her go. Brenda played for a few hours by herself and then went into the cavernous formal dining room to wait for her father. Two places had been set at either end of the enormous table. The best silver had been polished and the footmen were in full livery. Brenda sat down. But there was no sign of her father. Finally the butler announced that Mr. Frazier was "ill"—probably the discreet butler's euphemism for dead drunk—and wouldn't be down at all. Brenda ate dinner alone.

On June 27, 1926, Clara Duff Frazier died in her bed at 826 Fifth Avenue. She had been suffering from cancer of the intestine. Her will stipulated $50,000 bequests for each of her two nieces and her sister. She left her jewelry and furniture to her son. Most of her money—about $4 million— would be tied up in trust funds, which could never be touched until the death of her granddaughter, Brenda. The will stipulated, however, that Frank could spend the income from the trusts, about $50,000 a year. In the event of his death, the income would go to Brenda. (If she was still under twenty-one, it would be held for her until she came of age.) The capital itself, however, was beyond her grasp. Although she would one day try, Brenda would never be able to break the trusts.

36

Clara Duff's will fulfilled her husband's wishes. Frank Sr. had been determined that his son, whom he once described as the only bad investment he had ever made, would never dissipate the family fortune. More important, Frank Sr. wanted to ensure that Brenda Watriss would never touch his money.

CHAPTER THREE

Within months of Clara Duff Frazier's death, Big Brenda decided to challenge the custody ruling. She demanded to have Brenda full-time. What ensued was a six-year legal war. Dozens of people testified in courtrooms and law offices in America and in Europe. Detectives hired by both Frank and Big Brenda were summoned to give reports on their spying. Household servants were stolen away by one side to testify against the other. The ostensible legal issue was which, if either, parent was "fit." But the bickering centered on charges of adultery and alcohol abuse, with diversions caused by a flurry of scurrilous side issues.

Frank Frazier was convinced that Big Brenda's motive for starting the proceeding was mercenary. Now that Clara Duff was dead, Brenda's inheritance was certain, and Frank suspected that Big Brenda was trying to get some of it—with the child in her custody full-time, Big Brenda would find it easier to claim it. Frank's suspicions were probably justified to an extent, but the matter was more complicated than that. For her part, Big Brenda sincerely believed that Frank Frazier was an unfit father. She insisted that she would never have agreed to joint custody in the first place if Clara Duff had not been around to exert a "moral influence" in her son's home.

The Watrisses initiated their case by hiring two private detectives, John De Vries and Julius Braun. De Vries's first assignment was to visit Frederick J. Christmas, Frank Frazier's English valet. The Watrisses had told De Vries to do whatever was necessary to get information about Frazier. Eventually, that meant paying Christmas a substantial bribe. Initially, it just meant flirting—De Vries knew that Christmas lived with another man, and suspected that he was homosexual.

One day in April 1927, De Vries rang the doorbell at Frazier's Park Avenue apartment. When Christmas—who was just then packing Frazier's clothes for a trip to France—opened the door, De Vries, posing as a claims investigator for an insurance company, explained that he was looking for Frank Frazier's cook, who had broken her arm in a car accident. The two men chatted for a while, and De Vries invited Christmas to dinner.

Over the next year, De Vries pursued Christmas in a seemingly ardent courtship. In May 1927, he sailed to France on the same ship with Christmas and Frazier. At sea for a week, the friendship between the valet and the detective grew. They strolled together on deck and visited each other's stateroom. By fall, back in New York, they were going to the theater together. One day De Vries told Christmas he could get him another job, working for a "Mr. Millard," at $150 a month, slightly more than Frazier paid him. On October 27, Christmas quit Frazier's employ. But instead of reporting to his new job, he left with De Vries on a whirlwind tour of Canada.

They flitted from Montreal to Quebec to Ottawa to Toronto, staying in the best hotels and dining at the most elegant restaurants. They visited museums, art galleries, and historical monuments. After Canada they went to Boston, and then to Havana for three weeks. De Vries paid all the bills. During the two-month trip, the detective pumped Christmas for information about Frazier's habits, drinking problem, and love life, reporting all the sordid details to his partner, Julius Braun, in New York. On April 1, 1928, Christmas went back to England, sailing first-class on a Cunard liner. But every month for the next five months, Braun sent him a check for $150.

While De Vries wooed Christmas, Julius Braun courted Frazier's other servants. On January 13, when Frazier was in Palm Beach, Braun went to his Fifth Avenue apartment, where Clara Malm, one of Frazier's cooks, was acting as caretaker. Malm, fifty years old and suffering from stomach ulcers, was not happy working for Frazier. She claimed that her duties—supervising renovations in the apartment—left her no time to go to the hospital for X rays, or to see her doctor. On January 14, the day after Braun visited her, she quit. On January 15, Braun gave her a check for $150 and sent her, with Mrs. De Vries, to a resort, the Sunset Lodge, at Lakewood, New Jersey. The women stayed there for four weeks. For several months, Malm continued to receive monthly checks of $150, plus $30 for expenses.

Braun also hired Rosa Parkkinen, a cook whom Frazier had abruptly fired in May 1927 because he disliked the way she prepared roast beef gravy. Parkkinen was on the payroll for two months, collecting $300, although she didn't do any work. Similarly, Thomas Boylan, an ex-chauffeur of Frazier's, got a five-day trip to Richmond, all expenses paid, plus $200. Braun even hired a French detective whom Frank Frazier had hired to watch the detectives watching him. The detective, Georges Pion, had worked for Frazier one summer in France. His job was to watch the entrances to the hotel to see if Frazier was being followed, and to ask hotel employees if anyone had been seeking information about Frazier. After Pion signed a statement that Frazier conducted himself like a perfect gentleman throughout the summer, Braun paid him 3,600 francs to recant it.

By February 1928, Big Brenda and Fred Watriss were confident they had enough witnesses to prove Frank Frazier's unfitness as a father. On February 8, they filed a petition in Palm Beach County Circuit Court to set aside the joint custody agreement and win total custody of Brenda. The petition was a vituperative attack on Frazier's character. The Watrisses claimed Frazier wasted his annual income of approximately $250,000 "in a life of riotous living, for the purchase of intoxicating liquors, upon immoral women and in other vices and dissipation." They accused him of living a life of "idleness and shame," of doing no work, and of not really loving his daughter. During the time Brenda was in his custody, the petition continued, "she has been practically all the time in the care and custody of servants." Brenda, who was six, was at an age "when she should be constantly in some good school," the petition charged. "But . . . the defendant takes the child to Palm Beach in the winter where she cannot receive constant or proper schooling.''

Frank Frazier retaliated with predictable fury. He already had the brothers Duchemin working for him. Now he hired another private detective, a former policeman known as Captain Tunney. Working with Harry A. Usher, Frazier's secretary, Tunney rounded up a herd of witnesses, mostly disgruntled servants from the Watriss household. On March 21 Frazier filed an answer to his ex-wife's charges, castigating the life-style not only of Big Brenda, but also of Fred Watriss and even Lady Jane. He accused his wife and her new husband of living a home life that was ''sophisticated in the extreme.'' He accused Big Brenda of being an ''inveterate gambler at cards,'' of entertaining men, and of ignoring her daughter. He said Watriss was a heavy drinker. Lady Jane, Frazier claimed, had ''loose standards of conduct and an unwholesome method of living,'' which made her unfit to associate with his daughter. The Williams-Taylors and the Watrisses, he said, ''persistently endeavored to poison the mind of Diana'' against him by making ''false and cruel statements.''

During all this maneuvering, Brenda was still shuttling back and forth between her mother and father. As the date for the first hearing in the case approached, Big Brenda and Fred Watriss moved to a rented house in Palm Beach, where Brenda visited them occasionally. W. A. Paisley, a young attorney who assisted Big Brenda's lawyers, went to a dinner party there and found himself charmed by the object of this fight. During the meal, ''the little girl came out and curtsied,'' Paisley recalls. ''I never forgot it.''

He remembers Big Brenda as ''a very charming lady.'' Frazier, he says, ''was a typical alcoholic. But he never came to court drunk. He'd be in quite good shape. He [used to] drink way into the night, and the next morning, to sober up, he'd eat ice cream.''

Drinking was a major issue. Although the case came up at the height of Prohibition, the question was not *if* Brenda's parents drank, but how much. Each side portrayed the other as maintaining a household dominated by alcohol. One maid said she once saw Watriss drink a few whiskeys behind a screen in the dining room while the children were eating.

Another maid described Big Brenda as a blowsy lush who often returned from bridge parties giggling and red-faced. One servant said Lady Jane took her first drink, a brandy and soda, every morning at 11 A.M. Descriptions of Frazier's drinking orgies took up hundreds of pages of testimony.

The first hearing in the case began on January 11, 1929, at the county courthouse in West Palm Beach. Judge Curtis E. Chillingworth, who had handled the couple's divorce trial, heard the case. Tall and gawky, "Chick" Chillingworth resembled a crane, with a thin neck and arms that were too long for his shirt sleeves. Known around the courthouse as "the Big Judge," he had a reputation for meticulousness and austerity. Every morning at 9:29 A.M. he would stand outside the door to his courtroom, studying his watch, waiting for the stroke of nine-thirty so he could mount the bench and pound his gavel. Whenever he got impatient with a long-winded lawyer, he would drum his fingers on the bench, glaring sternly from behind rimless glasses. Years later, Chillingworth's integrity would cost him his life. On June 14, 1955, the judge and his wife, Marjorie, were drowned at sea by two hit-men hired by another judge whom Chillingworth was investigating for corruption.

Big Brenda was the first witness called, and she stayed on the witness stand for five hours. She described how she met and married Frazier and the details of their divorce. She denied that she and Watriss had had an affair before they were married, denied that she and Watriss were heavy drinkers devoted to social activity, and denied that she neglected Brenda. She said she wanted full-time custody of her daughter because she didn't think Frank was a fit father.

"I think [Frazier] supports [Brenda] liberally as regards money, but I don't think he sees very much of the child," she said. "I think his housekeeper and the governess look after her very well. I don't know who she is likely to meet in Mr. Frazier's home. I don't know who she is thrown with. I am only fearful of whom she may be thrown with."

Frazier testified next. Referring to his daughter as Diana, he said he was closely involved in her upbringing while she was in his custody. He said he had daily reports about her from his housekeeper, Mrs. Reilly, and from the governess. He claimed he saw her himself several times a day. He said he wanted to develop Brenda's talent for drawing and eventually send her to a good boarding school, where she would be exposed to outdoor sports and simple, wholesome values. Brenda should be educated in the United States and be completely American, he added.

Asked by his lawyer what Brenda meant to him, Frank said, "She just means everything in the world to me, that's all. I get a tremendous thrill every time I see her, every time she comes to me and touches me. I think of nothing but what she is going to turn out to be when she gets to be a woman, and I am always trying to think of something that will turn out to her advantage."

Lady Jane also testified. She boasted that she sunbathed nude in Nassau with her granddaughter. She said she smoked cigarettes, not a pipe, as apparently rumored. When asked to identify one of Clara Duff Frazier's letters, Lady Jane replied, "I get dozens of letters from maids like that." She called Brenda's governess "a damn fool." When Fred Valz, the Watriss lawyer, started to object to a question asked her by another lawyer, she snapped, "Oh, let him alone, he's so silly."

Lady Jane used the witness stand as a soapbox for advertising her social importance. She volunteered that one of her ancestors was of "a magnificent standing and a great lady." She talked of her "very great friends" in England, and spoke of her daughter's education in Europe, "where she was adored, as she was everywhere else." Referring to her husband's position as head of the Bank of Montreal, she said, "as the [wife of] the head of such an enormous institution, I suppose I entertain more than any woman in Canada, except the Governor-General's wife." Suddenly she picked up a newspaper that was folded in her lap and began reading out loud: "We see here Lady Williams-Taylor taking a morning walk in front of her magnificent winter residence on the Bay of Nassau in the Bahama Islands."

Hours of testimony were devoted to the adulterous ways of the various principals. One hearing in June 1929 was moved to the American Consulate in Paris, apparently to accommodate the many French witnesses. Both sides produced squads of French detectives and chambermaids whose stories of illicit sex droned on for days. The Duchemin brothers,

Hippolyte and Marcel, recounted their observations of Big Brenda and Watriss at the Hôtel Grand Cerf at Évreux four years before. In an attempt to discredit the French detectives, the Watrisses went back to Évreux and personally inspected the rooms. Next they enlisted a housekeeper, the local sheriff, his assistant, and even one of the architects who designed the hotel to make the same inspection. All were produced to testify: it would be physically impossible to see anything through the keyholes and windows under the circumstances the detectives described.

Adultery was also the major subject of a hearing on May 20, 1929, at the Bar Association Building in New York City. The hearing lasted two days, and fifteen witnesses were called. One of the first to testify was Wilson Thompson, a Pullman porter on the night train that Big Brenda and Fred Watriss had taken from New York to Montreal. Under direct examination by John Jackson, Frazier's attorney. Thompson testified that he was in charge of the sleeping car on June 29, 1925, and that he had had advance orders to have compartments C and D ready for occupancy at 9 P.M. Soon a woman occupied C and a man moved into D. Ten minutes after the train left New York, the woman asked Thompson to close the upper berth in her compartment and put a sheet over the window. The man in D then had him unlock the connecting door between the two rooms. After identifying a photograph of Big Brenda, Thompson was asked by the Frazier lawyer if the man who had occupied compartment D on June 29, 1925, was sitting in the room. Several people, Fred Watriss among them, were sitting in a semicircle in front of the witness chair. Starting at the extreme left of the room, Thompson looked at everyone in the semicircle, turning his head 180 degrees until his eyes finally reached Fred Watriss: "I think this gentleman over there, sitting in the last seat there," Thompson said.

Valz was furious. He turned to Jackson. "Will you stipulate in the record that [Thompson] is a Negro witness?"

In a brief later filed in Florida, Robert H. Anderson, one of Watriss's lawyers, argued that "it is incredible that an attempt would be made at the trial of a cause in this country, where the racial characteristic of the Negro for mendacity is so well known, to prove a fact by one of their number where it was denied by respectable white people."

Plenty of "respectable" white people had worse things to say about Big Brenda. A group of Frazier-recruited servants testified that Big Brenda and Watriss led dissolute lives, rising at noon, drinking, and staying out late. Isabel Armstrong, Big Brenda's former personal maid, testified that both Mr. and Mrs. Watriss drank too much, and that the food provided for their children was "sometimes really not quite as good as the staff had." She also claimed that Brenda's clothes were cheap and inappropriate. On cross-examination, Fred Valz tried to show Armstrong's snobbishness:

Q. Will you describe the clothes that Mrs. Watriss furnished that you state were poor?
A. She bought them at Altman's.
Q. What was the matter with them that they were so poor?
A. Well, they were not what I would buy for my niece . . . poor quality and poor style . . . and they made [Brenda] look like nothing on earth.
Q. What kind of a store is Altman's?
A. I would call it a middle class store.
Q. You do not approve of people of Mrs. Watriss's station dealing at a place of that nature?
A. No, well, especially for [Brenda] because they have got money to make her look as she should look.
Q. But you really think she should have expensive clothes?
A. Yes, I do. She was a child belonging to a rich man, and I think she ought to always look nice.

As the matter of *Frazier vs. Frazier* dragged on, the bitterness between Brenda's parents grew. Their vitriol clogged the courts with petitions, counterpetitions, and motions of all kinds. A final settlement was impossible. Meanwhile, Brenda was still traveling back and forth between her parents' homes.

She loved her father; but she felt guilty when she was with him, as if she were betraying her mother. Every summer the Watrisses petitioned the court for permission to take Brenda to Murray Bay, Canada. Judge Chillingworth always approved the trips over Frazier's violent objections.

In the fall of 1929 Frank Frazier started to believe that Brenda, then eight, was on his side. She even wrote a letter to his lawyer, offering to intervene on his behalf in court:

Dear Mr. Jackson,

I must ask you if you think that the Judge will dicide for me to stay with Mummy because if you think he will I will either have somebody tell the truth and say that I want to stay with Daddy I did not tell Mummy yet because she would set up a arguement if I did. And do you think that by any chanse I might be asked if you think so let me know it. If you can help it don't let anybody see this letter. If Mummy haddent done what she did it could have stayed the way it was couldent it. Give my best love to Mrs. Jackson.

love from Diana

At the same time there was much evidence to support Frazier's fears that the Watrisses and Williams-Taylors were trying to turn the child against him. Isabel Armstrong said Big Brenda talked to Brenda a great deal about her "ruined Daddy." The mother told Brenda that Frank had "turned them out of house and home" and that he was crazy. Armstrong said that Big Brenda even asked her to spy on Frazier when Brenda was in his custody and to record exactly how much time he spent with his daughter.

The Williams-Taylors also hinted to Brenda that Palm Beach, where she spent every winter with her father, was an unsuitable place to grow up. As Sir Frederick wrote on February 1, 1928:

My dearest [Brenda],

As I am not such a good writer as you I am using a machine so that you may spell out the words without difficulty.

I want to tell you how glad I was to get your letter and to hear that you can swim and dive and float and bicycle ride. There is not much swimming in Montreal just now, as it has been down to 20 degrees below zero, with mountains of snow in every direction. That may sound very chilly to you, but remember that a cold climate makes hardy people, and I am strongly of opinion that in some ways it would make a stronger, hardier, healthier girl of you if you spent your winters in Montreal with your grandfather, rather than down in your warm part of the world where you are liable to become soft and tender and unfitted for a northern temperature. Mademoiselle will explain all this to you.

I had a long talk with Muffy and Minty [apparently the family dogs] about you this morning, and we all three agreed that it would be very nice if you would come up and see us much oftener than you do. You see we all three know that this house belongs to you and that Grandpa and Muffy and Minty are just living in it and keeping it going until you take possession.

Your Granny is now at the far end of the world; yesterday, she was in a country called Java, where the coffee comes from, and in a few days she will be among the Cannibal Islands where they used to eat people, but they have given that up now because they can get canned goods so very cheap. You may be sure they will not eat your Granny anyway, because for one thing she wouldn't like it. Anyway, they liked to eat coloured people better than white people. They say they taste better. When you come up to see me in Montreal, you must bring your bicycle with you and then we can ride together on the mountain.

Please remember me to Mademoiselle and hoping you will like the photograph I am sending you.

Believe me Angel face, Sweetheart,
Your adoring Grandpa

By 1930 the Williams-Taylors had moved back to England, where they had bought Ramslade, a three-hundred-year-old estate outside of Bracknell, in Berkshire. On February 17 that year, the Watrisses asked the judge to let Brenda spend the summer there with her grandparents. Frazier objected on grounds ranging from Brenda's health to patriotism:

The defendant respectfully represents to the Court that the climate of England is notoriously damp and disagreeable, and conducive to colds and respiratory disorders. The testimony has established that Diana is susceptible to bronchial trouble. Sir Frederick and Lady Williams-Taylor have moved or will shortly move their residence to England, and if the prayer of the petition is granted, Diana will come in frequent contact with Lady Williams-Taylor, whose association is not wholesome for the child. . . . Diana is now

*nearly nine years old. She is unusually bright for her age.
The older she becomes, the more susceptible she is to unwholesome influences and examples . . . if the petition is
granted Diana will be influenced against her father and in
favor of England as compared to the United States.*

Judge Chillingworth, himself the father of three daughters,
did not agree, and once again he granted the Watrisses' request. On May 28 Brenda, along with her mother, stepfather,
stepbrothers, grandfather, Mademoiselle Ducolomb, and Griffiths, the family chauffeur, sailed from Montreal on the *Empress of Scotland.* They landed at Southampton on June 3 and
drove to Ramslade, arriving at midnight. Lady Jane met them
at the door, and after a light supper they all went to bed.

Ramslade, set on 140 acres of rolling hills, was dotted with
lakes, croquet lawns, and tennis courts. It was idyllic for
children. Brenda and the boys had a boat, bicycles, and
their own play cottage. "Three times a week we go riding in Windsor Great Park which is beautiful. . . . We see
herds of deer and white goats. And sometimes see Prince
George go up in his aeoroplane," Brenda wrote in her diary
that summer.

Brenda visited her English cousins, saw Madame Tussaud's
wax museum, and toured the Tower of London, where her
mother's friend Lord Gough commanded the Irish Guards.
She pasted pictures of herself and her relatives in her diary,
amid postcards of British monuments and royalty. "Mummy
had dinner with the Prince of Wales," she noted in one entry.
And in another: "Sir George Crichton was very kind to us
and arranged for us all to go over the private apartments at
Windsor Castle which very few people are allowed to see.
We saw the room where the King and Queen have lunch and
breakfast. Their little sitting room, the suit of armour worn
by Henry the VIII and lovely pictures."

Brenda returned from England in September to find that
she had a new stepmother. On June 10, Frank Frazier had
married his nurse, Marjorie Affleck. Sick and faltering, Frank
was undoubtedly fond of the nurse. Yet he immediately used
the marriage to strengthen his position in the custody case.
In an amendment to his petition, filed soon after the wedding,
he described his wife's impeccable character and credentials.

Then he produced nineteen witnesses who testified that Marjorie possessed the patience and loving nature of a natural mother.

The Watrisses retaliated by trying to sully Marjorie's reputation. After accepting bribes from Braun and De Vries, five employees in the building where Marjorie had lived before her marriage testified that she entertained men in her apartment.

Soon after the marriage, when Brenda left to be with her father in Palm Beach, Big Brenda insisted that the governess, Mademoiselle Ducolomb, go along to help the little girl adjust to her new stepmother. Marjorie soon became convinced that the governess was being used to turn Brenda against her father. "It is the feeling, and it is the atmosphere that is there when Diana and Mademoiselle and her father are together," Marjorie said. "It is the same when I am there. I will ask Diana if she would like to go to the movies, and she will say, 'I would love to, Marjorie.' And I will send her upstairs to get her coat and hat, and when she comes down Mademoiselle has her by the hand and has her own hat on. I have never been allowed, unless I insisted on it, to take Diana out of that house once this whole season."

Throughout all this time, Brenda had never been called to testify. In 1930 Big Brenda had asked Judge Chillingworth to put the girl on the stand, but Frank objected, arguing that it might be damaging to her. The judge agreed it was not a good idea; he said he would hear Brenda's testimony only if he could not otherwise decide the case. But the following year, in February 1931, Big Brenda renewed her request, saying that although Brenda was only nine, "she has the intelligence, understanding and demeanor of a much older child, with which fact your petitioner verily believes the court will become immediately impressed after seeing and hearing her."

Frazier realized that the judge was going to ask Brenda to testify. He suggested that it be done in a manner that is "the least disturbing" to a nine-year-old child and that the testimony be taken informally, outside the courthouse, without lawyers for the parents or the parents themselves being present.

Early in 1931, Judge Chillingworth signed an order to take Brenda's testimony, and on February 24 Frank Frazier's chauffeur drove Brenda to the county courthouse in West Palm Beach. Accompanied by her governess, the nine-year-old child was led into Judge Chillingworth's chambers. Her parents were not there, but their lawyers were.

Two weeks earlier, Big Brenda had come to Palm Beach in preparation. Since then she had seen her daughter only twice—both times in a restaurant. But the mother's influence was still overwhelming to the child. Brenda's testimony was a total rejection of her father. The stratagem Frank Frazier had thought would help him win the case, his marriage, had backfired.

Although her father had been kind to her, Brenda said she believed she "would have a better time" with her mother. Beyond that, most of her objections centered on her stepmother and seemed to echo the snobbishness of Lady Jane and Big Brenda. Brenda said she wouldn't love her stepmother because "she has been too common." Brenda regretted that "when I am married, I will always have to think he married a trained nurse." She told Judge Chillingworth that Marjorie married her father "for money more than anything else," and referred to one of Marjorie's friends as "not what I call very ladylike."

She said she thought her father should have asked her consent before he married. Her mother, she said, told her that Mrs. Frazier "has very few friends." Brenda also complained that Marjorie had "very bad table manners." Brenda admitted that she learned her own good table manners as much from her father as her mother, and then offered that she "would much rather speak French than English."

Under questioning from the lawyers, she said her father showed no interest in her schooling or drawing. "Hasn't he taken you on his knee and asked you to show him pictures you have drawn and suggested things to draw and encouraged you?" one of the lawyers asked Brenda. She answered, "No, I wish he would take some interest in it; it is about time, I have been drawing for some time." She said that it was at her father's urging that she had written the letter to his lawyer John Jackson. Frazier's lawyers, dismayed at the little girl's testimony, tried to show that she had been influenced by her mother and grandmother. One asked Brenda whether her mother had talked to her about the case.

A. No, . . . she never said anything to me.

Q. Your Daddy has always been truthful to you, hasn't he? So far as you know, he has always told you the truth, hasn't he?

A. I don't think always, no.

Q. Do you think your Mummy has always told you the truth?

A. Yes, far as I can remember she always has.

Q. Has your mother or Mr. Watriss tried to make you feel unkindly toward Mrs. Frazier?

A. No, Mummy thought I might like her, but I didn't a bit. She is very common. Mummy asked if I liked her, and I didn't, a bit.

Q. Has your Mummy told you that Miss Affleck married your Daddy for money?

A. No, she did not say that; it was quite my own idea. I thought so because I didn't see that she liked him at all and I thought probably that was it. She bought about eight pairs of shoes in about one week down here last winter and I would like to know why she was working if she had money to get everything she wanted.

Q. Has your Grandfather Frederick or Grandmother Lady Jane tried to make you feel unkindly toward your father?

A. Not a bit.

Q. Now, Brenda, think right well and tell the Judge whether or not your Mummy has ever spoken badly of your Daddy.

A. No, all she said was that she and Daddy were not friends, and he said the same thing. She has never spoken of Daddy otherwise.

Q. She has never told you that he was a very bad man?

A. No.

Q. Are you sure of it?

A. Sure of it.

Brenda was lying, of course. Big Brenda had spoken for years of Frank Frazier's wickedness, his drinking, his womanizing, his lack of concern for his daughter. She had obviously coached Brenda and coached her well. Brenda loved her father and was devoted to him, but she was terrified of defying her mother. Thirty years later, Brenda told her psychiatrist that one of the greatest regrets of her life was her lying to the lawyers and Judge Chillingworth. "Brenda was a little mannequin, a little puppet with a ventriloquist mother," says her psychiatrist. "Brenda had a great, great love for her father. It took [her] years to overcome the fears implanted by the mother, but he was a great man in her eyes."

On November 17, 1931, Judge Chillingworth awarded custody to Brenda Watriss. He did not issue an opinion, explaining that "no useful purpose would be served by any statement of my views, conclusions or findings." Frank Frazier was allowed "reasonable" visiting rights, but was not to have Brenda in his home for more than two weeks a year. The judge continued the $750 monthly child support payments and also charged the entire cost of the four-year proceedings to Frazier.

Ten days later, on November 27, Frazier filed an appeal with the Supreme Court of Florida in Tallahassee. More than a year later, in January 1933, after reviewing 4,000 pages of testimony contained in eight volumes, a five-judge panel reached a decision. The justices agreed with the lower court that Brenda's welfare and schooling required some modification in the split-custody agreement. But it found that the two-week limit on Frank's custody deprived him of "practically every vestige of his parental right to reasonably associate with and enjoy the companionship of his only child." The court extended his custody to three months a year. The nine-page decision left little doubt as to how the justices felt about either parent:

> That the father has an unusual feeling of affection for his only daughter has not been successfully refuted. Indeed this trait appears to be one of the few commendable characteristics he has shown in an otherwise sordid career. Neither parent appears to have been in the past, nor appears to be now, any paragon of virtue in parenthood. Nor can it be said that the mother of the child, even under the improved conditions claimed to exist since her last marriage, is on this record entitled to any more consideration as a parent than is the father.

Two members of the panel dissented. One of them, Justice Buford, wrote: "The record abounds with undisputed proof that . . . the father here . . . availed himself but little of any of the pleasures or privileges of the society or control of the child . . . he left her to the care, society, and control of persons employed by him for that purpose, while he pursued . . . conduct in which she could not participate."

After the decision, Brenda saw her father only occasionally, at his apartment in New York. "The visits, on which my [governess] reluctantly took me, were stiff and awkward," she recalled later. "When my father sent me clothing, it was put away as unsuitable for a girl my age. At times, when I felt affectionate toward him, I felt guilty toward my mother. When I clung to my mother, I felt guilty toward my father. I had two different parents in two different homes, yet psychologically, I was an orphan."

By February 1933, Frank Frazier had lost not only his daughter, but also what was left of his health. Suffering from throat cancer, he nonetheless pretended in his letters to Brenda to be busy and cheerful. In one letter he described his fishing trips and golf games, and closed with "Lots of love to you, and be sure to write soon to Daddy."

By spring, he was too ill to pick up a pen. Marjorie wrote in his place:

Dear Diana,
    Ten days ago your father picked up an influenza germ and has been in bed since—he's having his ears irrigated which is the reason he has not written you. He is much better however and just as soon as he is able to get out of bed will write to you. I expected to have a nice snapshot of your father and Taffy to send you today, but Joe thought Taffy needed a shave and cut off his whiskers which makes him look a little queer so your father wouldn't let me take his picture.
    Do keep well, and write to us when you have a spare moment. Lots of love from us both—

                                                            Marjorie

On June 21, Frank Frazier was operated on for throat cancer at a hospital in New York. He died twenty-four hours later.

Frazier's death, at age fifty-one, did not end his bitter feud with Brenda Watriss, however. His will named Marjorie as his daughter's guardian. It also stipulated—despite the custody ruling—that if Brenda lived with her mother or the Williams-Taylors instead of Marjorie, all the income from a small trust he had established would be reinvested as capital, until Brenda reached age twenty-one. If any court declared this provision illegal, Frazier instructed that the income from the trust then go to Yale University to establish a fund for medical research called "The Frazier Fund."

This "spite clause" was little more than that. Frank had no control over the income from the four large trusts set up by his parents. That income had already been earmarked for Brenda. The four trusts, along with about $800,000 in cash and property, comprised the bulk of his $4 million estate. The one trust established by his will was valued at only $280,000, and the income it threw off came to a comparatively meager $8,000 a year.

But these were facts the press virtually ignored. The news of Frazier's "unforgiving" will burst into the headlines in Palm Beach and New York. Like Barbara Hutton, another "poor little rich girl," Brenda was the perfect Depression-era symbol. She was worth $4 million, but she couldn't touch the money, the tabloids incorrectly reported, if she lived with her mother.

Sometime after her father's death, Brenda told Palm Beach County Judge Richard P. Robbins that she wanted to live with her own mother, and on July 8, 1933, the judge appointed Big Brenda her guardian. It is unclear exactly how the court avoided carrying out the intent of Frank Frazier's will. It is possible that his widow, Marjorie, declined guardianship of Brenda; or perhaps the trustees of the will, to whom Frank had given absolute discretion in carrying out the terms of the "spite clause," decided that the clause should be ignored. What happened to the money from that trust is unknown. Most likely it was reinvested, as Frazier directed, and eventually turned over to Brenda. Yale never sued to collect it.

Judge Robbins's decision appointing Big Brenda guardian was handed down several days after a hurricane, and reporters went wild comparing the weather to Brenda's "storm-tossed courtroom existence."

A reporter for the *Daily Mirror* interviewed Big Brenda over the phone at a resort in the Catskills where she was vacationing with her husband and daughter. He asked her how she felt about forfeiting Brenda's inheritance: "Yale is a lovely institution," Big Brenda said crisply. "But I don't want it to get [Brenda's] money."

CHAPTER FOUR

As 1933 PASSED into 1934, Brenda Watriss began to keep a diary. In it she recorded the details of her daughter's social life—which included a busy party and dating schedule that Big Brenda herself had orchestrated.

Brenda was not yet thirteen then, but she looked and acted much older. She waltzed at the St. Regis dressed in floor-length pink chiffon. She smoked cigarettes and stayed out all night. "In those days that was unheard of," says James Watriss. "For a girl her age and in that time, Brenda lived a very free and uninhibited life." She had her own French lady's maid, a woman named "Slater" whom Big Brenda had hired to replace Mademoiselle Ducolomb. Brenda wore heavy makeup and expensive jewels. Manicures, pedicures, and dress fittings were as much a part of her life as school, which she often missed because of colds and other illnesses. But Big Brenda wasn't particularly concerned about her daughter's education. Of her mother's attitude Brenda wrote: "I had a little talent for music and my teachers said I had a great talent for art, but these were important only as a matter of being well-rounded. You do not become a grande dame in high society by playing the piano or painting seriously. I was pretty good in my classes, but that was all together unimportant. Indeed . . . it was possibly dangerous; it might disqualify me for marriage to someone who was a brilliant catch, but unfortunately stupid."

Big Brenda was a crude, sloppy woman, still dominated by

her own mother, and, as her diary entries show, she had an astounding inability to separate what was important from what was trivial. Although she liked to paint bird portraits, generally she was bored by serious pursuits. Curiously, however, she enjoyed housework, and looked forward to vacations away from the servants so she could do her own laundry, which she described as "my favorite occupation." She was enormously fond of food, especially cake. After one binge, she described herself as looking "absolutely pregnant I'm so fat." When she went from 132 to 142 pounds in one year, she began a diet, one of many. But like all her attempts to lose weight, it failed. "Overeating agrees with me—the minute I cut out sweets, I feel awful," she rationalized.

Big Brenda's relationship with Fred Watriss was an improvement over her union with Frank Frazier, although there were some strains on this marriage too—strains sparked in large part by disagreements over how Brenda should be raised.

Most of Brenda's friends loathed her mother. "Brenda had a wonderful personality," says Esme O'Brien Hammond. "She was a very good artist and painter. She could even do cartoons. But she had a terrible life. Her mother was awful. She was a big, tough Mae West type. Brenda didn't get along with her, and I didn't like her."

"Brenda's mother was really evil," adds Jane Will Smith. "The only thing she lived for was the reflected glory she got from Brenda."

Later in life, Brenda herself seemed to blame most of her problems on Big Brenda. Her psychiatrist accepted this view. "Brenda's mother was too self-involved," he says. "All the psychic economy available to her to extend to relationships were [used] on her mother and herself. They were a duo like Siamese twins. How could she take care of a child who didn't exist? It was a horrible state of affairs."

But in fact, Brenda's relationship with her mother was more complicated than this. Gertie Folmsbee says Big Brenda deeply loved Brenda, whom she affectionately called "Ewee," short for "ewe lamb." "I think Brenda had a lot more attention given her than other girls of her [social] class," says Folmsbee. "Her mother was very fond of her."

The Watriss brothers also remember Big Brenda as a caring, if somewhat superficial, woman. Says Fred Watriss, Jr.,

"Big Brenda was really quite a nice person, generous and fond of people." Jimmy Watriss recalls that she encouraged the boys to call her "Mummy," and did try to be a good mother to them. But her relationship with her stepsons was tainted by her strained relations with Fred Watriss, Sr. Says Jimmy, "Big Brenda pushed Brenda. That was the biggest sore point with my father. I know that he didn't like it. There were bad feelings about it. He thought Brenda should be a normal child."

Big Brenda and Brenda were close and dependent on one another, but it was a closeness without mutual understanding and trust. Big Brenda's main goal in life was social success, a goal she inherited from her mother. Lady Jane's ambition, however, was redeemed by her personal dash, her wit, her forceful personality, whereas Big Brenda was a snob in the most conventional sense—she was obsessed with pedigrees and family fortunes.

Big Brenda was thrilled, as she noted in her diary, that "everyone raves about Brenda's beauty and charm." Brenda was less impressed with herself, and, even as a child, had a self-deprecating sense of humor. At dinner one night at the home of her friend Jerry Pendleton, someone at the table mentioned a young woman who was such a great beauty that she left people breathless. Without missing a beat, fourteen-year-old Brenda remarked, "The only way *I* can leave people breathless is to punch them in the stomach."

As soon as her potential for social success was apparent, Brenda felt "destined—doomed would be a better word—to be the most popular, sought-after debutante who ever broke a masculine heart. When I went to a party, nobody asked me afterward whether I had had a good time—only how many boys had danced with me. When I was still very young, a college boy asked me to a college prom—I forget just where. There was no question of my thinking about such problems as whether I was old enough to go, or really wanted to go. I accepted as a matter of course, then found that I was two to three years younger than any other girl or boy at the dance and had such an utterly miserable time that I never again—alone among all my acquaintants—went to another. But I would never have dared tell my mother that I was unhappy."

Throughout her life, social situations always made Brenda

anxious. Every dinner party, every dance, every charity ball "was anxiety-provoking," says her psychiatrist. "She was the shiest, most scared little girl. [She] thought she was completely unattractive." Big Brenda, in her blindness, never realized how unhappy Brenda was, and continued to push her. When another girl came along who was perceived as competition for her daughter, Big Brenda got in the way of the two girls' friendship.

One of Brenda's best friends at the time was Cobina Wright, junior. Cobina and Brenda had been playmates since kindergarten, and they had more in common than beauty. Both had dramatic, unhappy childhoods and ambitious, domineering mothers. Cobina's mother was the singer-actress Elaine Cobb, known on stage as Madame Cobina. After her divorce from an impoverished writer, Owen Johnson, Cobina senior married multimillionaire William May Wright.

Cobina junior grew up on Long Island in a pink stucco mansion with pink gravel in the driveway, a small golf course in back, and her own playhouse. It was a fairytale childhood, until Wright lost all his money in the 1929 crash. Later he and Cobina senior were divorced in a sensational trial that shared headlines with the Lindbergh kidnapping and the Gloria Vanderbilt custody case. Afterward Cobina junior saw her father only once—years later, when her youngest son was born.

On their own in Manhattan, the two Cobinas lived as nonpaying prestige guests in a suite at the Waldorf-Astoria. Cobina senior started a Saturday-night supper club at the Waldorf and became a torch singer at Mon Paris. At twelve, Cobina junior went to work as a Powers fashion model. She considered Brenda, whom she affectionately called "Ben," terribly spoiled. Cobina remembers staying with the Watrisses on East Seventy-fifth Street for two weeks: "Once we were playing a card game in Brenda's room and her mother came in with a big box and said, 'Here, Brenda, I have something for you.' Brenda answered, 'Not now, Mummy, we're playing. I'll look at it later.' When her mother insisted, Brenda opened the box for a peek. It was a gorgeous mink coat. Brenda seemed unimpressed. She simply said, 'Thank you, Mummy' and went back to what she was doing. I was very envious."

Though she considered Cobina her best friend, Brenda felt

competitive with the pretty blonde. She talked about the rivalry to Patricia Walsh Chadwick, a young woman who worked for her in Boston. "Brenda never got over it," says Chadwick, now a banker in Manhattan. "It was a social game, encouraged by the rivalry of the two mothers. I don't think Brenda loved Cobina. All I ever sensed was a genuine jealousy. She would tell tales about how Cobina thought she could outdo her. It had to do with a dress, or a ball, or a man. That was the level it was on. I don't think Brenda had too many friends."

Despite her adult furs, jewels, and sophisticated black gowns, Brenda at age twelve was an emotional infant. In February 1934, as her mother planned a trip to Miami, Brenda grew increasingly agitated. Big Brenda—hardly more than an emotional infant herself—seemed flattered by her daughter's distress, writing in her diary:

> [Feb. 26.] I spent all morning having a permanent at Michael's. B went with me—she really feels terribly at my leaving her—the sweet thing—follows me around like a puppy—I lunched with Fritz Mailer and then went to Bloomingdales and . . . got a lot of odds and ends. Sat with Freddie—we dined together. I have been asked out every night.

> [Feb. 27.] Miss Lockhart, the great numerologist, came at 11 to see me. She was extremely interesting and said there [would] be drastic changes in my life this year—Brenda is almost in tears at the thought of my going tomorrow—I hate leaving her—she is my life and I do so want to bring her up a kind and intelligent person—Freddie looks really better— Willis Booth came in at 6:15—Ash and Martha.

> [Feb. 28.] Brenda slept with me and did not go to school as we had lunch at 12:45—I had a million things to do— Brenda came to the station. Also John the butler. . . . She cried big crocodile tears. . . .

"The only way I could gain any semblance of love and acceptance was to submerge my own desires in my mother's, to be the totally dependent and passive tool of my mother's whims and ambitions," wrote Brenda. "She liked me when

60

I was 'good,' when I obeyed Mademoiselle and caused no trouble, when I showed that I adored her and was charming to her friends. I knew in the way children know such things, that I myself did not count, that nothing at all really counted very deeply in the superficial kind of life my mother and her friends were living.''

Sometimes, however, Brenda's hidden resentment toward her mother erupted in fights. Once when Fred Watriss was out of town, he wired that he would arrive home at 11:30. Brenda took the message, but forgot to tell Griffiths, the family chauffeur. Big Brenda, who was suffering from a painful abscess in her leg, had to take a taxi to the station to pick him up. She quarreled with Brenda, and they didn't speak for several days. Big Brenda wrote of the incident in her diary, ''This question of rows with Brenda is killing me. She can't stand any criticism, has hysterics, too painful . . . making me upset and nervous, which my leg is doing without any extra help. . . . Brenda and I have not met. She has to apologize. I am not very happy at the situation. . . . It's very sad for her if she goes through life so relentlessly—she won't apologize—I'm upset, and I imagine she isn't too happy.''

Brenda's relationship with her mother was strained by the fact that they were often apart. When Big Brenda wasn't traveling to Nassau, California, Montreal, England, or French Lick, Indiana, she was socializing in New York. She had lunch and dinner dates nearly every day. The rest of her time was filled with the business of society—teas, bridge parties, shopping, plays, and charity balls. Her social obligations escalated when her parents came to town, as they usually did several times a year.

On April 30, 1935, the Williams-Taylors were in New York to celebrate Big Brenda's birthday. ''We all lunched at the Ritz with Daddy—Being my birthday I had 28 for dinner—grand party had great fun—they left at 2:30 A.M. Have lovely presents and flowers. Daddy gave me $200 to pay for my two false teeth!'' Big Brenda wrote. The next evening, Big Brenda and her mother dined with Lady Jane's latest beau, George MacDonald, at his apartment. MacDonald was tall, blond, and handsome and had made a reported $32 million fortune buying and selling utilities in New York State. He became board chairman of the Federal Home Loan Bank of New York in 1932 and was also a powerful Catholic layman, serving as trustee of both St. Patrick's Cathedral and Catholic Charities of the Archdiocese of New York.

After dinner, Lady Jane, Big Brenda, and MacDonald took a train to the Sea View Golf Club in New Jersey, arriving at 12:30. "Had a heavenly day at Atlantic City—never have I laughed more—George is a divine companion and such a sense of humor—we have a grand suite—sitting room, etc. and our dinner up there. . . . G. MacDonald is a wonderful host—we then spent the entire afternoon at Atlantic City again; dined at 7:30. . . . Mother, George Mac and I again took the [train] at 9:30 back for New York—all weeping that our little jaunt was over. . . . ''

Big Brenda's financial dependence on her daughter exacerbated the tensions between them. Although Fred Watriss had survived the 1929 stock market crash, he lost money in the mini-crash of 1933. With his health failing—he suffered from a painful case of phlebitis—he had virtually retired by 1934. In a prenuptial agreement, Watriss had set up a trust fund for his wife that guaranteed her an income of $15,000 a year, the same amount that Frank Frazier had paid her in alimony. Big Brenda thus had enough money to live on, but not enough to continue her grand style of entertaining and traveling. For that she needed Brenda's money.

The details of Big Brenda's use of the money were laid out in New York County Surrogate's Court in February 1934, when she petitioned to have her daughter's guardianship transferred to Manhattan, where she lived. The petition went to Surrogate James Aloysius Foley, one of the court's two powerful judges, who annually handled half-a-billion dollars in estates.

Of the approximate $100,000 in income earned in 1934 by Brenda's five trusts and other property, Big Brenda asked for $19,204 to pay for Brenda's maintenance and education. In addition, she asked Surrogate Foley to charge Brenda one fourth of the Watrisses' annual household expenses, or $11,296.50. Five people lived at East Seventy-fifth Street, but since Brenda's two stepbrothers were away at boarding school or camp most of the year, Big Brenda felt this was fair. The total she requested was thus $30,000 a year, the same amount that had been granted her by Judge Richard P. Robbins in Palm Beach County Court. The rest of the income from the trusts—$70,000—would be reinvested as capital.

Attached to the petition was a list of itemized expenses:

Clothing	$3,600.00
Music	600.00
School	1,500.00
Skating and Dancing lessons	100.00
Governess	1,500.00
Doctors and Medical Supplies	1,500.00
Dentists	2,400.00
Secretarial and clerical services, insurance, attorneys' fees and miscellaneous	1,500.00
Club dues	400.00
Charitable contributions	250.00
Gratuities	200.00
Christmas gifts	250.00
Amusements, Parties, etc.	1,200.00
Traveling and Summer Vacation	3,500.00
Books, Toys, School Supplies, etc.	600.00
Pocket money	104.00
	$19,204.00

Household Expenses:

Servants, including chauffeur and extra help for parties	$10,180.00
Maintenance of automobiles, including supplies, insurance and depreciation	4,500.00
Interest on mortgage	6,600.00
Taxes	5,000.00
Insurance	500.00
Gas and Electricity	700.00
Ice, coal and wood	1,600.00
Laundry, dry cleaning, window and carpet cleaning	2,000.00
Elevator inspection	156.00
Telephone	450.00
Cuisine	7,000.00
Ash removal and miscellaneous extra expenses	500.00

Repairs to house	3,000.00
Replacement of glassware, linen, draperies and curtains, kitchen equipment, etc.	3,000.00
	$45,186.00

One fourth of above total: $11,296.50

total $30,500.50

On June 6, 1934, Surrogate Foley signed an order authorizing Big Brenda to spend $30,000 of her daughter's money. Courthouse reporters, bored by routine lawsuits, pounced on this unusual story. Their enthusiasm, however, far exceeded their devotion to accuracy: "HEIRESS, 12, GETS $2 WEEKLY DESPITE $8,000,000 FORTUNE" announced the *Journal-American*. (The reporters arrived at the $2 figure by dividing the number of weeks in the year into Brenda's $104 annual allowance for pocket money.) The Watrisses were vacationing in Murray Bay, Canada, when the first stories appeared. Big Brenda wrote in her diary on September 10, 1934: "Another long article about Brenda and her blasted reputed millions—it is so wicked."

In May 1935, soon after she finished the school year at Miss Hewitt's, Brenda sailed for England to spend the summer with her grandparents and to be presented at the Court of St. James's. She was barely fourteen, two years younger than the English debutantes, but Lady Jane and Big Brenda couldn't wait to launch her in society. She was already gaining a reputation as a great beauty—although her square face, with its full cheeks and thin lips, wasn't classic, nor was her figure perfect. "Brenda wasn't really beautiful," says her stepbrother Fred Watriss. "She just was done up to look beautiful." Her appeal was the opposite of that of bony blondes like Marlene Dietrich and Greta Garbo. There was nothing awesome or intimidating about Brenda's beauty.

She had a sweetness to her face, a warmth that was enhanced by luminous dark eyes. But Brenda's greatest asset was her striking coloring. She had flawless, translucent white skin, the type of complexion that Colette once described as "milk in shadow." Her hair was wavy dark brown and under nightclub lighting seemed to take on a bluish tint. Later, newspaper reporters and some of Brenda's friends started to think her hair *was* blue-black—an example of how her image had begun to erode her identity. In any case, the dramatic contrast of white skin and dark hair became her trademark, defining forever the "Glamour Girl" look, a style still copied by such contemporary beauties as Gloria Vanderbilt.

In London, Fleet Street reporters, well acquainted with Lady Jane's flamboyance, fought to interview her granddaughter. Still shy despite her popularity, Brenda tried to thwart the publicity by explaining her fear of kidnappers. But this had the opposite effect. Under the headline . . . DREAD OF PUBLICITY LEST KIDNAPPERS GET ON HER TRAIL . . . a *Daily Mail* reporter wrote:

> *Miss Frazier, a slim, petite figure with crisply curling hair of a rich chestnut shade, twisted her many charm-hung bracelets about a slender wrist. Then, nervously lighting a cigarette, she said:*
>
> *"Everywhere I go I am afraid to have it published where I am staying, or with whom. At home all such information about me is rigidly suppressed."*
>
> *She was firm in refusing to say how long her visit to London is to last, and when she is expected to return home.*
>
> *Miss Frazier, who is much sought after by the younger social set, is taking a busy part in the remaining functions of London's social season. Most mornings of the week she is to be seen riding in the Row.*
>
> *Although still officially a schoolgirl (she has not yet finished her studies), Miss Frazier is a very "grown-up" person with a manner which suggests that she is well equipped to handle the great wealth that will soon be hers.*

In certain ways, Brenda was indeed grown-up. Encouraged by her grandmother and mother, she was having sexual relationships with men by the time she was fourteen—perhaps earlier. Both Big Brenda and Lady Jane encouraged Brenda to share their detached, unemotional attitude towards sex. (To one acquaintance who met them in Nassau, Lady Jane and Big Brenda "looked like two old harlots, very painted and mean.") Making Brenda available sexually was a way of advertising her to the field of eligibles. "Look at what Lady Jane got as a result of sleeping around," says Victoria Kelly.

"In her mind that was obviously the way to get places. [Lady Jane] had the kind of personality that she could do it, get away with it and be a great success at it. Not everybody can take it. She didn't associate it with hurting anybody."

"When she was six or seven years younger than she should ever have had a [sexual] experience, her mother led her to it by the hand," says Brenda's psychiatrist. It is difficult to know how this was accomplished. As one possible explanation, the psychiatrist offers a story about one of his patients who may or may not have been Brenda.

When this patient was twelve years old, according to the psychiatrist, she traveled to Europe with her mother. On the trip they visited a castle, where a sixty-year-old nobleman lived alone. The nobleman desired the little girl, so the mother brought her to his bed that night. The next morning, as the child emerged from the old man's room, the mother asked, "How big was his cock?"

Just how intimate Brenda was with the men she met in London is unclear. But her scrapbook for that summer in Europe is filled with notes and telegrams from admirers. One, Fritz Wilson, sent her a bouquet of flowers, with a message, "Divine creature, some lilies. Darling, I hope I meet you once again." Another swain, a member of London's Author's Club, wrote her a poem on club stationery:

A Treasure

Britain to the U.S.A. gives thanks,
Not for specie or credit from banks,
Not for crooning, not music and song
Not for Crosby or Senator Long.
But thanks—since Sam thought fit to lend her
For the loan of a treasure called Brenda.

That summer Brenda became close to a man twice her age named Tommy Weldon. Weldon—tall and homely with a huge hook nose and awkward, storklike limbs—seemed an unlikely choice for a romance, but he apparently managed to charm her. After she returned to the States, he sent her a letter, which she pasted in her scrapbook and kept until the end of her life. In the letter, which is sexually suggestive, Weldon refers to his lack of interest in women his own age ("I'm so used to schoolgirls by now") and closes by expressing a longing to hear from Brenda "regarding your future plans, i.e., are you going back to the nursery!!!"

For the next two years they continued to see each other in New York, London, Paris, and Nassau, in a romance that Big Brenda seems to have encouraged.

In the fall of 1935, Brenda entered Miss Porter's in Farmington, Connecticut, a fashionable finishing school that trained girls for lives of leisure, not work. The school was founded in 1843 by Miss Sarah Porter, the daughter of a Congregational minister. Farmington, as the school is commonly called, boasted beautiful grounds, exquisite pre-Civil War buildings, and a dairy farm with "a grade-A milk herd to nourish its grade-A students." The school's Victorian attitudes about girlhood prevailed throughout the thirties. Every morning the girls were awakened by maids, who would enter their rooms calling, "Good morning, young ladies," before slamming the windows shut. The girls were not allowed to shop in town, nor were they permitted to wash their own hair. That was done by an old woman who came in once a week. Another woman visited twice a month to teach the girls etiquette.

Farmington was known for its well-trained, dedicated teachers. "They were sensitive to the personal problems of almost every girl," says Nancy Perkins, class of '35. "There was a lot of subtle teaching of values, such as compassion." The school was less well regarded from the standpoint of scholastic rigor. Classes started at a leisurely 9 A.M., and attendance was loosely monitored. Legend has it that on snowy evenings girls would hang out of the windows, trying to catch cold so they could be sent to recover at their parents' homes in Palm Beach. "Girls who wanted to go to college weren't encouraged to go to Miss Porter's," recalls Anne Cox Chambers, the newspaper publisher who was one of Brenda's classmates. "It was a finishing school. We studied art, history, English, French, music. We didn't have to do math or science. We didn't have to do sports." Adds Jane Will Smith, "If you could keep breathing, you could graduate from Farmington in those days.'' Actually, only those girls who earned a certain number of points received diplomas. Most girls never graduated. They simply left.

On the morning of October 3, Brenda and her mother took a train from New York to Hartford, where Griffiths met them in the family Lincoln for the drive to Farmington. Another student, Amanda Cecil, and her father accompanied them. On their arrival, Big Brenda inspected Brenda's room and chatted with her teachers. When it was time to leave, the mother and daughter roles seemed reversed again. Big Brenda burst into tears and fled outside to the car. She and Mr. Cecil rode back to New York, stopping in Westport for a consoling cup of tea.

Brenda's classmates remember her as a pretty girl, although quite plump. Jane Will Smith recalls that Brenda in those days was ''a little fat. She had a plump round face, and big legs and big arms.'' Anne Cox Chambers says of Brenda at fourteen, ''She was absolutely beautiful; she had this blue-black hair and white skin.''

But her beauty was marred by her unattractive legs. They were not the legs of a great debutante. They were shapeless and had had since her childhood a tendency to swell at the feet and ankles, a condition called edema, whenever Brenda was nervous or upset. Sometimes her feet would swell to three times their normal size and would cause such soreness that Brenda had to take a taxi even to travel a few blocks. Often she couldn't sit through lunch in a restaurant without putting her feet up. From adolescence on, she had several hundred pairs of shoes in different sizes to accommodate the changing shape of her feet. Some days they would be normal, other days the size of grapefruits. ''It wasn't just piano legs,'' says Anne Cox Chambers. ''It was a real deformity, like elephantitis. We all felt so sorry for her.''

The swelling plagued her until death, and none of the dozens of doctors she saw could diagnose the problem. ''She had some of the finest doctors in the world. But nothing we did for her really did any good,'' recalls Dr. Robert Hanned, a family practitioner who treated Brenda in her forties. ''She was a very proud and vain person. And the feet were ugly. Almost up to her knees. I used to give her injections of a mercury product drug—no one uses it anymore. But that's the only way we ever got any of the fluid out. But none of us really believed in what we were doing. The edema remained a mystery and a problem.''

Brenda's psychiatrist believes there was nothing organically wrong with Brenda's legs, that the swelling was caused solely by stress: ''It was a simple symptomatic [example] of the things that go wrong with people with severe neurosis. It was merely water retention. Something happened to the water balance in her body. There is a connection between hormones and water balance. After all, hormones are the messengers of the psyche. As she got well, her feet got well.''

Since she was six, Brenda's legs had been of great concern to her mother and grandmother. As a child, Brenda recalled, ''I was not only plain but rather awkward and my feet were always swollen, which must have seemed like the last straw to my mother. She was forever taking me to new doctors.''

One decided that the swelling could be cured by lengthening her heel cords, the Achilles' tendons. ''Poor Brenda has to have an operation on the tendons of her legs—they are too short—there is no use worrying, but I do,'' Big Brenda wrote in her diary on November 14, 1936.

On December 3, Brenda checked into the Le Roy Sanitarium, a small private hospital at 40 East Sixty-first Street that was popular with society women because the food came from the fashionable Colony Restaurant next door. She was operated on the following day. First the orthopedic surgeon, Dr. Arthur Krida, made incisions in the backs of her legs, exposing the tendons. Then he elongated the tendons by partially slitting the tissues, stretching them, and then suturing them back together. This operation is done today only as a last-resort treatment for such conditions as clubbed feet and chronic tendonitis, but it was common in the thirties.

The procedure lasted an hour and fifteen minutes. Big Brenda, Fred Watriss, and Tommy Weldon—Brenda's British beau, who was in town to visit her—stayed until 9 P.M. at Brenda's bedside. When she finally came home three weeks later, Brenda was still wearing casts on both legs. A nurse had to carry her up to her bed, and she ate Christmas dinner in a wheelchair. The casts were removed on December 28, and she was fitted for steel braces, which she wore for six months.

Brenda's friends believed the operation was mostly cosmetic. Says Audrey Gray Chapin, "I remember seeing her before the operation, when she told me she was going to have it done. She said, 'You've seen my legs. They're unsightly, and it's not a big operation. I've got to have it done, it's just a question of time.' " Decades later, Brenda told one of her nurses that her mother had the operation done so she could wear high heels.

Although Brenda's legs looked the same after the operation as they did before (except for stocking seam scars on the backs of her calves), some acquaintances imagined a vast improvement. Brenda's remade legs became part of the myth that built up around her at the height of her celebrity. Anne Cox Chambers remembers seeing Brenda after her debut and being "shocked and admiring of her legs. They looked fine. I heard the doctors told her the operation might cripple her. I was admiring to think that she'd gone through all that knowing she might never walk again."

But Dr. John C. McCauley, Jr., the late Dr. Krida's partner, says the operation definitely was not cosmetic. Dr. McCauley and other orthopedic surgeons say there is no way that lengthening the heel cords could improve the shape or appearance of a woman's legs. "It was a mechanical problem. She needed to have more flexibility in her heel cords. She may have been having trouble with calluses, or clawing of the toes," he says.

Still, the doctors who treated Brenda in later life could never justify the surgery. "I didn't see any scientific rationale for [the operation] on Brenda," says her psychiatrist. "I thought it was a tortuous waste of months of her life. The whole thing was just ignorance and cruelty. Her feet [were swelling up] and her mother thought it was unattractive. I'm not saying [the doctor] was ignoble. He might have been an ethical person with some crazy theory about how this would help. But there was no reason for the operation."

The psychiatrist believes the operation caused long-lasting psychic injury: "By crippling her for a number of months, it may have encouraged her to be a cripple for the rest of her life. This may have started all the hospitalizations that were to come. Being an invalid met an inner need that she hadn't yet discovered. She wanted to be sick so she could be mothered. To become a baby, to regress and have everyone mother her to make up for that huge vacuum of her childhood, was the dominant theme of her life.''

Instead of going back to Farmington after the operation, Brenda spent the next eight months traveling with her mother. From January 19 to March 17 they were in Nassau with the Williams-Taylors and Tommy Weldon. Over the Christmas holiday in New York, Weldon and Brenda had grown close. ''Brenda has no other thought in her head but Tommy Weldon,'' Big Brenda wrote in her diary. Weldon had traveled to Nassau before Brenda, and when she arrived at the island with her mother at 7:30 in the morning, he met their boat. For the next two months Tommy and Brenda had a gay time attending Nassau's fashionable parties, though Weldon had occasional bouts of jealousy. Once, at a dinner they attended with Big Brenda, Tommy got mad because Brenda sat and talked to Marshall Field IV, a descendant of the founder of the Chicago department store.

In April, Brenda and Big Brenda sailed to England for the Coronation of King George VI. Tommy met them in London and followed them to Paris, where he showed up at their hotel on June 9, Brenda's sixteenth birthday, with a cake. ''He is a darling,'' wrote Big Brenda.

After spending the summer in New York and Murray Bay, Canada, Brenda sailed for Europe on September 1. She stopped in London before starting school in Munich, and apparently broke up with Tommy Weldon. ''Daddy cabled that relations were severed between Brenda and Tommy Weldon,'' Big Brenda wrote in her diary.

Brenda did not see him again for several years. Once, before she married Ship Kelly, Weldon was in New York and called Brenda. ''She was so excited, she was hysterical,'' recalls Jane Will Smith. By this time Weldon had married, but that didn't seem to concern Brenda. ''When I asked her what all the excitement was about,'' says Smith, ''Brenda said, 'Oh, I'm sure he's still in love with me. I was so in love with him.' ''

In the thirties, upper-class English girls went to Munich for their traditional year abroad. Florence and Paris were still popular, but Munich, with its favorable exchange rate, was the cheapest place in Europe for young ladies to acquire a patina of cosmopolitan culture. Many affluent Americans soon followed.

Most of the girls lived in small, picturesque residences run by impoverished German noblewomen whose families had lost their fortunes in the postwar upheaval. Brenda and her mother visited a couple of these little schools in June, finally deciding on one run by Baroness Laroche. "The Baroness," as everyone called her, lived in a stone house at 121 Königinstrasse, at the far end of a quiet, shady street. "It was a modest little school and not at all fashionable," wrote Brenda. "But my grandmother and mother were impressed because Iris Mountbatten, a cousin of Britain's royal family, had been going there."

The atmosphere was casual and easygoing. During the day Brenda and her classmates, four English girls, studied French, German, and piano. In the evenings they went to the opera and concerts. There was a cook and a maid, Annie, who served their meals and made their beds. Annie also walked Brenda's dog, a dachshund named Hobeit. The girls slept in bedrooms upstairs, while the Baroness slept on a couch in the living room. The Baroness was in bed at 9 P.M. every night, and never knew if her pupils sneaked out to meet their boyfriends.

Brenda adored Germany. "Munich was a new kind of life," she wrote years later. "It was such a leisurely pace, with no pressures, no social whirl. People there went to the opera not because they wanted to be seen in a new evening gown, but because they loved the music. I was enchanted by the school and the parks and the modest, but dignified baroness."

The girls skiied at Bayrischzell, and on the weekends toured Bavarian castles and baroque churches. They all had bicycles and occasionally pedaled into town for their lessons. Brenda's German teacher was probably Fräulein Eva Marie Baum. Although rumored to be Jewish, she claimed to be a devoted Nazi. One of her former students, Mrs. John Weaver, told author David Pryce-Jones that Eva Baum "was always talking about Hitler, but on other subjects she was an inspired teacher."

Unity Mitford was also a student of Baroness Laroche's. She had studied with the Baroness in the early thirties. Although it is not known whether Brenda knew her, a picture of Unity is pasted in one of Brenda's scrapbooks. Unity and Brenda did, however, have a mutual friend in Iris Mountbatten. In 1937, the year Brenda was in Munich, Iris and Unity were occasional companions.

One of the celebrated daughters of Lord and Lady Redesdale, Unity was immortalized as a "Bright Young Thing" in Evelyn Waugh's *Vile Bodies*. She was pro-Nazi, and, while enrolled with Baroness Laroche, spent much of her time at the Osteria Bavaria restaurant, hoping to meet Hitler, who routinely lunched there on Fridays. "Day after obsessive day," wrote David Pryce-Jones in his biography of her, she acted "a lady's version of a prostitute, waiting for the pickup." Indeed, her virulent anti-Semitism, plus her Nordic looks (she was so white and tall that she reminded one acquaintance of a marble statue), soon attracted Hitler. One day at lunch she was summoned to his table, and thereafter became a fixture at his tea parties and political rallies.

Hitler and Unity were widely rumored to be having an affair. Eva Braun, the dictator's mistress, was so jealous of Unity that she refused to sit next to her at Nazi functions. In fact, however, Unity's relationship to Hitler was probably platonic. Unity's sister was married to Sir Oswald Mosley, founder of the British Union of Fascists, and Hitler probably valued Unity as a vehicle for propaganda.

Mary Gerard Leigh, one of her classmates at Baroness Laroche's, told David Pryce-Jones: "Unity slept next door to me, and I could hear her talking in her sleep. She'd suddenly scream out, and I complained to the Baroness about it, as well as about the portraits of Hitler all over her room, which she would salute. She used to bring SA or SS men back and ask them to spend the night, but probably there was no sex in it. The maid was shocked, and the Baroness would speak with horror of it."

Unity wore a black shirt and carried a dainty pistol in her handbag. She told people she was practicing to kill Jews. Instead, she shot herself. It happened in the Englischer Garten, in 1939, soon after war had been declared between Germany and England. Amazingly, she survived, but soon afterward tried to kill herself again by swallowing her swastika brooch. Hitler rushed to her side, and agreed to help her return home. She died in England in 1948, when the bullet, still in her skull, shifted.

For the privileged girls in the little residences, there was scant awareness of the horrors beneath the surface of Nazi Germany. Audrey Gray Chapin, who attended Countess Harrach's school in 1936, recalls: "We used to see all the funny SS men in front of the opera house, the galleries, the monuments. They'd parade up and down the boulevards at night with torches, and we'd think, 'Oh! what a fabulous parade!' We didn't know what was going on. And the Countess certainly didn't tell us. Imagine if she talked and we told our fathers and it got back to [the Nazis]?"

Her sister, Milo Gray, who attended Anna Mongeles's school, remembers one unsettling incident. "There was a monument called [the Denkmal], that was guarded on all sides by soldiers. Nobody was allowed to walk by it unless you gave the Heil Hitler sign. We Americans thought that was absolutely idiotic. We were foreigners. Why should we make the sign of this political party? So we tried to run by the statue, while giving the salute in a sloppy way. Once a soldier stepped out and made us go back to do it the right way. That kind of scared us."

Munich was not only headquarters for the Nazi party but also Hitler's home base. He spent most weekends there. On Fridays, in addition to the Osteria Bavaria restaurant, he would go also to the Carlton tea rooms and chat with the English and American girls. Hitler realized the public relations potential of so many aristocratic foreigners in Munich. Sometimes he would invite the girls to tea parties in his apartment in the Prinzigenstrasse. The curtains were always drawn, even on sunny days, but the flat would be brightened by bouquets of fresh flowers. A large globe sat on a stand in the center of the living room. Hitler served the girls cream cakes, which he never ate himself.

At other times, he would entertain the girls in restaurants. Audrey Gray Chapin recalls having tea one afternoon at the Four Seasons with Hitler, Goering, and Goebbels. "They looked like the three Marx brothers. Hitler asked me, Did I know the Rockefellers? Did my father live in a skyscraper? I got the sense he was trying to influence us. He was terribly impressed by the English, the way they dressed, also the

Americans. I thought he was an absolutely ridiculous little man. But we had no sense of the monster that he was, or of what was about to happen in Germany or the world. Goering and Goebbels called him 'Führer,' never Hitler. At the tea there was an English girl. Hitler asked her if she knew Windsor. Did her father know Windsor? Did she like the Wagner festival? He was quizzing us about ourselves and our families. He'd smile when we all said we loved Germany. Then Goering got up and said, 'The Führer has an appointment.' And they all jumped up like Jack 'n the boxes.''

Later in life, Brenda told people that she too had had lunch once with Hitler, although it is more likely she only sat near his table in a restaurant. "One night during dinner we were having an argument about Hitler,'' Brenda's friend Alexander MacLeod recalls. "All these students in the restaurant were staring at us. I said, 'You know, Brenda, Hitler may have been a monster, but he was a genius.' She said, 'Oh, come on. I knew him. I had lunch with him. He had bad breath.' ''

On December 14, 1937, Brenda went home to celebrate Christmas with her family. She convinced her mother to let her return to Laroche's for another term, and she went back to Munich the following February. But on March 10, Big Brenda's diary notes, "Brenda cabled she was leaving for England owing to [the] political situation in Germany—[it] looks bad.'' Then, on April 10, 1938, Fred Watriss died in Boston from complications after hernia surgery. Big Brenda was in Nassau when it happened. Because she was busy visiting her family and friends, Big Brenda hadn't seen Watriss in two months and she undoubtedly felt guilty as well as grief-stricken. She broke the news to Brenda in a letter:

Ewee darling,
. . . poor Papa died at 2:30 this morning. I am in misery, it's all so sudden and horrible—he was unconscious from 8 last night, but if the plane had left [earlier] I might just have seen him. . . . I have not called you dear, on purpose— what's the use—and Watkins advised writing you instead.

I will have a cross of violets from you three children in the middle of the blanket of flowers—darling, I have regrets I did not go to Boca Grande—but . . . what's the use of regrets. . . . The funeral is on Tuesday at St. Thomas and later the burial at Roslyn—you come home at the end of April, darling. I'll see about it in a few days. . . .

Your devoted
Ma

Brenda came home May 1. She still hoped to return to Europe that fall. Going to school in Munich had given her a sense of purpose. She had been learning to speak German and developing her artistic talents, filling her sketch pads with drawings of the city. But Big Brenda had other ideas—all of which revolved around a large, lavish coming-out ball planned for December. Now that Brenda's beauty had blossomed, "My grandmother and mother had the tool they needed," wrote Brenda. "I myself do not care for the face I had in those days. I [feel] embarrassment for the falsity of that fixed smile and pity for the strain I see in those eyes. But others decided I was a glamour girl." Brenda begged her mother to abandon plans for the debut. She didn't care about social status. Also, she was dreadfully shy. Although Brenda liked being popular and being written about in the newspapers, the prospect of being the center of attention at a big formal event frightened her and brought out all the insecurities of her childhood.

But Big Brenda was adamant. "You'll be very sorry if you don't have a debut," she told her daughter. "You'll be much happier if you do."

PART TWO

DEBUTANTE

CHAPTER FIVE

I'm established now for '38
With the title of glamour and
reprobate
I've won a position in Vogue and
Harper's;
For a hundred bucks I'll advertise garters.
A scent called Sarong alone
I possess,
Plus a maribou jacket and a
sequin dress.
I give the impression of savoir-faire,
Everyone I meet gives me an inward scare.
They think I'm fast and they
think I'm bad,
For my favorite man is an invariable cad.
I grit my teeth and smile at
my enemies,
I sit at the Stork Club and
talk to nonentities

> Brenda Frazier, 1938
> (quoted in *Life* magazine,
> December 6, 1963)

Twenty-five years after her debut, Brenda Frazier opened the red leather album containing photographs of her celebrated party. She had not looked at the album for years, and as she turned the pages, pausing over each black-and-white photograph, she began to feel a sharp pain in the muscle above her left collarbone. "It suddenly occurred to me that this muscle often hurts me," wrote Brenda. "It's an apt remembrance of that debutante season, when I held my head as straight as if it were in a vise, fearful to move it lest I disarrange my hair. It's the sort of painful souvenir that many girls . . . acquire as a result of being pushed too far and too fast in adolescence. I doubt very much that many girls . . . really enjoy being pushed into social functions. [But when] the honor and fate of the entire family are hanging on the outcome, the tension becomes unbearable."

In becoming a debutante, Brenda was embarking on a fiercely competitive ritual with roots that go far back in history. Anthropologists can trace the tradition back to the coming-of-age rites of ancient times, whereby parents served notice on their communities that a daughter was nubile and ready for marriage. More directly, the custom is derived from the rituals of the old European courts, particularly the court in England. For centuries, young daughters of the peerage and gentry were presented at grand evening balls called "courts." Indeed, before World War II, British society could be neatly defined as those people eligible for presentation before the Queen. Although married women were also presented, the custom mainly involved young girls. Once they had "bent the knee," they were invited to all the important parties in London, presumably to meet potential husbands, whose own social worth had been sealed by presentation at the King's levee, the male side of the ritual. By encouraging the marriage of upper-class girls to upper-class men, this system helped perpetuate the British aristocracy.

Even the origin of the word "debutante" evokes this emphasis on marriage. The original French word "début" was used in bowling and billiards to mean "from the mark." In the seventeenth century the noun "débutante" was coined to mean someone who "leads off." As Cleveland Amory explained in *Who Killed Society?*, since "debut" "was an expression used with jouer—to play—understood, it was rather like our modern expression . . . 'to play for the mark' or 'goal,' and allowing the substitution of a husband for the mark or goal, the word is still, in the sportive sense, going strong.''

After World War II the courts and levees were replaced by presentation parties, far less grand affairs that Queen Elizabeth II abolished entirely in 1958. By then the concept of elaborate court debuts, and their blatant celebration of aristocracy, had gone out of fashion. (Today an invitation to one of the Queen's large royal garden parties is considered the seal of upper-class social standing.)

It is impossible to know exactly when the debut custom started in America, but it was certainly underway by the late seventeenth century. At that time, American society consisted of those people closest to the British peerage. Americans were still essentially English in thought and values, and they participated in all British traditions, including the presentation of their daughters at court. Indeed, the first American debutante to bow before British royalty was Pocahontas, the daughter of an Indian chief. Pocahontas, by then the wife of English gentleman John Rolfe, came out in 1616, at the court of James I. A few years earlier, the young Indian maiden had shocked British soldiers by turning cartwheels in the nude, an act of deb outrageousness that may still be a pacesetter.

By the eighteenth century, when America was starting to develop its own national character, the idea of the aristocracy, and of who belonged to it, had begun to change. Instead of strictly following the English model, American society began to include families with a high position based on achievement, education, and community service. That rather meritorious notion changed in the nineteenth century, when America became rich. Soon society meant people who had money, preferably for at least the preceding generation, and who were willing to play the social game. In a nation without ''the pomp and the purple, the throne and the diadem,'' as social historian Dixon Wecter wrote,''the social game is a vital means to success, and . . . the only security against being forgotten.''

One of the great creators and celebrators of this system was Ward McAllister, the son of a lawyer in Savannah, Georgia. McAllister rose to eminence largely because he was the only man of his time willing to devote himself, as Wecter noted, to society's trivia—"the study of heraldry, books of court etiquette, genealogy and cooking, getting up balls and banquets, making of guest lists and the interviewing of ambitious mothers with debutante daughters." For a long time society in America meant McAllister's "Four Hundred," a theoretical list he devised by calculating the number of people who fit, literally and figuratively, into social empress Caroline Astor's Manhattan ballroom. "If you go outside that number," McAllister once told reporters, "you strike people who are either not at ease in a ballroom or else make other people not at ease." The number, however, turned out to be completely arbitrary. When finally challenged by reporters to identify his four hundred, McAllister could come up with only about three hundred names. The list was published in *The New York Times* on February 1, 1892.

Debutantes have always been symbols of caste, and their debuts have been celebrations of social position. Until McAllister's time, the typical debut was a dignified afternoon reception at which the debutante received guests at home with her mother and father. Often an informal dinner party followed, and then a dancing or theater party for the family's intimate friends. The average debutante was eighteen years old, although Southern belles came out as early as fourteen. Following her debut, a girl was expected to marry as soon as a suitable man proposed.

But the practice of holding debuts outside the home started as far back as 1870. That year, New York socialite Archibald Gracie King persuaded the owner of Delmonico's to rent him a large room for his daughter's debut. This decision, as Cleveland Amory wrote, "was a point of no return. The die was cast, and there followed a steadily increasing emphasis of the public nature of the debut and the loss of its private meaning."

The Gilded Age was underway. Lavish debut balls held in restaurants or hotel ballrooms soon became common practice. These parties caught the taste of the time: romanticism spiced with materialism and snobbery, "the mean admiration of mean things," as Thackeray put it. Sometimes events made the vulgarities terribly obvious. When James Paul presented his daughter to Philadelphia society around the turn of the century, he had ten thousand Brazilian butterflies hidden in gossamer nets against the ballroom ceiling. The insects were to be released at the climax of the evening. Unfortunately, they succumbed to the heat before the appointed hour, and ten thousand dead butterflies rained down on the revelers.

At the same time that debutante balls were becoming more lavish, the debut season was becoming more complex. In New York, for example, the season started with the Autumn Ball at Tuxedo Park in October and moved through the opening of the Metropolitan Opera and a series of charity balls, to climax during the Christmas holidays in a flurry of private debut balls. All this extravagance started to present a problem to the families at the top. It was also becoming harder to tell who was a true-blue debutante and who an upstart, since any family with enough money could throw a party for a daughter and call it a debut. One solution in the cities where the coming-out tradition was strongest was to insist that a girl be invited to certain dances sponsored by the Wasp elite in order to rank as a real deb. In Baltimore the anointing party was the Bachelor's Cotillion; in Charleston, the St. Cecilia's Ball; and in New York, the Junior Assembly, which was actually a series of three dances. The Philadelphia Assembly, at which George Washington once danced, remains to this day the hardest to crack. Founded in 1748, it is the oldest debutante ball in the nation.

Another way to keep the top in place was to insist on attendance at the "right" school. In Boston, that meant the Windsor School, Miss May's, or Beaver Country Day. Girls who attended these schools were automatically sent questionnaires by Miss Mary Porter, the Back Bay's social arbiter, who asked for the names of their parents and the expected date of their coming-out parties. The questionnaire, addressed to "Dear Little Bud," was inevitably followed by a deluge of advertisements from caterers, florists, stationers, and dressmakers, also addressed to "Dear Little Bud."

In New York, friendships formed at Miss Chapin's or Miss Hewitt's Classes often provided vital contacts with girls whose mothers were on the dance committees, including the one for the Junior Assembly. But an even surer route to the Junior

Assembly was through the Metropolitan Dancing Class. "The Met," so called because the classes for "subdeb" and "pre-subdeb" teenagers were held each year at the Metropolitan Club, selected only sixteen girls from a field of four hundred aspirants.

Even with these barriers, however, it was becoming hard to know which debs were true bluebloods. In 1938 Maury Paul, the *Journal-American*'s society writer, listed 400 debutantes, while the *World-Telegram* endorsed 350. Social secretaries Mrs. Huntington Tappin and Mrs. William H. Tew found only 270. And the high priestess of debutante arbitration, Juliana Cutting, recognized a mere 100. That was the number of girls invited each year to the Junior Assembly dances.

Not surprisingly, the cost of debuts rose quickly over the years. During the boom following World War I, debuts were flashier than ever. In 1929 Mr. and Mrs. William Robertson Coe, looking for a suitable way to celebrate the debut of their daughter Natalie, transformed the Ritz Ballroom in New York into a replica of the family's South Carolina plantation. The Coes had a colonial façade constructed with red brick and white pillars. They brought in box hedges and cedar trees. The ballroom floor was laid with a carpet of real grass, and the ceiling was painted to simulate blue sky.

Extravagant debuts even survived the stock market crash. In 1930, Woolworth heiress Barbara Hutton came out in a $60,000 spectacle featuring four dance bands, a forest of silver birch trees, and Rudy Vallee, whom she imported from California. One of the most costly debuts of all time was held the same year at the Mayflower Hotel in Washington, D.C., in honor of Helen Lee Eames Doherty. The night before Helen came out, her stepfather, gas and oil magnate Henry L. Doherty, gave Ford cabriolet automobiles with hunting scenes painted on the sides to twelve of Helen's best friends and one absent friend, the King of Spain.

Lost in all this fuss and expense was the debut's original purpose: to find a husband. Young ladies were no longer presented to a pool of eligible bachelors, but to a sea of college boys. According to one survey in the thirties, only 30 percent of the season's debutantes married within the year, and about 20 percent the following year. *Fortune* magazine thought this was startling enough to write an article about it in 1938: "From the society into which a New York girl makes her debut today, adults and especially men—marriageable or otherwise—have almost completely disappeared. So have they in Boston, where debutantes are now presented to the Harvard undergraduate body, minus freshmen. They have disappeared because the social game costs time and money. It flourishes where there is most leisure for caste and least pressure for cash. Which means that the social game is possible for men in Charleston, say, but a hardship for harried New Yorkers."

By the 1930s, the deb party was trying hard to hold on to the traditions that remained. In New York, the great arbiter of the custom was Juliana Cutting. As the city's impresario of parties, Miss Cutting organized coming-out balls, weddings, and other fetes for some of the world's richest people, including Marjorie Post Hutton and the Prince of Wales. Her power was based on a series of lists, containing data on some two thousand eligible males whom she deemed suitable guests, and therefore sound husband material. Each day she devoted several hours to updating this information, noting all births, deaths, marriages, divorces, changes of address, schools, clubs, and so on. Her lists were based on years of research. Muss Cutting started watching boys when they were still in short pants at dancing school, and then followed their social careers through the "presubdeb" and "subdeb" network of dances, until they were in college.

Each fall, almost every young man who owned a tuxedo and went to school in the East received this note in the mail: "Miss Cutting would like to have your full name, also nickname, if any, and the address to which you wish invitations sent for the coming season, in order that you may receive any invitations sent you by her office." Privately, Miss Cutting abhorred the custom of inviting three boys for every girl to debuts. She blamed it on the rise in alcohol consumption that put so many young men out of commission by mid-evening. Her own recommendation was a boy and a half to a girl for a dinner dance, and two to one for a supper.

But Miss Cutting was not one to buck tradition. The granddaughter of real estate heir Robert Livingston Cutting, she had come out herself in 1890 in the era of candlelit ballrooms and formal dance cards. At the time she seemed headed for a life of well-married ease. But her family lost its fortune before she found a husband, and she was forced to go to work. First she taught ballroom dancing. Then, in November 1922, she went to work at Mrs. Thomas A. Blackford's Fifth Avenue secretarial bureau. Eager to make more money, she went into business for herself in 1924, opening an office with one assistant in the Bankers Trust Building on Madison Avenue. Two weeks later she was so swamped with commissions that she had to hire another assistant. By 1939 she had moved up to a six-room suite and seven assistants.

At sixty-nine, Miss Cutting resembled a plump pouter pigeon with a round, lineless face and a corona of fluffy white hair. She had a reputation for severity and would not tolerate any misbehavior. The poor boy who got drunk on the stag line was immediately dropped from the list. Miss Cutting also kept meticulous records on the debutantes, rating them along with the boys as "A," "B," or "C," depending on their pedigree, wealth, and personal charm. All this information was neatly typed on pale blue paper and kept in a looseleaf notebook. Her calendar showed the scheduling of debuts up to two or three years in advance.

Anyone could look at the calendar for free, but Miss Cutting charged hefty fees for her other services. To plan an entire party—a service that included sending out invitations, hiring an orchestra, planning decorations, buying flowers, and renting a ballroom—she charged up to 20 percent of the total cost. She also received commissions from florists, caterers, orchestra bookers, hotel managers, and stationers.

Just to look at one of her lists cost anywhere from $50 to $500, depending on which list one wanted to see. Most girls who had large debut balls bought all three lists. A client did not have to be "A" caliber herself to look at the "A" list. She only had to be willing to spend "A" list prices.

Although Miss Cutting was part of old New York society, she agreed to plan a debut for anyone who hired her. "One cannot live in this democratic country without feeling that every mother has the right to ask the best for her daughter," she once told a reporter. In fact, she seemed offended if a party was organized without her. After another reporter wondered if all debutantes asked her advice, Miss Cutting snapped, "Well, they better."

It was the fashion at deb balls in the thirties to have twice as many boys as girls. This made every dance a cut-in—a ballroom practice started during World War I, when soldiers going overseas found that there were not enough girls to go around at big farewell parties. For years the custom was deplored by Juliana Cutting as the ballroom equivalent of divorce.

By the 1930s, cutting in had gotten "totally out of control . . . a regular Frankenstein monster," wrote journalist Alice-Leone Moats in her 1933 etiquette book for debs, *No Nice Girl Swears:* "The stag line has ceased to be a line and has become a large block in the middle of the room—a regiment of young men who take up most of the floor and make dancing almost impossible. The effort to dance with attractive girls only is usually too much for a stag, as he can't go two steps without being cut in on, and then comes the exertion of darting into the crowd again in search of a partner—on the other hand . . . no stag will take a chance on getting stuck with any girl and having to spend the evening with her." Sometimes desperate stags waved dollar bills behind the girls' backs, hoping to induce other boys to cut in. Miss Moats reports that one deb, catching her partner in the act, snapped, "Make it five, and I'll go home."

In addition to the stags, most deb parties had a number of so-called Ballroom Boys, young men—often impoverished aristocrats—who picked up a little cash by escorting lonely dowagers to parties. Ted Peckham, now a Manhattan antiques dealer, started the city's first escort service of this type in 1935, after observing legions of ladies going out alone. Peckham's escorts were paid $10 until midnight and $15 every two hours after that, except on New Year's Eve, when they got $25. Like Miss Cutting, Peckham did not tolerate any shenanigans. If a youth made a pass at his date, or got drunk, he was dropped.

The turmoil in the world of debutantes was only a symptom of a larger turmoil afflicting the top reaches of society. Who really belonged? Social barriers started crumbling after

World War I and in some areas were reduced to rubble by the 1929 crash. The 1930s were the Golden Age of social-climbing. Behind the elaborate debut were the aspirations of a newly rich class, "attempting to seize, even by casual symbols . . . [the] guiding wisdom . . . of being rich gracefully," wrote Wecter. In response, the old aristocracy "folded in upon itself," according to *The New York Times,* and thus lost its "real power and prominence to [the] new arrivals."

These new arrivals were a brilliantly gaudy group whose status rested not on property and ancestry, but on personal style and self-promotion. They sprouted in the Jazz Age and, like Fitzgerald's Dick Diver, pursued useless lives in Manhattan speakeasies and French cabarets. As a group they came to be known as "Café Society," a phrase coined in 1919 by Maury Paul after he observed six people from wildly different backgrounds dining out together. "Society isn't staying home and entertaining anymore," Paul once said. "Society is going out to dinner, out to night life and letting down the barriers—that I should see a Widener, a Goelet, a Corrigan and a Warren all together. It's like a seafood cocktail, with everything from eels to striped bass!"

After the crash, when scores of social families had to fire their servants, close up their mansions, and entertain in restaurants, Café Society started to eclipse polite society. Soon, with the repeal of Prohibition, New York went "café mad." Caroline Astor would turn over in her grave, wrote Maury Paul, if she could "see the manner in which celebrated and supposedly exclusive ladies of fashion fall over each other in their frantic efforts to obtain advantageous tables in the various restaurants and cafés." The home dinner party, he believed, was now a bore; in fact, "certain razzle-dazzle souls always make a point of refusing invitations to dinner parties in private residences."

Café Society flourished in Manhattan's nightclubs. Its chief votaries, wrote social observer Lucius Beebe, "were four or five hundred professional celebrities ranking from grand duchesses to couturiers, stage and screen characters, tavern keepers, debutantes, artists, commercial photographers, wine salesmen, literary lights, proprietors of love foundaries and professional nightclub lushes."

These people became famous because they had their own Boswells—dozens of them, scribbling away in the gossip columns of newspapers. Society's old guard had been reported on for years, but suddenly stories and items started to appear about the people who were going out at night—raffish types, drinking, cavorting, and carrying on. Quickly there was great demand for this new type of reporting. After all, the things these night people did and said were probably more interesting than an account of the guest list at Mrs. Vanderbilt's tea. As for the stars of Café Society, they loved the attention.

Publicity was replacing patrimony as the nation's number-one status symbol.

The revolution was tied in with a dramatic change in American journalism. Newspapers had had their excesses, the jingoistic posturing of yellow journalism at the turn of the century being perhaps the most notable example. But for the most part, American reporting was sober, straightforward, impersonal. All that started to change at the end of the nineteenth century, and the emergence of a new type of newspaper was signalized by the first issue of the New York *Daily News* on June 26, 1919. Here was something readers hadn't seen before. Instead of a summary of the world's major events, the front page flashed a picture of the Prince of Wales and an announcement in bold type that he planned to visit Newport in August. The back page was covered with beauty pageant contestants, and pictures were scattered throughout the paper. The stories were short and emphasized personal details over ideas.

Soon tabloids were appearing all over the country, elbowing aside the more conservative broadsheets in the fight for readers' attention. In New York City alone, three tabloids had been founded by 1924. Technology quickly gave these scrappy newspapers another boost. The development of Leicas and other small German cameras made it possible to take candid pictures in settings with very low lights. Suddenly a peek inside the shadowy nightclub world was available to the bricklayer and his wife in Brooklyn. The tabloids started carrying unposed shots of stars and celebrities in the Stork Club, El Morocco, and the Monte Carlo. For the public, the pictures were the next best thing to being there.

The tabloids also opened up new styles of reporting. For years, papers had been covering the major events of society: the balls, teas, marriages, and births of the top families. The coverage was quiet, respectful, passive. In the twenties that started to change, as Walter Winchell and other columnists began to write stories about the lives and loves of the famous. Some of the reporting was impudent, even hostile. And yet, for a time, even the tabloids held the line on not reporting gossip—that is, rumors that could not be clearly established as fact. According to one account, the gossip barrier was breached by the New York *Evening Graphic,* one of the most sensational and scandalous daily newspapers ever published. For a time, even the *Graphic* held out: Though it regularly carried lurid illustrations of violent crimes and doctored photographs, it refused to print gossip. For example, the editors would not run a story about a rumored divorce until the case made it to court.

Walter Winchell, who at the time wrote a column for the paper, is said to have changed all that by one day sneaking in an item about the rumored marriage of a Broadway actor. When the walls didn't come tumbling down, Winchell and his editors realized they were onto something.

Winchell was the most powerful of this new breed of journalist. He was a sixth-grade dropout and a one-time vaudeville hoofer who started out by writing the *Daily Newsense,* a chatty newsletter about showpeople that he tacked to theater bulletin boards. The creator of the *Vaudeville News* saw the material and hired Winchell for twenty-five dollars a week. From there he went to the *Evening Graphic* and, in 1929, to William Randolph Hearst's New York *Mirror.* As Stanley Walker, city editor of the New York *Herald Tribune,* wrote in *The Night Club Era,* Winchell "brought to his job the perfect equipment—great energy, an eager desire to know what was going on, a lack of conventional breeding and experience, a mind delightfully free of book learning, and an unquenchable desire to be a newspaper man. If his background had been different, he would have been so befuddled by canons of what some people call good taste that he would have revolted at some of his best stuff."

Winchell cultivated both gangsters and politicians. J. Edgar Hoover assigned FBI agents to be his bodyguards. Winchell, dressed in a blue suit and snap brim fedora, held court every night at the Stork Club, "the joint," as he called it.

In 1933, Winchell brought his gossip to the radio with a Sunday night program. Every week one third of the adult population listened to him rail against "Hitlerooting U.S. senators" and the "Ratzis," or discuss what "moom pitcher star" was dating which "sweedee pie." Few could escape Winchell's lance. One item in the thirties, for example, read, "Edna St. Vincent Millay, the love poet, just bought a new set of store teeth." When *The New Yorker* magazine reported that 41.2 percent of Winchell's items were inaccurate, Winchell retaliated with the completely inaccurate charge that the magazine's editor, Harold Ross, didn't wear underwear.

With his contacts in show business, politics, and the underworld, Winchell often wandered far and wide in his reporting. Not so the other preeminent gossip of the time. Maury Paul rarely ventured beyond the confines of society. Paul came to New York in 1914 and worked as an anonymous columnist for the old *Evening Post* and *Daily Mail*. Within a few years he had become the nation's leading society writer. He studied carefully for his trade, spending hours examining family histories in the library and walking the streets memorizing addresses. He also learned to play the phone like a virtuoso, squeezing items about weddings, funerals, and divorces from reluctant dowagers. Soon he became a fixture at the best Fifth Avenue parties, and an intimate friend of some of society's top families.

Paul, who was short and fat, lived with his mother in a penthouse apartment. He employed an assistant, Eve Brown, and a personal factotum, dubbed "Adonis" by Brown. Paul ordered all his clothes, even undershirts, from London. Sometimes he had his shoes shined three times a day.

His prose was as fancy as his clothes. To Paul, people didn't fall in love, they "succumbed to the darts of that greatest of sharpshooters, Dan Cupid." On a sunny day, "Old Sol reigned." Wealthy dowagers had "oodles of ducats," and a sugar daddy was a "Grand Old Provider, or G.O.P." But nothing inspired Paul so much as a juicy divorce—that is, in his terms, the sad result of "the marital barque foundering in the matrimonial seas."

At one time Paul wrote for four newspapers: the *Evening Journal*, the *Evening Mail*, the *Journal-American*, and the *Evening Post*. Paul's career seemed threatened in 1922, when Arthur Brisbane, editor of the *Evening Journal*, fired him for being too mean to the people he wrote about. Subsequently the *Evening Post* dropped him after a society woman complained to the district attorney that Paul had tried to blackmail her. But then William Randolph Hearst offered Paul $250 a week to write exclusively for him. Hearst became interested in the columnist when he found Marion Davies engrossed in Paul's column. If Marion loved Maury, reasoned Hearst, so would everyone else.

At the start of his career, Paul worked out of his own private office at 11 West Forty-second Street. The office, which had an anteroom wallpapered in dollar bills, was a gift from a fan. Paul used the office to entertain his friends, whom Eve Brown later described as "fragile, slim youths with high complexions and curly hair, boys with an airy manner, trailing clouds of perfume."

Perhaps because he grew up in but not of Main Line Philadelphia, Maury had a schizophrenic attitude toward high society. It was reflected in his style, at once fawning and mocking. In his column he would talk about the "lovely Mrs. So-and-so," or the "beauteous Miss So-and-so." But one day, after Eve Brown commented on a particularly attractive female visitor, Paul waved his hand dismissively. "No woman is beautiful," he said.

Maury's snideness earned him the sobriquet "Mr. Bitch." But he remained on good terms with most of the people he wrote about, some of whom gave him wildly expensive gifts: a station wagon, a $5,000 mortgage on a country home, a rare Aubusson rug.

He was the master of discreet innuendo. Unlike Winchell, who ran laundry lists of raw, unrelated items separated by three dots, Paul would pick one or two special tidbits and weave them into a story.

Julian Gerard, who sometimes worked for him, says of Paul's technique: "Maury had a wonderful gift. He would take a situation, say, something that happened the night before at someone's house, or at a party, and he would make a story out of it. He didn't have a great deal of space to do it in, but he'd find a way to make it a story."

Although Winchell and Paul were the kings of gossip writing, they were not its only practitioners. In 1938, New York City supported fourteen daily newspapers, and most of them employed at least one gossip columnist. (A few, such as *The New York Times*, held out against the trend.) The competition for news was fierce. Given that, and also the fact that gossips were usually not the most creative of writers, a series of gossip conventions was soon invented.

One convention involved the Society Heroine. Every year reporters looked for a girl to symbolize Café Society and to be an ornament and a focus for their columns. Traditionally, they settled on one of the more flashy debs. The point was not only to celebrate the girl, but also to categorize her, thus elevating her sexuality, as Betty Fussell wrote, "from the vulgarity of burlesque to the chic of high fashion." To accomplish this, the reporters created a series of "types." The first type, in the twenties, was the "Girl of the Year," epitomized by Millicent Rogers, a combination flapper-deb who shocked proper society by marrying Count Ludwig Salm, an exotic nobleman twice her age.

In the thirties, styles changed. With the Depression, the flapper-deb idea gave way to "the Poor Little Rich Girls," whose unhappiness seemed as bottomless as their fortunes. The queens of this group were Doris Duke and Barbara Hutton. Doris was worth $70 million. Hutton, who was raised by an uncle after her mother's death and her father's remarriage, lived up to her youthful billing by marrying miserably seven times.

Another type created by the press was "Glamour Girl No. 1," a phrase coined by Maury Paul but rarely used until Eleanor Young came along in 1936. "Cookie" Young, the only child of a self-made railroad baron, Robert R. Young, was a sexy black-haired beauty, an "exotic blossom," as some columnists put it. Her debut at her parents' Newport villa was the party of the year, but her story ended tragically in 1941 when the plane she was in with a young Greek shipping heir crashed into the surf at Matunuck Beach, Rhode Island.

The next glamour deb was Gloria "Mimi" Baker. Her coming-out party at her mother's Sands Point estate overlooking the Long Island Sound was described by Maury Paul as the "ultimate" in deb balls: From the "thousands and thousands of lighted lanterns hanging in the floodlighted trees to the dahlia-banked terraces leading down to the t-r-e-m-e-n-d-o-u-s dance floor built over the swimming pool, everything was on the bigger and better scale."

"Glamour" was the perfect buzz word for the thirties. As an idea and a label, it captured the public's imagination and lingered in the cliché-ridden world of the gossip column. Like "charisma" in the sixties, or "survivor" in the seventies, "glamour" was hopelessly overused, yet its elevation to a cliché tells something of the era. The Depression was a time of escapism—of *42nd Street*, the Big Bands, and Walt Disney. America, as portrayed by the chroniclers of popular culture, was a dreamy, never-never land in which everyone was carefree and rich. Hollywood created a glittering world where even stenographers lived in houses with marble foyers and vast living rooms. People flocked to the movie theaters to see Busby Berkeley's chorus girls prancing around the screen dressed up like dollar bills.

To anxious families struggling to make ends meet, the rich were more dazzlingly remote than ever. The public was fed an endless string of columns about glamour girls and boys who seemed to live in nightclubs and had nothing better to do than drink champagne and dance the "Flat Foot Floogee." The cult of glamour was so ubiquitous that it even touched politics. In 1939 *Life* called Thomas E. Dewey "Republican Glamour Boy No. 1," and Attorney-General Frank Murphy "New Deal Glamour Boy No. 1."

Glamour represented money and mystery, and it was symbolized by beautiful, privileged debutantes. Writing in the *Journal-American* in 1936, Maury Paul told his readers that he had spotted a perfect example:

> *Among those in the Ritz's Japanese Garden yesterday was Brenda Frazier, a schoolgirl who won't make her debut un-*

*til about two years hence. The dark-eyed and VERY pretty
Brenda was lunching with her mater, Mrs. Frederic Watriss.
And appeared deeply intrigued by all the social activity. It
may seem a bit early, but I—here and now—predict Brenda
Frazier will be one of the belles—if not THE belle of her
season.*

CHAPTER SIX

Two years later, when Brenda returned from Europe, Paul's prediction still sounded like just another example of a columnist's puffery. One night in the spring of 1938, she dressed up in black silk and pearls and went to the Stork Club with Julian Gerard, a Yale student. "Who is that lovely girl?" Chick Farmer, the nightclub's photographer, asked. "That," Gerard answered proudly, "is the glamour girl of the year."

At first, no one but Gerard seemed to know it. Brenda shopped at Bendel's for dresses and lunched at fashionable restaurants without anyone asking for her autograph. On a trip with her mother in the summer of 1938, she rode around the edge of the Grand Canyon in a bus and toured Hollywood's movie studios without being recognized by the other tourists or written about by reporters.

In June 1939 *The New Yorker* sent out a young reporter, E. J. Kahn, Jr., to try to get to the heart of the matter. He filed this report: "The properties of glamour are not in themselves very impressive. In Brenda's case they are a small, thin mouth; wavy blue-black hair, which she is incessantly combing; deep-set staring eyes; and round, full cheeks, over which she sometimes pulls a few stray locks of hair while having her picture taken or portrait painted. Consistently late hours have given her face a brittle doll-like look, much as if her features had been painted on. Some of them, of course, have. She uses a deep-red lipstick, to match her long fingernails, which she manicures herself. She lengthens her short eyebrows by pencilling them down in a curve around the corners of her eyes. . . . If Brenda looks pretty much the same in all her pictures, which are usually somewhat flattering, it is probably because she has the habit of raising her eyebrows, which makes her seem continually amazed. She talks in a high, shrill voice. Among her own set, which for the most part deals conversationally in social trivialities, she is regarded as an intellectual leader. 'She talks about life and things,' they say.''

During the summer of 1938, several pictures of Brenda taken at the Stork Club by Chick Farmer appeared in the New York papers. She was photographed at the Greentree Fair on Mrs. Payne Whitney's lawn in Manhasset, Long Island, and with Julian Gerard at Belmont racetrack. Still, Brenda was virtually unknown outside New York. But by September the publicity was starting to explode. "Miss Frazier No. 1 Glamour Girl of Season," announced the headlines across the country. Stories about her appeared in such unlikely places as the Milton, Pennsylvania, *Evening Standard,* the Baltimore *Sun,* and the Saginaw, Michigan, *News.*

Brenda's overnight fame baffled even the reporters who helped create it. "There is no more rational explanation of her astonishing rise than there is for a crowd which will gather and peer anxiously into the sky just because a man on a street corner happens to stretch his neck," wrote E. J. Kahn, Jr. "Nobody . . . ever elected Brenda to the exalted position of glamour girl. She simply got there, and neither she nor anyone else knows exactly how."

Brenda's home that summer was the fourth floor of the Carlton House, where she and her mother had moved after the death of Fred Watriss. Their five-room apartment was divided into two suites; the larger one, for Brenda, overlooked Madison Avenue, and the one for Big Brenda fronted the Ritz-Carlton's Japanese Garden. Mother and daughter each had her own sitting room and bedroom. Big Brenda's sitting room had robin's-egg-blue walls, apricot chintz upholstery, and exquisite inlaid wood screens. A life-sized portrait of herself hung above a crystal vase that often overflowed with yellow chrysanthemums. Brenda's sitting room had a baby grand piano, a radio, and a portable bar. All the rooms were crowded with eighteenth-century antiques, rare Chinese porcelains, jade lamps, and a collection of rose quartz. Brenda's bedroom was painted pink, and much of the wall space was covered with mirrors. Her amazing collection of dresses (her evening gowns alone numbered several dozen) and furs hung from poles fitted into the sides of an enormous closet. Her shoes and evening slippers, of which she owned hundreds of pairs, were kept in glass-faced cabinets in the hall.

The kitchen was used only rarely, because Brenda and Big Brenda ate most meals out. When they did dine at home, they usually ordered room service from the hotel kitchen. Years later, Brenda told her friend Betty Blake that she resented living in a hotel. "I remember Brenda one day saying that her mother never made a home for her," says Mrs. Blake. "It bothered her that they lived in a hotel, and that they didn't have a summer place. I think Brenda felt that her mother used her money all the time and lived off her."

They employed a staff of three: Griffiths, who drove their black town car; Slater, the gray-haired English lady's maid; and Gertie Folmsbee, the factotum, who had an office off one of the sitting rooms. In addition to overseeing the family's complicated finances and keeping a file on Brenda's party invitations, Gertie had to answer the endlessly ringing phone. She was the mediator between Brenda and businessmen who wanted to produce Brenda Linen, college boys who wanted dates, and reporters who wanted interviews. Gertie also opened Brenda's fan mail, which came in at the rate of ten letters a day from around the country and the world. Some of the letters weren't addressed, but simply sent to New York with a title on the front: "Brenda Frazier, No. 1 Glamour Girl," or "Brenda Frazier, $4,000,000 debutante," or "Brenda Diana Duff Frazier, The World's Prettiest Debutante." She got one letter from Europe addressed to "No. 1 Glamour Girl, U.S.A.," and another with nothing but her picture pasted on the envelope and "Long Island, N.Y." written underneath.

Not all the letters were billets doux; some contained obscene proposals, and others dirty pictures. Many of them were pleas for money. A thirteen-year-old boy requested a hundred dollars to buy a car. A girl in the West wanted Brenda to finance a Louis XVI bedroom set. A struggling musician asked for a piano. College boys everywhere invited Brenda to their proms, offering, if necessary, to pay Mrs. Watriss's expenses as chaperone.

Brenda's typical day that year began at noon. Lying in bed, drinking the coffee brought to her by Slater, she would phone her friends. Later, she'd lunch at an expensive restaurant, usually having three shrimp and a glass of brandy or champagne. The Stork Club was one of her favorite spots, because the owner, Sherman Billingsley, offered debs lunch for just a dollar, hoping to attract the girls and the publicity that pursued them. In the afternoon Brenda would attend charity ball committee meetings, go shopping, or see a movie.

Diana Barrymore, who also came out in 1938, described the committee meetings: "You sat around dressed up like a mannequin, and discussed plans for the next ball. You screened the boys who were to be invited. That was only protocol, because you had been carefully screened yourself or you wouldn't be here, in the home of Mrs. Vincent Astor, planning the dance. If you were snobbish, the boys were even more so, more careful where they went, and with whom they were seen." Like Diana Barrymore, Brenda considered the charity committees a waste of time. "I have always thought it was disgusting for a group of people, all of whom had at least a million dollars, to sit around and discuss at great length how they could give a charity ball that, with luck, might raise $1,500."

For Brenda, like many of the top debutantes, coming out was a full-time job. "Being a debutante, to put the matter crassly, is a business . . . it is certainly not a pleasure," Brenda wrote in *Life*. It was a business with something grim about it, a competition for attention that the reporters encouraged. For the top debs, success was measured by the number of clippings in their scrapbooks. The game could get rough. It was not uncommon for a girl to approach Walter Winchell or Maury Paul with nasty stories about other debs (one oft-told tale was that this or that girl was sleeping with a Stork Club waiter). The idea was to sabotage a rival's popularity.

In addition to this sort of back-stabbing, a certain amount of physical stamina was needed just to complete the debutante season. *Fortune* estimated that during the height of the sea-

DEBUTANTE

son, December 16 through January 7, the average girl put in
140 hours on the dance floor and danced 70 miles. She ate
18 plates of scrambled eggs and sausage, drank 12 quarts of
champagne, and endured 20 hours of beauty treatments.

That fall, the first real measure of Brenda's influence came
on October 28 at the Velvet Ball, one of the biggest deb events
of the year. The gala's ostensible purpose was to raise money
for the New York Infirmary. But its real goal was publicity
for the Velvet Guild, an association of velvet manufacturers,
which picked up the tab for the ballroom rental, decorations,
and orchestra.

The ball was designed to be a re-creation of a gala at the
court of Louis XIV. The dances, including a lilting "Hoop-
skirt Waltz" and a polka mazurka, were professionally cho-
reographed and rehearsed by the debs, whose parents watched
their performance from tables set up around the massive dance
floor. King Louis was portrayed by *New Yorker* cartoonist
Peter Arno. Wearing an elaborate brocade costume and a large
wig of cascading black curls, he observed the proceedings
from an ornate throne on the stage of the grand ballroom.

Brenda, who had been picked as the debutante chairman
of the ball, led the debutantes' grand march and the Quadrille
of Coaches. The boys played horses, with reins draped over
their shoulders; the girls, holding small whips, were the driv-
ers. Brenda was unquestionably the star of the show. Whereas
the other girls wore fussy ball gowns with flounces and bows,
and adorned their hair with orchids and ribbons, Brenda wore
a simple pale pink strapless gown. She wore nothing in her
hair; her only jewelry was a pearl and diamond necklace.
The pictures, published in newspapers and magazines across
the country, sparked a strapless gown craze that endured for
years.

A week after the Velvet Ball, Big Brenda took Brenda to
Nassau for a rest from the press. Already the mother was
getting concerned about all the attention her daughter was
getting. There was to be little rest, however. Seven photographers had met their plane when they landed in Miami. On
their return to New York, they were greeted by more photographers and a bigger surprise: the November 14 cover of *Life*
featured a picture of Brenda in her now famous pink strapless
gown. The photograph had been taken at a Velvet Ball com-

mittee meeting, and the magazine had somehow acquired a print of it.

Big Brenda claimed to be appalled. "I was furious about Brenda's photo being on the cover of *Life,*" she wrote in her diary. She got in touch with the magazine's founder and publisher, Henry Luce, who paid her a late-night visit at the Carlton House, promising to do "something in the way of an apology," according to the diary. What he did, if anything, is not known.

The incident probably illustrates Big Brenda's ambivalence about her daughter's publicity. On the one hand, the attention was welcome, an affirmation of Brenda's status. On the other, Big Brenda's main goal was to be accepted by the Old Guard—and the Old Guard still thought publicity vulgar. Aristocratic girls were supposed to have their names in the paper only five times: when they were born, when they came out, when they were engaged, when they married, and when they died. One of Brenda's friends and fellow debs, Edith Gould, says her father fined her every time her name appeared in the paper. "It was chic to be written about by Cholly Knickerbocker. But the last thing you'd want would be to have your picture on the cover of *Life,*" says Victoria Kelly. "[Big Brenda] probably felt about *Life* the way you'd feel about *The National Enquirer* today."

It is also possible that Big Brenda didn't like the specific picture *Life* chose. It was not particularly glamorous—Brenda had on little makeup and no jewelry. For once she looked like the immature teenager she was. There is no further mention of the episode in Big Brenda's diary, although she was delighted by one of the article's effects: a rise in Brenda's already burgeoning popularity. Big Brenda noted in her diary on December 3, "Ewee had about ten young men call on her—what a gal!"

For the most part, Big Brenda reveled in her daughter's publicity. "Brenda certainly likes being popular," she once told a reporter. "So do I. We all love it. There is no problem being the mother of a popular deb. It is the mothers of the others I'm sorry for. It must be awful to be the mother of a flop." Big Brenda never hired a press agent, as many of Brenda's acquaintances believed. She didn't need to. But she did employ Burrelle's clipping service. In one six-month period it found five thousand items about Brenda. Her mother had them mounted in huge green leather scrapbooks.

Big Brenda made sure that Brenda was on the town and in view. "Brenda's mother forced her to go out at night," recalls Esme O'Brien Hammond. "Brenda would be in bed, not feeling well. Her legs bothered her a lot, after that operation. Her mother would come into her bedroom and say, you're going out; you're going to El Morocco and the Stork Club. Get up. You're just pretending to be sick." One morning Brenda and Jane Will Smith, who often stayed at Brenda's apartment, were sleeping in Brenda's bedroom when the phone rang. Jane grabbed the receiver and, imitating a snooty British accent, said, "Miss Frazier's secretary here." The caller identified himself as a reporter from the *Daily News* and asked if he could speak to Brenda. "She's in Saudi Arabia, and she won't be back for three weeks," Jane said, and hung up. Just then Big Brenda came in and said she was waiting for the *Daily News* to call. When Jane announced that she'd "got rid of them, Mrs. Watriss blew her stack and I blew mine. I told her 'you're making your daughter into a public drinking fountain. You don't know what you're doing to this beautiful daughter of yours. You're ruining her life. The only reason you want to do it, is so it will reflect on you.' She told me never to darken her door again. Brenda meanwhile was cowering in the corner in tears. And I said, 'I don't think I ever want to come in your apartment again.' There was screaming and yelling and more screaming and yelling, and I pranced out and went home. Of course, Brenda was on the phone a little while later, pleading, 'You've got to come back.' So I told her to come to my house, and she spent a couple of nights with me. Poor Brenda kept saying that I didn't understand, that that was her mother's attitude. And I said, 'I understand perfectly. It's terrible!' "

Jerome Zerbe, El Morocco's roving photographer, tells a similar story: "I saw Mrs. Watriss about four or five days before Brenda's debut, at a party at Frazier Jelke's. She was complaining bitterly about all the publicity. Of course, she was loving every minute of it. Anyway, I said to her, 'Well, there's one way of settling that very easily. Just cancel the debut and give the money to charity.' Oh, God, she was furious. And the next day, her secretary called up and said,

'Oh, Mr. Zerbe, this is an embarrassing thing for me to do. But Brenda's mother tells me that your invitation was sent by error.' ''

Brenda herself was flattered by the attention. She admitted in her *Life* memoir years later that she had enjoyed the publicity. "I was a fad that year—the way midget golf was once a fad, or flagpole sitting. The publicity came by itself, without any encouragement. But of course my mother did nothing to discourage it. She loved it. . . . So, for a while—to my great shame—did I." Lady Keith, a former wife of Howard Hawks, Leland Hayward, and Lord Keith, a British banker—says she can always pick out the celebrities who enjoy their fame. "It is the way they get out of a car or walk into a restaurant, always managing to spot the camera and having their smiles on by the time the camera spots them. Brenda was like that. I think she enjoyed the notoriety and the publicity. She was well aware of who she was and that she was a star."

Victoria Kelly agrees. "My mother always loved publicity. She pretended she didn't, because no one likes to say, 'Gee, I love having my picture taken.' But if there was ever anything written about her [even toward the end of her life], she saved it. My mother loved every minute of her debut year. I never met anyone who knew her in those days who thought she didn't like it."

As intoxicating as the publicity was, it was dangerous. Grace Davidson, a Boston newspaper woman who got to know Brenda in her forties when she looked like a parody of her debutante self, says, "I had met Brenda in 1938 at the Stork Club, and I thought she was already beginning to look like a freak." For anyone who lives in the public eye, image begins to erode identity. For a frightened, weak, seventeen-year-old girl, the constant attention was devastating. Brenda came to know herself through what she read. The publicity robbed her of an identity and turned her into an oddity.

Around the time of her debut, Brenda also developed an eating problem—something that would haunt her for the rest of her life.

In an effort to remain fashionably thin, she got caught up in a cycle of starving herself, then binge eating, followed by self-induced vomiting—the anorexia and bulimia that have become such familiar female ailments today.

Brenda had always had a difficult time with food. She had been chubby until she was thirteen, when Big Brenda, worried about the effect on her daughter's social life, started pressuring her to lose weight. Dieting was terribly difficult for Brenda, especially since her mother, who was overweight herself, always had plenty of chocolates and other sweets around their apartment.

Eventually Brenda discovered a way to eat as much as she wanted and remain thin: she forced herself to vomit. Brenda's friends tell stories about her eating a huge lunch in a restaurant and then going into the ladies' room, sticking her finger down her throat, and throwing up. More often she did it at home. Later in life, she was capable of consuming virtually the entire contents of a refrigerator at one sitting and then purging it all.

But if there were troubles ahead, no one was stopping to point them out. In 1938, Brenda Frazier was the best advertisement for just about everything. Almost every charity and every debutante committee in New York wanted her as a member. A perfume, Sarong, was created in her honor. Department stores borrowed her likeness for fashion illustrations. A Woodbury soap ad featured a picture of Brenda in a strapless gown, and a testimonial from Cholly Knickerbocker: "I've often noticed that the Society 'lovelies' who go in religiously for a Woodbury Facial cocktail at the zero hour of 5 P.M., are usually the Glamour Girls who are the toast of the stag line in the romance hours later." Brenda even endorsed Studebakers, though she didn't drive a car and went everywhere by taxi or chauffeured limousine. She said in the ad, which included two pictures of her, "Driving my Studebaker is really thrilling. It's such an alive motor car." In most cases Brenda cooperated with the ads and was paid a modest fee, but occasionally she found herself an unwitting endorser.

One evening, at the opening of the Iridium Room at the St. Regis Hotel, a photographer, trying to get an unusual shot, asked Brenda if he could take a picture of her dunking a doughnut. She complied, and the picture appeared in several newspapers and two national magazines. The delighted doughnut industry picked up the picture as an advertisement.

So did Shell Oil, which argued in an ad that to be a good dunker you had to dunk doughnuts made in a machine oiled with Shell.

The doughnut picture opened a new angle for one enterprising reporter. He consulted the arbiter of etiquette, Emily Post, who pronounced that Brenda's doughnut dunking was socially correct. In sitting rooms up and down Fifth Avenue, however, Brenda's dunk was considered seriously déclassé.

The doughnut-dunking incident, society reporters thought, was the main reason Brenda was not invited to the Junior Assembly, a series of three subscription dances sponsored by New York's Old Guard. Actually, as a member of Café Society, not polite society, Brenda was probably never considered by this symbol of Wasp elitism. Big Brenda, however, desperately wanted Brenda to go to these dances, and the previous year she had sent her daughter to talk to one of the Assembly's committee women.

Brenda was also turned down by the conservative Junior League, which in 1938 asked only one fifth of the debutantes to join. Esme O'Brien Hammond, who had been rejected by the Assembly in 1937, explained, "The problem was we were too show biz." Brenda, however, was invited to the Bachelor's Cotillion in Baltimore, and consequently brought a wave of publicity to that bastion of the Old Guard.

As the day of her debut approached, Brenda's name was in the papers almost every day. Even the *Daily Worker,* the newspaper of America's Communist party, wrote about her under the headline "$8 Million Glamour Girl Has Serious Side—Once Read a Book." But the fact that Brenda was one of America's most unproductive idols didn't deter enterprising reporters, who managed to build stories around her decision to wear a hat or visit the hairdresser.

Charlotte Johnson, who did Brenda's hair, remembers that her booth at Sattler's Salon was jammed with male reporters whenever Brenda came in. While Charlotte waved her hair with a curling iron, Brenda would patiently answer questions from the mob of journalists. "Who says you have to put your hair up?" began one story under the headline "Debs Declare Thumbs Down on Hair Style." "The debutantes aren't doing it. 'I put mine up for a fashion magazine,' Brenda Frazier,

No. 1 Glamour Girl of this year's crop, said. 'But I've worn it down ever since.' "

Other stories discussed Brenda's feet. "It's tough being New York's No. 1 society glamour girl—tough on the feet," wrote the Associated Press. "With a rueful 'ouch!'—rubbing a daintily shod foot still sizzling from 5 A.M. festivities, Brenda Frazier, 17, told today how it feels to be known as America's most famous debutante. She said: 'I love it. But, golly, my feet hurt!—a tea dance this afternoon, out again tonight, then dancing later.' The dark-eyed heiress to a fortune variously estimated at between $3,000,000 and $8,000,000, with an income of $200,000 a year, said she looks on all the ballyhoo as 'just a lark.' "

Since Brenda's appearance at a party, nightclub, or restaurant usually sparked a frantic reaction from the press, other celebrities found that a sure way to get their pictures in the paper was to go out with Brenda. There's no reason to doubt that Bruce Cabot, Errol Flynn, Mickey Rooney, and Joan Crawford genuinely liked Brenda. But it seems unlikely that these stars would have spent time with an amiable but unaccomplished teenager if she hadn't been the reigning Glamour Girl No. 1.

It was a measure of Café Society's arrival and Brenda's own celebrity that she even beat the Old Guard at its own game. Since its founding in 1883 the Metropolitan Opera had been a toy for the extravagant rich. As Peter Conrad wrote, the very design of the opera house, which "contrived to snub anyone not in a box," favored social ostentation over music. Society dowagers, who always arrived late and chatted throughout the opera lest anyone doubt that their status placed them above the musicians, looked like walking jewelry displays. Maury Paul referred to them as the turreted tiara set. Over the years their baubles got bigger and brighter. Once Mrs. Frederick Vanderbilt, determined not to be outdone by anyone, removed the famous Vanderbilt pearls from her neck and looped them around her waist. At the end she attached a gigantic lump of sapphire, which she kicked ahead of her like a soccer ball as she advanced to her box.

On November 21, the Met's opening night in 1938, the curtain went up on Verdi's *Otello*. At least 4,400 people jammed the auditorium. Four hundred standees were packed in back of the seats; five hundred more had been turned away at the door. Reporters and photographers milled about. A pile of discarded flashbulbs littered the lobby. Maury Paul, in white tie and tails, a red carnation in his lapel, stood in an upper tier using binoculars to study the action in the diamond horseshoe. He scribbled his observations in a notebook with a jewel-banded gold pencil. Outside on Thirty-ninth Street an excited crowd waited for the "grandees," the elegant aristocrats who never showed up until the first act was well underway.

At around eight-thirty, limousines started pulling up to the curb. Out came the dowagers, like plump pheasants trussed up in expensive furs. First came Mrs. George Kavanaugh, as Paul reported the next day, "ablaze with ALL her diamonds and supported by two bodyguards." The high priestess of high society, Mrs. Cornelius Vanderbilt, arrived at eight-fifty with her niece, "the Vanderbiltian Debbie," Rosemarie Warburton. Wearing her trademark headache band and diamond stomacher, Mrs. Vanderbilt smiled majestically, and the crowd applauded. As she strolled toward her box, a photographer shouted, "Here she comes, boys. The season is open!"

But that was nothing compared to the frenzy sparked by Brenda Frazier. She arrived with her mother after a dinner at the St. Regis Hotel. They were dressed in contrasting costumes that seemed chosen for the photographers. Brenda wore a simple white satin dress and white ermine jacket with a spray of white orchids on the shoulder. Her hair was parted on the side and held in place by a diamond clip. Big Brenda wore a black fringe dress, black suede gloves, and a black chinchilla cape. In her hair were two tremendous black aigrettes. When the two Brendas arrived, they were met by a barrage of popping flashbulbs and excited shrieks from the crowd. At one point the cheers grew so wild that several furious Met employees poked their heads outside to hush the mob. "Please remember that an opera is going on inside," scolded one usher. As the Brendas tried to enter the opera house, where they were guests of Frazier Jelke's in Box 6, their path was completely blocked by excited admirers. "Dreadful!" Big Brenda said as she plowed her way through the bodies. "Dreadful!'

By late November, Brenda's popularity had reached such a level that Barclay Beekman of the *Mirror* complained to his readers, "I just can't keep her name out." It was still a month away from the Christmas holidays and the height of the debutante season, but reporters were already fighting over who had discovered her. The *Journal-American* published a Chick Farmer photograph of Brenda above the headline "THE SHOT THAT MADE BRENDA FRAZIER." In the caption Farmer boasted, "This is the shot that made the country Brenda Frazier–conscious. When I first saw Brenda I thought she was attractive, but when I developed this very first shot in a nightclub, I knew she was destined for page 1. My camera, not I, discovered her."

Maury Paul, who probably invented the columnist's "you-read-it-here-first" boast, wasn't about to be one-upped. On November 27, 1938, Paul arrived at his office ready to work. First he went to his file cabinet and pulled out a copy of his 1936 item predicting that Brenda would be "the Belle of the 1938 season." Then, as he did whenever he wrote a column, he took off his jacket and hung it over the back of his chair. Next he unclasped his gold wristwatch, removed his platinum ring with the blood-red ruby, and unbuckled his gold belt. Finally he unzipped his fly and let his huge stomach spill out comfortably over his trousers. Paul arranged a piece of yellow copy paper in his typewriter, placed his chubby index fingers on the keys, and began to type:

> *In thumbing back through some files I came across [a column] written more than two years ago after encountering 1938-39's No. 1 "Glamour Girl" and her mother lunching at the Ritz.*
>
> *I well remember the afternoon—and how impressed I was with Brenda's good looks, and how I marveled at her ultra-sophistication.*
>
> *It would appear I was the first to realize she was a "Glamour Girl" in the making. . . .*
>
> *Brenda has become a newspaper and magazine "personality" in the public's eyes. And she belongs to the public created for her just as much as if she were a "movie" star, or an operatic diva.*

I feel for Mrs. Watriss, knowing how much she dislikes having her only child publicized so persistently.

But after all, it isn't every season the writers and photographers have such a comely, glamorous subject as Brenda Frazier to write about, and to "shoot at." . . .

Out of 400 debutantes of the current season, more than 219 have yet to get their photographic likeness in the papers or so much as an editorial mention.

That should cheer up Mrs. Watriss on "Blue Monday" afternoon as she peruses, with horrified optics, the columns and columns of "notices" pasted in Brenda's scrap-book.

Frankly, that scrap-book "ain't nothin' " yet.

Wait until the debutante season really begins.

CHAPTER SEVEN

On December 27, the day of Brenda's debut, a cold rain thrashed New York City. In the late afternoon, Griffiths took Brenda's black Chrysler Imperial and picked up Charlotte Johnson at Sattler's hairdressing salon. Carrying a large curling iron and a portable gas stove on which to heat it, Charlotte entered the Carlton House and took the elevator up to the fourth floor. Inside the apartment she walked down a marble corridor to Brenda's bedroom and opened the door. There was the Deb of the Century, churning in her pink satin sheets, her delicate white face remade by illness into a puffy red mask.

Brenda had the flu. She had first felt ill on Christmas Day and had stayed in bed while her mother attended a service at St. Patrick's Cathedral and a party at the Vanderbilts'. Two days of rest hadn't improved her condition, and, on top of everything else, her feet were very swollen. Her condition had sparked an enervating argument with her mother—the outcome of which was certainly obvious beforehand to both women. Brenda insisted she was too sick to attend her debut, and she begged her mother to call it off. This suggestion infuriated Big Brenda. After all, she had spent thousands of dollars and months of planning to introduce Brenda to society the right way. People such as Henry Luce, Mrs. William Randolph Hearst, and Douglas Fairbanks, Jr., had promised to be there.

Big Brenda had also released Hal Phyfe's stunning predebut

portrait of Brenda to eager society editors across the country. Papers everywhere published the picture, which showed Brenda in her debut gown from Henri Bendel.The dress had a skirt of floor-length white duchesse satin, a tight bodice, a hoop skirt, and a sash of frothy ostrich feathers cascading from the waist. She was posed standing against a backdrop of white plumes made into Christmas trees. Her shiny dark hair was set in a soft halo of waves; her mouth was held in a serene half-moon. The effect was dreamy, other-worldly. It was the perfect picture of a Society Goddess. The debut, Big Brenda hoped, would be her daughter's apotheosis.

Big Brenda refused to believe that Brenda was too sick to go out. "It's just a cold," she snapped. Had she been more sensitive, she would have seen Brenda's malady for what it was: sheer terror. Brenda later wrote of her pain: "It was the clammy, headachy, stomach churning terror that being the center of so much attention often arouses in even the most confident and extroverted of 17-year-old girls—something I myself certainly was not."

Big Brenda had been planning the party for more than a year. In October 1937, she had visited Surrogate Foley to discuss using some of Brenda's money to pay for the debut. Big Brenda waited almost two hours to see him. Finally he called her into his chambers. How much money Big Brenda requested is unknown, but she must have been terribly disappointed when he granted her only $15,000—barely enough to cover the cost of the ballroom rental and flowers. A practical, conservative man, Foley probably disapproved of extravagant debut balls. Although most newspaper accounts said the debut cost from $50,000 to $75,000, Big Brenda "could not possibly have afforded such a sum," wrote Brenda. In later life, she told people that the party cost between $16,000 and $20,000.

Two months later, Big Brenda and Lady Jane paid a call on social secretary Juliana Cutting. Big Brenda probably bought all three of Miss Cutting's lists. She also hired her to handle invitations. Two thousand were sent out on engraved stationery. The debut was to be held at the Ritz, where New York's most patrician young women traditionally came out. Big Brenda had rented the hotel's entire ballroom suite, including the large foyer, the Palm Court, and the Oval Room.

As was the custom at all-night society parties, she also rented dozens of nearby bedrooms so exhausted guests would have a place to nap and repair their appearances. Big Brenda encouraged her friends to bring their servants to the party. The maids and valets would work the bedrooms, mending torn tailcoats and broken zippers, while the butlers would be paid fifteen dollars each to help the Ritz staff serve dinner.

Unlike Barbara Hutton's "Valley of Diamonds" or Natalie Coe's "Southern Plantation"—debuts held at the Ritz in previous years—Brenda's ball had no overall theme. Nor were there any spectacular decorations. For one debut in 1937 the Waldorf-Astoria's roof had been covered with thousands of yards of white satin, and a plaster fountain with neon lights was built in the center. For Brenda there were beautiful, stylishly arranged flowers. Constance Spry—the famous English florist who had designed the floral set for the wedding of the Duke and Duchess of Windsor, and had just opened a Madison Avenue shop—transformed the ballroom suite into a moonlit garden.

Brenda's ball was to start at 11:30 P.M., a late hour that some socialites believed was designed to maximize attendance. Harry Cushing, a polo player and cousin of Gloria Vanderbilt's, recalls that many Old Guard families wouldn't let their daughters go to the debut of a relative upstart like Brenda. "I remember people talking and saying, 'Are you going to Brenda Frazier's debut?' And others answering 'Well, the food's going to be good; it's going to be a great party. But Daddy doesn't want me to go.' There were other parties that night for girls the mothers and fathers knew; girls who were more socially acceptable. So Brenda was very smart. She had hers very late, because her mother was worried that — if they started it early, you'd be able to shoot ducks in the place."

Because of her illness Brenda didn't go to any of the other deb parties held that day. She missed an afternoon tea dance at the Sherry Netherland for one girl, a supper dance at the River Club for her good friend Catherine Gamble, a party at the St. Regis for another friend, Alice Fleitmann. Nor did she show up at any of the dinners given in her honor, not even the small supper for thirty-eight that her mother attended in a restaurant.

Still, Brenda did begin getting ready. When Charlotte arrived, Brenda sat up in bed and slid a lacy bed jacket over her nightgown. "I don't know how I'm going to get through this," she told the hairdresser. But she got up, sat at her mirrored dressing table, and let Charlotte wave her hair into soft loose curls—one step in an interminable toilette that included manicure, pedicure, facial, bath, and makeup.

While Brenda languished in her bedroom, a young girl in Brooklyn named Edythe Friedman was preparing for another kind of debut. The daughter of a man who designed trimmings for draperies and clothes, Edythe had skipped several grades and at fifteen was a freshman at Brooklyn College. She hoped for a career in journalism and was one of the few girls who worked on her college newspaper, the *Vanguard.* She was having trouble convincing her editors, all upperclassmen, to give her challenging assignments. Then she had an idea. She would go to Brenda Frazier's debut and write a firsthand account of the party. She had written Brenda asking for an invitation. When Brenda hadn't responded, Edythe decided to use her *Vanguard* ID to get in as a member of the working press. It would be her first effort covering a real story side by side with real reporters.

Edythe was not yet allowed to date, so she arranged to have a girlfriend go the party with her. In the afternoon she packed up her good clothes and rode the subway to the friend's home in Manhattan. Once there, she changed into a plaid taffeta gown and black suede pumps and tied a black velvet ribbon around her neck. Then her friend backed out: she didn't have a press card, and she was afraid she'd be turned back at the door. So Edythe had to go alone. Not knowing what time a society debut began, she walked over to the Ritz at 9:30 P.M., and was told by a doorman that the Frazier party would not start until eleven-thirty. For the next two hours she walked aimlessly around the neighborhood, her dress hitched up under her polo coat, as she shivered against the subfreezing temperatures and biting winds.

Big Brenda, who had been at a dinner party since six, returned to the apartment at ten forty-five. Dressed for the debut in a black net gown covered with sequins, she wore a huge diamond tiara atop her tightly curled hair, three long strands of pearls around her throat, and white orchids pinned at her shoulder. When she arrived, the scene on Forty-seventh Street resembled a Broadway opening. A gaggle of photographers huddled on the sidewalk beside a swelling crowd of onlookers. At the curb, men in silk top hats and tails stepped out of shiny stretch limos. Beautiful teenagers in grown-up gowns blinked into bursts of popping flashbulbs.

Upstairs at the Carlton House, Brenda was stepping into her creamy satin gown. Her mother helped her clasp a diamond necklace around her throat and a four-strand pearl bracelet on her wrist. Finally, at eleven-twenty, mother and daughter walked down the long corridor that linked the Carlton House to the Ritz Towers.

Emil Coleman's orchestra was playing "Manhattan" to the empty ballroom when Brenda and her mother entered. White lights concealed in the ballroom ceiling iluminated thousands of fragrant flowers. On the balconies on either side of the room, mammoth Louis XVIII urns overflowed with gilded leaves, lilies, and golden pears, grapes, and apples. Garlands of white and yellow blossoms hung from the stairway balustrades, and sprays of Easter lilies and gold-veined cellophane leaves flanked the downstairs entrance to the suite. The foyer was lined with towering cornucopias packed with California lichen moss, gladioli, and more lilies.

Standing before a gigantic cornucopia of fresh flowers and a table stacked with corsages that had been sent her that day, Brenda dutifully took her place in the receiving line between Big Brenda and her stepbrother Freddie Watriss. Her swollen feet, stuffed into her satin evening slippers, throbbed with pain. So did her head. With one white-gloved hand Brenda clutched a bridal-type bouquet of orchids. With the other she puffed frantically on a cigarette through a long white holder, until the first guest was virtually at arm's length.

One of the first to arrive was Mrs. Cornelius Vanderbilt, weighed down by a satin brocade dress, ropes of pearls, and a tattered gray fox stole that she wrapped around her neck for warmth. Her son, Cornelius "Neily" Vanderbilt, whose book criticizing high society later got him dropped from the Social Register, arrived escorting two socialites. Elsa Maxwell came in a black velvet dress and elbow-length black gloves. Condé Nast showed up, as did Doris Duke, Douglas Fairbanks, Jr., Peter Arno, and Ralph Holmes. Noticeably absent were Lady Jane and Sir Frederick, who remained in Nassau because Sir Frederick was ill. Only one of Brenda's paternal relatives appeared, a great-aunt named Ida Spear, who had not seen Brenda since Frank Frazier's funeral in 1933. Mrs. Spear did not appear to be having a good time. "I fear Brenda's being spoiled," she sniped to one guest. "I loathe all this spectacular notoriety."

The day before the party, Big Brenda had called her friends on the phone and asked them to wear their showiest jewels. Vaults throughout the city were opened for the occasion—here were the priceless Burden pearls, the Rothschild diamonds, the Rhinelander emeralds. There were also dozens of glittering tiaras, despite a time-honored rule of etiquette against the wearing of tiaras in hotels. Fifteen detectives, disguised in white tie and tails, were paid twenty-three dollars each to mill about and guard the finery.

Brenda, her mother, and Fred Watriss stood in the receiving line until 1 A.M., when Big Brenda ordered supper to be served in the Oval Room. Guests wandered into the restaurant and sat wherever they pleased. White-jacketed waiters served the three-course meal: black bean soup; breast of chicken with Madeira sauce, wild rice, and purée of peas; and chocolate and vanilla ice cream in individual molds, tiny cakes, and coffee.

By 2 A.M. the party was in full swing. In the Grand Ballroom three big mirrors with white light playing over them like moonlight reflected a blur of diamonds and velvet. Waiters struggled through the mob carrying trays of sloshing champagne. The guests broke one thousand dollars' worth of glassware. One glass careened off a stair railing and showered a girl with wine. So much champagne was drunk that forty waiters spent all their time doing nothing but uncorking and pouring. Eventually the guests had emptied all two hundred cases and more was carried up from the hotel's wine cellar. "Three pints a person should be sufficient!" grumbled Adolph Jeanet, the Ritz's banquet manager.

Two orchestras played throughout the night. In the ballroom, Emil Coleman's twenty-four piece ensemble played "De-Lovely," "Mountain Greenery," and Brenda's favorite

Cole Porter tune, "Get Out of Town." In the Palm Court, Alexander Haas's six-man gypsy band, in red coats to match the poinsettias, played mostly rumbas. The men outnumbered the women three to one and made every dance a cut-in. Brenda probably danced with a hundred men, most of whom she had never seen before and would never see again. Although her swollen feet ached, she bravely endured the Lambeth Walk, the Big Apple, the Shag, and dozens of rumbas.

Guards were posted in the Ritz lobby, and two secretaries from Juliana Cutting's office sat at a folding table in front of the door, checking invitations. Reporters, except for Maury Paul and Dixie Tighe, were barred. So were all photographers but one, Jay Te Winburn, hired by Big Brenda as the official debut photographer. Still, a swarm of paparazzi managed to sneak in. Some hid behind pillars and flower arrangements, but as the evening wore on, they grew brazen. As Brenda whirled by during one dance, an uninvited guest tapped her partner on the shoulder and asked if he could cut in. Brenda smiled and her partner obligingly stepped aside. The young man guided Brenda toward a corner and whispered in her ear. Brenda's face froze. "No," she said emphatically, "you can't take my picture."

Eager for a society scoop, the *Daily News* secured tailcoats and rented a room at the Ritz for six of its best-looking men. When the party was well underway, the newsmen strolled casually into the packed ballroom and mingled with the guests. Hiding behind potted palms, they pulled out cameras from inside their jackets and began snapping pictures. One young man sneaked onto the bandstand and pretended to be a musician. But before he could take any pictures, he was recognized by another photographer, a Russian who had also crashed the party. He reported the *News* man to Brenda, who had them both thrown out. Another *News* man sat atop a box overlooking the dance floor, making goofy faces at Brenda to grab her attention. She stared at him blankly for a minute and then turned away.

A third *News* man crept up behind Winburn, and as the fast-working photographer laid down one spent plate of film after another, the *News* man picked them up and slid them under his coat. Then he sauntered out of the ballroom and rushed his booty to the *News*. Meanwhile, Winburn, who had taken sixty shots using flashbulbs, appeared pop-eyed before Mrs. Watriss to announce that eighteen plates had been stolen.

Another uninvited guest who had no trouble getting in was Edythe Friedman. She simply walked up to the Ritz doorman and flashed her orange *Vanguard* press card. "Okay," he muttered, motioning her inside. Edythe walked through the receiving line. "How do you do. I'm Edythe Friedman," she told Brenda. "How do you do," answered Brenda, looking past her to the next person in line. "I had the feeling that Brenda was kind of tired. She looked subdued," says Edythe. "I thought, 'Is she so used to this that she takes it as a matter of course?' I was a little disappointed that she wasn't more excited. She seemed reserved, apart, even bored. I sensed that she wasn't really enjoying it."

Edythe was also disappointed by the ambiance of the party. "It was elegant, but shallow. There didn't seem to be a lot of friends there. Nobody seemed to know anybody else. It wasn't warm. Dinner was sort of informal; there wasn't a waiter behind everybody. I expected it to be more formal, yet friendlier and warmer. I guess I expected pheasant under glass and a waiter whisking away the first course. For some reason I thought everybody would know everybody else. But of course, there were two thousand people there."

Most of the conversation, Edythe observed, was typical party chitchat. Among the debs: "Didn't Brenda look too divine in her white gown—but then Brenda always looks just right." The older people commented on Brenda's charming manners: "Imagine, after being laid up for so many days! Now that it's over, she ought to take a long rest." Edythe drank her first glass of champagne (to her it tasted like ginger ale) and danced with her first society swains, lithe, smooth-skinned boys who bowed elegantly and asked, "Care to dance?"

At 4 A.M. Big Brenda ordered a buffet breakfast to be served: ham and biscuits, hot fruit, chicken hash with bacon crisscrossed on top, coffee. By this time some of the calla lilies and many of the guests had faded. One elegant old gentleman fell asleep in a chair, a stale glass of champagne on a butler's tray in front of him, a white napkin tucked behind his white tie. At 5 A.M. Edythe Friedman observed that "Brenda was still dancing. Once when I passed close by her on the floor I noticed that her eyes were shut, but she opened them when someone cut in and continued to rumba with as much zeal as she had shown at the beginning of her party."

Around 6 A.M., as the party was winding down, several boys set up an obstacle course in the middle of the dance floor with empty champagne bottles. Then the waiters brought in electric cars, the kind used for rides at amusement parks. As the boys raced the cars around the polished parquet, Brenda sat quietly at a table holding hands with Peter Arno and chatting with a gaggle of admirers. Occasionally she pulled her compact from her evening bag, dabbed some powder on her face, and reapplied her liver-red lipstick.

Hotel guests who came down for breakfast at six were shocked to see the party still in progress. Finally, at six-thirty, Big Brenda stopped Coleman's orchestra. Douglas Fairbanks, Jr., draped a tablecloth around Brenda's shoulders and she sat huddled in its folds, puffing on a cigarette. Years later, Brenda recalled the final moments of her party: "Doug said I was shivering; that the hall must have grown cold. But the hall was not cold at all. I was shivering from exhaustion."

As Brenda said good-bye to her last guests, commuters on the way to work read the first excited accounts of her party. Several hours before in Washington, D.C., President Franklin Roosevelt's niece, Eleanor, had come out at the White House. But Brenda's coming out was the national event: fourteen hundred aristocrats from the United States and Europe had come to pay homage to this seventeen-year-old girl. The ball was news not only in New York, but also across the country and the world. Brenda made the front page as far away as Seattle. The San Francisco *Chronicle* announced in a banner headline, "BRENDA IS FINALLY OUT, NOW WE CAN ALL RELAX." The party was also news in Germany, Canada, and England. She made *Life* and the "National Affairs" section of *Time*. She was the lead story on the society page of *The New York Times*. It reported:

> *Miss Brenda Diana Duff Frazier made her debut last night at a ball given in the main ballroom suite of the Ritz Carlton by her mother, Mrs. Frederic N. Watriss. It was the largest*

debutante dance of the season thus far, the hundreds of guests including many older friends of Miss Frazier's family, as well as the majority of the younger members of society who have participated in the holiday entertaining for debutantes.

In contrast, Maury Paul's account in the *Journal-American* bristled with hyperbole:

> *Diamonds sparkled, champagne corks "popped," a small army of musicians played—and Brenda D. D. Frazier, the No. 1 "Glamour Girl" of the 1938-39 season, slid down the debutantal ways into the New York social seas last night at the Ritz Carlton.*
>
> *Brenda made a graceful splash as she officially entered society's ranks at one of the largest balls of the winter.*
>
> *And, as she received the 2,000 guests, arrayed in white duchess satin, combined with ostrich feathers, eye-compelling brunette Brenda again asserted her right to the title: "New York's Most Beautiful Debutante."*

Unlike Paul, most of the reporters assigned to write about the party weren't there. They relied for their accounts on information released by the family and interviews with Brenda's guests. Consequently, the stories were filled with inaccuracies about the food, the decorations, and the party's costs, widely overestimated at $50,000 to $75,000. One of the biggest mistakes appeared in London's *Daily Mail*, which reported that the party featured an act from the Broadway show *Hellzapoppin.*

Not surprisingly, the *Daily News* had the best coverage. "BOW'S A WOW," gushed the *News* over an article keyed to a two-page spread of pictures developed from Winburn's film. Here was the whole story: Brenda greeting Mrs. Vanderbilt and Elsa Maxwell, Brenda being kissed by an anonymous admirer, Brenda being pulled by the arms in opposite directions by two young men.

One of the most accurate accounts was that of Edythe Friedman, who wrote her story in longhand on ruled paper and sent it to the *World-Telegram*, the paper her father brought home from work every night. It immediately appealed to the *Telegram*'s editors, but they were more interested in her adventure than her story. They sent a reporter to Edythe's house for more details, and a photographer arrived to take a picture of her in her taffeta gown. It was published under the headline "Everyday Girl." Suddenly Edythe herself was a celebrity. Other newspapers interviewed her. She even appeared on the Parks Johnson and Wally Butterworth "Vox Pop" radio program, along with a socialite who discussed divorce in the Smart Set. Edythe reported that Brenda's party was "magnificent . . . Brenda was lovely . . . the men were good-looking."

As she had originally planned, Edythe's story was printed in the Brooklyn *Vanguard,* under the headline " 'I Crashed Brenda Frazier's Party': Edythe Gives Dope on How She Did It." "In evening dress and slippers, I roamed the town for two hours," wrote Edythe, "and more than once I lost my nerve deciding that nothing was worth this (this being a howling wind and a temperature of 20 degrees above). At last 11:30 rolled around and with chattering teeth and trembling knees, but with head held high, I entered the hotel, presented my press pass from Vanguard (yes, that's all there was to it) and walked in. I introduced myself to Brenda and her mother, who smiled sweetly and murmured polite 'how do you dos.' "

Today Edythe is a travel writer living on Long Island, and the mother of two grown sons; but she still keeps a copy of the story in a scrapbook stored in her attic.

The *Daily News* ran its report of Brenda's debut next to a story headlined "HUNGRY MOTHER ATTEMPTS SUICIDE." Such tragedies were common during the Depression. But at no time in history were debutantes more glorified. The disillusioned and bewildered nation felt a deep need to take life lightly. Even the *News,* the great paper of the working class, rushed to defend Brenda's extravagance. In an editorial entitled "OH, PISH TUSH," the *News* wrote:

> It's a trifle tiresome to listen to the current complaining by various brands of share-the-wealthers over the fact that Brenda Diana Duff Frazier's coming out party a couple of nights ago cost somewhere between $20,000 and $50,000.
> We're not, God wot, social butterflies. But if this blowout didn't share some wealth with quite a few people who could use it, what would?

Some shrewd guesser has figured out that the money was whacked around about as follows, or in these proportions: Supper, breakfast and ballroom rent, $7,500; champagne, $1,500; Scotch, rye and soft drinks, $1,000; music (25-piece orchestra; 6-piece gypsy band), $2,500; private detectives, $350; decorations (including fifty dozen calla lilies, several hundred poinsettias, 1,000-odd chrysanthemums), $1,000; tips to 100 waiters, twenty captains and five banquet master's assistants, $1,000; 300 stags, $500; social secretary's fee, $2,500; breakage, $25.

Most of the money went, in other words, into active circulation among people who in turn spend it soon. . . .

Permit us to suggest that the share-the-wealth thinkers save their brain sweat for an endeavor that really matters; namely, the long, slow endeavor to bring about a more equitable distribution of wealth and wealth control in this country. The deb parties are just bubbles on the beer, anyway, and they do put a little money into active circulation.

The newspaper accounts made Brenda's party sound like a smashing success. Big Brenda was ecstatic. She noted in her diary the next morning, "It was a great success. I danced all night after 1 [A.M.]. . . . Brenda looked lovely in her white satin and feathers. . . . " But Brenda was miserable. "I hated every minute of my debut," she wrote in *Life.* "I fell into bed afterward, in such a state of collapse, that I still can't remember what happened all the next day."

Now that she was officially "out," Brenda hoped the publicity, the attention, the commotion, would stop. Her mother, however, had different ideas. The next step was to capitalize on Brenda's triumph by arranging a brilliant match for her. "Unless I married well, the whole [debutante] year would have passed in vain," Brenda wrote. "I was bred and trained to be married, run a household, give parties and rear daughters to have their own debuts, and sons to dance with a new generation of debutantes."

PART THREE

SYMBOL

CHAPTER EIGHT

To the nation struggling under the yoke of the Depression in the winter of 1939, Brenda was a dazzling symbol of hope. She was beautiful, rich, young, and celebrated. She traveled by chauffeured limousine, dined out with movie stars, and danced at El Morocco until 5 A.M. When she entered a nightclub, "the crowd parted like the Red Sea," recalls Brenda's friend Gerald Groesbeck. "Everyone who was with her loved it. We all used to bask in her fame."

On February 4, when she sailed for Nassau for a vacation, the event was covered with all the fanfare usually reserved for a royal crossing. By noon a crowd of photographers and reporters had gathered at the Eleventh Street pier where the S.S. *Munargo* was docked. Other reporters were on board already, interviewing Brenda. The previous night she had danced at the Stork Club until four in the morning with Yale student Harry Wilson. Still she looked "fresh as a daisy, her big eyes bright and clear and her complexion as pink and white as they come," wrote one reporter. On board, the dancing started up again at a bon voyage party for Brenda. Wearing a simple black dress and black pumps, Brenda did the conga to the ship's four-piece band, while Big Brenda served drinks from a folding table laden with liquor and buckets of cracked ice.

Reporters asked Big Brenda why she and her daughter were sailing on the family-class *Munargo*, instead of a luxury liner more befitting a Glamour Girl and her mother. "I have my own ideas on economy, and this is one of them," she said. The press also grilled Billy Livingston, who had been invited along to stay with the family in Nassau. "Brenda's no flop, but she's no fiancée either," Livingston told a reporter from the *Daily News*. "Don't say we're engaged. I'm just her friend." "An old friend," Big Brenda corrected. "I invited him to come to Nassau with us so Brenda could have someone her own age to play and swim with." Harry Wilson, who had to go back to New Haven for classes, came on board for the party. As he and Brenda chatted alone in a corner of the ship's lounge, Billy told the reporter that he wasn't plotting to steal Brenda's affections. "I'm just going down for my health," he said.

Brenda signed autographs and had her picture taken chucking a baby under the chin. The *Daily News* ran the picture in its Sunday feature supplement under the headline "Chucking a Cherub! The Chucker is Glamour-Gal Brenda." At 1 P.M. the *Munargo* pulled out from the pier and glided down the Hudson, with one unexpected passenger aboard—twenty-seven-year-old socialite Ogden Hammond. He had met Brenda at a cocktail party just twenty-four hours before. Now, in the frenzy of the bon voyage party, he had forgotten to disembark.

Poor Harry Wilson was left standing alone on the pier, holding two mink coats, one belonging to Brenda, the other to her mother. He had promised to return the coats to the cedar chest at Brenda's apartment; Griffiths was waiting to drive him back to the Carlton House. But watching the ship pull out, Wilson was suddenly overcome with emotion. He had dated Brenda every night for a week, and now he would not see her for almost two months. Noticing that the reporters were watching him closely, Wilson put on a pair of dark glasses, but he couldn't hide his tears. They flowed uncontrollably, while the reporters scribbled away.

As a college student, Wilson didn't have a chance with Brenda. Her relatives hoped that she would marry someone either titled or famous. Douglas Fairbanks, Jr., at the time one of the nation's most popular movie stars, remembers how Big Brenda approached him. "It was all done by indirection," he says. "But it was made very clear to me that she'd make it worthwhile for me to marry Brenda if there was a sign of attraction. She suggested that a happy settlement could be made." Fairbanks was not interested. Brenda, he said, "behaved and was made up to be years older than she was. It was too much. She was seventeen, but she looked twenty-seven. One felt sorry for her. She was made to look so cosseted and protected, like a bird in a gilded cage."

In 1939 the trip to Nassau took four days. In recent years the picturesque harbor town, the capital of the Bahamas, had become a fashionable winter resort among the English and American aristocracies. Politically, the island was said to be run by a cabal of corrupt white businessmen, led by Sir Harry Oakes, a successful gold prospector who'd fled to the Bahamas to escape taxes. Socially, Lady Jane ruled. She had been spending the winters there with Sir Frederick for many years, and by the late thirties she had established a true monarchy. One evening at a party given by Oakes, Lady Jane was holding court on the patio when a young princess, the Ranee of Pudukkotai, swept into the room in a cloud of chiffon. She hurried over to Lady Jane, curtsied deeply, and exclaimed, "To the Queen of Nassau." Lady Jane extended her white-gloved hand and motioned the Ranee to rise, "accepting the compliment as her just due," as one reporter covering the party observed.

Lady Jane was a charter member of the ultra-exclusive Porcupine Club on Hog Island and also an active member of the Emerald Beach Club on the mainland. Great rivalry existed between the two clubs. The Porcupine was favored by the Americans, and the Emerald, of which Sir Frederick was president, by the British. Although the Porcupine had better beaches, better food, and more charm, the Emerald was more accessible. Jane went to both clubs, where she entertained at elaborate beach buffets featuring native music and burning palm trunks.

In 1938 the Williams-Taylors had built a spectacular estate called Star Acres atop a ridge overlooking a golf course. Outside, the house had shell-pink walls, sea-green shutters, and cedar shingles. Inside, it was as elegantly furnished as the couple's London townhouse. Among Nassau socialites the house was rumored to contain a million dollars' worth of antiques. The drawing room was filled with treasures from Jane's travels: lamps of jade and amethyst amber, a rare oriental Chippendale mirror, Chinese paintings on glass. The centerpiece of the room was a larger-than-life portrait of Jane by England's royal portrait artist, Simon Elwes.

The dining room sat sixteen, and Lady Jane frequently gave large luncheons, which began promptly at 1 P.M. If the guests or the food were delayed even a few minutes, Sir Frederick, a stickler for punctuality, was known to stomp angrily out of the house. After lunch the guests would play bridge in the green-tiled card room or relax in the library, which was filled with rare books and autographed pictures of English royalty. The most astounding piece in the room was a portrait in oils of Adolf Hitler, signed by the Führer. Hitler had given it to Lady Jane in Munich in 1934. "I got it at lunch one day," she liked to tell her astonished guests. She kept the picture proudly on display throughout the war. As Brenda later said, "It made very little difference to my grandmother whether a man was a beast or a hero, as long as he was a head of state."

When the *Munargo* docked in Nassau on February 8, the Williams-Taylors' chauffeur met Brenda, her mother, and Billy Livingston at the pier and drove them to Star Acres. Two six-hundred-pound eagles flanked the entrance. The car drove through an antique wrought-iron gate and wound up a hill lined with red hibiscus, orchids, and tropical shrubs.

At sixty-eight, Lady Jane was as strong and vibrant as ever. But Sir Frederick, now seventy-six, seemed to have shrunk and faded. One Bahamian friend, Valeria Moss, remembers that "Lady Jane was always well made up. She looked quite smart, even in her seventies. Sir Frederick, too, was always very turned out. He was very slight; he had a small face, with a little pointed mustache and a little goatee." He used to stroll on the beach in a straw boater, a plaid jacket, and a black Count Dracula–type cape that billowed out from his shoulders in the shore breeze. No longer able to play golf, he liked to show people his gnarled, arthritic hands and say, "See, they are frozen in a position to hold a club."

Although Brenda had said she was going to Nassau to rest, her appointment book for February shows lunch and dinner dates almost every day, plus a flurry of parties, teas, dances, picnics, and yachting trips. What was more, the publicity blitz hardly let up. Pictures of Brenda soon began to appear in the New York papers: Brenda leading the band at a night-club called The Jungle, Brenda doing the Hurdle with Billy Livingston, Brenda dressed as a Hindu princess at a party in her honor, Brenda sunbathing on the beach.

The press also kept daily tabs on her love life, a subject of great interest to Big Brenda and Lady Jane. Mrs. Robert Holt, one Bahamian friend of the family, recalls, "I felt so sorry for little Brenda. It was as if she was for sale. They tried like the devil to get her married to a title."

Much of their scheming was chronicled—sometimes accurately, sometimes not—by the papers. At one point the reporters were intrigued by the Honorable Edward Astley, one of a group of titled Britons that included Lord Astor, Sir Victor Sassoon, and the Duke of Sutherland, who flocked to Nassau each winter.

Edward Astley, handsome and urbane, was from one of England's oldest families. The Astleys claimed seven hundred years of ownership of a Norfolk estate. The family, which Edward heads today as Lord Hastings, can be traced as far back as 1236, when Sir Thomas Astley, Knight of Astley Castle, married Editha Constable of Melton Constable.

When Astley and Brenda appeared together at a ball at Nassau's Victoria Hotel, reporters assumed they were serious. But then Helen Rich, a society writer in Miami, wrote that Astley "was disconsolate and disapproving" when Brenda danced with another man at a Nassau nightclub. Astley was furious and wrote Rich an angry letter. Maury Paul picked up the spat for his column:

> It now appears that the Hon. Edward Astley, whose name has so frequently—and, as I've always pointed out, erroneously—been connected in a romantic way with Brenda Frazier, is "hoppin' mad" over the way ink-slingers from New York to Nassau have made it appear he's trying to land the wealthy "Glamour Girl" for his bride.
>
> In a slightly ungallant letter to Helen Rich, who rates as the cleverest and most widely read society scribbler in Miami (hi-yah, Helen!) the Hon. Edward lets off steam—the substance of which seems to be that he wouldn't have Brenda for his bride—even if he could.
>
> Tut tut and a few woof-woofs!

When someone more interesting entered the romantic sweepstakes, the press soon forgot all about Edward Astley. Howard Hughes had pulled into Nassau harbor on his yacht, the *Southern Cross*. "Everyone knew that Hughes and Brenda would find each other," says her friend Gerald Groesbeck. "All of us in the New York group just sat around the Bahamian Club and waited for it to happen. . . . I think it was a Sunday, in late afternoon, at around five or six. Brenda came in, then Hughes. I didn't actually see them shake hands, but I'm sure that was the evening they met. Three days later they were in the hay."

Brenda's appointment book shows that she had daily dates with Hughes during her last two weeks in Nassau. They went to picnics at the Emerald Beach Club; they dined with Dorothy Thompson, the newspaper reporter; they danced until dawn at the Jungle Club. Hughes, who was staying at the British Colonial Hotel, also took Brenda up in one of his planes. One day they flew to the Exuma Cays, and another day to Palm Beach, where Brenda visited her father's stone villa, then occupied by Herbert Pulitzer, third son of the newspaper publisher Joseph Pulitzer.

Brenda and Howard had much in common. In 1939, both were at the height of their celebrity. Both loved the idea of fame but were repelled by the actual attention it sparked. Like Brenda, Hughes was naturally shy and feared large parties. Observing Hughes at a social function, one writer noticed that "when standing, he inclines his head out and down and looks at the ground. Seated, he clasps his hands between his widespread knees and stares at his knuckles."

To Brenda—still shy, and uncertain, and only seventeen—the thirty-three-year-old Hughes seemed to have the courage she lacked. To Hughes, Brenda possessed the ideal combination—the beauty and glamour of a movie star and the polish of a socialite. Of all of Hughes's other famous girlfriends—Carole Lombard, Ida Lupino, and Katharine Hepburn, to name a few—only Hepburn had this magic duality.

Hughes was possibly also interested in Brenda as a potential actress. He had a history of wooing young beauties, giving them expensive acting and singing lessons, and promising to make them stars. Hughes introduced Brenda to his friend Pat di Cicco, a talent scout for MGM. When reporters saw the three of them dining together in Nassau, a flurry of stories appeared speculating on whether Brenda would sign a movie contract. Barclay Beekman of the New York *Mirror* reported that MGM had offered Brenda a five-year contract for $500,000. "Then a rival company wired Mrs. Watriss that the deb could write her own ticket," Beekman wrote. "Two agents are waiting in New York, ready to hasten to Nassau the moment Mrs. Watriss decides to consider either offer, but Mrs. Watriss said, 'Brenda doesn't know anything about acting.' 'Leave that to us,' was Hollywood's answer. 'She photographs perfectly. She can be taught to act.' 'My daughter's a successful debutante. I wouldn't want her to be a flop in the movies,' is Mrs. Watriss's realistic reply to both companies."

Pat di Cicco claimed he was not troubled by Brenda's lack of talent or ambition. "There's no doubt that she photographs well," he told one reporter. "MGM is satisfied that she has more assets than the average person in pictures. If she should decide to settle down and act in the movies, I think she would do more than very well. This is the first time I have seen her, and I am very much impressed."

When mother and daughter returned to New York at the end of March, Big Brenda issued a release to the papers that Brenda had decided to reject the MGM offer. "Frankly, I've always been opposed to it," she said. However, Lady Keith says that MGM may have rejected Brenda after giving her a screen test. Lady Keith thinks that Brenda was eager to be in the movies. "She was so starstruck. I don't imagine that she would have given up the opportunity," says Lady Keith. "But once they gave her a screen test, they may have realized that she had no acting talent, no screen presence."

Brenda's failure to become a movie star did not diminish Hughes's ardor, however. In April he followed her to New York, where he lived in his huge yacht, anchored in the Hudson River. They went out together almost every night. James Watriss, who was studying at the Boeing School of Aeronautics in 1939, remembers visiting Brenda and her mother one evening when Brenda had a date with Hughes. "She was very upset because Hughes talked aviation to me, while she sat waiting to go out on her date," he says. Brenda was fond of Hughes, but to her friends he seemed, at thirty-three, old and stodgy. "Howard came to dinner at the Carlton House," Billy Livingston recalls, "and we had room service upstairs. It was just the three of us. He was kind of stuffy and not much fun. As a joke, I got a waiter's uniform from the Carlton House and wheeled in the dinner. Then I made everything go wrong. I dropped the peas, and I remember serving and slopping the soup. Brenda was laughing so hard. But Howard didn't think it was terribly funny."

Hughes did, however, have his own peculiar sense of humor. For a while he sent daily boxes of flowers to Brenda. One day, Esme O'Brien Hammond remembers, "Brenda opened the box in front of her mother. There at the bottom was a ring box from Cartier, with the two Cartier seals enclosing it. Brenda opened the box while her mother stood there wide-eyed. Inside, there was nothing but two aspirins! Brenda thought it was hysterically funny. I don't think her mother did. I presume she needed those aspirins after that." Another day a box of flowers arrived with a large necklace box. Inside was a half-used bottle of cough medicine.

Eventually Hughes proposed to Brenda. She claimed she turned him down because "he was a little too mysterious." But her psychiatrist believes Hughes's proposal was never serious. "I think Howard proposed to every girl he shacked up with. This was his way of winning them. I know he never really proposed. If he had, she would have married him. She wanted him. And she might have had a better life than she had. Howard Hughes was probably the biggest disappointment in her life. She didn't win him. He was too crazy to be won. But she tried. This was really the heroic figure for her. The powerful man. The pilot, the inventor. He was the image of her father."

After a few months they stopped going out together, and Brenda never saw Hughes again. Years later, when they were both living as recluses in Boston, she tried to call him, without success. Hughes, fleeing California in 1966 to avoid millions of dollars in state taxes, had moved to the fifth floor of the Ritz-Carlton Hotel in Boston, a city he hadn't visited in forty-six years. The trip to Boston was the first time he had been out of his Bel Air home in more than four years. Four months later, Hughes left as mysteriously as he had arrived, to settle permanently in Las Vegas.

Big Brenda was actually pleased when the romance with Hughes was over. She preferred another of her daughter's suitors—Peter Arno, the *New Yorker* cartoonist. Arno was twice divorced, and seventeen years older than Brenda.

If Brenda was Queen of Café Society, Peter Arno in those days was King. He was tall and lean, with striking square-jawed looks. Reporters liked to describe him as "debonair," a favored ideal of the time. Arno owned seventeen suits, fourteen pairs of shoes, and three dozen shirts, and was a fixture of the best-dressed lists.

His normal routine was to sleep every afternoon until two, work until the early evening, and then go out every night to clubs and private parties. Sometimes he appeared with his own shakerful of dry martinis. Arno was often written up in the gossip columns, frequently described in the presence of young, beautiful women. He was as well known for his violent escapades as he was for his *New Yorker* cartoons. Once Cornelius Vanderbilt, Jr., waving a revolver, chased him down the street after catching Arno embracing Mrs. Vanderbilt. Another time, during a party at the Embassy Club in Hollywood, Arno got into a fight with Drexel Biddle Steel, an actor who Arno claimed was annoying the cartoonist's female companions. After Arno punched Steel, one of the actor's friends struck Arno on the side of the head, knocking him unconscious.

He had been born Curtis Arnoux Peters, the son of a New York State Supreme Court judge. Partly to protect his family and partly to disassociate himself from them, he changed his name. In 1923 he dropped out of Yale to start a band that featured a young singer named Rudy Vallee. Two years later *The New Yorker* bought Arno's first cartoon for thirty dollars. Much of his work satirized the rich. He created the Whoops Sisters, two obscenely alcoholic old maids, and his drawings of drunken dowagers, lecherous patricians, and dotty socialites helped establish *The New Yorker*'s reputation for urbanity and originality.

Though he partied with the rich and used them in his cartoons, Arno claimed to be disgusted by the members of New York society. "At no time in the history of the world have there been so many damned morons gathered together in one place as here in New York right now," he said in 1937. "The town squirms with them. Vain little girls with more alcohol in their brains than sense. Take a look in any nightclub or the fancy restaurants around lunch time. . . . Those people make me mad, the young ones more than the old ones. You don't do good work of this sort unless you're mad at something."

That anger was part of what attracted Brenda to Arno. She liked bullies. Only an exaggerated male—a heroic pilot like Hughes, or a lady-killer like Arno—could please her. Yet Brenda did not seem like a sensual woman. One of her friends, Audrey Gray Chapin, sensed that "Brenda was not passionate. She was like an old lady at eighteen. I don't think Brenda was good in bed at all. [But] one of the things she'd like in her sex . . . was someone who was like a truck driver, who would slap her, who would throw her right down on the mattress and screw her while she cried, 'Help, help, help!' "

"Brenda loved derring-do stuff," adds her psychiatrist. "She would have loved pirates. She would have loved being raped. Oh, her fantasy life was so full of what she really wanted."

"She was so naïve sexually, that's what made me wonder, how could she have had the sex life she was supposed to have had?" says Victoria Kelly. "She would read a [contemporary] book and she wouldn't even know what half the [sexual expressions] meant. A lot of men found her incredibly boring. She didn't appeal to a lot of men because she was very painted. She was like a doll." Victoria guesses that her mother made love because it was the only way to be close to her boyfriends. "She probably liked the emotional aspects of it, but not the sexual," says Victoria.

A boyfriend of Brenda's recalls getting a desperate call from her once at three-thirty in the morning. Sobbing, Brenda explained that she was all alone—her mother was away on a trip—and she asked the young man to come over. He woke his mother, and the two of them rushed to the Carlton House. Peter Arno had just left Brenda's apartment. They had had a terrible fight, and he had hit her, leaving Brenda with a black eye.

Still, Brenda came to think about her affair with Arno as a happy experience. "She loved Peter Arno," says her psychiatrist. "She had a wonderful relationship with him. He was demanding, there was a mean streak in him, but he still was quite nice to her, and gave her fulfillment.''

During the thirties the world of celebrity in New York existed in a few flashy nightclubs, where every night the brightest stars of entertainment, literature, government, society, and sports gathered to see and be seen. ''It was a good time in New York,'' says Angelo Zuccotti, the maître d' at El Morocco. ''In those days it was fashionable not to have responsibility. People would stay out until 4 A.M. and then go to Reuben's for breakfast.'' The city's newspaper columnists wrote obsessively about goings-on in the nightclubs, and the public eagerly devoured their reports.

As symbols of glamour and power, nightclubs were taken very seriously—and especially so by celebrities. When Leland Hayward separated from his third wife, part of the settlement included division of space at El Morocco. To avoid embarrassing encounters, Hayward got one side of the main room and his ex-wife got the other. In those days, says Rudy Stanish, Paul Mellon's former cook, ''it mattered as much to be a part of Café Society as it did to be alive.''

There were many Manhattan nightclubs, but only two were important: El Morocco and the Stork Club, which Walter Winchell called ''the New Yorkiest place in town.'' Every night, celebrities gathered in the mirror-lined Cub Room. Ordinary mortals were seated in the dining room next door, which was crowded and noisy. This allowed the common people to watch the celebrities watching themselves and gave the Stork its magic. ''If you were at the Stork, you would not have to think. You would just watch The People and listen,'' wrote Ernest Hemingway, one of the Stork's regulars when he was in New York.

The Stork Club was owned by Sherman Billingsley, a boyish, mild-mannered man who had been born in the back of a grocery store in Enid, Oklahoma. Billingsley had dropped out of school in the fourth grade, and made his way by selling beer to the local Indians. Oklahoma was a dry state, and he peddled his wares from a red wagon covered with a blanket, and, for purposes of camouflage, topped by his two-year-old nephew. ''Now Sherman,'' Billingsley's brother would advise him, ''you just pull your wagon down by the Indian Village and you just stand there. When an Indian takes a bottle of beer out of the wagon, you take fifty cents off him.''

At sixteen, Billingsley and his brother Fred opened a drugstore in Oklahoma City, where they sold bootleg liquor. Then Sherman moved to Missouri, a wet state. By day he worked as a wholesaler of legal liquor. At night, bumping along the dark dirt roads in his car, he smuggled liquor into nearby Omaha, since Nebraska was a dry state.

Billingsley came to New York in the twenties and opened a speakeasy called the Stork Club on West Fifty-eighth Street. Next, he moved to East Fifty-first Street, off Park Avenue. Socialites named Vanderbilt and Astor started dropping in for drinks. Politicians and Hollywood stars soon followed. After the repeal of Prohibition, the club moved to East Fifty-third Street, where its legitimate incarnation was an immediate hit. "I should have thought up a good story on how and why I named [the club]," Billingsley said toward the end of his life. "Actually, it started as an unnamed speakeasy. . . . Somebody left a toy bird and somebody else put it behind the bar. It looked like a stork and soon the regulars were referring to the Stork Club. When repeal came, I just kept the name."

At the height of his success, Billingsley was rumored to make an average of $3 million a year, some of which he lavished on favored customers in the form of expensive gifts— perfume, champagne, solid gold compacts encrusted with diamonds, even cars. The Stork Club catered to the debutantes and their escorts. "We used to go to the Stork for lunch," recalls Billy Livingston. "Then we'd sit around and play backgammon or gin rummy and suddenly it would be time for cocktails. So we'd go home to change and [after dinner] at eleven o'clock we'd end up back at the club."

Every night Billingsley moved through the crowd with exquisite poise. To all customers he was considerate; to famous ones he was worshipful. After following Billingsley around one night, Damon Runyon wrote in *Cosmopolitan* magazine:

As he passes through the Stork Club, Mr. Billingsley is constantly followed. Fred Hahn, a former waiter, stays near him and watches every move he makes from seven o'clock in the evening until closing time. . . . Every few minutes he passes him a slip of paper with a message on it. "Doris

Symbol

*Duke has just come in," the message may read. Or "Do
you want the music to stop at three fifteen?" Mr. B will
glance at it without interrupting his conversation and shake
his head or nod. "Governor Green of Illinois and Bing
Crosby are here; both want Table sixty-one." He scribbles
a solution and hands it to Hahn while he asks Leon Henderson about the stock market. He passes another table and
stops to say hello, rubbing his right index finger against the
side of his nose. Hahn knows this means a gift of perfume
for each lady at the table, just as the adjustment of the
handkerchief in Billingsley's coat pocket means free champagne and a turn of the ring on his little right finger means
no check for this party.*

Billingsley peppered his conversation with "golly" and
"gee," eschewed alcohol and cigarettes, and refused to wear
black tie, dressing instead in conservative business suits.

His homespun, good-ol'-boy image belied his shrewdness.
Not only was he an expert in the care and feeding of celebrities, he also had a talent for publicity. He employed two
crews of press agents, one that worked all day, and one that
worked all night. He hired a full-time photographer, the ex-
radio singer Chick Farmer, whose job was to take pictures of
famous and beautiful customers and then sell them to the
newspapers. The pictures usually showed a Stork Club ashtray or some other identifying symbol.

The Stork's best advertisement was Winchell, for the columnist used the club as his night office. He arrived every
evening around eleven and stayed until four or five in the
morning, holding court at a choice table just inside the entrance. He would accept calls at a telephone at the table while
talking to an endless stream of celebrities, politicians, and
fans. Sometimes, in search of more privacy, Winchell would
receive people in the Stork Club barbershop, located in a loft
building next door and accessible through a secret passageway inside the nightclub.

An evening out often began at the Stork Club, but it usually
ended at El Morocco. The Stork Club catered to a young,
energetic crowd, while El Morocco attracted an older group
and was widely regarded as New York's most sophisticated
nightclub. This reputation had much to do with the club's

137

decor. El Morocco had two main rooms. One was evocative of a sultry desert night, with blue-and-white zebra-striped banquettes, flattering pink lighting, twinkling stars over the dance floor, and palm trees with cellophane leaves climbing up electric-blue walls. The other, the red velvet Champagne Room, was "candlelit and schmaltzy."

John Perona, El Morocco's owner, once explained the origin of the zebra stripes, which became the club's signature: "It was speakeasy days and those prohibition agents would raid you and they loved to take an ax and break up the place. So I told my first decorator to do something simple, just paint the place in stripes. No use having a lot of silk and satin for those raiders to destroy." When Perona tried something new by redecorating in pink, business plummeted. He worked frantically and had the stripes back in forty-eight hours.

"El Mo," as it was called by nightclub habitués, had the aura of a private club. There was no phone, so outsiders could not call for reservations. It had its own newspaper, the *El Morocco No News*, and its own photographer-press agent, Jerome Zerbe. The columnists Maury Paul, Leonard Lyons, and Lou Sobel were there every night. Perona banned Winchell from the club after the columnist printed an item that Perona had been killed in an automobile accident in Europe. "No nightclub in the world . . . conveys by mere mention [the] association . . . of platinum lamee aloofness that the Villa Perona achieves," wrote Lucius Beebe in the first issue of the *No News* in 1933. Having Zerbe take your picture against the stripes was an important status symbol in Café Society. When stars such as Marlene Dietrich returned to New York after a trip to Europe, their agents would send them to El Morocco to be photographed.

In theory, anyone who could afford the two-dollar cover charge could go to El Morocco. But in reality, only a few were welcome. Maintaining social distinctions was primarily the work of El Morocco's imperious headwaiters, who, as *Time* reported, "ate $5 bills while riding home on the subway." Once a waiter asked showgirl Peggy Hopkins Joyce to sit in a cramped room to the left of the entrance. "I refuse to sit in Siberia," she said. From then on, anyone shown to "Siberia" was socially dead.

El Morocco's success, like that of the Stork Club, was built on its owner's ability to attract the right people. When Perona, a former busboy from Italy, opened his first restaurant in New York, one of his best customers was Luis Firpo, the Argentinian heavyweight. Perona, who had a puffy face and dark, buttonhole eyes and who dressed like a gangster in chalk-striped suits, had once been Firpo's sparring partner. Two hours before he fought Jack Dempsey, Firpo went to Perona's and ate two helpings of spaghetti, a steak smothered in soft-boiled eggs, three raw eggs, and six hunks of spumoni ice cream. This feat attracted other celebrities, and the restaurant's reputation was made.

Perona next opened a speakeasy called the Bath Club, which moved to the East Side and became El Morocco after the repeal of Prohibition. The theme of the new club was "an oasis for parched New Yorkers," according to the New York *Herald Tribune*. Perona suggested the name "Morocco," and "El" was added as a whimsical tribute to the nearby Third Avenue elevated line.

Perona loved to surprise people. Once, after a young woman admired the pink fixtures in the club's ladies' room, Perona sent his plumber to install a similar set in her apartment. Not all his surprises were welcome. He liked to sneak up on male guests, plant matches in their shoes, and then light them. As his startled victims jumped about wildly, Perona roared with laughter.

This was the world Brenda moved in. It was a world of childish pranks, massive egos, too much alcohol, too little sleep. It was a world with lots of chatter, but little worthwhile conversation; lots of romancing, but little love. On any given night at the Stork Club and El Morocco, you might find Clark Gable, Joan Crawford, the Duke of Windsor, Irving Berlin, Cary Grant. All would be photographed, all would be written up. Yet the celebrity whose light shone brightest of all in that nighttime world was Brenda Frazier, then an eighteen-year-old girl.

After observing one of her entrances at the Stork Club, British journalist C. V. R. Thompson wrote:

> *A hubbub of chatter spreads like fire through dry brush across the whole room. Flashlight bulbs are exploded. It seems as if some people are about to cheer, others, outsiders*

*who have found their way into our preserves, about to boo.
Brenda Frazier has come in.*

*She stands still waiting for a choice table, and every face
is turned in her direction, as if all had been watching a
tennis match which had suddenly stopped. As she passes my
table, the other girls seem to become dowdy and passé. As
soon as she sits down she pulls out a comb and draws it
slowly and carefully through her luxurious black hair. Then
a dab of powder on her already too pale face. Then a streak
of liver red lipstick. She is beautiful. Not as beautiful as her
pictures, of course. That wouldn't be possible. But beautiful
all the same. In a few moments she is sipping champagne,
and toying with a dish of shrimps while she listens seriously
and earnestly to whatever nonsense her escort is telling her.*

A year after her debut, Brenda's fame was as intense as
ever. Babies were named after her. She made all the "most
admired" and "best-dressed" lists. The Children's Welfare
League, a prominent New York charity, hailed her as America's model "All American Girl." A panel of experts, including Elsa Maxwell and the photographer Horst, picked her
as one of the world's most glamorous women. Brenda won
the award for "making the debutante the most attractive
woman alive." Two portraits of her by the famous English
portraitist Dorothy Vicaji were displayed at the Hotel Pierre.
A white-petaled, crimson-lipped orchid presented at the 1939
International Flower Show was named after her.

She became a fashion symbol, setting styles that were in-
stantly imitated. Girls copied her clothes, her hair, and her
posture, a slightly stooped stance called "the debutante
slouch." She became the idol of New York's homosexual
community. It wasn't uncommon at drag balls to see dozens
of young men dressed in strapless ball gowns, black wigs,
and white pancake makeup. In the thirties, an entrepreneur
sponsored costume parties for homosexuals on boat rides up
the Hudson River. Many of the men dressed up like Brenda.
When the boat returned to a West Side pier, the police would
sometimes raid it, which led to some sorry and comic scenes.
Some of the passengers would jump overboard to avoid arrest. "It was really funny to watch all these guys almost
drowning in their hoop skirts," recalls Andy Gillespie, a New

Yorker who observed one of the raids. The men who were caught would be locked up overnight for dressing as women. Released the next morning, they would have to endure stares and taunts as they traveled home covered with cosmetics and dressed like Brenda Frazier.

When Brenda went out, she was often mobbed on the street by strangers. Schoolgirls waving autograph books rushed her at the entrance to Bergdorf Goodman. Taxicabs chased her limousine down Park Avenue. Once, in a department store, a woman flung open the door of the dressing room Brenda was using. "I've just got to look at you," the woman said. During the 1939 Easter Parade, as Brenda and her mother left St. Thomas Church, on Fifth Avenue at Fifty-third Street, that chilly morning, someone in the throng on the side street yelled, "There's Brenda Frazier!" Suddenly the crowd on the street surged into the Fifth Avenue group. The *Daily News* reported that two hundred "yelping women clawed each other and their menfolk practically climbed on each other's shoulders" to glimpse the glamour girl. Brenda, who was wearing a black mink coat and a black bonnet with a gigantic bow tied under the chin, pushed nervously to her car, but the door was blocked by a dozen admirers. It took three policemen and two burly onlookers to clear the way.

"Brenda epitomized the way I wanted to look and be," says public relations woman Letitia Baldrige. Out-of-town soldiers on leave in Manhattan took taxis to the Carlton House, where Brenda lived, and stood anxiously outside the entrance, as if waiting for their sweethearts to appear. Strangers confessed their sins and sorrows in letters to her. The public seemed to think she belonged to it—an appropriation of intimacy that is probably even more common with celebrities today.

In his book *Intimate Strangers: The Culture of Celebrity* Richard Schickel wrote: "Most of us retain, in most of our private and professional dealings with people we don't actually know, a sense of their otherness, a decent wariness that protects both ourselves and the stranger from intrusion. But that shyness . . . is not operative when we are dealing with celebrities. Thanks to [the media] we know them, or think we do. To a greater or lesser degree, we have internalized them, unconsciously made them a part of our consciousness, just as if they were, in fact, friends.''

Soon enough, Brenda's fame had made her a suitable hook "on which to hang everything from humor to obscenity.'' She was lampooned by the *Harvard Crimson* in an article entitled "The Anatomy of a Debutante.'' She was impersonated in a Columbia University revue by a football player who wore a strapless gown and white pancake makeup. She became the subject of a popular limerick:

> *There was a young man from Eurasia*
> *Who toasted his balls in a brazier*
> *Till they grew quite as hot*
> *As the glamorous twat*
> *Of Miss Brenda Diana Duff Frazier.*

She and Cobina Wright, junior, were satirized on the *Bob Hope Radio Hour* by a comedy team that portrayed two crude, man-chasing old hags, "Cobina Fright'' and "Brenda La-Frenzy,'' who spoke in rasping Brooklyn accents.

Once Brenda and a group of friends went to a football game at Princeton. *The Princeton Tiger,* the campus humor magazine, dedicated the issue being sold that day to "Frenda Brazier.'' As Brenda sat in the stadium, hawkers selling the magazine walked through the bleachers calling out "Frenda Brazier.'' "Everyone there knew who she was,'' says Brenda's friend Gus Ober. "It was very embarrassing.''

Predictably, some of the publicity became hostile. The Erie, Pennsylvania, *Times* wrote on April 13, 1939: "Brenda Frazier, the over-ballyhooed glamour girl who has been filling the social and gossip columns in New York for the past six months, actually didn't spurn a movie offer as first reported, but the movie company, after looking her over and screen-testing her, decided that her figure, especially her limbs, weren't glamorous enough.''

In the Midwest, where Depression-dazed farmers were struggling against mortgage foreclosures, Brenda's frivolity was particularly aggravating. She was a convenient scapegoat for what was wrong with "the system.'' A February 23, 1939, editorial in the Chariton, Iowa, *Herald Patriot* was typical of several attacking her celebrity:

We're becoming rather bored with a number of things.

But most of all we're tired of pictures of Brenda Duff Frazier.

The continued cold weather has become as monotonous as the Spanish Civil War and the Sino-Japanese struggle. Polls and quizzes have reached the point of creating only mystified yawns.

But most of all we're tired of pictures of Brenda Duff Frazier. . . .

We've seen Brenda Duff being the No. 1 debutante. We've seen her being a home girl, a play girl, a glamour girl—in fact every type of girl except perhaps the girl friend of the whirling dervish. We've seen her starting somewhere, enroute, and returning. We've seen her as she is morning, afternoon and night.

Now Brenda Duff Frazier is a pretty girl. And she probably is a nice person and no doubt finds the task of keeping photographers from the door as difficult as the job most of us have with the wolf in that respect.

Maybe she's tired of pictures of Brenda Duff Frazier, too.

A mocking anti-debutante backlash broke out in New York, where a Protest Glamour Girl No. 1 was chosen by a committee of twelve men about town, including Peter Arno and Lucius Beebe. They picked a blond model named Wilma Baard, the nineteen-year-old daughter of a tugboat captain who had spent her infancy on a barge. Her protest debut at a Manhattan nightclub aimed to prove that a poor girl could make as spectacular a debut as a rich one.

Among those especially annoyed at the debs were women who made their living being glamorous. Outside a fashion show where debutantes were acting as models, a group of professional models walked a picket line carrying signs that read:

Helena Rubinstein We Protest
As Fashion Models We're the Best
We've Better Figures, Better Faces
Keep the Debbies in Their Places

At first, Brenda regarded her celebrity as a joke: she never thought it would continue beyond her debut. When it did, she began to be deeply affected by the experience. Brenda understood quite well the publicity dynamic around her, and she even understood the hostility. The public's intimate yet impersonal embrace of her was particularly painful. It confirmed what she'd always really believed about herself: people liked her for her money, her fame, her connections. She herself was really unimportant. Even as a child, says Gertie Folmsbee, "Brenda had this idea that the only reason people liked her was because of her money. I used to tell her, 'That's silly. People like you for yourself.'" All her life she "felt that she had to buy affection," adds her psychiatrist. "Her generosity was pathological. It wasn't unusual for her to give one of her nurses a mink coat. I told her that this wild, reckless generosity was misplaced. There were genuine ways of giving, instead of trying to buy the goodwill of a transient, someone she'd never see again."

One night, as Brenda sat with friends at a Broadway nightclub, the master of ceremonies decided to introduce the celebrities in the audience. The comedian Ben Blue was introduced first. As the spotlight illuminated his face, everyone applauded. They applauded also for Sonja Henie. Then Brenda was introduced. As she stood up, blinking into the spotlight, there was some applause, but just as many boos. Brenda sat down with her face burning, but secretly agreeing with the audience. "I'm not a celebrity," she thought to herself. "I don't deserve all this. I haven't done anything at all. I'm just a debutante."

CHAPTER NINE

O<small>N ANOTHER NIGHT</small>, the Stork Club organized a little game, the sort of silly extravaganza that Sherman Billingsley was fond of staging: Dozens of balloons were released, some containing a $100 bill or a gift certificate for another prize— perfume, jewelry, a puppy. While the balloons bobbed through the club like bubbles in champagne, willowy debs glided after them, hoping to catch one. On the dance floor nearby, couples swayed to Cole Porter tunes, while Walter Winchell, who would exaggerate the evening's excitement in the next day's column, took notes at Table 50.

While the balloon chase was still going on, Brenda Frazier walked in. Everyone tried hard not to stare as she sat down and started combing her hair. A waiter poured her a glass of champagne, compliments of the house, and Brenda removed a gold swizzle stick from her purse. It opened like a palm tree, and a spray of gold spokes shot out of the top. She swirled it through her champagne and the bubbles disappeared. Tallulah Bankhead was there that night with a date, John "Shipwreck" Kelly, a former football hero. Suddenly Tallulah jumped up and popped a balloon that had been floating above her head. Out dropped a $100 bill. "Watch me, I think I'll have some fun," she said to Shipwreck. The couple walked over to Brenda's table, where Tallulah handed the glamour girl the bill. "Here, I thought you might need this," she said. "Thank you very much, Miss Bankhead. I can use it." Brenda glanced at Shipwreck, who was studying her intently. "What a pretty girl you are," he said. "I might call you sometime."

At twenty-nine, Shipwreck Kelly was the Joe Namath of his day. A farm boy who became a University of Kentucky football hero, he moved East after college and played professionally for the New York Giants and the Brooklyn Dodgers. Like Tom Buchanan in *The Great Gatsby*, he was "a national figure, in a way, one of those men who reach such an acute limited excellence at twenty-one that everything afterward savors of anticlimax."

Ship, as he was called, looked like a poster artist's idea of an athlete: tall and barrel-chested, with cool blue eyes and a fleshy, square-jawed face. Though his professional playing career did not last long, he became a fixture in Café Society, bringing to it a small-town geniality and a definite sexual heat. He was friendly and amusing in a vulgar sort of way. One day, while waiting for actress Joan Fontaine to dress for their date, Ship grew impatient. As the actress recalls in her memoir, *No Bed of Roses*, Ship flung open the door to the bathroom, where she was splashing in the tub, and dove in beside her, still wearing his suit, tweed overcoat, wristwatch, and shoes. Ship loved to shock. Once he took a maid from the Bel Air Hotel in Los Angeles to one of Norma Shearer's fancy Hollywood parties. Another time, while sunning himself during a boat ride with photographer Jerry Zerbe, he suddenly grabbed Zerbe's hand and placed it on his crotch. "Now you know why the girls love me," Ship said.

Although his rich New York friends liked to romanticize Ship's Kentucky farm origins, he had grown up as pampered and privileged as most of them. He had been born in Springfield, Kentucky, in 1910; his mother died when he was just three weeks old, and he was raised by his maternal grandparents, John and Prudence Simms. The elderly couple divided their time between a prosperous tobacco and mule farm and a large frame house in town, near the local Catholic church.

Ship's father, Richard Kelly, remarried and had five more children before his death in 1919. "Shipwreck always seemed to hold a grudge [against his father]," says a relative, Mrs. Leon Simms. "He couldn't understand why his father gave him away. But it was out of necessity. It was the Depression, and Richard Kelly was having a hard time. Also, he didn't want to take Shipwreck away from his aging grandparents. He knew how much they loved Shipwreck."

John and Prudence Simms "were bigshots, if farmers can be bigshots," says Kelly. "Of course, that's all they had in Kentucky, were farmers." John Simms, whom everyone called "Dude," was the first man in Springfield to own a car—a convertible Studebaker. He rode along the dirt roads while his black chauffeur drove.

Ship had no chores around the farm; Dude Simms employed eighteen black servants to do the outside work, and six more servants to work inside the house. Dude also employed a young black man named Jim whose main duty was to play with Ship—to take him hunting and fishing and to teach him how to ride horses. Ship and Jim were very close. Then one day Jim ran off with a horse breeder who had come to town for the county fair. Ship never saw him again.

Even as a small boy, Ship had a reputation of being irreverent and fearless. At St. Mary's, a parochial boarding school he attended in St. Mary's, Kentucky, Ship once put a live skunk in a priest's desk. When the priest opened the drawer during class, the skunk jumped out. "Only one person in this class could have done this," said the priest, looking straight at John Kelly.

At the Springfield public high school, Ship was the star of the football team. Notre Dame recruiters courted him, but Kelly decided to attend the University of Kentucky to be near his elderly grandmother. She never went to his games, but before each one she would light a candle and say the rosary.

On the college football field, Kelly became known as much for his brashness as his talent. "A good many upperclassmen resented the cocky freshman with his wisecracks and airy disregard of traditional respect for their wisdom and seniority, although they liked him," wrote a reporter from the *Herald Tribune*. "The kid would brag about what he was going to do to the varsity in scrimmage, and then go out and ring up two or three touchdowns even though the entire team was ganging up to stop him." His teammates nicknamed him "the Wrecker," and after Ship worked one summer on a steamship, a sportswriter started calling him "Shipwreck." On the field Ship didn't disappoint. *The Kentuckian*, the University of Kentucky yearbook, gushed that Kelly was "possibly the fleetest grid star in the South and one of the nation's outstanding backfield men."

Off the field, too, Ship had his accomplishments. During his junior year, he sparked a scandal by becoming involved with a divorced woman seven years his senior who was also the mother of three young children.

Ship's closest friend in college was "Duke" Johnston, a son of Percy Johnston, a native Kentuckian who became chairman of the Chemical Bank and Trust Company in New York. Duke was handsome and well built, but uncoordinated. "It was difficult even for him to sit down," says Ship. Poor Duke loved sports, though, and Ship got him named manager of the football team. They became great friends, and Duke brought Ship home with him to Montclair, New Jersey, every summer. "Duke's old man would come to all the games and bring some of his friends," says Ship. "One of them gave me a bearskin coat after a game. It was a hell of a game, and a hell of a coat. It was a big, black bearskin. The guy took it off right there in the dressing room. He said to me, 'Here, when you get your clothes on, put this on. You can have it.' "

After graduation, Ship moved East and lived with the Johnston family. Percy Johnston found him a job at the Chemical Bank, but banking bored Ship. "I didn't do anything but sit on my ass," he says. After a few months he quit and signed up to play pro ball for the New York Giants. He played four games and then became ill with a bizarre muscle disease. While recuperating in Kentucky, Ship heard that the Brooklyn Dodgers, a professional football team, were for sale. With money he inherited from his family, plus a loan from the Chemical Bank, Ship formed a partnership with Chris Cagle, a former West Point football star, to buy the Dodgers. He paid $75,000 for a franchise. Ship's first season with the Dodgers was a "disaster," according to one reporter. Ship calculated that as half-owner and non-salaried player on the team, each gridiron appearance cost him $500.

Eventually Ship sold his share in the Dodgers and moved into Manhattan. He shared a two-bedroom duplex apartment overlooking Central Park with steel heir Dan Topping. Topping paid most of the rent. Ship had already made some society contacts through Percy Johnston and football. But Dan

Topping introduced him to the elite's innermost set in New-port and Palm Beach. During the day Kelly sold insurance policies for the Home Insurance Company; at night he went to El Morocco and the Stork Club, picking up showgirls and actresses.

At the time they met, both Brenda and Ship were dating other people. Brenda was seeing Peter Arno and going with him to nightclubs and parties several evenings a week. Ship's girlfriends were a wide selection: actresses, models, and so-cialites.

Ship was used to making quick conquests and then moving on, but his romance with Brenda developed slowly. At first he courted her by phone. The conversations grew long, as Brenda and Ship found they had lots to talk about. Eventually the pace of their relationship picked up. Ship took Brenda to a dinner party on November 19. The next day they met at the Carlton House for lunch.

Ship was smitten. "There was something about Brenda that was different from any other woman I'd ever met," he re-calls. "I loved everything about her, the way she looked, the way she walked, the way she talked, the way she smelled—like mashed carnations. There was a niceness about her that other girls didn't have."

For Brenda, Ship seemed an odd choice. He could be crude, unsophisticated, provincial—not the perfect match for a glamour girl. Indeed, some of her friends thought that Ship tarnished her image, that he took away some of her magic, and that she never got it back. But Brenda was strongly drawn to him. Something about his All-American flash, his sweet-ness, his naïve confidence, attracted her. Though in her life-time she had affairs with many men, Shipwreck Kelly was probably the only man she really loved.

After their first date, they went out almost every night to dinner parties, plays, and nightclubs. During the day, Ship could be spotted haunting restaurant foyers looking for Brenda. The press soon picked up on the budding romance. "It looks like the real thing," announced one paper, over a picture of the couple. A caption beneath the picture noted that it was the twenty-third night in a row they had visited the Stork Club.

Unlike the delighted press corps, Big Brenda was disappointed by the relationship. "She wanted Brenda to marry Howard Hughes, or someone like that," says Ship. Not surprisingly, Kelly resented Big Brenda and never really got along with her. "To me, Brenda's mother was the biggest bore. She wasn't anything. She looked like the washerwoman waiting for the tub," he says. "But she went overboard trying to be something. Brenda was so famous, and Lady Williams-Taylor was so famous, that she felt a little out of place." With Fred Watriss dead, she was also lonely, and her loneliness drove her into the company of Brenda and Ship. Sometimes she joined them for dinner. Many nights, after Brenda went to bed, Big Brenda cornered Ship for long chats in her sitting room.

Ship's relationship with Lady Jane was less ambivalent. He liked her, and she adored him. Ship "and his Irish charm had my Grandmother Williams-Taylor wrapped around his finger," wrote Brenda. But Ship was not fond of Sir Frederick, whom he first met in Nassau at the end of January. Brenda and Ship flew to the island to stay the rest of the winter at Star Acres. When they arrived, Sir Frederick, disdainful of Ship's Kentucky background and probably concerned because he seemed not to work, refused to let him sleep in the house. Ship checked into a hotel owned by Anders Ostergren. (He was a successful liquor importer who, the year before, had named Ship as a correspondent in a divorce suit against his wife.) Later, when Sir Frederick got to know Ship better, he offered him a room at Star Acres. Ship refused. Brenda sometimes visited him at the hotel, and years later he told his daughter, Victoria, that this was where they had made love for the first time.

In the languid luxury of Nassau, the romance deepened. Holding hands and sipping champagne, they fished off a friend's yacht, and then watched the sky turn pink at twilight from the veranda of the Emerald Beach Club. They played golf and romped in the surf. At night they went to little dinner parties in private homes or to galas at the governor's hilltop mansion.

"It was a very quick and immediate romance in which they each met the other's needs and goals. Each wanted to be like the other and each [chose] the other in order to have a weakness reinforced," says Brenda's psychiatrist. "He saw in her a beautiful, difficult-to-obtain woman who was glamorous. She saw in him all the bravado she lacked. He was an athletic figure for her. He was an All-American. She was so passive and timorous and fearful. He was the bold guy. She always had to put on a front. She had so much anxiety. She had anxiety in almost every situation. He knew no fear.''

Whatever the unconscious motives in the attraction, Brenda and Ship were genuinely in love. The following winter, when Brenda went to Nassau alone for two months, Ship wrote her nearly every day, using their pet names ''Muzzie'' and ''Duzzy'' in the letters. ''You can't possibly realize how desperately lonely and how miserable I am without you,'' he wrote in one brief note. '' . . . the nites are terrible.''

Although the press had reported that Brenda and Ship were engaged (and even secretly married) a few months after they had started dating, the couple didn't decide to marry until June 1941. One of Brenda's closest friends at the time says the decision coincided with Brenda's discovery that she was pregnant. She had been in this condition a few months before, and her mother had arranged an abortion, which was performed in Brenda's bedroom at the Carlton House. Years later, Brenda told Frances Griffin, one of her lady's maids, that she—rather than her mother—had insisted on the abortion. ''She was so young, and she hadn't been going out with Ship that long when it happened—maybe three months,'' says Griffin. ''Maybe she didn't know whose baby it was.''

Although in later years Brenda talked about her first pregnancy and abortion, she never discussed being pregnant at the time of her marriage. Jane Will Smith says Brenda's pregnancy ''was just assumed'' by the hastiness with which the wedding was arranged and by Brenda's and Big Brenda's attitude. ''The mother [implied] that otherwise she wouldn't have allowed her to marry Ship,'' says Smith. ''[Big Brenda's] attitude was, 'I've got to go through with this.' '' Big Brenda had raised Brenda to marry a prince, or a Vanderbilt, or a Whitney. Ship wasn't considered good enough.

It's possible that Brenda only thought she was pregnant, or that she lied to her mother about being pregnant so that Big Brenda would let her marry Ship. ''Brenda told me she was having terrible fights with her mother over the marriage,'' recalls Jane Will Smith.

The family factotum, Gertie Folmsbee, and Brenda's close friend Esme Hammond say that Brenda was not a pregnant bride. Ship also insists that Brenda wasn't pregnant at the time of the wedding, but he admits that the marriage was Big Brenda's and Lady Jane's idea. "I never asked Brenda to marry me," he says. "Her grandmother and mother got together one time when I was at the house and said, 'Why don't you all get married?' I said, 'Well, I don't know, I never thought about that. Maybe Brenda wouldn't want to marry me.' And Brenda said, 'Oh, yes, I would, Ship.' "

Even if the marriage was forced, it started out full of love. "You could see when they were together that they were in love, and I think she loved him until the day she died," says Jerome Doyle, a close friend and for many years Brenda's lawyer. "Long after they were divorced, whenever Brenda was in serious trouble, she'd call Ship. He was like her father, her adviser."

Nevertheless, the marriage also started with problems. Lady Jane and Big Brenda insisted on running the show. Brenda felt as powerless as she had during her parents' custody battle ten years before.

On June 18 Big Brenda leaked the news of the upcoming wedding to Maury Paul. The only thing Paul loved more than a messy divorce was a society wedding. "Maury was completely sincere when he began babbling of the wonder and glory of some rococo marriage," wrote his assistant, Eve Brown. "If a marriage involved a 'name' like Astor, Gould or Vanderbilt, of course it was played big. If it involved Maury's Café Society friends, there was no stopping him." The more vulgar the wedding, the better. But even if the family tried to get away with a simple, quiet affair, Eve wrote, "Maury, howling with glee like the Three Furies, dragged it out into the open by its hair making news of its very conservatism."

That afternoon, in the late editions of the *Journal-American*, Paul broke the society scoop: "The U.S.A.'s No. 1 'Glamour Girl' abdicates! Brenda Diana Duff Frazier, who won her 'Glamour Girl' crown in 1938 and has worn it so gracefully for *three* social seasons, will become the bride of John Simms Kelly before the close of the present month." Paul cited the war and a general desire to avoid publicity as Brenda's reasons "for insisting upon a wedding marked by utter simplicity." He delighted in contrasting Brenda's debut ball, "the largest and most costly debutante ball of that season," with the impending wedding, which would be "the smallest and most unostentatious nuptial event of June, 1941." He noted that Mrs. Watriss pleaded with him not to write more than a few lines about Brenda's engagement. Paul ignored the request and wrote: "That wouldn't be playing fair with the wide public interest in every move of our No. 1 'Glamour Girl,' who still receives between 800 and 1,000 'fan letters' weekly from all parts of the earth."

The day Paul's story appeared, the switchboard at the Carlton House was jammed with congratulatory calls to Brenda. By 6 P.M. the hotel had put an extra operator on to handle the backed-up calls. While Gertie Folmsbee manned the phone, Brenda, her mother, and Lady Jane plunged into a frenzy of arrangements. Since the wedding was on June 30, twelve days after the engagement was announced, there was no time for formal, engraved invitations; instead, telegrams were sent to friends and relatives.

During her brief two-week engagement, Brenda's days were occupied by dress fittings, photo sessions, and beauty treatments. She hated the idea of a formal wedding—it reminded her of her coming-out party. On the wedding day itself, "I felt as I had the night of my debut—tense, under terrible strain," Brenda later wrote.

Big Brenda insisted that the ceremony would be simple, and it was. Only twenty-five close friends and acquaintances attended. Surrogate Foley was there, along with Paul Flato, the society jewelry dealer, Charles Tiffany, owner of the Fifth Avenue store, and George MacDonald, Lady Jane's boyfriend. Sir Frederick, who was gravely ill but would hang on for four more years, remained at home in Canada.

Though the wedding was small, Brenda still played the role of a Glamour Girl bride. Lady Jane and Big Brenda delighted society writers with the news that Brenda's gown was made from the last bolt of Parisian slipper satin to leave France before the war, and her veil from the last bit of "wind" illusion to be imported from England. Designed by Herman Patrick Tappe, the simple dress had a square neck, short train, and three-quarter-length sleeves. The veil fell from a Celliniinspired crown of wax orange blossoms and pearls and was pulled back and caught at the back of her head. Each blossom of her bouquet of lilies of the valley was wired to give the effect of intricate, pearl-studded lace. The only jewelry she wore was earrings, a small gold bracelet, and her engagement ring—a huge emerald flanked by diamonds. The newspapers reported that the ring had once been owned by an Indian rajah.

At 4 P.M. an organist played Wagner's wedding march, and the guests gathered in Big Brenda's sitting room around a temporary altar set up in front of the fireplace. The flickering glow of tall white candles in crystal candlesticks atop the mantelpiece rippled over Brenda's face as she knelt at the altar with Ship. The couple promised to love, honor, and cherish each other. Society photographer Hal Phyfe clicked away. The best man, society golfer Tommy Tailer, stood at Ship's side. Brenda's only attendant was a ten-year-old relative, Helen Alexander, who wore a Kate Greenaway dress of white net trimmed with lace collar and cuffs. Big Brenda wore a gown of French-blue crepe de chine, a hat of magenta straw, and a corsage of deep purple orchids. Lady Jane was attired in a gown of bois de rose crepe with a moss-green hat trimmed with pink rosebuds.

The room was fragrant with expensive perfume, summery lilies, and yellow roses. The Reverend Joseph Flannelly, administrator of St. Patrick's Cathedral, used a sermon to tell a small moral tale. He described the New Testament story of the wedding feast at Cana in Galilee, where Christ performed his first miracle by turning water into wine. The wedding, Father Flannelly told his hearers, was remembered because of the presence of Christ, not because of the celebrity of the bride and bridegroom; in fact, the name of the bride at Cana and what she wore were not even recorded.

Afterward, waiters carrying trays of champagne entered through the french doors, and the guests drank to the couple's health. When Brenda and Ship left the apartment for their reception downstairs, they were greeted by popping flash-bulbs.

The dozens of photographers, reporters, and newsreel cameramen who had gathered in the corridor outside Brenda's apartment were anticipating a journalistic field day. ''Hadn't

Brenda been the most glamourized glamour girl of the decade? Hadn't she cooperated splendidly with the press since her debut?'' wrote one reporter on the scene. "Wasn't there a world of readers all prepared for and entitled to this, the happy-ending story? But no. It was, sorry no pictures, sorry no reporters. No this and no that from the policemen, private detectives, city detectives, hotel detectives, waiters, secretaries, doormen, etc., who spent the afternoon at the Ritz Carlton protecting Brenda from her former allies, the ladies and gentlemen of the press.''

To avoid going out in the street to get to the Ritz's Crystal Room, where the reception was to be held, the bridal party filed through a narrow corridor on the fourth floor of the hotel. As Brenda walked along, pulling her rustling train, she was met by more photographers and newsreel cameramen. "A nice smile, Mrs. Kelly," one called. "Look this way, Brenda," pleaded another. Then someone said, "Miss Frazier, are you happy?" Not knowing her voice was being recorded, Brenda snapped, "No, can't you see? I'm utterly miserable." She was being honest. But she immediately regretted the statement. Years later she recalled the moment: "There might have been some baffled movie audiences that week, but the words I spoke never reached the screen. Our best man, Tommy Tailer, stayed behind to argue and bargain with the newsreel people. He finally persuaded them to throw away that piece of film in return for a promise that Ship and I would . . . pose and answer all their questions."

At the end of the hall the bridal party took an elevator—decorated for the occasion with green brocade drapes—to the kitchen, where a red carpet had been laid. The stoves, sinks, and pots and pans were concealed behind pale green draperies, hung to form a narrow, fifty-foot-long passageway to the Crystal Room.

The bridal party stood at the foot of the Crystal Room's grand staircase, one floor below the street-level ballroom where Brenda had had her debut. The air-conditioned room, softly lit by candles, was filled with summery delphiniums, pink foxgloves, and ferns. A three-tiered bridal cake, the tiers separated by pillars, and topped with a large bell, stood at the center of the buffet table.

People lined up to congratulate the couple. Flashbulbs exploded as Mrs. Cornelius Vanderbilt, in a red print dress with matching hat, Doris Duke, and G. Creighton Webb, who hadn't missed a society wedding in sixty years, came down the stairway smiling at the newlyweds. The guests were announced by the butler of one of Big Brenda's friends.

As Irving Rose's orchestra played "Make Believe," Brenda's favorite tune, the Kellys moved out onto the dance floor. Then the orchestra switched to "In the Still of the Night," Big Brenda's favorite song. Brenda turned to dance with the best man while Ship waltzed with the bride's mother.

Reporters were barred from the reception. For two hours they stayed in the office of the hotel's press agent, Maximilian Elsner, Jr., waiting for the newlyweds to fulfill their promise. Elsner gave them sandwiches and beer, but nothing printable. Finally, at 7 P.M., they were told they would be allowed in the ballroom to take pictures. Brenda and Ship posed for a few minutes and then rushed back through the kitchen to the freight elevator. Not satisfied, the press ran after them but missed the same elevator. What happened next was described by a reporter from the *Daily News*:

> When the next elevator stopped at the familiar fourth floor, heavy guards wouldn't let anyone off. Trigger-quick, the 15 newspapermen crushed into the elevator, commandeered it to the fifth floor, and, just like in the movies, streaked down the fire escape stairs to catch their prey on the fourth floor. But the detectives were too quick and again the way was barred. We were trapped because the fire escape stairway door had locked behind us. But the end of the afternoon was near. Quite suddenly and politely, the detectives opened the way and cameras focused and then Brenda and Shipwreck got safely away.

At midnight the newlyweds arrived at LaGuardia Airport, where they were booked on a flight to San Francisco, and from there to Honolulu. Forty well-wishers had gathered behind the aluminum chain-link gate outside the terminal. While the couple posed for photographs as they boarded the airplane, a reporter asked Brenda if she had any advice for American girls. "Don't be foolish enough to be tagged with the title of Glamour Girl," she said adamantly.

Just a few hours earlier, Eleanor Young, Glamour Girl No. 1 of 1936, had been killed in a plane crash on a Rhode Island beach. Eleanor's death and Brenda's marriage seemed to reflect the end of an era.

Europe was consumed by war, and American youth, even New York's nightclub habitués, were exhibiting a new seriousness. Young men who a few months before "had done nothing more strenuous for a living than order wine in loud, testimonial tones," as E. J. Kahn, Jr., wrote, were now learning how to handle guns. Young women who so far had devoted their lives to dressing up and going to parties now donned uniforms and joined the women's branches of the armed services.

At such a time, extravagant debuts were unseemly. By 1942, the private deb ball had been virtually abandoned. That year New York's top hundred debs came out at a mass Christmas party at the Ritz. The expenses for the dinner dance were paid by Coty cosmetics. The newspapers were filled with stories about how parents used the money they saved to invest in war bonds.

"It would seem that glamour girl Brenda Frazier will go down in social history as the last of the glamour girls who came out in a burst of glory," wrote one columnist soon after Brenda's wedding. "I'm glad to be able to report that the erstwhile debutante is now a hardworking girl, serving her country. There are no idle women anymore, which is one good thing the war has brought about."

Brenda had not married as well as Lady Jane and Big Brenda had hoped, but she had married, and that, after all, was the whole point of being a debutante. Ship was not rich or titled, but he was charming, he loved Brenda, and he was well known in New York, and as Mrs. Kelly, Brenda could still rise to the top of society.

PART FOUR

WIFE

CHAPTER TEN

IF LIFE WERE a movie that could be played back and stopped at any point, Brenda surely would have lived hers in the freeze frame of summer 1941. That season she had it all—beauty, money, health, and love.

The Kellys' languid Hawaiian honeymoon lasted through July and most of August. Ship, in bathing trunks, and Brenda, in a floral two-piece bathing suit, a fragrant orchid behind her ear, lounged by the side of the pool. Servants brought them tall iced drinks. Later, they swam and played golf, then sipped cocktails on a moonlit veranda. Thousands of miles away from New York and the scene of her celebrity, Brenda could finally relax. She realized, says Ship, that "she enjoyed not being photographed and written about."

On August 13, when the Kellys returned from their honeymoon looking tanned and healthy, Brenda vowed to stay out of the limelight. "No more nightclubs for me," she firmly told the reporters who met the Kellys' flight.

The newlyweds moved into an apartment on East Fifty-seventh Street. While Ship went off to work at the Home Insurance Company, Brenda donned crisp wool suits and veiled hats to attend war relief committee meetings and ladies' luncheons. One morning New York *Post* reporter Earl Wilson interviewed Brenda at the Waldorf-Astoria, where she had joined other socialites to plan a benefit for Navy Relief. As Brenda sat in a folding chair in a corridor outside an office, she talked to Wilson about her new life. She said that she got up every day at eight-thirty, planned menus with her servants in the mornings, attended meetings in the afternoons, and went to the movies at night. At one point Brenda interrupted the interview to get an ashtray from the office. When she returned, she lit a cigarette and said, "This kind of life is a lot better for me than the old, and ever so much more interesting. Frankly, I always felt pretty much of a fool when they were photographing me in the nightclubs. There were always people there who had done things and deserved to be noticed. But what had I done?"

Brenda told Wilson that she had learned a lot about charity work from Mrs. Vincent Astor, who just then burst out of the war relief office. "Sweetheart, I have to go now," she said to Brenda, kissing her on the cheek. "See you Tuesday, Angel." Although Brenda had disavowed nightclubbing, she admitted to Wilson that her value as a fundraiser stemmed from her Café Society contacts. One night Brenda, Ship, and George Jessel toured the clubs, selling tickets for a Navy Relief Show at Madison Square Garden. They raised $2,000. "I got quite a lot of donations," Brenda told Wilson.

Several times a week, Brenda visited her mother. Big Brenda was still living at the Carlton House, although she had moved into a smaller suite after Brenda's wedding. Mother and daughter shared a limousine and chauffeur, whose salary was paid out of the income from Brenda's estate. Big Brenda still received about $15,000 a year from a trust fund set up for her by Fred Watriss. But the money the surrogate court gave her annually out of Brenda's inheritance—$52,000 in 1939—would end in June 1942, when Brenda turned twenty-one. Big Brenda, however, had been preparing for that day. Since 1934, according to Ship Kelly, she had been stashing some of the inheritance money away.

In mid-November, Brenda's pregnancy was reported in the press. The columnists wrote that the baby was due in May, but Jane Will Smith believes that Brenda was already about six months pregnant. In late November, Brenda went into premature labor, and her child, a son, was delivered dead, according to Smith. "The whole thing was handled so oddly," she says. "The family was trying to hush it up." Smith says that Brenda told her the child was delivered at home by her gynecologist, a Dr. Watt. Only after the stillbirth was she taken to LeRoy Sanitarium to recuperate. After her recovery, Brenda discussed the ordeal with Smith. "Brenda was very upset about losing the son. They were going to call him Christopher. She also talked about how physically hurt she'd been. Brenda said, 'They almost killed me trying to save the baby.' The baby came out in pieces and she was in agony. They had a terrible time getting her back in shape. Her insides were cement, and she couldn't go to the bathroom for a few days."

Brenda never mentioned the tragedy to her daughter, Victoria, although she told Victoria about her earlier abortion. If it was true that she was pregnant at the time of her marriage, then she must have been deeply ashamed of having been a pregnant bride. She didn't want anyone to think that Ship had had to marry her.

By mid-December Brenda had recovered, at least physically. The Kellys spent the holidays in Miami, where they shared a rented house on Pine Avenue with director Howard Hawks and his new bride, Nancy (now Lady Keith). The couples put up a Christmas tree in the living room, and on Christmas morning the husbands surprised their wives with two fluffy puppies. A servant took color movies as the couples lounged around the house, swam, and visited friends. Hawks later edited the film in Hollywood.

Lady Keith recalls how Ship doted on his young wife. "He treated her like she was a baby doll, some fragile little thing." Ship removed the front passenger seat and the entire back seat of his car and installed a chaise longue so that Brenda, whose legs still swelled painfully from edema, could travel with her feet up.

It is possible that Brenda was acting out her frustrations and unhappiness at having lost a child. In any case, Lady Keith remembers her being particularly petulant that vacation. "She was decent and nice, but amazingly spoiled," says Lady Keith. "She was like an old baby. I thought that she was silly, not that I was so serious myself. She had no curiosity except about the most superficial things."

Brenda spent much of her time languishing over movie magazines. "She was well aware of who she was and that she was a star," says Lady Keith. "She had her way about everything, and if she wasn't getting her way, she'd stamp her foot, she'd cry. I remember one night the Duke and Duchess of Windsor were giving a dinner at Government House in Nassau, and Ship didn't want to go. Brenda did, so she threw a tantrum. He was very patient, very good, very sweet to her. 'Darling, why do you want to go?' he said. 'It's just going to be all the same people.' But I think in the end they went.''

After the holidays, the Kellys returned to New York and resumed their heavy social routine. The war for them was largely confined to the stories in the newspapers and on newsreels, although Ship's civilian status was an embarrassment at Fifth Avenue parties. All the other fashionable young men had traded their dinner jackets for fatigues. Why hadn't Ship? Billy Livingston, home on leave from the army, recalls wondering about this after encountering Ship. "I was a lonely little private crossing Park Avenue when a town car stopped at a light, and I heard my name called. There was Ship sitting in the back seat. He had a morning coat on, and gray striped trousers." He told Livingston, teasingly, that he was on his way to Long Island to visit his polo ponies.

Actually Ship had tried to join the army but was rejected because of an injury: several years before his marriage he had broken his leg in four places while trying to catch a football. "I could have just sat on my ass [and lived off Brenda]," says Ship. "She had plenty of money. But I wanted to do something."

A solution came in the form of undercover work for the FBI—a job that included one of the most bizarre espionage assignments of the war. Ship ended up doing most of his spying on Ernest Hemingway.

When World War II broke out, several rival American intelligence services belonging to the State Department, the FBI, the army, and the navy fought to control counterespionage in South America. In 1940 President Roosevelt created a new department of the FBI, the Office of Special Intelligence Services (SIS) to oversee the spy network in the Western Hemisphere. (Later Roosevelt created another civilian cloak-and-dagger organization, the Office of Strategic Services, OSS, to cover counterespionage in the Eastern Hemisphere.)

J. Edgar Hoover named Jerome Doyle to head the Washington office of SIS's undercover operation. Doyle was a young attorney who, after finishing Yale Law School, had worked briefly for the FBI in 1934. Later, during a stint prosecuting criminals as an assistant U.S. attorney for Manhattan's Southern District, Doyle had polished the tough, confident style that Hoover loved and encouraged. One day, soon after he took over as head of SIS, Doyle got a call from Hoover. The FBI chief said that he wanted to use Shipwreck Kelly as a spy in South America. Hoover, who liked the drama and mystery of nightclubs as much as he enjoyed more important intrigue, had become friendly with Ship and Brenda over drinks at the Stork Club. After being rejected by the military, Ship had asked Hoover to let him serve the country by working for the FBI.

One evening in June 1942, Doyle arranged to meet Brenda and Ship at the Shoreham Hotel in Washington, D.C. He knew them only from photographs, but as he entered the hotel's restaurant, he spotted them dining with the U.S. ambassador to Mexico and his wife. Doyle was immediately impressed by Brenda's looks. "She was much more voluptuous than people realize," he says, recalling the first time he saw her. Brenda and Ship excused themselves from the table and retired to their suite with Doyle. Over the next two hours they discussed Ship's assignment. Brenda told Doyle, "Wherever Ship goes, I go too." And Doyle conceded that her beauty, money, and social connections might enhance Ship's undercover work. Doyle recalls, "I told them that we had decided to send them to Havana. Ship was to get acquainted with all the important people in Cuba and find out in a discreet way what was going on." He was to be known as agent #357.

Havana in those days had a transient population of idle millionaires and celebrities from the United States and Europe who had been drawn to the island by its tropical climate and languid life-style. One was Cathleen Vanderbilt, who along with her half-sister, Gloria Vanderbilt, shared the bulk of a $5 million fortune left by their father, Reginald. In 1940 the twice-divorced Cathleen married a prominent Cuban newspaper publisher, Martin Arostegui, and settled permanently in Havana. Mrs. Arostegui may have been the richest expatriate in Cuba, but Ernest Hemingway was the most famous. Attracted by the Gulf Stream's abundant marlin fishing, Hemingway and his third wife, Martha Gellhorn, had settled in 1940 at Finca Vigía, an elegant country home on the outskirts of Havana.

During the war the tone of social life for the expatriates was set by the U.S. ambassador, Spruille Braden, who had made and lost a fortune in real estate and oil before entering government service. He was a bit of a blowhard, but a popular figure in Havana nonetheless. A "good shot," he drank martinis and danced a graceful samba, despite his bulky frame. Batista once called him "more man than diplomat."

Braden did his best to promote American interests, but by the time the war was underway the mood in Havana was strikingly anti-American. *Diario de la Marina,* Cuba's leading newspaper, was run by a wealthy Spaniard whose editorials attacked America at every opportunity. Even worse, Nazi spies were infiltrating Cuba with forged passports, aided by thousands of Spanish Falangists. Offshore in the Caribbean, German submarines were stalking Allied tankers and cargo ships. Frightened Cuban fishermen claimed that crewmen from German submarines had boarded their boats, demanding food and water.

Richard O'Connell, who worked for the army's Cuban intelligence organization from 1942 to 1945, recalls that a few German spies were caught and executed on the Isle of Pines, just off the Cuban coast. But much of the intelligence work consisted of mundane spying on troublesome soldiers and prostitutes. "We used to go to the bars and nightclubs looking for people with loose talk," says O'Connell. "We were trying to spot the civilians who were asking too many questions and soldiers who were talking too much. We'd tell the military police, 'Pick that guy up and tell him to go home.'"

Brenda and Ship moved to Havana in the summer of 1942, assigned to live there by the FBI, which paid Ship about $800 a month, plus expenses—a total that was barely enough to maintain Brenda's wardrobe. The Kellys used her money to rent an elegant house overlooking the ocean on a private beach. It was flanked on one side by the home of the British ambassador to Cuba, and on the other by General Manuel Benítez, the flamboyant Cuban chief of police. The house had an indoor swimming pool and five bedrooms, each with a private dressing room and bath.

As soon as the Kellys arrived in Havana, they were besieged with invitations from the highest levels of Havana Society—Mr. and Mrs. Alfonso Fanjul, local social leaders; Cathleen Vanderbilt Arostegui; Ambassador and Mrs. Braden; Robert Joyce, the second in command at the embassy. The Kellys spent a lot of time at the Havana Country Club, where they sometimes saw Robert Joyce's wife, Jane. She remembers the Kellys as a pleasant but unremarkable couple. "She was very pretty and nice. He was charming and funny, and he used to cheat at golf a bit," Mrs. Joyce says.

Over time, the Kellys' social scene became strongly eclectic—it included diplomats like Braden and Joyce, millionaire expatriates like Winston Guest, Spanish Civil War heroes like Gustavo Durán, and, of course, Hemingway. Ship also became very friendly with his next-door neighbor, General Benítez, who, before becoming chief of police, had spent some time playing Latin lovers in Grade-B Hollywood movies.

By most accounts the Kellys were very happy in Cuba, though there is some evidence that Brenda drank heavily during the year she lived there. As a debutante, she had usually limited herself to an occasional glass of wine or champagne. After she met Kelly, her drinking escalated. Alcohol, after all, was part of the texture of upper-class life in New York, Nassau, and Havana.

Harry Cushing says that his mother, Cathleen Arostegui, and Brenda were frequent drinking companions in Havana despite the difference in their ages (Cathleen was thirty-seven, Brenda twenty-one). "I don't think my mother was a very good influence on Brenda," says Cushing. "My mother was a drinker, and Brenda was a drinker. The country club was very important, as it is in Latin countries. Everyone sat around drinking. I think that was the main thing in Cuban life."

For Brenda, the pattern was dangerous. She was attracted to alcohol. It took away her pain. When she was drinking she could forget her unhappy childhood, her anxious girlhood, her empty life.

Moreover, she could drink steadily throughout the day without appearing drunk and was able to convince herself and everyone around her that she did not have a drinking problem.

Brenda may have inherited a tendency toward alcoholism from her father. For more than a century, doctors have noted that alcoholism tends to run in families. (Today researchers report that about 40 percent of all alcoholics may have been born with biological traits that predispose them to the disease.)

When people asked Ship why he was in Cuba, he had two ready stories: sometimes he said he was selling insurance policies for the Home Insurance Company; other times he said he was a sales representative for a tractor and bulldozer manufacturer. "The idea," says Doyle, "was that he was embarrassed about not being in the war, so he and Brenda wanted to get out of the country."

No one in Havana knew that Ship was working for the FBI except the bureau's legal attaché, a rigid bureaucrat named Raymond Leddy. Ship reported directly to Leddy, who reported to Hoover. Though there were plenty of spies around in the fall of 1942, Ship and Leddy were the only two FBI agents in Havana. (The following April, regular FBI agents arrived, and the Kellys were sent to Mexico.)

"Kelly was no great spy," says Doyle. "But he was able to feed [Hoover] all this stuff he was picking up at dinner parties, and it gave the ambassador a jump on his rivals." Ship seems to have occupied himself principally by spying on his old friend Ernest Hemingway.

Shipwreck Kelly had known the novelist since the early thirties, when Hemingway had watched Ship play football for the Brooklyn Dodgers. Later, they became sparring partners at a gym on West Fifty-seventh Street. Before the war Ship had visited Hemingway in Key West and Havana, and hunted quail and shot pigeons with him. Through Ship, Brenda, too, had met Hemingway. It hadn't taken her long to figure out the novelist's insecurities. She later told a reporter that she thought Hemingway "was a forceful man, yes, but when one realized how physically strong he wanted to be, you knew he wasn't very strong inwardly."

As the war continued, Hemingway became more restless and eager to be a part of it. He approached Braden with an elaborate plan to set up a counterespionage ring in Havana to

A
TYPICAL
EVENING
(9 P.M. TO 6 A.M.)

The Williams-Taylors' house in Montreal.

Brenda's mother and grandmother at the time of the former's debut in 1907.

*Brenda's father,
Frank Frazier,
in Manchester,
Massachusetts, 1922.*

*Frank Frazier (at top) and
"Big Brenda" (third from top)
with friends, Manchester, 1922.*

*Brenda at her grandparents',
Manchester, Massachusetts, 1922.*

GLAMOUR TAKES A HOLIDAY. Miss Brenda Frazier sails from New York on the Munargo to visit her grandmother, Lady Williams-Taylor, in Nassau.

Glamour girl No. 1.

Glamour to Freckles

None other than Mickey Rooney was the escort of Brenda Frazier at a Manhattan dinner party. Mickey is pictured turning on the charm which Brenda seems to be able to take in her stride.

Screen Star Meets
Four Glamour Girls

William Holden, of Golden Boy Film, Has Dinner with Wealthy Debutantes— Party then Adjourns to Stork Club

By PATRICIA COFFIN

Four golden girls met a golden boy last night when T. Burt McGuire introduced William Holden, juvenile star of the motion picture Golden Boy, to a quartet of wealthy debutantes. The party met for dinner at the apartment of Kenhrick Gillespie, Burt's uncle, who lets his nephews spend the summer there while he is in Southampton. The girls were pretty Pat Fenn, dark-haired Jane Melton, glamorous Maude Overall and peppy Mary Graham. They greeted Bob Gamble and Harold Van Rosen as if they were long lost friends. Every one of the young people is summering in Southampton, and see each other daily.

Pat, who wore her "lobster dress," an effective red, black and white chiffon number, told Van that Eric Ridder's engagement to Tommy (Elsie-else) Tucker "is definitely official; he has bought the ring." Maude looked very ethereal in a gray and white chiffon dress which wound up in a veil. Jane discussed tomorrow's party at Canoe Place Inn with Burt, who will be her escort. Mary promises to be one of the most popular debs of the season with her ready wit and impish expression.

The party went to the Stork Club after coffee and brandy. Brenda Frazier was there at a ringside table with Dea Hudson Amsuldown, estranged wife of Phil Amsudown. They were accompanied by two handsome Englishmen and there was nothing unusual in the picture until Peter Arno walked in with Marie Wilson, the actress. He was given an adjoining table. Peter and Brenda barely spoke and in less than 15 minutes Arno left.

* * *

"Driving my new Studebaker is really thrilling"

says popular young socialite

MISS *Brenda Frazier*

"It's such an alive motor car," says Miss Frazier. "It's so responsive to the touch and it's finished and styled so smartly! Raymond Loewy, who had a hand in designing it, certainly is to be complimented."

ONE look at the smooth, sweeping, impressive lines and flawless appointments of this new Studebaker Land Cruiser and you understand why it's such a favorite with the smart younger set.

Possibly no new car of the year has won such extensive and enthusiastic social approval as this roomy, restful-riding Studebaker Land Cruiser. And it's one of the most money-saving of all cars to operate.

You can count on Studebaker's unique master craftsmanship to keep this distinctive Land Cruiser running smoothly and satisfactorily for many years.

See it and drive it now at your local Studebaker dealer's. Use your present car as part payment—easy C.I.T. terms.

BORN TO THE PURPLE BUT CHARMINGLY DEMOCRATIC is young Miss Brenda Frazier whose beauty and graciousness have become an American legend. This popular young woman proudly and competently drives her new Studebaker Land Cruiser many hundreds of miles each month.

Distinctively smart new **STUDEBAKER LAND CRUISER**

AVAILABLE ON COMMANDER SIX OR PRESIDENT EIGHT CHASSIS

DEBUTANTE BRENDA DIANA DUFF FRAZIER

November 14, 1938.

Brenda with Joan Crawford at the Stork Club, 1938.

*With David Niven and John Perona (center)
at El Morocco.*

Brenda Frazier

New York, N. Y.

An address was not necessary.

Her debut: the Ritz Ballroom, December 27, 1938.

The debut, continued.

Brenda with Peter Arno, 1938.

With Shipwreck Kelly, Palm Beach, 1940.

The wedding of Brenda Diana Duff Frazier and John "Shipwreck" Kelly, June 30, 1941.

The bride and her mother at their apartment in the Carlton House.

Brenda and Ship in Havana, 1943.

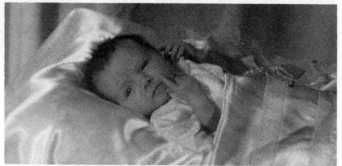

Brenda and Ship's daughter, Victoria, 1945.

Victoria and her father (right) at Meadowood, 1946.

The house at Meadowood, 1946.

At El Morocco, 1948. Left to right: the Ayesha of Jaipur, Ship Kelly, "Bubbles" Holmes, the Maharajah of Jaipur, and Brenda.

Cocktails with Brenda. A drawing by Alajalov.

Brenda and Pietro at a beach near Rome.

Brenda in Naples with Pietro and Victoria and Victoria's nanny, Eva Moorcock.

Wedding day at Why Not, Brenda's house at East Harwich on the Cape, March 3, 1957.

Brenda and Bob Chatfield-Taylor.

Brenda and Alexander McLeod on their way to a dinner party in Boston, 1977.

ferret out Nazi spies. Braden discussed the idea with the Cuban Prime Minister, then gave Hemingway his approval and furnished some supplies. Their understanding was that Hemingway's operation would end when the regular FBI men arrived in April.

Working out of a guesthouse at Finca, Hemingway assembled a rag-bag fraternity of jai alai players, waiters, fishermen, and aristocrats, loosely held together, as Carlos Baker wrote, "by the force of Ernest's personality and liberal infusions of wine, spirits and pesos." He called his spy ring the Crook Factory. It had been operating for only a few weeks when Hemingway—who at the same time was editing an anthology of combat journalism called *Men at War*—decided he wanted to do some real fighting. He approached Braden with another idea: to transform his fishing vessel, the *Pilar,* into an armed Q boat that would cruise the coast hunting for German submarines. Hemingway and his crew of eight would, as Baker describes the plan, pretend "that they were scientists gathering specimens for the American Museum of Natural History. If and when halted by a Nazi submarine, they would wait until the enemy boarding party had emerged on deck and the craft had closed with the *Pilar* to a distance of fifty yards. Then, on signal, Ernest would rev up his motors, close the gap to 20 yards, and begin shooting. The heavy machine guns would mow down deck personnel while Ernest's crewmen, trained for the purpose, would lob grenades down the conning tower and, if possible, arm and heave one of the short-fuse bombs into the sub's forward hatch. Ernest told Braden that he could find the right men. All he needed to make his romantic dream come true was good radio equipment, arms and ammunition and official permission." Braden, remarkably, was enthusiastic about the idea, and in June the *Pilar* went on its first expedition.

Not surprisingly, Hemingway sighted only a few submarines in his adventures, and sank none. The mission was ridiculous, as Martha Gellhorn—who had to endure the rowdy drinking parties and Hemingway's "mastodon" hangovers that typically followed a sub-hunting spree—recognized, and it couldn't be taken seriously.

But that's exactly what the FBI did. Hoover was jealous of Hemingway because of his relationship with Braden, and considered the novelist disloyal to the bureau. Raymond Leddy, the FBI's main man in Cuba, hated him even more. Hemingway had once referred to Leddy as "a member of the Gestapo." "This goddamn stupid business of looking for German submarines," as Doyle put it, gave the bureau a reason to keep an eye on the novelist. "Hemingway was a free-lance wild man, and [the FBI] wanted some sort of control over him, some way of finding out what Hemingway was up to," Doyle says.

Recently Hemingway scholar Jeffrey Meyers obtained the dossier that the FBI kept on Hemingway beginning in October 1942, two months after Ship and Brenda arrived in Havana. The dossier reveals that the FBI tried to sabotage Hemingway's espionage activities by claiming that they were completely worthless. The agency also tried to prove that Hemingway was a Communist.

By spending time with Hemingway, Doyle says, Ship was able to gather most of the initial information in the FBI dossier. "Ship isn't given credit for it, because he was undercover, but [the FBI] was getting [its] information about Hemingway 90 percent of the time through Ship," says Doyle.

In the lengthy Hemingway file, Ship is the direct source for only one confidential memorandum. This memo, dated August 13, 1943, was written by Leddy to Hoover, and half of it has been blacked out. The remaining portion states:

> Sis #357 advises that Mr. Hemingway of whose intelligence activities under Ambassador Spruille Braden the Bureau has been previously advised, is currently engaged in writing a book based on his experiences in that work. Hemingway states that all of the people whom he had known during the last year in Cuba in connection with intelligence work will appear in his book, including Ambassador Braden. We are not yet informed as to what role the representatives of the F.B.I. will play, but in view of Hemingway's known sentiments, [we'll] probably be portrayed as the dull, heavy-footed unimaginative professional policeman type.

Hemingway later boasted that he could spot "these inescapable FBI men . . . all trying to look so average, clean-cut young American that they stood out as clearly as though they had worn a bureau shoulder patch on their white linen or seersucker suits." But at the time he never suspected Ship. Years later, however, Hemingway did find out, and confronted Ship. "Ernest felt that it was wrong that I was working for the FBI and didn't let him know it," says Ship.

In April 1943, sixteen regular FBI agents took over the Cuban assignment, and in September the Kellys returned to New York. Brenda was pregnant again, and again she lost the baby, this time at three months. While awaiting Ship's next overseas assignment, the couple lived at the Plaza Hotel and resumed their busy social life.

Within a few months they were off again to Mexico, then Chile, Brazil, and Argentina, where they dined with Juan and Evita Perón. What Ship's exact duties were at this point is murky. But one of his assignments, he claims, was to befriend the owner of a Brazilian snake farm who was smuggling snake venom to Japan in the moldings of suitcases, the venom to be used as a snakebite antidote. Ship says that after he visited the owner several times and gave him some cash, the smuggling stopped.

In Argentina, Brenda, who was now twenty-two, became pregnant again, and for the first time proved able to carry the child to full term. As the date of their baby's birth approached, the Kellys returned to New York and moved into a townhouse on East Sixty-sixth Street.

In their absence, Big Brenda had married for the third time. Her new husband, Henry Pierrepont Perry, was a retired stockbroker. Big Brenda had been lonely after the Kellys moved to Cuba, and remarried for companionship more than anything else. "I don't think Brenda's mother liked Perry too much," recalls Jane Will Smith. "But he was social; he had money. That was enough. And after Brenda got married, she needed someone."

On June 9, 1942, Brenda had turned twenty-one and taken control of the income from her father's trusts, which were then worth about $2 million. She also received $1 million outright in cash and securities. Brenda's possession of the Frazier fortune seemed to embolden her, at last publicly. Doyle recalls hearing Brenda talk to Big Brenda "as if Brenda was the mother and the mother was the child. I think Brenda realized how silly her mother was.''

Yet Brenda still felt completely dominated by her mother. Brenda was "too nice" (and, no doubt, too repressed) "to go against her mother's wishes," says Esme Hammond. It was Lady Jane, however, who ruled both women. "The grandmother was behind everything, and she could be kind of ruthless to get what she wanted. Big Brenda was caught in the middle," says Gertie Folmsbee.

On November 26, two weeks before her baby was due, Brenda was rushed to Doctors Hospital, and the next day she gave birth by cesarean section to a healthy seven-pound, five-ounce girl. The Kellys named her Brenda Victoria.

The child's arrival was hailed like a royal birth. Radio programs were interrupted to announce Brenda's motherhood. Telegrams, flowers, and presents poured in from friends such as Cardinal Spellman, Toots Shor, and Irving Berlin. "Delighted that you completed that forward pass," wrote publicist Steve Hannagan. "Please stop giving the Stork free publicity," cabled John Perona, the owner of El Morocco.

With a baby at last, this young society family needed a country estate, and Ship soon found one in Oyster Bay, Long Island. A sprawling, 160-acre farm called Meadowood, it featured horse barns, a swimming pool, and an elegant Georgian mansion at the end of a winding tree-lined drive.

Years before, Lady Jane had told Ship, "Set Brenda up in a big house and get her to running it and she'll be perfectly happy." Lady Jane, of course, was telling him what *she* had wanted as a young bride. "Nobody bothered to consult me," Brenda later wrote. "I would not have known how to answer if they had; I was merely a pawn in the game my grandmother and mother always had played."

CHAPTER ELEVEN

WITH AN INCOME of $200,000 a year, Brenda could afford to be a stylish pawn. At twenty-four, she had become the glamorous socialite of Lady Jane's and Big Brenda's fantasies, a baby-matron with expensive toys—a Bentley, Tiffany jewels, Mainbocher gowns, and a life-size dollhouse in which to display her treasures.

Meadowood was the picture of country elegance, with miles of white wood fencing imported from Kentucky, defining vast field of blue-grass lawns. Ship renovated the barns and went into business boarding racehorses. Among others, Jack Dempsey and Judy Garland kept horses at Meadowood. Meanwhile, Brenda hired society decorator George Stacey. He filled the rooms with polished antiques, flowered chintz upholstery, and bowls of fresh flowers.

She hired a staff of ten—a chauffeur, a chef, a butler, two downstairs maids, two upstairs maids, a lady's maid for herself, a valet for Ship, and a nanny for Victoria—and spent her mornings lying in bed, giving orders. Most afternoons, dressed in white gloves, pearls, and a fur coat, she made the forty-five-minute drive into Manhattan to meet a friend for champagne and chicken salad at the Stork Club. Most evenings she and Ship went out.

With the end of the war, Long Island began developing rapidly. New and better roads made the island accessible to New York City, and many of the area's great potato farms were plowed under and turned into subdivisions. Much of this new housing was middle-class, but the rich also rediscovered Long Island. They built new mansions and bought many of the old estates dotting the coast. Entertaining in an opulent style reminiscent of the twenties returned. In her scrapbook Brenda kept pictures of her friends' parties, and the record shows a monotony of high style, with the same sprays of gladioli on the tables, the same fixed smiles on the guests' faces, the same bartenders serving the same drinks in the background.

Sometimes undercurrents surfaced. As Brenda was driving away from a party one evening, she realized she had forgotten her coat. When her chauffeur, Gerald Kelly, approached the house to retrieve it, he saw the hostess on the porch making love with one of the male guests. They were lying on the chaise lounge—the hostess with her skirt hiked up to her waist, the man with his pants bunched at his knees. A few feet away in the living room, the hostess's husband was mixing drinks.

One night at a party honoring the Duchess of Windsor at the Locust Valley home of Mrs. George F. Baker, Brenda sat near William Woodward, Jr. After the party, Woodward drove home with his wife, Ann, and they retired to their separate bedrooms. Awakened by her dog in the middle of the night, Ann Woodward got up and, claiming she suspected a burglar, fired a shotgun into the darkness. The alleged intruder turned out to be her husband, whom she had fatally wounded in the head. According to one officer who investigated the killing, the couple may have quarreled because Bill was flirting with Brenda.

The Kellys did their share of entertaining, too. Brenda used the family silver and china and organized elaborate luncheons and dinner parties for ten or twenty people. Sometimes Bing Crosby and the Duke and Duchess of Windsor would arrive. Brenda seated her guests at a long table in the green-and-white dining room. At each place setting would be a silver cigarette lighter, a silver ashtray, and a silver box containing four or five Sherman cigarettes. After dinner, the guests would retire to the drawing room to play bridge on card tables set up around the room.

Brenda appeared to thrive in her role as hostess. She was always at the center of the party, chatting effusively and making everyone feel comfortable. "I'm very remiss not to have written my bread and butter letter before," Elsa Maxwell wrote Brenda after a weekend at Meadowood. "I had a divine weekend as you know. That's because you're a perfect hostess. In other words, you're a post-deb Duchess of Windsor."

Brenda's friends remember her as always exquisitely groomed for these affairs, with beautifully styled hair and freshly polished nails. Adds Mary Sanford, a central figure in that world, "Brenda seemed to do everything right. She never made mistakes."

At her parties, Brenda maintained her self-possession even when faced with near-disaster. One evening during dinner, a guest announced in a loud, authoritative voice that she knew who had killed Sir Harry Oakes, the Nassau businessman who had been murdered in 1943. "It was Harold Christie!" the guest shouted, not knowing that Christie was sitting at the end of the table. "And how do you know this?" demanded Christie, rising from his chair. Before the woman could answer, he collapsed on the floor with a heart attack. Brenda directed one of her guests to call an ambulance; meanwhile, she ushered everyone out of the dining room and got several bridge games going in the drawing room. To everyone's relief, Christie recovered.

The man presiding over these dinners was French, the Kellys' not-so-proper English butler. "He used to get drunk and take his teeth out and go to sleep in the silver safe," Brenda later recalled. "When he applied for the job, Ship said something to him about drinking. French said, 'I never touch alcohol!' Well, French was the biggest drunk we ever had. And if he wasn't interested in the people coming to dinner, he wouldn't put his teeth in. And he had only one tooth. One night I said to him, 'Mr. and Mrs. Vanderbilt are coming to dinner.' This was big business. He couldn't wait for Uncle Willie! So Ship and I were in hysterics. His teeth were in; you've never seen such service in your life! But if he didn't think somebody was chic enough, he didn't bother."

Brenda probably tolerated French because she shared his values. The obsessions of Lady Jane and Big Brenda had become hers. She continued to seek out the Old Guard, and during the years she was married to Ship her address book was filled with Astors, Dukes, Phippses, Whitneys, and Vanderbilts, many of whom were a generation older than Ship and she. "Brenda *was* older than her age," says her friend Count Vasilli Adlerberg.

But underneath her ebullient hostess mask, Brenda was miserable. Going to nightclubs and being fawned over was mindless, passive activity. Entertaining was hard work. "She got very, very nervous," say her friend Lucienne Piro. "At one party she told my husband, 'I can't take it anymore.' He told her to go upstairs and relax." Gertie Folmsbee says that Ship enjoyed entertaining much more than Brenda did. "They would invite the Argentine polo team out to the house, and he'd be much more interested in the preparations than Brenda would be. A lot of the entertaining was just too much for Brenda. She was really very shy."

Brenda found it increasingly difficult to keep up with the social whirl. She told one of her lady's maids, Dorothy Caverno, that in one year she went to three hundred parties. To cope with this dizzying pace, she started taking drugs. Among the rich and their hangers-on, barbiturates and amphetamines were almost chic in those days. The Manhattan medical community was filled with "Dr. Feelgoods" who routinely and legally prescribed drugs to bolster their patients' moods and to make their lives easier and more pleasant.

"My mother would have bad headaches. She'd [go to a doctor] and end up with codeine," says Victoria. "She [also] took a ton of Librium, Ritalin, Dexedrine, Seconal, and chloral hydrate."

Pill-taking was accepted not only in New York society, but also in Brenda's family. Her mother took diet pills and her grandmother occasionally used cocaine. When she died, tiny gold boxes with grilles over the top were found among her belongings. Victoria suspects that Lady Jane kept her cocaine in these boxes.

It was clear that Brenda was unhappy with her life in her Long Island mansion, and Ship grew concerned. "She was drinking too much, and she didn't want to do anything," he says. "She just wanted to stay home and read and stay in bed." He tried to find projects to interest her. He built her a tennis court and spent hours hitting the ball to her. After Brenda had admired the flowers from a greenhouse owned by another socialite, Ship built a greenhouse for his wife. But as with everything else she tried, Brenda soon lost interest. "She went down and worked in the greenhouse for two or three months and she loved it, putting in different flowers," says Ship. "Then one day she broke two or three fingernails and after that she gave up on it. So I got rid of the men I'd hired to take care of it. From then on, whenever Brenda asked me for flowers from her greenhouse, I'd send the farm manager down the road to buy some from a professional nursery."

Just as Ship was troubled that Brenda had no true interests, she was worried that he didn't have a real career. "She used to say that he never finished anything he started," says the chauffeur, Gerald Kelly. Ship kept an office at Rockefeller Center, where he ostensibly conducted the insurance business he'd had before the war. He went in a couple of times a week, but there wasn't enough work to keep him busy. He spent most of his time on the golf course. "Ship wasn't the type to be tied to a desk," says Gertie Folmsbee, who handled the Kellys' finances and shared this Rockefeller Center office with Ship.

Nagged by Brenda to find a career, Ship came up with an idea: he'd be a screenwriter. After all, everyone said he told great stories, and he had lots of friends in Hollywood. So he sat down and wrote a screenplay based on the life of Eddie Bentz, a notorious bank robber of the 1930s. Brenda was thrilled. She asked Jerome Doyle, the former SIS undercover chief, who at this time was practicing law in New York, to leave his firm to produce the movie. Doyle recalls that Brenda courted him and his wife constantly, taking them to dinner again and again at the Stork Club. Finally he made it clear to her that he wanted to be a lawyer and "didn't want anything to do with the motion picture business. So once I made that clear, once that thing died, that was the last I saw of Brenda and Ship until after they'd separated."

Ship never sold his screenplay, a copy of which he still keeps at his home in Manhasset, New York.

The Kellys' erratic lives made them difficult employers, and few people could work for them long. Brenda went through a dozen chauffeurs in a few months; none of them could endure her constant lateness. Then Gerald Kelly, who had lately been an employee of a United Nations official, arrived. At six feet four inches tall and three hundred pounds, Kelly looked like a bodyguard, but he had an avuncular manner. Over the years he became much more than a chauffeur to Brenda. He was her confidant, her friend.

On his first day on the job, Kelly, driving her limousine, picked Brenda up in front of the house. Brenda stepped into the car cradling a huge bundle of mail. All the way into Manhattan, Kelly listened to ripping envelopes and crumpling letters. By the time they arrived at the Westbury Hotel, where Brenda kept a pied-à-terre, the back seat was filled with balls of paper. He cleaned it up while Brenda was upstairs. The next day the incident was repeated. This time Kelly ignored the mess. When Brenda got in the car, she was shocked to see wads of paper piled on the floor.

"Would you mind cleaning the car, Gerald?" she asked.

"I'll be glad to," he answered. "First thing in the morning."

"What do you mean, tomorrow morning?" demanded Brenda.

"I only clean the car once a day, first thing in the morning," Kelly said.

Brenda was furious. She didn't speak to him all the way home. But the next day, when they got to the Westbury Hotel, before going in, she handed him an envelope with all her mail neatly folded inside. "Throw this away, please," she said.

"From then on," says Kelly, "we got along just fine."

By this time the Kelly marriage was undergoing strains because of Brenda's and Ship's extravagance. "Brenda's mother had always told her she was an heiress, so Brenda thought of herself as being rich," says Jane Will Smith. They spent huge sums of money. At the beginning of each month, Brenda transferred cash from a savings account into a joint checking account. She and Ship, says Gerald Kelly, dug into this account "like it was an endless pit." Brenda spent it on clothes, buying dozens of tailored day dresses and bouffant evening gowns. Ship spent it on the stables and golf equipment. "The bills were fantastic," says the chauffeur.

One morning Kelly, who lived above the garage, awoke to find six new cars in the driveway. Ship had bought them at a party the night before. Brenda bought a car, too: a black limousine with a distinctive beige canvas top, so she could spot it easily among the other limousines in parking lots at parties. She designed her own trademark—back-to-back *B*'s—which she had engraved on the car's doors. Indeed, the car became a kind of emblem of their extravagance. Sometimes Brenda stuffed it with sixteen Louis Vuitton suitcases and took it on vacation. The Kellys drove it to Southampton for polo matches in the spring, and to Newport for golf and tennis tournaments in the summer. With Gerald Kelly at the wheel, and the beige canvas top rolled down, Brenda paraded down "Millionaires' Row" in Newport on warm summer evenings, cool in a white linen dress.

The Kellys traveled several months out of the year, following the social seasons around the country. They also took trips to Cuba, Haiti, and Nassau. In 1948 they visited England and France. It was Ship's first visit to Paris, and when they returned, Bing Crosby wrote and recorded a song for them with his sixty-five-piece orchestra. The song is to the tune of "How Ya Gonna Keep 'Em Down on the Farm":

> Oh, how ya gonna keep him down on the farm,
> After he's seen Paris?
> How ya gonna keep him on Long Island?
> Deep in that grass, flat on his ass?
> How ya gonna keep him at Oyster Bay?
> That's a mystery.
> A fellow used to worry lots when he went away.
> But penicillin cures it up in a day.
> Now he'll get a new one most every day,
> after he's seen Paris.

Their daughter, Victoria, accompanied them on some of these trips, but often she stayed home. Brenda wanted to be a good mother, but her depression and her escalating alcohol-and-drug problem interfered. Her maternal style was like her own mother's. She even hired her old baby nurse, Mabel Bishop, to take care of Victoria. Nanny Bishop was soon troubled to see Brenda behaving toward Victoria in the same way Big Brenda had behaved toward Brenda.

Once, according to Bishop, when Victoria was about two, the child was playing by the pool as her mother sunbathed.

Brenda had taken off her jewelry and placed it beside her. Attracted by the glittering baubles, Victoria picked up a bracelet. Suddenly Brenda jumped to her feet, grabbed Victoria, and slapped her violently across the face.

Victoria Kelly remembers her mother during this period as a glamorous but distant figure. "My mother never had anything to do with me except to say good morning and good night," she says. "I always had my own nanny and nursery and so forth. I never had breakfast with her, I never had lunch with her, I never had dinner with her. Every now and then, as a big treat, she'd take me to lunch at Quo Vadis, or I'd get to spend the night in her bedroom with her. [Sometimes] I would be brought downstairs all dressed up for tea in my special little chair with my special little tea set when she had people in for tea."

When they did spend time alone together, Brenda enjoyed dressing Victoria up like a doll and talking baby talk to her. "Brenda loved baby talk," says her psychiatrist. "Even with her boyfriends, it was always baby talk. The unrequited infant would come out at every opportunity."

On November 16, 1948, Big Brenda suffered a stroke in her apartment at the Carlton House. She was rushed to Doctors Hospital, but she died several hours later. She was fifty-nine. Her memorial service at St. Thomas Church on Fifth Avenue was a somber occasion until the organist, who had been playing gloomy hymns, suddenly broke into Cole Porter's "In the Still of the Night," one of Big Brenda's favorite tunes.

Brenda was twenty-seven when her mother died. For years afterward she spoke well of Big Brenda. "For my mother I feel only pity and sorrow," Brenda wrote in 1963. "She was such a charming woman, so intelligent, so witty. Above all, she was so very democratic. There was nothing whatever of the snob in her; she was willing to accept and to like anyone who had earned the right to be liked, regardless of origins. I often wondered what kind of woman she might have been, what she might have accomplished if her own childhood had been blessed with more genuine love and understanding." Of course, hardly any of this was true. Big Brenda was indeed a snob, and virtually no one remembers her as charming, intelligent, or witty.

But only toward the end of Brenda's life, after a decade of analysis, did she begin to talk about the deep ambivalence she felt toward her mother.

Big Brenda's death came at a time when the strains on the Kellys' marriage were becoming apparent. Gerald Kelly remembers fierce arguments between Brenda and Ship. Brenda would complain about Ship's spending. "And he'd holler and scream like you wouldn't believe," says the chauffeur. Ship could also be wildly unpredictable. When Gerald Kelly went to the garage one morning to get a car ready to take Brenda to New York, he found none there—Ship had sold all three the night before.

Today Ship insists that "no two people were any happier than Brenda and me. I never did anything to embarrass Brenda, like a lot of men do in their marriages. For so many years I never looked at another woman, never touched another woman. I tell you, we never spent a night apart."

But there are indications from other sources that the sexual side of their relationship was not altogether happy. "She told me once that Ship was always after her [for sex]," says one of Brenda's lady's maids, Frances Griffin. "That could have turned her off, or turned her off Ship, because she went on to have sex with others."

Her psychiatrist says that she completely turned away from Ship sexually. "With the marriage came the extinction of the romance," he says. "All the hot passion of lovemaking disappeared the evening of the marriage. From then on, she was the one at fault. She couldn't tolerate [the marriage]. And when he stopped being the great cocksmith—he couldn't even excite his wife—the great love evaporated. And so he became pathologically jealous. She was nice to others, but not nice to him. She took refuge in illness to avoid him."

The psychiatrist, a Freudian, argues that Brenda's childhood relationships deeply affected her marriage. Ship "represented her father and her great love for the father," the psychiatrist says. "She was so scared [in front of her father]. Her father had tried so hard to be pleasant to her, to eat dinner with her, chat with her, go fishing with her, go to the beach with her—he extended himself as much as he could—

and she was so scared, because of the authority of the mother. This would be disloyal. The very niceness of the father brought out how much she hated her mother. Ship was a representative of the father. Once they were married, now he was a member of the family. She was related to him. The difference between girlfriend and wife is tremendous. I've treated many couples who are on the verge of splitting whose courtships were pink and whose honeymoons were black.'' In the psychiatrist's view, Ship never understood the dynamics of the marriage. "Any evidence of esteem by a male of a higher social order was his reward in life. The fact that he could capture the prize woman was all part of this.''

Lady Jane was too lost in grief over Big Brenda's death to be aware of the Kellys' marital troubles. Now she was all alone. Sir Frederick had died four years earlier, and her son, Travers, had died in 1925, while serving with Canadian troops in the Sudan. According to newspaper accounts of his death, Travers was killed in the line of duty, but Brenda later told friends that he had shot himself. In a letter to Brenda, Lady Jane urged the Kellys to visit her: "You realize that you and Victoria are all I have now, as kind and sweet as people are, nothing and nobody can [console] me or fill her place as you do.''

The Kellys obliged Lady Jane by spending the summer of 1949 with her at the Canadian resort of Manoir Richelieu. During the winter they joined her in Nassau. Brenda and Ship rented a house next door to Ellin and Irving Berlin, who was writing a new musical. Sometimes when he had reached a snag in his composing he'd ask Ship to walk up and down the street with him. The two men would stroll side by side, without talking, but Berlin would whistle to himself. Finally he would say, "Well, Ship, I think you did me a good thing. I think I've got something. Now good night.''

Brenda and Ship stayed in Nassau five months. Victoria was with them, along with her governess, Brenda's maid, and Gerald Kelly. As in New York, Brenda and Ship went out to lunch and dinner virtually every day. While Ship played golf, Brenda lay in the sun reading or playing canasta with her grandmother. At night they went to movies or to parties, often with people from Brenda's mother's and grandmother's generation, who were attracted to Brenda and felt protective of her.

That winter, Brenda thought she was pregnant. Her doctor took a blood sample, and the following day Ship flew the sample to a Miami hospital for testing. "Ship left early for Miami, and I went on a picnic with Harold Christie, Grandma, Francis Williams. . . . we went to Lyford Cay," Brenda wrote in her appointment book on March 11. "Ship called me to say the test was positive and we are all very excited—I went to bed early and Victoria slept with me." But on April 2, Brenda miscarried. Counting her abortion, this was the fourth baby she had lost. "No more baby," she wrote laconically in her appointment book.

A few days later, Brenda resumed her busy schedule. The sameness of Nassau's social life was punctuated now and then by feuds, illicit love affairs, and even murder. "As a rest cure, I personally do not recommend Nassau," Brenda once wrote. "Some people come down here under the mistaken illusion that they will find a peaceful resort in which all worries will vanish like magic, and the sun will bring health and strength to their dissipated bodies. Unfortunately worries, encouraged by scandal, increase, and the sun is apt to result in violent sun stroke. At the end of the happy season you may possibly find one or two people still speaking to each other, but [if you could tell them] what you knew, [they] would not be speaking to each other."

By the time Brenda and Ship returned to New York in the spring, Ship was suffering from a horseshoe fistula—an abnormal rectal passage—caused by an injury. On June 18 he was admitted to Southampton Hospital for an operation. Ship's illness left Brenda deeply frustrated and brought out her neuroses. She wanted to be the baby, the fawned-over patient—a role her husband was now usurping. Ship's condition, says Jane Will Smith, "took all the play away from Brenda. People would call up in the morning and say, 'Well, how's Ship?' " Brenda couldn't wait to resume her place at the center of attention. The day after Ship's operation, she decided to have a cyst in her ear removed. Ship's surgeon, Dr. William Gaynor, operated on Brenda, and she spent the night in Ship's hospital room.

Brenda's cyst, however, couldn't compete with her husband's serious illness. Ship's fistula refused to heal, and on June 27 he was operated on again, this time at New York Hospital. Brenda moved into the city to be near him. Once her friends found out she was in town, they started asking her out to restaurants and nightclubs. "At night she would leave the hospital," says Jane Will Smith, "and go out. Everybody made her feel attractive. She found out she liked this [going out again]. She liked all this adoration, having a few drinks, going to a bar." Men started pursuing her again, says Lucienne Piro, "and she probably got a little excited."

It was a return, in a small way, to her glory years, when the attention of her suitors and the press had bolstered her sense of self-worth. Since her marriage to Ship, things had changed. Her friends thought she was losing the most precious thing she had: her "glamour."

"It faded gradually," say Count Vasilli Adlerberg. By 1950, the Deb of the Century had been reduced to a subordinate clause in the gossip columns. ("The picture of Joanne Connelley on *Life* magazine is the most glamorous since the days when Brenda Frazier was the toast of the town" was a typical item.) At age twenty-nine, Brenda felt like a has-been, an afterthought. When she arrived at socialite Cynthia Foy's wedding at St. Bartholomew's Church on Park Avenue, the photographers lining the sidewalk didn't even recognize her. "It can't be anybody important," mumbled one as Brenda walked by.

Ship's illness opened up a chance for her to try to capture something of what she'd lost. Café Society had none of its prewar excitement—after four years of war, the country was too industrious, too eager to get on with serious life—but many familiar faces still gathered at the Stork Club and El Morocco. Brenda's reappearance as a regular was probably seen as a hopeful sign by the nightclubbers; things might be made as they had been.

Ship may have sensed what was going on. One day he sent Brenda a note on hospital stationery, telling her how much he loved her and promising to "make up" for "the hell of a time I am causing you" when he got home.

After a third unsuccessful operation in September, Ship went to Lexington, Kentucky, for a fourth. Brenda, Victoria, the governess, and Gerald Kelly checked into a nearby hotel.

Brenda was restless and bored, and two weeks later she returned to New York. Back on the scene of her previous success, Brenda surrounded herself, says Ship, with "that glamour bullshit group—all those people who flattered her, all those sycophants. It was hot-shit for some of those peasant girls to be out with Brenda Frazier."

Brenda also started seeing other men. Some would come to Meadowood to play tennis and swim. Others would arrive at the cocktail hour, filling up the drawing room like the stag line at a debut. Brenda told Frances Griffin that she had slept with at least one of them. "Brenda said that she had cheated on Ship; that she lied to him and made up excuses about where she was going," says Griffin. (Some of the couple's friends and employees say that Ship was the first to stray, that he had begun an affair with another woman before Brenda started seeing other men.) But most of her guests were platonic friends. Indeed, some of them were homosexual.

Throughout her life Brenda had a number of homosexual friends. They were attracted by her money and fame; she was attracted by their nonsexual devotion. "She was afraid of sex," says her psychiatrist. "What could be her refuge from it—homosexual men. They were safe. And they became her little children. It doesn't matter what side of the coin you're on if it's a mother-child relationship you're looking for throughout life. You're either the mother or the child. Always this duality. But if she didn't get enough devotion from them; if they weren't ass kissers, boot lickers, then she'd have nothing to do with them."

One of Brenda's heterosexual friends was George Atwell, the brother of her friend Edwina Atwell. George was tall, blond, and attractive in the slightly sinister style of Errol Flynn. The Atwells had lost their money during the Depression, and George had been forced to sell his polo ponies, his passion. He became a flamboyant drunk. Sometimes he carried a pistol, once pulling it out during the dessert course at a dinner party and threatening to shoot down the chandelier. Another time, at a large tennis party at Meadowood, he pulled a gun from his jacket and waved it in the air. Ship had to grab it out of his hand. "Lots of girls were mad about George," says Jane Will Smith. "But I didn't think he was handsome. I thought he was creepy. He was a kind of lounge lizard. He would arrive and just sit. He'd tell you how great he was, and how great you were.''

Atwell's bad-boy bravado greatly attracted Brenda, however, and they began an affair. Their relationship was cemented in part by their mutual interest in alcohol and drugs. Brenda was drawn to people who drank. Most of the men she became involved with had alcohol problems. Many of her butlers and cooks drank.

Jane Will Smith remembers visiting Brenda in the early fifties. "She had a bed all full of beautiful pillows and by it were tables, tables, tables, and on them pills, pills, pills,'' says Smith. "I said, 'Brenda, what are all these pills?' and she said, 'Oh, that's for this, and this is for that.' Then she said, 'These are marvelous that George Atwell gave me. He told me if I took them I'd feel marvelous, and I do. They're absolutely marvelous. Do you want one?' Of course, I didn't even know what they were. [But] Brenda started taking pills to go to sleep and pills to wake up, pills for digestion and pills to go to the bathroom, and pills to be happy and pills to be sad, and pills to be.''

Through all this, Ship was still in the hospital in Kentucky. When he recovered, Jock Whitney sent his private plane to pick him up in Lexington and fly him home. Brenda met the plane in New York. "On the way in we had a talk,'' Ship recalls. "She said, 'Ship, my friends tell me I'm losing my personality living out on a farm.' '' He wanted to stay together, and he wanted to continue living at Meadowood. He like hanging around the stables, and he liked living near the Meadowbrook golf course, where he spent a lot of time. But Brenda had already made up her mind to leave Ship.

She bought a seventeen-room duplex apartment at 563 Park Avenue. She went to nightclubs every night and "got back into that whole life she lived as a debutante,'' says Ship. She continued seeing George Atwell and also dated a handsome Englishman named Francis Williams.

Ship stayed at Meadowood until Brenda moved all the furniture out of the house and into her apartment. Then he moved into the groom's quarters at the stables. When Brenda finally sold Meadowood, Ship went to Nassau. He met a beautiful Russian girl with whom he began an affair. "I was so broken up,'' says Ship. "I wanted to get Brenda out of my mind.''

And that was the end of their marriage.

It might have been less sad had it ended in some terrible fight. Despite their problems, Brenda and Ship still seemed very much in love. Their friends were shocked by the breakup and expected them to get back together. Thirty years later they are still debating its cause.

Lucienne Piro: "When Brenda was first married to Ship, she seemed happy. Ship was a very good husband. That social life of theirs ruined everything."

Count Vasilli Adlerberg: "When Brenda married Kelly, it was a little astonishing. I don't know what she saw in him. She was interested in society, in life, in museums, galleries. But he was never that sort of international man. Mentally, she was very much above Kelly. I think she began to realize that he didn't fit into the picture at all. He ruined the [glamorous] image everyone had of her and her life. [Some people] would say, 'Oh, he's a bore, let's not invite them.'

"She saw what Ship is and then she tried to change him, which is impossible. She thought she could make him popular or agreeable. She tried and then saw that nothing could be done. People avoided him. He never laughed; he was gloomy. And then he'd be envious if he saw that you talked to her. Brenda liked to be flattered. She liked to have men around her, and he didn't like that. Even if you're jealous, you don't show it. Poor man, he couldn't understand her attitude."

Frances Griffin: "Brenda told me that Ship embarrassed her. He wasn't of her class. He was gruff, and he would sometimes come out with these [vulgar] remarks."

Betty Blake: "I didn't think Ship was quite good enough for her. He sort of came out of nowhere, you know. He didn't have any background or family. I think she should have married somebody with maybe a little more sensitivity. But I think he did love her, and I think she did love him. It was a strange sort of marriage. He was an adventurer, and he was older than she. She should have married some college boy, somebody we all knew."

Victoria Kelly: "I don't think she ever cared for anybody as much as she cared for Daddy. When he got sick, she should have stayed with him, but she didn't. She went to New York, and these social people got her under their spell, and that was the beginning of the end. She was very insecure, and suddenly she was on her own surrounded by people who were telling her what to do and how to do it, and it just got worse and worse.''

Writing in *Life* years later, Brenda herself assessed her relationship to Ship with perhaps undue harshness: ''I have never known the true meaning of love. A girl with my kind of upbringing cannot possible understand such an emotion. She is too immature; she has never been allowed or aided to grow up and know what real love means. I thought at the time that I loved everyone—all my beaux, all my relatives, everyone I met. But I loved them only because I wanted them to love me, because the faintest sign of rejection by another person, even a nightclub doorman whom I might never see again, brought back all my old childhood feelings of being unwanted and depressed. I was indeed terribly fond [of Ship. But] I never loved anyone as a person—as a human being, with virtues and faults and a personality I had deliberately and maturely selected as desirable.''

For whatever reason, Brenda shed Ship—though not entirely. While they separated in 1951, they didn't officially get divorced until 1956—a measure of Brenda's ambivalence about the breakup. Nonetheless, she was determined to recapture her glamour. All that Brenda had to sustain her was the memory of her reign as Glamour Girl No. 1. Her image was inseparable from her identity. Fame had projected Brenda completely outside herself. The press taught her who she was, and she desperately wanted to believe her clippings.

But the cost of clinging to her glamour turned out to be very high. She sacrificed her family. Years later, when she was close to dying, she told one of her nurses that the happiest time of her life had been when she was married to Ship, after Victoria had been born. The trouble was, Brenda said, she had not realized it at the time.

PART FIVE

SHADOW

CHAPTER TWELVE

THE WOMAN WHO walked out of the marriage with Ship Kelly was a far different person from the one who had walked into it. Nine years had passed. Brenda was only thirty when she moved back to New York, but her life had changed dramatically, at least on the surface. For the first time she was on her own, living in relative obscurity. Photographers and reporters no longer pursued her. She had lost her mother, who had dominated the first half of her life. She was also losing her looks. The bloom of her early twenties had given way to forehead lines, deep creases on the sides of her mouth, puffy eyes, and a slight slackening of the jawline. But what she had lost in prettiness she had gained in character. It was an interesting face, a face that betrayed the difficulty of her life.

For one thing, she was deeply in debt. Brenda told Donald Chase, one of her secretaries, that she and Ship never paid their bills regularly. Once, she said, Ship gathered together their mountain of unpaid bills, opened the basement door, and pushed the pile down the stairs. Whatever bill landed on the top was the one he paid first.

"I'm not sure of the exact figure, but my mother was in debt hundred of thousands of dollars," says Victoria. "When she and Daddy were together, she bought an incredible amount of clothes, even with her income and life-style. She also spent . . . on travel, the house, servants, and me. She spent more on me when I was little than when I grew up.

"It's a good thing that third-generation trusts are illegal because [trusts] really cause ill will. Everyone resents everyone else. My mother resented terribly the fact that she couldn't have it outright. She resented me because I was going to have it outright, and she used to say, 'You won't have my worries. You'll have the whole thing.'"

Jerome Doyle convinced her to hire a professional financial manager, who put her on a strict budget and monitored her expenses for the rest of her life. "She was spending more than her income," says the financial manager. "She didn't know what her income was. It took many, many years to get a budget going. We had to liquidate some of her net worth. She borrowed money from friends. She borrowed money from banks." Brenda got in trouble only once after that, in the early sixties, when the stock market dipped. She tried, unsuccessfully, to get the Frazier trusts broken, so "she had to borrow money and she had to sell a couple of [diamond] clips," says Victoria Kelly. "That was the only close time we ever had. But we never starved. We were never destitute. In fact, we never changed our way of living."

Money wasn't Brenda's only problem. After she and Ship separated, she began having chronic bouts of depression, partly due to the breakup of the marriage. "Things really started to go downhill after she and Daddy broke up," says Victoria. "He kept her in control and away from bad influences [like drugs]." Partly the depression was due to the loss of another great influence on her life. On December 6, 1950, around the time the Kellys' marriage was collapsing, Lady Jane died in Nassau at age eighty-two. Brenda had resented her grandmother and her domineering ways, but she had also depended on her, just as she had depended on her mother. Without Lady Jane and Big Brenda to help her steer a steady course through a socialite's life of parties, entertaining, and decorating, Brenda started slipping into her own troubled world.

She began to spend more and more time in bed, sometimes not getting up until three in the afternoon. Even when friends arrived to take her to lunch, she'd nestle in her satin sheets until the last moment. "I would arrive and Brenda would still be in bed with her makeup on," recalled one friend, Anne Slater. "There would be books piled on the bed, and her clothes were laid out. There were maids in and out. After we'd have half a drink, I'd say, 'Darling, don't you think we should go to lunch?' Then she would get out of bed and put her clothes on. We'd go to the Polo Lounge at the Westbury Hotel. She'd have a chicken sandwich, which she wouldn't eat, and a couple of daiquiris.''

On some days she never got out of bed at all. If she had appointments, she would cancel them, usually giving a very flimsy excuse. "Brenda would call me [in the morning] and invite herself to tea," recalls Diana Vreeland, who was her neighbor. "Later, I'd get a message from her secretary: 'Miss Frazier has found that her Fabergé picture frames aren't quite clean. She's going to stay home to polish them.' ''

If she needed an accessory—a handbag, or a belt, for example, to go with an outfit that she was planning to wear that evening—she'd send her chauffeur, Gerald Kelly, to the store. "I did a lot of shopping for her. I used to buy handbags for her on approval at Tiffany's, and I used to buy belts for her," says Kelly. "I'd put them around my head. And if they fit around my head, they'd fit around Brenda's waist."

Brenda's eating problem became more pronounced. "She ate strange foods," say Constantin Alajalov, a friend of Brenda's and an artist known for his *New Yorkers* covers. "For dinner she'd have only oysters and clams. Then she'd go home and eat out the icebox—pickles, junk food, but nothing wholesome." In her teens, Brenda had only occasionally forced herself to vomit, as an emergency measure to keep her weight down. But later, in her twenties, she got caught in a vicious circle of binging and purging, followed by periods of starvation, or anorexia nervosa.

Today both the binging and purging—so-called bulimia— and starvation—anorexia nervosa—are familiar female maladies. The diseases often start as a diet that gets out of control. After weeks of starving themselves, anorexics will often give in to the urge to eat, triggering a binge. With that, their worst fear, overeating, has been realized, and they force themselves to throw up. In Brenda's case, the disease was triggered by pressure from her mother and grandmother to shed her puppy fat and become a glamour girl. Although she had periods of anorexia beginning in her teens, Brenda's main problem in her early life was bulimia. By her late thirties, however, she had begun to starve herself regularly, and photographs of her show a woman who looks as if she has just been released from a concentration camp.

When Brenda first became ill, many doctors did not even recognize anorexia as a serious medical disorder and were unsympathetic to their anorexic patients. Nor did parents commonly realize the true nature of the situation. There is no mention of Brenda's problem in her mother's diary for the years 1934–38. It is likely that Big Brenda was not aware of it or, if she was, did not understand its seriousness. Brenda herself apparently did not realize how common her problem was: in a rare moment when she acknowledged suffering from the disease, she told a servant, "I invented it."

In the last decade or so, bulimia and anorexia nervosa have been carefully studied, and doctors are starting to recognize some of the underlying emotional causes of these related illnesses. For their victims, weight loss is only superficially the goal; the real effort is to gain control over their lives. The disease enables the anorexic to prove that she "can do something nobody else can, and that she is, therefore, not ordinary, not average," in the words of Dr. Hilde Bruch, professor of psychiatry at Baylor College of Medicine and one of the country's leading authorities on anorexia.

The severe loss of weight also satisfies the anorexic's need to return to childhood. With the weight loss, her menstrual flow stops, her breasts shrink, and her other feminine curves disappear. She returns to an easier, safer, preadolescent time.

In the first years after the breakup of her marriage, Brenda's friends became terribly worried about her. She was always in bed. She had surrounded herself with servants whom she paid to ignore her drinking and drug-taking. Her bizarre eating habits were becoming more apparent. Doris Lilly, author of *How to Marry a Millionaire*, remembers seeing Brenda at a dinner at the St. Regis Hotel in the fifties. "I was writing a column for the New York *Post* then. All my life I'd heard of Brenda Frazier, and here she was. She was drinking pink ladies, and pushing the food around her plate. She'd put food on a fork, then raise it to her mouth. But she never put the food in her mouth. She was just giving the impression that she was eating it."

Brenda's relationship with her daughter was deteriorating.

They rarely spent time together. Every afternoon when the child got home from school, she would go immediately to her room, take a bath, and put on a bathrobe. Thus scrubbed and combed, she would be brought in to her mother's bedroom to say hello. Victoria spent most weekends in those years on Long Island at the home of Jane Will Smith. "Her mother was having all these affairs, and I didn't think it was good for Victoria to be exposed to it," says Smith. "My husband would pick Victoria up on Thursday night in New York and bring her out to Southampton for the weekend. Once, on a Monday morning, my husband said to me, 'I don't know whether I'll be home tonight. I've got this business meeting.' We had an apartment in New York. And then Victoria said, 'Why don't you stay at Mummy's and sleep with Mummy. Everybody does.' "

Probably at the suggestion of her friends, Brenda started visiting a psychiatrist, Dr. Louis Hausman, a professor of neuropsychiatry at New York University School of Medicine. He treated her with drugs and shock therapy. "I never got the statistics on how often Brenda was getting shock therapy," says the psychiatrist who treated her later in life. "But it was practically every time she went [to the doctor's office]. They'd give her one or two or five or six [shocks]. It didn't destroy her brain. She had enough brain left over when I met her. She had remarkable acuity and a very high IQ."

Gerald Kelly says the treatments left Brenda exhausted. "I had to take care of her after she had the shock treatments. She had them in the doctor's office, and I would pick her up afterward. She came out one time, and I took one look at her and said to the doctor, 'What the hell did you do to her?' Her hair was standing on end almost. She looked really drained. She wasn't lucid. I said to her, 'You don't need this stuff, you got everything to live for.' "

Brenda certainly didn't think so. To her, alone in New York in 1951, the present seemed suspended between a faded past and an empty future. She had little to sustain her except the memory of a brief, glorious fame. But the memory did sustain her—at least, she thought it did. She was obsessed by her former celebrity, and finally—after all, Dr. Hausman didn't seem to be doing her any good—she decided to try to recapture it.

The setting for her comeback was the Park Avenue apartment she purchased soon after leaving Ship. In the library she set up her own salon, a place where she would be the star, where she would be sought after and treasured, just as she had been in 1938. Brenda was having an affair with George Atwell, the dashing alcoholic who shared her interest in drugs, but her apartment was often filled with male admirers.

Most afternoons at cocktail time a crowd of men gathered in Brenda's library to chat and sip drinks. At around 6 P.M. Brenda would appear dramatically at the top of the staircase to greet her guests. The room reflected both her love of beautiful things and her inclination toward sentimentality. There were fine pieces of English furniture, a flowered chintz sofa, and oil paintings—including one of Brenda over the mantel. Mixed in with this were a ceramic poodle sitting next to the fireplace and a stuffed beaver plopped on the desk. The coffee table supported bowls of nuts, chocolates, and Sherman cigarettes. A butler carried drinks on a silver platter. A maid answered the constantly ringing phone.

The gatherings became known as Baker's Street, after Sherlock Holmes's Baker Street Irregulars. The men in Brenda's salon were a diverse group. There was Constantin Alajalov, Vasilli Adlerberg, Jerome Doyle, George Atwell, David Selznick, Jr., and Patrick O'Higgins, who later wrote a biography of his employer, Helena Rubinstein. Brenda kept a guest book—a green leather album in which her admirers wrote poems and pasted in photographs, newspaper clippings, telegrams, calling cards, cartoons, and letters. The focal points of the book are Alajalov's lively, imaginative drawings depicting Brenda as an exquisite mouse surrounded by dozens of faceless swains bearing gifts of flowers and jewelry.

Men flocked to her, attracted more by the myth of Brenda Frazier than by the woman herself. "I think so many men were interested in her because she was a celebrity, and they hoped some of it would rub off on them," says Alajalov. "There was nothing particularly impressive about her. She was just another attractive woman who was startling-looking because of her white skin and black eyes and black hair. I wouldn't have called her beautiful. But Brenda's personality was very attractive—she was charming. She seemed to be very well read without having read anything. She was very good-natured; she had a big heart; she liked to giggle.''

One of the men who became obsessed with both the myth and the woman was Count Vasilli Adlerberg. When Brenda first met him, he was doing publicity for the Sherry Netherland Hotel. Later he became a jewelry broker for Harry Winston, one of New York's largest jewelers. ''Vava,'' as he was called, was tall and lanky, with a receding hairline and a bushy mustache. He dressed in beautiful clothes, smoked a pipe, and had a dignified fastidious manner.

Vava came from the Swedish branch of an aristocratic Russian family and had been a captain in the Czar's fusiliers. While fighting on the Russian front in 1914, he had been shot in the stomach, and afterward was transferred to Paris, where he lived during the Bolshevik Revolution. Later he went to Manhattan, where he found work greeting guests in a hotel.

One of Vava's closest friends in New York was Serge Obolensky, a Russian prince who became a Manhattan hotel executive and an international socialite. Serge's family had been aides to the Czars for many centuries and claimed direct descent from Rurik, the Viking sea lord who reputedly founded Russia in 862. As a bright young prince growing up in a baroque villa outside St. Petersburg, Serge hunted wild boar, rode horses through deep forests, and went sledding on mammoth ice hills.

Serge joined the cavalry of the Imperial Guards and, after war broke out, was wounded on the front in 1915. When he woke up in a hospital in Yalta, a beautiful nurse was standing over him. She was Catherine Bariatinska, daughter of Czar Alexander II. Although Catherine was much older than Serge, they fell in love and were married. Serge subsequently studied agriculture for two years at the University of St. Petersburg, but his future as a gentleman farmer was shattered by the Bolshevik Revolution of 1917. Suddenly his picture, with the words ''Wanted Dead or Alive'' blazoned across it, was looking down from posters tacked on meeting hall walls, and he fled the country in disguise.

The Obolenskys lived first in Paris, then London, where they were divorced in June 1924. The next month Serge married Alice Astor, daughter of financier Jacob Astor, and several years later the couple moved to New York. Serge worked in the foreign department of Chase Securities Corporation and became a flamboyant social figure, dressing for dinner in a tunic and cloth boots, a shiny sword strapped to his waist. "He was terrifically charming, very much the courtier," says Diana Vreeland.

He was also very much the soldier. When World War II broke out, Serge, at fifty-one, joined the U.S. Army. He rose from private to colonel and won both the Bronze Star and the Croix de Guerre for his daring jumps behind enemy lines.

After the war he went to work as head of public relations for the Plaza. His job was to polish the hotel's image, and his technique was simple: He persuaded his rich, elegant friends to frequent the hotel, and he threw parties that attracted other rich, elegant people.

In a way, Serge was Vava's sponsor. Vava's flawless manners fit in well with the formal atmosphere at the Plaza, and Serge hired him as his assistant. When Serge moved to the St. Regis, and subsequently the Sherry Netherland and the Ambassador, he took Vava with him.

But at times it seemed that their chief occupation was going to nightclubs and parties. "I take it for granted that a primary objective in the lives of men is to have a good time," Serge once told a reporter.

Along with Alajalov, Vava and Obolensky spent most summers at the Southampton estate of Angier Biddle Duke, great-grandson of Washington Duke, founder of the tobacco empire. Duke had given his old garage and barn to the Russian bachelors (Serge had been divorced from Alice in 1932), who turned them into apartments. During the day the men hosted luncheons and beach parties. At night they sat in at the Dukes' formal dinner parties, joining distinguished guests such as Jimmy Stewart, Cary Grant, and Henry Ford II.

There was something slightly mysterious about Vava. He lived alone in a small Fifth Avenue apartment and was very secretive about his past. In New York he did not seem interested in any woman except Brenda, who was twenty-five years his junior. Every afternoon he showed up at her apartment, where he sat quietly in a chair, "jealously watching his rivals," says Alajalov.

One of those rivals was Patrick O'Higgins. He was tall and red-haired, with a blotchy complexion and a penchant for tweed jackets and hunting caps. O'Higgins had grown up in Ireland, and served as a captain in the Irish Guards during World War II. After the war he moved to New York. He was working as a travel editor for the feature magazine *Flair* when he met Helena Rubinstein at a cocktail party in 1950. Soon afterward he went to work for her. His salary was $7,000 a year, and at first his job consisted principally of sitting in her office and rising only to open and close the door. As the years passed, he became her secretary, nurse, bodyguard, and social director. His biography of Rubinstein, published in 1971, six years after her death, portrays "Madame" as a monster who ruled her cosmetics empire with nepotism and terror.

O'Higgins escorted Brenda to parties and promised one day to cowrite her memoirs. But he could not compete with Vava. The Russian bought Brenda expensive jewelry and sent her a bouquet of violets every day. "I used to run into him all the time, walking solemnly toward Brenda's apartment carrying great bunches of flowers," recalls Diana Vreeland. "I'd say, 'Vava, darling, you're in love! you're in love!' " Vava had been raised in the traditions of the Russian grand dukes, who often imported flowers from France for their sweethearts. He thought "this was how one should behave," adds Alajalov.

It never occurred to Brenda that a workingman couldn't afford such extravagances; she had no sense of the value of money, and anyway, she was thrilled by presents—like her scrapbooks of newspaper clippings, they confirmed her worth. "Brenda was very susceptible to presents," says Alajalov. "The physical size and the cost impressed her too."

During this time her collection of gold and jewelry began to grow dramatically. Eventually she would own fifty-seven gold cigarette cases, thirty-six gold picture frames, gold toothbrushes and toothpicks, a gold manicure bowl, gold swizzle sticks, and gold clocks, most of which arrived as presents. She had a charm bracelet with tiny handmade Fabergé eggs, some encrusted with diamonds and sapphires, and priceless black-and-white pearl drop earrings that had once been owned by the Rothschild family in Paris.

All of Brenda's bedroom and bathroom accessories were gold. "Every single one of her handbags had solid gold handbag chains," says Victoria, and even "her evening bags had a few jewels in them, like sapphires. People have joked that the Queen of England probably didn't have jewels like my mother's. Very few people in the world have what she had. [Maybe] Madame [de] Pompadour.''

The jewelry gave her a sense of power and worth that she got from few other things in life. When she died, Brenda left five hundred pieces of jewelry stored in a safe five and a half feet tall with separate drawers for diamonds, sapphires, rubies, emeralds, and pearls. ''She loved her jewelry, and she really looked after it,'' says Victoria. ''She didn't just toss it in the drawer. And even if she left it out overnight, it would be left out on top of a piece of velvet with a piece of velvet on top of that.''

Gerald Kelly started carrying a gun to protect the walking gem display that was his employer. Maintaining Brenda's jewelry was one of his most important responsibilities. ''Sometimes she'd want her pearls restrung,'' says Kelly. ''She'd take them off in the middle of the street and say, 'Gerald, take these downtown and have them restrung.' When I took them to the jeweler, I'd have to count each one, and I'd get a receipt for it; and when I picked them up, I'd have to count each one. And that [diamond ring]. She'd tap it and say, 'I think that's loose.' Then, she'd take it off, give it to me and say, 'Have this fixed.' ''

Her favorite necklaces were the ''stop-and-go pearls''—two strands of grape-sized pearls, one with a huge ruby clasp, the other with a huge emerald clasp. Each strand of pearls cost about $50,000 in 1953, but the clasps were fakes. (Brenda could not have afforded genuine stones that size.)

Brenda tried to find herself in the adoration of her Baker's Street beaux. After drinks and conversation, one or two of them would take her out to dinner and to a nightclub. Brenda would often carry her Maltese terrier under her arm—a gimmick surely designed to attract the photographers who had once trailed her wherever she went. Her celebrity had dimmed. But she was about to meet a man who would thrust her back into the public eye.

CHAPTER THIRTEEN

ONE AFTERNOON in 1951, Brenda got a call from a man she didn't know. In heavily accented English, he told her his name was Pietro Francesco Mele, and he said a mutual friend had suggested they get together. "I hear you are the most glamorous girl in town," said Pietro. "For this I'd like to meet you." Brenda was intrigued—his title of Count may have had something to do with it—and she invited him up for a drink.

Pietro Mele was twenty-eight, short, well built, and darkly handsome, with thinning brown hair. The only son of one of Italy's wealthiest families, he had the easy confidence of a natural nobleman. His father—who died in 1947—had been an Italian senator and had owned a chain of department stores in southern Italy. Pietro's mother, who had been an Italian congresswoman, was from the prominent Matarazzo family, which had made a fortune in textiles, coffee, and real estate in Brazil. In Rome he lived with his mother, Countess Ida Marcello, in a mansion near the Borghese Gardens. The gracious house was filled with polychrome marble floors, Venetian antiques, and neoclassical sculpture, including a large Venus by Antonio Canova.

During the war, Pietro had joined the Italian resistance as a volunteer paratrooper. Afterward he had embarked on a career as a filmmaker and photographer of exotic cultures. He became quite successful. His documentary about Tibet had won an award in the 1949 Venice Film Festival. He went on to film *Pacaya,* a documentary about the Amazon, and documentaries on Afghanistan, Saudi Arabia, and Bhutan for Italian television. Over the years, Pietro's films and photographs have been displayed at museums around the world, including the Museum of Modern Art in New York. But at times the film work seemed only a sideline for Pietro. Although he had studied law, literature, and philosophy at the universities in Rome and Naples and considered himself an intellectual, he had a reputation as a playboy, earned, in large part, because he liked the things playboys liked: fast cars, dangerous sports, and beautiful women.

In Rome, Pietro was known for his violent swings of mood and fist. According to one perhaps apocryphal story, when he entered a nightclub, three waiters were assigned to his table so they could grab him if he started trouble. "Fighting is Pietro's peculiarity. He's fought more people than Joe Louis and Jack Dempsey combined," says Harry Cushing, who knew him in Italy. Pietro was naturally belligerent, especially when fueled by alcohol.

"Today men don't do anymore the military service, men don't do anymore the war. That has been forgotten of what is supposed to be a man," says Pietro, explaining his attitude toward fighting. "Man isn't made for the peace. All those famous peacemakers, they're all killed, no? Why has Kennedy been killed, Martin Luther King, Gandhi? If they loved so much the peace, why have they been killed? This thing of peace is just stupid propaganda. It's false. You can't go against the rule of history. History says that each twenty or thirty years there is a war."

Pietro's fighting ways continued in New York, where, indeed, it fit in rather well at places like El Morocco. Nightclubs, after all, were the children of speakeasies, and brawling was part of the scene. Even the stars did it. One evening a drunken Humphrey Bogart arrived at El Morocco carrying two toy pandas. Refusing to check them at the door, he seated them at his table and ordered drinks for them. When two debutantes tried to play with the bears, Bogart grew infuriated. Then a young man sitting at a nearby table rose to defend the girls. Bogart slugged him and then started flinging plates across the room.

Pietro recalls fighting at El Morocco with Porfirio Rubirosa, the Dominican playboy. "He was dancing with an Italian girlfriend of mine. I was dancing with somebody else. And to show me that he was dancing with my girlfriend, he did like this to me [made a fist] very close to my face. I left the girl there and I said to Rubirosa, 'Would you care to come outside with me?' " They fought and afterward resumed dancing with their dates. From then on, says Pietro, "Rubirosa and I were very good friends."

From the start, Pietro and Brenda were strongly attracted to each other. The first night he went to her apartment, Pietro says, he was immediately drawn by Brenda's "elegance and personality. She was very aesthetic. Probably the least thing I liked about Brenda was [her celebrity]. How could I understand someone who was famous for a coming-out party?"

Brenda liked Pietro because he was different from Ship—he was passionate, he was rich, and he tried to dominate her. "He was very domineering," recalls Jane Will Smith. "Suddenly Brenda was under new management. For her that was the charm. He was a father figure. He'd tell her, 'You can't wear that dress; go change,' or 'I don't want you wearing rubies tonight, wear emeralds.' If she didn't do what he wanted, he'd throw the most awful [tantrums]."

Over the next few years, Brenda and Pietro flitted back and forth between Italy and New York. When he was in Manhattan, Pietro kept a room at a hotel, but he spent most of his time at Brenda's apartment. ("He'd disappear for a few hours, and then he'd come back," says Gerald Kelly.) When she was in Rome, she stayed at his mansion, or at the Grand Hotel. They also traveled to Nassau, Capri, and the Dolomites. They visited Clark Gable in Portofino, and the Duchess of Marlborough in England. At the end of Pietro's four-month expedition to the Amazon in 1952, Brenda met him in Peru for a celebration.

In their travels, they staged a series of noisy public fights that sometimes ended, Brenda's friends insist, in violence. "[Pietro] was a sadistic bully," says her psychiatrist. "He beat the living hell out of her and degraded her, and she went back for more. He was good-looking, he had money, he was aristocratic. That didn't attract her. She met plenty of them. She liked him because he was a bully." Today Pietro denies that he ever hit Brenda, saying, "You should never hit a woman, not even with a flower.'' Their fights resulted from the clash of two stubborn tempers. Brenda was very difficult and demanding. She was used to having things her way, and she wanted Pietro to stay with her, as he once said, ''thirty hours a day.'' Yet on many days she didn't want to get out of bed.

Pietro was infuriated by Brenda's inertia. He was also wildly jealous. ''My mother was always surrounded by tons of people,'' says Victoria. ''I think she was excited by Pietro, but she had some safe friends she didn't want to lose either.'' Victoria remembers helping her mother burn telegrams from Brenda's admirers so that Pietro wouldn't find them. Once, in a restaurant in Rome, when movie actor Bruce Cabot greeted Brenda by kissing her on the cheek, Pietro picked up a cream pie and hurled it in Cabot's face. ''It was too much of a kiss,'' Pietro explains. Victoria, who sometimes traveled with her mother and Pietro, recalls the lengths he'd go to to control their lives. ''It was unbelievable,'' she says. ''He would cancel our plane reservations so we couldn't leave Rome. Once in Positano he was going to throw my mother out of a window. It wasn't a very high window, and at the time it didn't really bother me, because this kind of thing was an everyday occurrence.'' Another time, in Rome, on the day Brenda and Victoria were scheduled to fly back to New York, Pietro hid Victoria so she and Brenda would miss their plane. ''He took me to the zoo,'' recalls Victoria. ''He said, 'Do you want to go out?' Of course I wanted to go. I remember he called my mother from the zoo. He kept me out long enough so we couldn't make our plane back to New York.''

Brenda loved his extravagance. He gave her lovely jewelry, including a necklace of carved emeralds and a huge pin in the shape of a bouquet of violets, with amethyst petals, diamond centers, and emerald leaves. The day after one fight he returned with a peace offering from Tiffany's: a pair of diamond earrings. When Brenda refused to accept the jewels, Pietro threw them out the window. Presumably, a passer-by walked off with them, because they were never recovered. Another night, in Italy, ''Pietro took all his brand-new camera equipment and threw it out the window at four o'clock in the morning,'' recalls Victoria Kelly. ''It made a terrible crash. My mother would lock us into our hotel room to get away from him. But that wouldn't stop Pietro. He'd climb onto the balcony in the next apartment and get in through our kitchen window. Then they'd have another argument."

Both Brenda and Pietro were drinking a great deal at this time, and drinking no doubt accounts for some of their unhappiest moments. Brenda had moved beyond champagne and was concentrating on vodka; she was also drinking more often. Indeed, she could not function without liquor, which was beginning to dominate her life.

One evening Brenda and Pietro went to a restaurant in Rome with several friends, including Harry Cushing, his father, Harry Sr., and Vava Adlerberg. Adlerberg, then in his fifties, was determined to win Brenda away from Pietro and had taken a leave of absence from his job to follow her to Italy.

"That night Pietro was really awful," recalls Cushing. "He was insulting Brenda all through dinner. Snide remarks. Whatever she said, he'd disagree with. I knew Brenda liked this. It was part of her pattern. She was just sitting there smiling. Then Vava said, 'If I were twenty years younger, I wouldn't allow this lady to be insulted'—meaning that *I* should do it. Finally Vava said, 'I'm going to have to do something!' And rather than have him do it, I decided I might as well because Pietro would have knocked out Vava. So there Pietro and I were, fighting on the floor, while this little orchestra in the corner was playing dinner music. Finally I pushed Pietro through the bass drum. My father was laughing hysterically, but I was hoping someone would grab Pietro, because he's like a bull and he would have killed me. The waiters pulled us apart. I thought we'd get thrown out, but they knew Pietro well, and we simply went back to the table and continued eating dinner to the music of this little orchestra playing without a drum."

During 1952 and 1953 Brenda spent several months in Italy, accompanied by Victoria, the governess, Eva Moorcock, and Gerald Kelly. In photographs of her travels that year, she looks happy and healthy—even slightly plump—swimming in a pool near Rome, dining al fresco in Positano, sightseeing in Venice. "With me she was very happy," insists Pietro. "With me she skiied. With me she swimmed, with me she went sailing by boat. With me she ate a lot of spaghetti."

Pietro says he tried to get Brenda to stop drinking and start a career. He taught her how to type, and she practiced in messages to him: "Amore mio, You can see that I can type if necessary so I am a little nervous in case you might decide to get me to type for you—I would need a year to practice so don't attempt it for the moment and do your own!"

Victoria was also fond of "Uncle Pietro." "He was a very kind, sweet person, probably one of the kindest, but just very messed up," she says. He gave her extravagant presents: live rabbits at Easter; an electric car that traveled twelve miles an hour; a motorboat with *Victoria, N.Y.* blazoned across the bow; and a huge stuffed giraffe.

That summer Brenda drew a picture of herself with Pietro and Victoria riding in a car with a picnic basket in the back seat, and a highway lined with trees stretching out before them. Underneath she wrote: "The Ready-Made Family."

"I think that was enough for her," says Pietro, explaining why he and Brenda never married. They also had a complication with the Church. After Cardinal Spellman read about their affair in the tabloids, he called Brenda and told her that Pietro, as a Roman Catholic, couldn't marry her because she had been previously married.

"I don't know if Brenda wanted to marry me," says Pietro. "I don't know if I wanted to marry her. I don't know. It's a strange thing, this question of marriage. You never really marry the person you love. There's a difference between the love of marriage and the love out of marriage."

At one point though, marriage was at least being considered. Pietro's mother came to New York and visited Lucienne Piro, one of Brenda's closest friends. "She wanted Pietro to marry Brenda," recalls Piro, "but she said, 'Brenda has to be cured first because she's mentally confused.'" Pietro's mother thought Brenda should go to an asylum to get rid of her problems, probably her drinking and her anorexia, and she wanted Piro to help her get Brenda committed. Piro refused.

During the summer of 1953 in Italy, the fighting between Brenda and Pietro grew so violent that Brenda decided to return to New York. After fleeing Positano in the middle of the night, Brenda, Eva Moorcock, Victoria, and Gerald Kelly arrived in Rome at 6 A.M. and started packing. Kelly left on a ship with her Ford station wagon and luggage, and Brenda made plans to fly home with her daughter and the governess a few days later. When Kelly's ship reached Cannes, he received an urgent telegram, seemingly from Brenda, directing him to return to Rome immediately. He called her, explaining, "I can get the luggage off, but I can't get the car off."

"What the hell are you talking about?" demanded Brenda.

"I've got your cable here in front of me to take the car and luggage off in Cannes and come back to Rome," said Kelly.

"I didn't send you any cable," said Brenda.

Pietro had sent it and signed Brenda's name.

A few days later, Brenda returned home. Pietro followed her, and soon they made up and resumed their dangerous pattern of arguing violently and going to nightclubs. On November 10, 1953, Brenda and Pietro's fighting exploded into a tawdry public scandal. In Brenda's apartment that evening, Pietro argued with her about her drinking. In a fit of temper, he grabbed the vodka glass out of her hand and flung it into the fire. The vodka burst into flames. "See what liquor does to your body," he said. Later they had dinner at Le Coq Rouge—a picture of them snapped that night by the house photographer shows an edgy, unsmiling couple—and afterward they toured a few nightclubs in Greenwich Village.

At around two-thirty in the morning Gerald Kelly was waiting outside one of these clubs when Brenda suddenly appeared alone on the sidewalk and jumped into her limousine. "Let's go," she demanded. As Kelly sped home, he noticed in the rearview mirror that a taxi was following. When they arrived at 563 Park Avenue, Pietro bounded up to the limo. Brenda and Pietro started screaming at each other. Pietro later said that they were arguing about Latins versus Americans, and that he was defending the Latins. Gerald Kelly testified in court that they were arguing about whether Pietro would go up to Brenda's apartment for a nightcap, and that Pietro, shaking his fist at Brenda, had shouted, "If I don't go up, you don't go up."

Somebody, perhaps a neighbor awakened by the noise, called the police. When they arrived, Pietro bolted into Brenda's building, took the elevator up to her apartment, and ran into her bedroom. Brenda went up and talked to him privately while three policemen waited in the hall.

Suddenly Pietro ran out of Brenda's bedroom and into an adjoining room and tried to slam the door shut. One of the policemen wedged his foot in the door and managed to get inside the room. He tried to grab Pietro, but "he was slippery as an eel," Patrolman William Murray later recalled. Finally Pietro was caught. But as two officers led him out of the apartment, down the elevator, and into the street, the officers fought with their captive. The police claimed that Pietro kicked one patrolman, Duncan Christie, in the groin. A newspaper photographer waiting outside snapped Pietro in the middle of the fight. In the picture, which appeared in the tabloids the next day, Pietro's eyes are almost shut, his nose is smashed, his custom-made striped gray flannel suit is awash with blood.

One of the policemen admitted that he hit Pietro once with a blackjack to subdue him. But the cops insisted that most of Pietro's injuries occurred when they were trying to put him into the police car. He "placed his feet up against [the car] in an attempt to resist. His leg gave way, and his face struck the side of the car," Christie later testified.

But an Italian journalist, recounting Pietro's side of the story, wrote that "the cops went after him and started to beat him up before he even attempted to defend himself." At first, said Pietro, he tried to run away, then he swung and kicked in self-defense. Pietro also said that the policemen continued to beat him while he was handcuffed.

The police couldn't get Pietro into their squad car, so they pushed him into Brenda's limousine and sped off to the East Fifty-first Street station, where Pietro was booked for felonious assault against a police officer. At the station house Pietro was calm, even jovial. He told officers that he was an Italian newspaper photographer, a dirt auto racer, and a director of several Italian movies. He said that he was scheduled to drive for Ferrari in the Pan-American road races in Mexico the following month. (He had had Brenda's double-B monogram engraved on the doors of his black car.) He denied kicking any cops. "I wouldn't do a thing like that," he said.

During an impromptu press conference later, reporters asked Pietro how long he had known Brenda.

"You ask Brenda. I'm only a newspaper photographer."

"Are you the Pietro Mele who has been linked romantically with Brenda?"

"No. You've been looking up the clips."

"Are you the Pietro Mele who directed two film documentaries, one of which, on Tibet, won a prize at the 1949 Film Festival?"

"No, I am not. But I know him."

Pietro was held in the city jail until one-thirty the next afternoon, when four men from the Italian consulate paid his $1,000 bail. On his release he went straight to the hospital, where he was examined by William Gaynor, the doctor who had operated on Ship. Dr. Gaynor found Pietro to be in a "dazed condition" and badly banged up, with abrasions on the skull, a broken nose, and an enormously swollen forearm. "Mr. Mele has been placed on bed rest for further observation," the doctor reported.

Pietro was in the hospital for a month, and the trial was delayed several more months to give him time to recuperate fully. "Who turned on the switch when Mele's head was in the meat chopper?" asked the judge who delayed the trial after reading Dr. Gaynor's report.

For a decade Brenda had been a cameo player for the tabloids, but the arrest changed that. The No. 1 Glamour Girl and her "No. 1 Boudoir Brawler" were headline news. Quick-thinking reporters had a fine time called Pietro a "Roman Ruin," and the "Human Vesuvius," and describing his nose as a "Roman wreck." The New York *Post* referred to him as "an Italian globe-trotter who when in New York did as the Romans do."

Pietro's plight became a kind of cause célèbre for the Italian-American community. Across the country, men and women named Mele sent him letters, presents, and bottles of whiskey. One wanted to form a Mele Club. As for Brenda, "the accident," as Pietro calls it, did not deter her ardor. She visited him in the hospital, once sneaking into his room in the middle of the night to bring him some vanilla ice cream. She called Igor Cassini, who had taken over the Cholly Knickerbocker column after Maury Paul's death, and asked him to "be kind to Pietro" in his column. She told other reporters who called that she would be glad to date Pietro again. "He's a poor, unfortunate, hotheaded boy," she said.

Brenda did complain bitterly about Pietro to her friends, and insisted that the arrest had greatly embarrassed her. Still, she could not bring herself to break up with him. She was genuinely fond of Pietro, and besides, as Esme Hammond says, "Brenda could never let any man out of her life."

One evening, after Pietro was released from the hospital, he called and begged Brenda to meet him for a drink. Brenda called Jerome Doyle, who was acting as her lawyer, and asked his advice. "He's desperate to see me," Brenda said. Doyle told her not to go, but she went anyway. Late in the evening she met Pietro in the bar of the Essex House on Central Park South. Pietro urged her to have the case against him dropped. When Brenda explained that it was out of her hands, Pietro became angry. According to newspaper accounts, he slugged Brenda under the left eye with such force that her chair tipped backward and landed on the floor. Crying, she stumbled out of a side door, where Gerald Kelly, who had been alerted by the hotel staff, was waiting. Later, Pietro denied hitting Brenda.

Around this time Brenda returned about $300,000 worth of jewelry Pietro had given her. The reason she did is a matter of some dispute. Doyle says Bulgari of Rome contacted Brenda and claimed that Pietro had charged the jewels to his mother, who now refused to pay for them. The store threatened to sue unless she gave the jewelry back. Brenda considered going to court, Doyle says, but he persuaded her to return everything. She opened her jewelry safe, weeded out all of Pietro's presents, and dropped them into an open suitcase held by a maid. Brenda was particularly upset about losing the violet pin, so the faithful Vava had it re-created by Harry Winston.

Pietro today says that Brenda simply returned the jewelry because their relationship was over. He insists that the jewels are now in a bank vault in Rome and he is saving them for Victoria.

This incident seems to have marked the turning point in Brenda's relationship with Pietro. A few days later a reporter for the *Daily News* found Pietro eating lunch alone in Theodore's Restaurant. "Crocodiles have more charm than most of the women I've met," snarled Pietro, adding that his romance with Brenda was finally over. "In the three years I knew her we only saw one movie and one play. I like fresh air and outdoor sports.''

He had already found someone else to share those interests. Her name was Madina Arrivabene, an Italian beauty with gold hair and a beautiful figure. She had been twice married, each time to an Italian count. In an age when most society women took their identities from their husbands, Madina was fiercely independent. She had kept her maiden name and had a thriving career as an artist.

Although the tabloids assumed that Madina and Pietro were having an affair (one newspaper later reported that they were secretly married), it is possible that Madina, who was a friend of Pietro's mother and still lives near the Mele family in Rome, had come to New York simply to keep an eye on Pietro. The two of them also may have had other things in mind.

In January the Manhattan district attorney's office heard a rumor that Pietro had sneaked out of the country. Two detectives went to his hotel; Pietro had indeed checked out and sent a truck to the airport. After checking all the plane reservations, the detectives decided that the trunk was a decoy. They looked next at the passenger lists of all the ocean liners leaving that day. Sure enough, Pietro was booked on the *Constitution*, which had already sailed for Italy.

Two assistant district attorneys went to court and got a judge to revoke Pietro's bail and sign a warrant for his arrest on assault charges. Then the prosecutors led two detectives, eight policemen, and a *Daily News* reporter aboard a small police launch and chased the *Constitution* down the Hudson River. They caught up with the ship near Swinburne Island, just three miles short of their limit of their jurisdiction. Climbing up a dangling rope ladder, the men boarded the ship and searched for Pietro. They found him lunching in the main dining room with a beautiful blonde wearing a patch over one eye. She was Madina Arrivabene.

A few minutes later, preceded by ten suitcases and followed by eight policemen, Pietro climbed down the rope ladder into the boat. Hundreds of puzzled passengers looked on from behind the steel rails. Madina begged the police to let her go with Pietro. When they refused, she grew furious. As the boat sped away, she could be seen running up and down the decks, wildly waving her arms and shouting in Italian.

Back in court in Manhattan, Pietro insisted that he had intended to return to New York for his March trial. He said that he was just planning a short trip to Italy to take his law examinations at the University of Rome, to wrap up a contract for a documentary film about Japan, and to visit his mother. The judge was not impressed. He impounded Pietro's passport and raised his bail to $2,500.

As the date of Pietro's trial approached, Brenda, who had fled to Florida to escape the scandal, grew more agitated. One day she called Doyle at his office in New York. Doyle was usually pleased when Brenda called. "I loved her voice," he says. "It was almost as deep as a man's, very sexy." But this time she was asking the impossible. She wanted him to get her excused from a subpoena to testify at the trial.

"Brenda, you're an American citizen. You can't avoid testifying," Doyle told her.

"Well, I'll go to Cuba and they won't be able to get me," Brenda threatened.

"I'll do what I can to help you. But you've got to come back to New York," Doyle said.

Doyle went to Brenda's psychiatrist, Dr. Hausman. The psychiatrist told Doyle he would not testify in court, but he signed an affidavit saying that Brenda had become hysterical when she was subpoenaed and that she would have a nervous breakdown if she were forced to testify. The affidavit disclosed that Brenda had been under Dr. Hausman's care for "underlying depression" for a year, and that she had been progressing satisfactorily until the incident outside her apartment on November 10. The psychiatrist's affidavit was apparently not an exaggeration. Soon afterward, Doyle picked up Brenda at Newark Airport; she was exhausted and overwrought. The next day, twenty-four hours before she was supposed to testify, the psychiatrist called Doyle to confirm what he'd already told him. "Brenda can't go on the witness stand," Dr. Hausman said. "She'll have a total nervous collapse and it might be permanent. It's too much of a risk."

On March 10, the day Pietro's trial was to begin, Brenda's feet were swollen to twice their normal size. She couldn't walk and was confined to bed. "I remember that day very well," says Gerald Kelly. "Her feet looked like sausages ready to bust." As Brenda rested at home under the watchful eye of two nurses, Pietro's case came before a three-judge panel in special sessions court.

He was charged with simple assault, a misdemeanor carrying penalties of a year in jail and a fine of up to $500. The earlier felonious assault charge had been reduced after Pietro's lawyers convinced a judge in a pretrial hearing that Pietro had been drinking on the night of the incident and that the police officers he allegedly assaulted were not injured seriously.

As the trial opened, Pietro, dressed in a blue suit, shifted restlessly in his seat at the defense table. Policemen wearing uniforms and grim expressions packed the front rows. "They weren't going to let this Italian get away with anything," says Doyle. After the opening arguments, Assistant District Attorney Robert Reynolds called his first witness, Brenda Frazier. Doyle rose and handed copies of Dr. Hausman's affidavit to the three judges. "Mrs. Kelly has great respect for this court and members of this court. But her doctor has advised her that she will suffer permanent mental injury if she appears today," he said.

The judges declared a recess and took the prosecutor into a back room for a conference. When they returned, the prosecutor announced that the state would withdraw the subpoena.

Gerald Kelly was the next witness. He testified that he had driven Pietro and Brenda on a tour of nightclubs on the night of November 10 and that they had argued in front of Brenda's apartment.

Then Patrolman Duncan Christie took the stand. He testified that Pietro had kicked him in the groin with his knee, and that he had been in the hospital for seven days.

On the witness stand the following day, Pietro denied that he had kicked Christie.

"You saw him fall to the ground with pain on his face, didn't you?" prosecutor Reynolds asked Pietro.

"I had pain on *my* face," Pietro snapped.

Reynolds called another officer from the East Fifty-first Street Station to try to establish that Pietro had had another quarrel with Brenda at her apartment the year before. These judges, too, were unimpressed. In a split verdict, they granted Pietro's motion for an acquittal.

As the judgment was read, Pietro sat at the defense table, his face scowling, his arms folded imperiously across his chest. Afterward he walked out of the courtroom with his lawyer, pausing briefly to talk to reporters. "I am very happy that the judges treated me fairly, and at the justice extended to me in this country," he said.

The press, however, was not happy with the verdict. In an editorial on March 16, the *World-Telegram* criticized the justices for freeing Pietro:

> At the time the affair Mele was one of the gaudier vagaries of the lorgnette and leisure set. A great to-do was made over the story of the Italian movie director, name of Pietro, bounding around the boudoir of Mrs. Brenda Frazier Kelly in a nocturnal session of hide and seek with the cops. . . .
>
> What about the injured policeman? The man, Duncan Christie, was hospitalized for seven days. For that he had redress coming. Regardless of the merits of the case against Mele, nobody, no matter how wealthy or prominent, has license to haul off and boot a police officer in performance of his duty.

Two days after his acquittal, Pietro raced to West Fiftieth Street at the Hudson River, where the *Queen Mary* was docked. Rain thrashed the giant liner as Pietro, hatless and carrying his suitcases, ran up the gangplank. Reporters who had gathered at the pier watched the ship pull out of the dock and glide down the Hudson, carrying Pietro forever out of Brenda's life.

CHAPTER FOURTEEN

Fᴜᴠᴇ ᴅᴀʏs ᴀꜰᴛᴇʀ Pietro left New York, Brenda was admitted to Doctors Hospital, where, according to newspaper reports, she was treated for a "a severe nervous breakdown" brought on by "the Mele mess."

Gerald Kelly had driven her to the hospital. "She was hysterical. She wouldn't eat, and she wouldn't get out of bed," he says. "She really cared about Pietro." What was more, the publicity about the case was devastating. For years she had relied on the papers to bolster her self-image. Even if, deep down, she didn't really believe what was written, there was still something intoxicating about seeing herself portrayed as beautiful, privileged, important. Pietro's prosecution changed that. The reporters had a new image to play with. Now, when she read about herself in the newspapers, she was as likely to see herself described as a wanton, a has-been, a "hollow-eyed and heartsick" invalid "living on a diet of slimming pills, sleeping pills and pills for exhaustion."

She had to do something—something that would either end her hopeless life or break out of the downward spiral she had fallen into. She decided to kill herself. It is impossible to date Brenda's first suicide attempt, but throughout the fifties and sixties suicide attempts became almost another addiction. Brenda's psychiatrist says she tried thirty-one times, and there may have been other incidents he didn't know of.

Almost everyone who knew Brenda at this time witnessed

one of her attempts or heard her talk about them. "Suicide was taken almost casually, my mother tried it so many times," says Victoria. Sometimes Brenda would slit her wrists with a razor or a piece of broken glass, and eventually she had railroad-track scars running along the insides of her wrists. More often, she took an overdose of pills from the vast assortment she was collecting.

"The glamour girl had had it," wrote Brenda in 1963, explaining why she tried to kill herself. "The debutante everybody was supposed to find so irresistibly fascinating could no longer stand herself. The high-society and café-society life which the rest of the world was supposed to envy was no longer worth living. I was supposed to have everything a young woman could ask for—and all it had brought me was despair."

Of course, no one who really wanted to die would fail as many times as Brenda did. "I'd say she wanted to die 49 percent, and wanted to live 51 percent," the psychiatrist says. "In all of Brenda's suicide attempts I saw this fortuitous advantage of the survival instinct. She always did something, perhaps unconsciously, to ensure that she was saved. She'd know that somebody was going to call her at a certain time and that they'd be astonished if they called and she was unconscious and couldn't come to the phone."

Once when Brenda was in the hospital she hid razor blades in get-well cards, knowing that her lady's maid was watching out of the corner of her eye. Suddenly Brenda jumped out of bed and ran into the bathroom screaming, "I'm going to kill myself and no one is going to stop me." While Brenda was in the bathroom, the lady's maid confiscated the blades.

One signal Brenda used repeatedly was to lock her bedroom door. This was an immediate warning to her servants and friends that she was planning another suicide attempt. During one Easter weekend, with a houseful of guests, Brenda locked her bedroom door. Her friends had to break it down. They found Brenda lying unconscious, her wrists slashed and dripping blood down the sides of the bed. Her two white pekingese, dyed red with blood, whimpered in the sheets.

The scene was lurid, but not fatal. Brenda lived to torment her daughter later that day. As Victoria was on her way out to church, Brenda threatened to slit her wrists again. "Wear my pearls," she told Victoria. "I want you to wear my diamond ring, because I won't be here when you get back." When the frightened child returned from church, Brenda was still alive and making threats. "Everybody took all the glass out of her room," Victoria recalls. "They said, 'We want you to spend the night with her because you're the only one she cares enough about that she won't try anything.' "

Brenda frequently used suicide attempts "to make someone with whom she had just had an argument feel awful," says Victoria. Once, when Ship was visiting, they argued, and he started to walk out the door. "If you leave, I'll kill myself," threatened Brenda. Victoria says that Ship "just got fed up and said 'Okay. Why don't you just open the window and jump. Good-bye, I'm leaving.' But all the way down in the elevator he was worried.

"I'm guessing, but I'd say my mother didn't care one way or the other if she lived or died," Victoria adds. "She was depressed. If she died, fine; if she came to, she came to."

Though Brenda's suicide attempts eventually tapered off, her intake of drugs never abated. Starting in the mid-fifties, she began keeping an enormous assortment of pills around her house. Her bedside table was a virtual drugstore filled with tranquilizers, pain-killers, diuretics, uppers, and downers. She had Dexadrine, Percodan, Ritalin, codeine, Librium, Seconal, chloral hydrate. If Brenda was traveling, she would carry her pills in a special red leather case from Mark Cross of London with a dozen plastic vials inside. "Sometimes she asked [the servants] to get the pills for her. But usually she'd fumble around for them herself. She'd know that she needed ten milligrams of this or that," says her friend Dick Gott.

No one knows for certain where Brenda got her drugs. Her friends speculated that she was bribing pharmacists; her servants accused one another of supplying her. "Different people [who worked for her] would know a doctor. They'd be able to get her a few [pills] here, a few there. I don't think any [one person] supplied her with a great number of pills," says Victoria Kelly. Brenda may have got some drugs illegally, but most of her pills were prescribed by doctors to treat real illness and pain caused by a panoply of ailments—edema, liver disease, insomnia, anorexia, depression, nausea, exhaustion, itching, tooth decay, and nervous tension. "She had symptoms over every part of her body," says her psychiatrist. "I think there was hardly a day that she was pill-free."

She had a copy of the *Physician's Desk Reference*, which she studied carefully for its information on drugs; she kept a list of the pills she was taking so she wouldn't poison herself unintentionally with lethal combinations. Usually she would take her pills with liquor, and she would rarely take Valium because she had heard that it mixed badly with alcohol. One morning her lady's maid, Dorothy Caverno, found Brenda passed out in bed, dozens of brightly colored pills scattered on the floor. Caverno was alarmed, but Brenda eventually woke up.

"I know how many pills to take to kill myself," she used to boast. Nonetheless, she occasionally took an inadvertent overdose or a bad combination. She'd be sick and feeble, and she'd have drunk too much. Bleary-eyed, she'd lost track of how many pills she'd taken, or what she had taken. Only the vigilance of her friends and servants kept her alive. If Caverno, for example, couldn't awaken Brenda from a deep sleep, she would hold a mirror under her nose to see if Brenda was still breathing.

With the departure of Pietro, Brenda became increasingly bitter about New York's social life. She blamed many of her problems on it. Since her marriage to Ship, she had been joylessly acting out the role of society matron. She still wanted to be invited to the right parties, but she no longer wanted to actually go to them—they were boring, and they revived all of her youthful feelings of anxiety. Life was easier lived in reclusiveness.

On a trip one summer, Brenda had fallen in love with Cape Cod and decided to buy a vacation home there, far away from the Manhattan social scene. After looking at several houses, she settled on a large gray-shingled home in East Harwich, overlooking Pleasant Bay. The house sat at the end of a long wooded drive. It had pink shutters and a heated swimming pool with an adjacent bathhouse. When a friend asked Brenda why she had purchased a house so far out in the country, Brenda answered, Why not? From then on she called the house "Why Not." She hired a kind, hardworking couple,

Joe and Helen Drozell, as caretakers; they would stay with her for the rest of her life. They lived on the grounds in a cottage that was a miniature version of the big house.

Soon Brenda started spending more and more time at Why Not. In 1955 she met a man with whom she moved there full-time. His name was Robert Chatfield-Taylor. Forty-six years old, he was tall and good-looking and, like all of Brenda's men, was strong, athletic, and devoted to masculine pursuits. A Yale dropout like her father, Bob had worked as a test pilot, a commercial pilot, and a rancher in Arizona. He was a passionate big-game hunter who loaded his own shotgun shells and invented a special rifle for shooting African buffalo. His hunting friends, who called themselves the "Marsh River Rats," nicknamed Bob "Brown Bear," partly because he was an authority on Alaskan bear and partly because he resembled a brown bear—large and dark, with a shuffling walk.

Bob loved guns. William Heisey, a doctor who treated him, recalls that Bob once came in for a checkup with a suitcase full of guns. "When he found out that I didn't have a gun, he was surprised. 'You must have a gun for protection,' he insisted. So he gave me a rifle. It was a Ruger .22. I used it to shoot squirrels.

"He had a first-class kind of life-style. I believe he drove a Porsche. He was into alcohol a bit, imported scotch. I remember I did an X ray on him and there was a bullet in his cheek. He told me that he had been grouse-hunting with a Belgian prince and caught a piece of shrapnel in his cheek."

Late in life Bob was once accused of using his hunting skills to kill a neighbor's cat, which had apparently been keeping him up all night with loud meowing. One morning it was found dead on its owner's lawn, shot between the eyes with a .22 rifle. The cat's owner accused Bob of the shooting. But after investigating, the police decided Bob couldn't have done it: there was no way he could have hit the cat from his bedroom window (a distance of about 120 paces) in the dark. Still, Bob's friends were convinced he was guilty. "He was such a good shot, as good as Balfour. We used to tease him [about killing the cat], and he'd get very indignant. 'God damn it, I didn't do it!' he'd insist," says a close friend.

Like Brenda's father, Bob was descended from a rich Chicago family. His maternal grandfather, Charles B. Farwell, had helped finance Marshall Field's original Chicago store. Later, in partnership with two other men, he had built the state capitol in Austin, Texas, in exchange for three million acres in the Texas panhandle. He also became a U.S. senator. Bob's mother, Rose, had been a great beauty. His father, Hobart Chatfield-Taylor, wrote novels, but was perhaps best known for his hyphenated last name. According to family legend, his childless uncle, William Chatfield, persuaded Hobart Taylor to take his name as a condition of inheriting his money.

Brenda was introduced to Bob by her stepbrother James Watriss. The two men had flown helicopters together for a company in California. Bob was twice married, once divorced, and the father of three children. He had recently moved to New York, following his separation from his second wife, Elinor. At the time he met Brenda, he was working as a sales representative for Olin Corporation's gun division.

With his chiseled features and patrician background, Bob seemed like a good partner for Brenda. But many of her friends thought him a bore. "Chatfield-Taylor was very handsome, but all he wanted to talk about was guns," says Jerome Doyle. "He was a social butterfly. His conversation was small talk. He didn't know anything about public affairs. He was a goddamn moron in my book."

Nonetheless, he was devoted to Brenda. For all her eccentricities and problems, she was still rich and famous. What was more, there was a mystique about her, a strange allure. Even if the physical glamour was fast deteriorating and turning into something freakish—her body was emaciated, her once vibrant features were turning skeletal—she still had an unmistakable dynamism, exercised, often as not, from her bed. It was almost as if, with her beauty wasting away, she had reached inside herself and re-created an aura of glamour by force of personality.

Dr. Robert Chatfield-Taylor, Jr., Bob's son, recalls that "Brenda could talk for hours on end, but I don't know what she talked about except day-to-day events. She would run over every event that took place during that hour for another hour. Who called, who walked through the door, every trivial thing. It wasn't particularly interesting, but when Brenda talked about things, they somehow became more interesting than they really were. Brenda was very intense, emotional, and opinionated. One of her nice qualities was that when she liked something, she really liked it, and when she disliked something, she really disliked it.''

Bob Chatfield-Taylor wasn't the only person drawn to this troubled, imperious woman. Throughout the last half of her life Brenda was surrounded by a retinue of admirers and acolytes, men and women, rich and poor. Some, like Chatfield-Taylor, Sr., were basically weak and ineffectual. Others were enormously successful in life. She held her fans in part by manipulation—the suicide attempts, for example, or her constant lateness. But beyond that, she had a magnetism that drew people to her. Bob Chatfield-Taylor "defined his life around her," says his son.

For Brenda's part, the relationship was probably less exotic. Unlike Ship or Pietro, Bob was easily dominated. The relationship was based on "her being the baby," says Esme Hammond. "He'd hold her and rock her while she curled up in the fetal position in his arms, crying."

Still, Brenda might never have married Bob if Ship hadn't pressed her for a divorce. As Brenda's life was growing darker, Ship's was growing brighter. Through golf and his friendship with Jock Whitney, he had met many famous people. He played golf with the Duke of Windsor and Baron Guy de Rothschild; he was invited to lunch with Truman Capote at the home of Babe and William Paley. He had affairs with beautiful women. One night, on a date with Joan Fontaine at El Morocco, Ship left their table for a few moments. When he returned, the actress was dancing with a short, homely foreigner. Ship walked up to the couple. "Joan, you must be awfully hard up for a dance," he said. The foreigner laughed. His name was Aristotle Onassis. The next day he invited Ship to lunch, and later for a cruise on his three-hundred-foot yacht, the *Christina*.

One day in 1956 Ship called Brenda and told her he needed a divorce. He wanted to marry one of his girlfriends quickly. Brenda did not object. At a hearing in Florida, Ship told a Polk County judge that Brenda had left him several years before, and that she refused to return despite his frequent pleas for a reconciliation. Under questioning from his attorney, Ship described the events leading up to their breakup.

"Well, I had been sick. I had a fistula and I was in and out of the hospital for a period of a year and a half. The last operation when I was in the hospital, my wife asked if she could go out with her friends, and I said that would be all right. I think she just got on the merry-go-round, when I was sick. When I got out of the hospital, she said she felt that there was another life she would like better. I had my last operation in Kentucky and when I met her in New York, she said, 'I think I would like to have a different life.' So she moved into town, and I stayed in the country. That's all."

Q. Did you ask her to come back and live with you in the home you had provided?

A. Yes, I have asked her different times to talk over our future, on account of our child and different things like that, and to come back.

Q. And you have made attempts as recently as six weeks ago to reconcile with your wife?

A. Yes, I asked her to come down and bring Victoria, our daughter. We would talk things over. As a matter of fact, she said she would come. Then she changed her mind and said she had to go to Cape Cod where she has a house.

Q. Did you do anything to provoke your separation?

A. I do not feel that I provoked this separation. I feel that I have been a good husband and father to my child and I did all I could to make a success of our marriage.

Q. What did she mean by a different life?

A. My wife travels in high social circles and there are constant rounds of parties and social affairs, leaving very little time for home life.

Q. And did that different life include you?

A. Excluded me completely.

Q. Did your wife give you any reason for desiring this different life of her own?

A. Nothing whatsoever. She has told me since that no one could have made her happy.

On April 13, Ship was granted a divorce. The decree awarded custody of Victoria to Brenda and gave Ship "reasonable" visitation rights. He was also ordered to pay $100 a month in child support.

Three months later, on July 10, 1956, in a simple ceremony in Brussels, Belgium, Ship and Catherine Manning Hannon were married.

Brenda was furious that Ship had remarried before she had, and she started pressuring Bob to get a divorce. Finally he took a leave of absence from his job and moved to Reno, Nevada. While he was en route, Brenda announced their engagement in the press. After six weeks, the time required to establish residency, he filed for divorce from his second wife, Elinor, on the grounds of mental cruelty.

Perhaps anticipating that her husband would file for divorce, Elinor had tracked down airline stewardesses and hotel clerks in Miami and Mexico City who agreed to testify that they had seen Brenda and Bob together.

On August 29, 1956, in an affidavit that preceded her counterclaim against Bob, Elinor charged that her husband had left her and their children virtually destitute, while spending a $43,000 inheritance "on his personal living expenses, including dues and other expenses at exclusive clubs of which he is a member, and expenses at nightclubs in New York City and elsewhere, and in courting Brenda Frazier Kelly."

The affidavit went on to state that Bob "is constantly in the company of said Brenda Frazier Kelly, and is spending large amounts of money in entertaining her. He introduced our daughter, Joan, to . . . Brenda Frazier Kelly, and informed Joan that Brenda Frazier Kelly was to be Joan's future stepmother. Since our separation, said husband has purchased for himself a new Chrysler automobile, which he uses principally in his courtship of said Brenda Frazier Kelly, since he does not require an automobile in his occupation."

Elinor claimed that although her husband was capable of earning "approximately $1,500 per month," and although he received a $6,000 annual income from various trusts, he had given her no money since August 1, 1956. She said she was forced to take a part-time job as a travel agent and sell the family piano in order to pay the bills. "Notwithstanding my efforts," Elinor claimed, "a suit was filed against me and my husband for the collection of a grocery bill incurred prior to our separation in the amount of $414.44."

On February 25, 1957, a Washoe County district judge granted Elinor a divorce, ruling that since the marriage Chatfield-Taylor had treated her with "extreme cruelty, entirely mental in character." The terms of the divorce were sealed, but Jerome Doyle says that Brenda agreed to pay Elinor's alimony and child support.

On March 3 Brenda and Bob were married by a Congregational minister in the living room at Why Not. The simple ceremony was witnessed by twenty-five close friends and relatives, including Brenda's daughter and her stepbrothers, Fred and James Watriss. Brenda looked worn and much older than her thirty-five years. Since the breakup with Pietro she had been starving herself again. Her pale blue brocade dress hung loosely on her bony frame; deep lines formed parentheses around her mouth.

She felt as bad as she looked. She had not slept the night before because, says Dorothy Caverno, "she didn't want to get married." She told Caverno that the moment she was married she realized she had made a mistake. Soon after the wedding, Brenda was rushed to Cape Cod Hospital, where she remained for about a month. She recuperated at home for several weeks after that, with nurses attending her around the clock. She told her servants that she had had exploratory surgery for a kidney ailment. Most likely she was also being treated for malnutrition. She seemed so sick and weak, says Helen Drozell, "that I thought she'd never last."

Brenda recovered, however, and in the spring the Chatfield-Taylors left on a honeymoon trip, first to Boston, where they stayed for two weeks at the Ritz-Carlton Hotel, and then to Florida. It was not a pleasant vacation.

Brenda was depressed and drinking too much. She had taken a lady's maid and a chauffeur with her. By the end of the trip she had fired them both. She told Dick Gott that she had also tried to kill herself during the honeymoon. Thirteen-year-old Victoria Kelly, who joined her mother and new stepfather on the trip, remembered their loud, public fights. During one argument in a restaurant, Bob jumped up and left. A few minutes later, Brenda announced, "I'm leaving." Victoria was left sitting at the table alone. A waitress approached the child. "Will you be ordering dinner?" she asked.

Victoria got up from the table and found her mother in the

lobby. Bob was outside in the car. "That night he drove us home, and she and I sat in the back seat," says Victoria. "None of their fights were ever about anything of any importance. She'd be in a bad mood. With Uncle Bob, it was usually money, how she supported him and paid for this and that. She'd throw it in his face at every possible opportunity.

"These fights used to happen [frequently] in restaurants. [We'd be] at Valley Steak House, and my mother would be screaming. 'I put your son through school, you son of a bitch,' and on and on. Your average American guy in Valley Steak House isn't going to put up with this. He doesn't know who she is. So he turns around and says, 'Would you shut up, lady, and stop using that language. I've got my family here, let us eat in peace.' She'd pay no attention. She'd just keep going. Usually she'd had a lot to drink, or she had taken the wrong combination of pills. That was when she was the most obnoxious, when she was mixing pills and alcohol."

By this time Brenda's drinking and drug-taking were out of control. She could not function without liquor and drugs, and she was nearly always high.

When Brenda and Bob returned from Florida, she set him up in a foreign-car dealership on the Cape. Says Joe Drozell, "It was just a place for him to go and get out of her hair." Yet Brenda would often phone Bob several times a day with trivial requests, demanding, for example, that he run out to buy her a tube of toothpaste. She would also get angry if he left town on a hunting trip, and she would inevitably punish him for leaving her. She told her friend Alex MacLeod that once while Bob was hunting bear in Alaska, she had the wall between their ground-floor bedrooms knocked down to create one large room for herself. On his return, Bob found all his belongings stuffed into a small room upstairs. She claimed that for his first dinner at home following the trip, she served him soup made from a douche solution.

Bob endured these incidents. He did everything he could to accommodate his difficult wife. Brenda sometimes reversed night and day, staying up until three or four in the morning, and "for a long time my father stayed up with her," says Bob Jr. "[Before he met Brenda] he defined his life by getting up at a certain hour, and having a barbecue at a certain hour, having a big porterhouse sirloin. I think keeping

Brenda's schedule was very difficult for him. It made working very difficult for him.''

Bob Jr. first met Brenda on his way from San Francisco, where he had been living with his mother, to St. Mark's, a prep school in Southboro, Massachusetts. His first impression of Brenda was that "she was someone who was in bed a lot. She stayed in her room most of the day and ran her household. She sat in bed and watched television. She was doll-like. She didn't have a normal life. Her life seemed totally foreign to me; it was the direct opposite of my own mother's life. My mother would go out four times a week and had hundreds of friends and was a very independent woman.''

For several years Bob Jr. spent the summers at Why Not, and he and Brenda became very close. "She talked to me a lot about herself. Maybe I listened to her more than other people did. She liked the idea of my being her son.''

As a mother, though, Brenda continued her pattern of uninvolvement. She rarely saw Victoria, who was boarding at Miss Hewitt's in New York, except on holidays and during the summer. When they were together, Victoria often found herself pitted against Bob Jr. If Brenda was angry with Victoria, she would ignore her daughter in favor of Bob Jr. More and more, Brenda's relationship with Victoria resembled her own relationship with Big Brenda. Brenda even fired Victoria's beloved nanny, Eva Moorcock, just as Big Brenda had fired Nanny Bishop. "I had a nanny I loved more than anybody in the world, except Daddy and Mother, but actually I loved her more than my mother. And my mother took her as a maid and gave me a witch of a French governess,'' recalls Victoria. "Nanny was living in the same house; but I had the witch, and Nanny was looking after my mother.'' Later, when Victoria got sick and Nanny Moorcock tried to take care of her, Brenda got mad and fired her.

The mother-daughter relationship was also strained by jealousy. As soon as Victoria reached puberty, Brenda regarded her as competition. "My mother just loved to keep me as chubby as possible,'' says Victoria. "Imagine if I had a gorgeous figure and hung around New York and had my picture taken, I'd be far more of a threat than [if I was] a large, 180-pound dumpling sitting somewhere feeling sorry for myself. We had fights about food. I'd be trying to diet and my mother would sabotage it in every way possible." Brenda would throw a tantrum if the servants did not give Victoria large portions of fattening foods. She would also be furious if Victoria lost weight. "She'd say I was going to get sick; I was going to get like her. She didn't want me to turn out like her. But anyone who knew the situation knew it had absolutely nothing to do with that," Victoria continues. "Everyone used to make her mad by saying, 'Oh, Victoria, you look so gorgeous. What are you now, a size four or a size six?' She'd go absolutely berserk. Because she took such pride in the fact that she was a four or a six."

Most of Brenda's day was occupied by managing her staff. Ed Gallagher, the owner of an employment agency in Wellesley, Massachusetts, supplied Brenda for years with a revolving army of servants: butlers, maids, cooks, chauffeurs, and secretaries. Many came and went quickly, driven away by her capriciousness and cruelty. A few who stuck it out, however, grew fond of her despite everything. And, though it was sometimes hard to tell, Brenda was deeply attached to them. Throughout her life, some of her closest, most intense relationships were with servants, and this was never more true than in her later years.

To her friends, though, Brenda liked to complain vigorously about the help, and she derived much pleasure from giving long, passionate accounts of the incompetence, drinking, and thievery of her servants. One evening Alex MacLeod tape-recorded Brenda as she warmed to the subject. "Once I had a roast chicken and I wanted the stuffing served around it [on the outside]," Brenda said. "The butler came in—I was always served first in the English style—and the chicken was lying flat on its stomach on the plate. It looked as though its backbone had given in, and it was lying there all flattened out. I looked at this and said, 'What in the name of God is that?' The butler said, 'Madam, that's the chicken you ordered.' And he couldn't keep his face straight. I said, 'Where's the stuffing?' And he said, 'I don't know.' Well, I went out to the kitchen, and [the cook] was Swiss or something, so I said, 'Would you kindly tell me what you did to that chicken?' And she picked the chicken up off the platter, and shook it at me, and said, 'There's the stuffing.' It was inside. The butler and someone else were in the pantry, and they were shaking [with laughter]. I said to her, 'Would you kindly unhand that bird. Whatever it is, it's awful. You're fired.' And I walked out.''

One butler she had for a time, of whom she was very fond, was an alcoholic, but curiously—for a butler and an alcoholic—he was unable to mix a drink. This amused Brenda. Her ability to joke about the drinking problems of this man and her other servants is an indication of how deeply she denied her own alcohol problem. Brenda continues on the MacLeod tape: "One day I said to him, 'Would you mind telling me something? We all know you're an alcoholic. Why is it you can't make any damn drink?' He said, 'Are you serious, Mrs. Taylor?' I said, 'Of course. It seems very odd to me that you can't make a cocktail.' He said, 'Mrs. Taylor, when I drink, I take a bottle of Four Roses and pick it right up. Do you think when I feel like drinking that I mix myself a white lady with an egg?' I started to laugh; so did he. He was in hysterics.

"Anytime I left [him], anytime I left the Cape, he went on a complete bender. He'd drink out the whole bar. But he'd replace it. Finally he said, 'It isn't fair to you. I'm going to do this more. It's a bad climate here for me, I'm going back down South,' which is where he originated. He was a divine guy, terribly, terribly nice. I think people thought my attachment to him was rather odd.''

Yet another alcoholic butler once disrupted a holiday dinner at the Chatfield-Taylors'. As Brenda described the incident to MacLeod, "I said to Bob, 'Isn't it nice, the butler is so good. But he looks sort of odd tonight. I don't know what it is.' Well, of course he was dead drunk. He couldn't even stand up.'' The wine was on the table, and the butler would step up every now and then to pour it. "He would go around and put one drop in everybody's glass. And I'd make faces at Bob to keep the bottle, which he never did, so the butler would go outside, throw back his head, and drink the whole bottle down. So I finally said to him, 'I have to speak to you. You're drunk.' He was holding onto the chair and weaving, and he said, 'Madam, I have never touched alcohol.' And I said, 'It seems to me, you're drunk right this minute.' And he said, 'No, madam, I never touch it!' So I said, 'I know a little differently, and something has to be done.' So I let him go.''

Brenda went on to discuss three chefs she had: "The first one was a drunkard, the second one was a drunk, too. The third was the best. He drank, but not too much. He would order the food. We had a freezer the size of a hotel's. This gentleman would fill the deep freeze up to the very top and then he'd go home in this station wagon in the evening. The next day there would be no food there. And I'd say, 'Why not?' And he'd say, 'Well, I'm going shopping.' And again the food would go. Well, he owned the store from where the food was coming. And he was ordering it every day, and then taking it home for himself and his wife. So he must have made a fortune, because it was some time before this little caper was found out.''

Brenda had bought the large house with its three guest rooms facing the bay in part because it was big enough for entertaining. She tacked up a notice in the linen closet explaining to the servants how to prepare each room for guests and how to unpack their suitcases. She kept a silver service and several butlers' uniforms with white jackets for day, black for night, and beige for a change of pace.

Sometimes she threw formal dinner parties to which she invited local friends such as her doctors, Paul Butterfield and Henry H. Hopkins, and Jacques Maroger, her painting teacher. "If Brenda had a party, she'd want everything on display," says Helen Drozell. That meant that the staff spent days polishing silver.

Once she insisted on lining the driveway with dozens of lighted candles even though it was a breezy night, and the servants were afraid the candles would start a fire. She'd order cheesecake from Reuben's in New York. She had bowls of fresh flowers everywhere. "Brenda had maybe 150 flower vases around the house, and when [Victoria's French governess] wasn't taking care of Victoria, she was taking care of the flower vases," recalls Bob Jr. "There were hundreds of things that could go wrong with the flower vases, and Brenda would get very concerned about it.''

Even if it was just a family gathering, Brenda made a big production out of dinner. Bob Jr. remembers that Ship once came to Why Not to visit Victoria. He had tickets for the

Ringling Bros. circus. "But somehow we wound up not going to the circus, because we were having dinner, and dinner was too late and somehow dinner was more important. It was more important to go to dinner than to the circus."

Like many anorexics, Brenda spent a lot of time thinking about food and planning meals. She read cookbooks and she loved to watch Julia Child on television. "She knew instinctively what ingredients were in food," says Dick Gott. "And I used to say to her, 'You know, if you'd go to the kitchen, you'd be the greatest cook.'" Instead of doing it herself, though, she'd prepare long, incredibly detailed instructions for her cooks. Often as not, the instructions would be violated, precipitating a new crisis with the help.

One Christmas night, a different sort of crisis broke up a dinner: the furnace exploded. "We had people coming to dinner," Brenda told Alex MacLeod. "I was talking to Joan Chatfield-Taylor in my room. We were having eggnog. And she was sitting on a sofa at the end of my bed, and I was sitting on the floor with one of my dogs. There was the most awful explosion you ever heard. Victoria was thrown off the sofa in the living room, and the table behind her went over. She went right over her head onto the floor. Joan was knocked off my sofa. Helen was [in the basement] getting more lights for the Christmas tree. She was just coming up when the furnace exploded. She was nearly killed. The walls and everything were covered in about an inch of soot. Everything was covered with this and here were the Butterfields and I don't know who else coming for dinner. I was in my bathrobe. Everybody was choking to death. Then the electricity went off. The firemen arrived, plus the police, who heard about it. There was nothing to cook with. There was no water." After electricity was restored and the Christmas tree relit, Joan Chatfield-Taylor stumbled and fell into the tree. "Her father never stopped playing chess to get her out. She nearly burned to death. He was playing chess right next to her. She crashed into the tree for some reason, and there was all these burning-hot bulbs. We yanked her out of it. That was a lovely evening."

After a while, Brenda's entertaining tapered off—mostly,

says Joe Drozell, because people got tired of waiting until midnight for dinner. Sometimes they never got dinner at all. One night she ordered dinner for seven o'clock. At the appointed hour, the butler went to her room to tell her that dinner was ready. Meanwhile, Brenda's guests were fidgeting in the living room. "Tell the cook to keep it warm," Brenda insisted. Several hours passed, and finally the infuriated cook stomped into Brenda's room. "You can serve yourself, I'm quitting. You expect it to be fit to eat at eleven when it's been ready since seven?" she shouted. Brenda ordered her to leave the room and start serving. "I won't!" said the cook. Brenda followed her into the kitchen. "I won't do it, I'm quitting right now," the cook said. Suddenly Brenda started picking up dishes full of food and flinging them across the kitchen. When she was finished, she surveyed the mess. "That'll keep you busy for a while," she said.

The next day Brenda's lady's maid Peggy Eldridge also quit. "One of the maids has been up all morning cleaning the bathrooms and Brenda said, 'Oh, they're filthy.' [Then Brenda] started in on me again, and I said, 'Good day. I'm going home now.' And she said, 'Are you coming back?' And I said, 'No, not today. And I don't know when I'm coming back. I don't have to take this kind of stuff.' She said, 'Oh, you'll come back, Peggy, they all come back to me.' I told her, 'You know when I'll come back. You look out this window, and when you see robins wearing rubber boots, you call me, and that's when I'll be back.'"

Joe and Helen Drozell also quit several times. A year after Joe started working for Brenda, he quit because of the long hours she demanded. He was working as a landscape contractor when Brenda sent her butler over to ask him to come back. He agreed only if he was put on a contract.

Everyone who worked for Brenda was a victim of her tantrums. Anything could set her off. Once she yelled at an employee for affixing a crooked stamp on a letter; another time she screamed at the cook for putting too much vinegar in the salad dressing. Once, when she found a paperweight out of place on the desk in the living room, she picked it up and hurled it at one of her lady's maids, narrowly missing the woman's leg.

When Brenda was in bed one night, she asked her lady's maid Frances Griffin to get her a nightgown. Griffin went to Brenda's bureau, where about fifty beautiful silk nightgowns were folded individually in tissue paper. As Griffin held up the nightgowns, Brenda rejected each one. Finally Griffin said, "Why don't you get it yourself?" Brenda scrambled out of bed, ran over to the drawer, and began tossing the nightgowns and tissue paper into the air. After they had scatted onto the floor, she screamed, "Pick them up!"

"No, Mrs. Taylor, I will not," said Griffin. "If my children had tantrums and did this, I wouldn't pick them up, so I'm surely not going to do it for you."

"Frances," Brenda yelled, "you work for me!"

This became a refrain in the household, a command from the Queen to her court. She had bought her servants' devotion and she demanded that they satisfy her every whim. Like the attention of the tabloid photographers in the thirties, the obsequiousness of her servants confirmed her worth.

Sometimes, after she cooled off, Brenda compensated for her cruelties with extravagant presents. She gave one of her secretaries a red wool Mainbocher dress and a silver fox cape to wear to a local policemen's ball. Most of her servants received expensive presents of gold jewelry and checks on their birthdays.

Of course, the money and gifts could not compensate. A lot of the help simply quit. But the Drozells and others who stayed with her for many years could never have survived her tantrums and craziness if they had not been attached to her. "By and large, the people [who stayed with her] fell in love with her," says Dick Gott. "She encouraged that. She put it on a much more personal basis than she should have. She'd want [the servants] to sit down on the bed and talk to her one minute, and the next minute she'd be screaming at [them] because they hadn't done something properly."

By the late fifties, however, the rotation of servants in and out of the household had begun to slow. Brenda's health was worse and she was spending more time in bed. Sometimes she would hide in her room for days, not even letting herself be seen by the people who brought her food. They would have to leave trays outside the door. "She would sleep for days to try to escape everything," says Joe Drozell. Even when she was awake and feeling well, she rarely ventured outside during the day. It was as if she knew she was peculiar and felt uncomfortable mingling with normal people. Sometimes at night the staff would see her outside the house, working in the garden, alone, with a flashlight.

CHAPTER FIFTEEN

In 1960 BRENDA decided to rent a suite at the Ritz-Carlton Hotel in Boston. At thirty-nine, she was becoming increasingly preoccupied with her body and all the things that were going wrong with it, and she wanted to be near good doctors. She also had a partially formed idea of becoming involved in Boston social life. And there was probably something else at play in Brenda's decision: Hotel living was a throwback to a happier time, when she and Big Brenda had lived together at the Carlton House in New York. But hotel living had become obsolete in the intervening years—as rare in the 1960s as satin Porthault sheets and Packard automobiles. In 1948 forty-five people lived at the Boston Ritz. When Brenda moved in, there were only a few permanent residents.

Brenda rented a suite of rooms on the fourth floor overlooking the Public Gardens. Her suite, which at the time rented for $200 a day, was one of the largest in the hotel. It had two bedrooms and a living room with French provincial furniture and a grand piano. There was no kitchen or kitchenette, so Brenda ordered all her meals from room service. Sometimes, if she got hungry late at night, she'd raid the communal floor kitchen where the other guests kept hors d'oeuvres and sandwiches.

The Ritz in those days was a model of Yankee rectitude and stuffy elegance. Women were not allowed to wear slacks in the public rooms, and the men had to wear ties. Though the rule had been discontinued by Brenda's time, for years the hotel would accept only guests who were in the Social Register or *Who's Who*. Civilians writing for reservations had to pass muster according to the feel of the quality of their stationery. The hotel had been founded in 1927 by a Harvard graduate, Edward Wyner, and until his death in 1961 he lived in an apartment on the top floor. Brenda, who gave five-dollar tips, was popular with the Ritz staff, but Wyner refused to meet her. "He'd heard of her reputation, and he didn't want to get mixed up with her," says Grace Davidson, a retired Boston newspaperwoman, who met Brenda through Charles Banino, the hotel's chef and general manager. "He thought she was bad news. He never liked to meet people who were notorious, although he liked their money."

One day Brenda called the Ritz's business office and, in a drugged slur, demanded to see Wyner. Wyner sent Banino. "Whenever Mr. Wyner didn't want to do something, Mr. Banino had to do it," says Eleanor O'Neill, Wyner's assistant. It was the start of a friendship that would last the rest of Banino's life. Banino was the son of an Italian farmer. He had started at the Ritz as the night sandwich chef in 1927 and quickly worked his way up to become head chef and then managing director of the hotel. Banino was short and rotund, with a smiling moon face and a bald pate, and was known for his romantic gestures—he would typically send a dozen red roses to his hostess after dining at a private home—and his devotion to French haute cuisine. He insisted that his waiters know every ingredient in every dish served so that they could intelligently discuss the menu with guests. He lectured on food to Ivy League women's groups, co-wrote *The Ritz Cookbook,* and participated in seminars at the Harvard Business School.

Banino was also an insomniac who rarely slept more than two or three hours at a time. Regular guests who had trouble sleeping often called him in the middle of the night, and he would bring them a cup of hot tea laced with Courvoisier.

When Banino answered the call that day, he found Brenda nearly unconscious. He called her doctor, Irwin Portner, who told him to feed Brenda black coffee and keep her up and walking so that she wouldn't fall asleep. As they circled her bedroom, Brenda told Banino she wanted to die.

"Why?" he asked.

"Nobody loves me," she answered.

"I love you," he said.

"What else could he say?" asks Grace Davidson. "So he kept walking with her. He was a wreck. He dropped about ten pounds. He was with her about eighteen hours. He saved her life, and she became a great friend of his."

After that the Ritz made certain that someone was always aware of Brenda. "The maids were always watching. The maids were going in to make up the room all the time. They could tell by the way she was acting," says O'Neill. "She'd always call one of us to say she'd [attempted suicide]. She'd call me or she'd call Mr. Banino, or she'd call the doctor, who'd call one of us. With me, she'd ask for Mr. Banino, so I'd have to find him. He was always in the kitchen. He'd call Dr. Portner, and then he'd go up. I'd say in the eighteen months she was here, she tried to kill herself four or five times."

Brenda's husband, Bob, had moved with her to the Ritz, but they weren't getting along. After Bob left on a hunting trip, Brenda called an Italian man she'd met during her affair with Pietro and asked him to fly to Boston to visit her. Brenda and Dorothy Caverno made the call from a pay phone in the hotel lobby so that it couldn't be traced on Brenda's bill. The Italian told Brenda he couldn't leave Italy that night, but he did show up in Boston a few weeks later.

Soon after Bob returned from his trip, Brenda kicked him out of the Ritz suite. Ruth Trader, one of Brenda's maids, was living with them, and she recalls the day it happened. "I was standing in the hall and I heard her say to him, 'I want you to get everything out of here'—meaning his bedroom. He didn't put up a fuss. I felt so sorry for him." Trader had been sleeping on the couch, but after that Brenda let her move into Bob's room. "She said she was going to get an exterminator to clean it out, he smoked so much," says Trader.

Bob returned to Why Not, and eventually the maid also left the Ritz. On March 16, 1961, Brenda was all alone in her bedroom. She sat up all night, thinking, she later wrote, "about what a travesty my life had been. It would have seemed that I had everything going for me; physical appearance, reasonable intelligence. . . . Yet now I was 39 years old and what did I have to show for my life? An adolescence

Shadow

and young womanhood full of tension and terror. Two broken marriages . . . a daughter whom I dearly loved—but whom, I now felt convinced, I had shamefully neglected.''

Brenda wrote a letter, making plans for the care of Victoria. At 5:30 A.M. she reached for a bottle of pills and swallowed every tablet inside. Then, as she had so many times before, she lay back against the satin pillows, closed her eyes, and waited to die.

But even this, probably her most serious suicide attempt, was really only a cry for attention and help. At the last moment she saved herself by calling the Ritz's operator, who alerted a doctor. He rushed to Brenda's room and revived her with a massive dose of stimulant. She was quickly moved to a private room at Faulkner Hospital in Jamaica Plains.

Brenda was by no means out of danger. Her liver was badly damaged; she had barely enough flesh on her body to stay alive. Two nurses sat by her bed round the clock so that if one had to leave, Brenda would not be alone, even for a minute. The nurses had less to do with Brenda's horrid medical condition and her doctor's fears that she would attempt suicide again than with her need for attention.

Her physician, Dr. Portner, was convinced that Brenda would die unless she received psychiatric help. He called a friend, a distinguished Freudian analyst, and asked if he would be interested in meeting Brenda. ''She's a fascinating woman,'' he told the analyst. ''She's charming, and lovely, and she's pathetic. She's managed to do everything wrong with her health, and now I don't think she'll live more than two weeks. She's hardly conscious, and she's so feeble and emaciated. She's in the hospital now, and her two stepbrothers are there, and her daughter and stepson. It's like a wake. I'd love you to go see her.''

The psychiatrist agreed. During their first meeting Brenda was nearly incoherent. ''I understood almost nothing she said,'' he recalls. ''But one thing was very definite—the look on her face. No matter how . . . incoherent she was . . . her face was a plea for help; it was so desperate a plea, so clear in its request. It reminded me of those pictures of starving little children with their arms out, pleading, 'Save me.' This message came through very strongly, and I said to her, 'I read clearly your message that you want help, and if you'll

237

take this wish seriously, and if you can get yourself to my office, I will accept the responsibility of treating you.' Brenda nodded. The psychiatrist left Brenda's room and told her family waiting outside, "What have you got to lose? You can arrange with the hospital to get an ambulance to take her to my office on a stretcher. There will be a little expense. But something has to be done, and if she can afford it, it should be done."

For the next several months, Brenda saw the psychiatrist every day. His office consisted of two small rooms attached to the rear of his spacious stone house on a quiet tree-lined street in a Boston suburb. The small waiting room was decorated with the kind of functional and inexpensive furniture typical of doctor's waiting rooms. A painting of Freud and artwork by the psychiatrist's patients hung on the walls. The examining room contained a desk, two chairs, and a couch.

For the first few weeks Brenda arrived in an ambulance. The attendants carried her into the waiting room on a stretcher and propped her up in an armchair against some pillows. Later she was driven to her appointments by her chauffeur, accompanied by two male nurses who carried Brenda into the office in their arms. It was a year before she could walk in by herself. "Even then," says her psychiatrist, "you'd look at these spindly legs with hardly any muscle . . . and you'd wonder how this skeleton had made it."

During the first three months of her analysis, Brenda lived at the Faulkner Hospital in a large room that she transformed into a hotel suite. She set up a bar with glasses and a silver champagne bucket. She brought in her clothes, her fur coat, her jewelry, and her bed linens. She had a refrigerator in her room in which she kept Jell-O, custard, and Great Western champagne. On some afternoons Charles Banino came over to cook her meals in the hospital kitchen. Brenda was allowed to leave the hospital during the day to visit her psychiatrist, and in the evening to go out to dinner. Sometimes she would not return until after midnight, tottering up the hospital steps in her high heels and fur coat, woozy from too much champagne, and carrying a bouquet of flowers that she had plucked from the hospital's grounds.

There was no medical reason why Brenda needed to be in the hospital for three months. Once she had recovered from her suicide attempt, she could have gone home. But Brenda didn't want to leave. To her the hospital's aura of concern was strangely comforting. "In the hospital, she was looked after," says Victoria. "She knew everybody couldn't quit. She knew . . . no matter what she did, how nasty she was, or if she had a fight, [the nurses] couldn't walk out."

Brenda needed a mother surrogate constantly in attendance, and at the hospital she discovered an endless supply. She cultivated the kindest, most patient nurses, some of whom she paid extra to stay up with her at night. She'd talk into the early morning hours, regaling them with stories about her debut and her "engagement" to Howard Hughes. When she was finally released, she called them up to take care of her at home. A few became devoted, long-term employees.

Within a few weeks of her starting analysis Brenda's condition began to improve. Going to the doctor gave her a reason to get out of bed. She began to make plans for the future. One of her primary goals was so stop spending so much money. In 1961 Brenda's medical bills alone were several hundred thousand dollars, almost her entire income. She was also spending a small fortune for her suite and room service at the Ritz.

As an economy measure, Brenda decided to move out of the hotel. On a drive with one of her nurses one day through Medfield, a small, quiet Massachusetts town, she came across a large abandoned house, hidden behind a row of pines and elms at the edge of a cemetery. The dilapidated white frame house, built in 1789, had black shutters and was surrounded by a white picket fence. Though there was something spooky about the place—particularly all those nearby tombstones—Brenda decided to buy it.

For Brenda, Medfield meant isolation, both physical and emotional. At first Chatfield-Taylor moved in with her, but soon afterward Brenda asked him to leave, saying, "Darling, you just can't stay here." Bob rented a small apartment in the harbor town of Manchester, Massachusetts (his sister Adelaide lived nearby), and he got a job as a pilot for a commuter airline. Bob Jr., who continued to live on and off with Brenda, supported the separation. "I thought my father would be happier flying airplanes than taking care of Brenda," he says.

Brenda and Bob never divorced, and they remained close friends until Chatfield-Taylor's death from cancer in 1980. Throughout Brenda's final decades, Bob played the role of dutiful husband. He usually visited Brenda once a week, meeting her at her psychiatrist's office and then taking her out to lunch and, sometimes, to a movie. The couple spent most holidays together. "He took other women out and there were other women who wanted to marry him," says Bob Jr. "But he was always in love with Brenda."

Brenda's Medfield house gave the appearance of a home in which a busy family lived. Crackling fires warmed the rooms; servants puttered in the kitchen. In the study a leather-topped mahogany desk held a card listing the most used telephone numbers—the supermarket, the dentist, the plumber, the laundress, and the Ritz Hotel. The opposite side of the card listed the numbers of various house telephone extensions, for Brenda had installed a phone in every room, including the garage. But there was no busy family here. Everything existed for Brenda alone, who, often as not, ruled the household from her bed.

Her hours were odd and chaotic, continuing the pattern established after her separation from Ship. It was not uncommon for Brenda to sleep all day and be up all night. Naturally, she insisted on her servants staying up with her. Often, just when her lady's maid and nurses were getting ready to go home, Brenda would get an urge to clean out closets or reorganize the kitchen drawers. Sometimes she would decide that her dresses were all on the wrong hangers, and she'd stay up all night with a servant, moving them to different hangers. The next night she would put them all back. "My eyes wouldn't stay open," says Celia Mohr, a nurse who endured many of Brenda's nocturnal projects. "Joe would say, 'Celia, here's a Dexedrine. If you can't stay awake, take it.' I'd get the bus at eight in the morning and fall right asleep."

Victoria recalls that "no one wanted to be the last one with her because then you usually had to spend the whole night with her, watching her sitting at her dressing table sorting things out. Everyone would try to ease out of the room. That's why she'd start fights with people to keep them there. She did this with everybody."

Brenda's daytime demands were equally impossible. Sometimes she'd send her chauffeur on a doomed search for Raven Red lipstick or some other long-extinct cosmetic. Other times she'd send him out to the local movie theaters to buy Milk Duds. When he return, she invariably complained that he had bought the wrong-sized boxes.

Still, there were times when Brenda found herself alone. During those times she stayed upstairs in her bedroom. For company she had her ubiquitous pills and several bottles of Great Western champagne in a small icebox. If she couldn't get anyone on the phone at the last minute to come over to cook for her, she'd sauté chicken livers in sherry in an electric fondue pot in her sitting room.

Her day typically began when one of her servants served her breakfast in bed—to eat, poached egg on toast, or cereal and milk; to drink, a split of champagne, or vodka and water. Sometimes she would not eat the food, but she always sipped the drink. Next she would have a Dexedrine to help wake her up, followed by a Librium or some other tranquilizer to calm her down. Then, if the Librium relaxed her too much, she'd take a Ritalin to pep herself up. Next she would take a bath, put on her makeup, and get dressed—an undeviating ritual that often took several hours and the assistance of one or two people.

Sitting in her silk underwear on a pink-velvet-cushioned brass chair in front of her dressing table, Brenda would put on her Glamour Girl mask—foundation, dark red lipstick, false eyelashes, rice powder, and sometimes a black velvet beauty mark under her eye. She would remove the pink plastic rollers she had worn to bed and comb out her hair. Her lady's maids would then bring in a selection of outfits, with appropriate shoes and gloves. For a while the maids kept ledgers in which they recorded the days she wore each suit, dress, and ball gown. After she was dressed, one of the maids would make a corsage for her out of three carnations. If it was cold outside, she would put on one of her twenty-two fur coats, and at last she was ready to go out.

By now, she was inevitably behind schedule. For years Brenda arrived an hour or two late for her psychiatric appointments, a habit that led the doctor to bill her not only for her appointment but also for the one after it.

In the car on the way to her appointment, Brenda usually

had a drink. She carried a glass in her handbag, and sometimes she carried a flask in the shape of a radio that often contained "fuzzies," a mixture of Cointreau and vodka. After her appointment, Brenda often stopped at a restaurant for a chicken salad sandwich and champagne, and later she might go to the pharmacy to pick up some pills. By the time she got home, usually at around three-thirty in the afternoon, she would be so exhausted that she sometimes passed out. Her maids learned how to groom Brenda while she was unconscious. They polished her toes as she lay unknowing in bed; sometimes they propped her up like a rag doll to roll her hair in curlers.

Brenda's psychiatrist insists that Brenda wasn't an alcoholic, and indeed her friends and servants say they rarely saw her staggering around drunk. And yet, by one accepted definition, an alcoholic is someone who organizes his or her behavior around drinking, and who continues to drink even though it causes medical or psychological problems. Frequently, after drinking, Brenda would collapse into a deep sleep in the middle of the afternoon—sometimes even in a restaurant. Over time, her liver was damaged. Although she occasionally stopped drinking—once in Medfield for almost a year—she could never give it up for good. Ever since her debut days, alcohol had been as much a part of her life as fresh flowers or chintz upholstery. Champagne and cocktails were at the heart of the nightclubs where Brenda spent almost all her evenings as a teenager. Over the years her drinking progressed. Nanny Bishop told one of the lady's maids that Brenda had had a drinking problem since age twenty-five. Excessive drinking, exacerbated by excessive dieting, was probably at least partly to blame for her three miscarriages. "You couldn't take [liquor] away from her or she'd be miserable," says Victoria.

Whenever Brenda was in the hospital, she would have her servants sneak liquor into her room in flower pots and witch hazel bottles. She took a drink the very first thing in the morning, and she drank steadily throughout the day. She drank in the car; she drank alone in bed. She hid vodka bottles behind the drapes in her bedroom. Sometimes she went to the dentist with a bottle of liquor in her handbag. "She'd have a drink before she came in, and if I went to check another patient, she'd [sneak] a drink," says Brenda's dentist, Dr. Murray Gavel. Occasionally she would pass out in the dentist's chair, and Dr. Gavel would have to wake her up. But Brenda, drunk and incoherent, wouldn't want to move. "Just give me the key, and I'll lock the door after you leave," she used to tell him.

Her servants and friends seldom saw her finish a drink. Usually she'd take a few sips and then order a fresh one. But she was dependent on holding a glass in her hand. Although her servants gently urged her to cut back and tried to dilute her drinks, Brenda always noticed and sent the concoctions back for more liquor. She was what members of Alcoholics Anonymous call "a high-bottom drunk"; that is, her alcoholism was so protected by money, sycophants, and a life free of responsibilities that she never reached "bottom," the point of physical, emotional, and financial ruin when many alcoholics at last decide to seek help.

Brenda's psychiatrist probably denies the extent of her drinking problem in part because he was focusing on her depression and her anorexia and in part because he did not know just how much she drank. Patricia Walsh Chadwick, the young woman who worked as Brenda's chauffeur in the summer of 1974, recalls that the psychiatrist seemed surprised when she told him that Brenda consumed several ounces of vodka every morning before her appointment. The Dexedrine kept her alert, and she'd drench herself in perfume to cover any hint of the smell of alcohol. She also managed to hide it by sheer force of will.

Again, even at her most feeble and vulnerable, she projected an image of glamour. Through the power of her personality she could create an illusion of sobriety, even of health and beauty. "She could make you think there was nothing wrong with her," says Ruth McCarthy, one of her lady's maids.

Reporter Bernard Weinraub, who interviewed Brenda in Medfield for *Esquire* magazine, was struck by the strong personality under Brenda's "Blanche DuBois" exterior. "She looked ghastly. Incredibly frail and skinny with a shrunken face. But given all that, in a funny way she was vibrant," he recalls. "There was a real strength there that you wouldn't expect. She smoked a lot and drank a lot of champagne. I remember going to the refrigerator and seeing no food, just bottles of champagne. But as soon as you began talking to her, she was fascinating.''

The power behind Brenda's physical ravagement is revealed in an eerie Diane Arbus photograph that accompanied Weinraub's article. The portrait shows Brenda, fully made up and wrapped in a fur bed jacket, lying against fluffy pillows. One perfectly manicured hand holds a burning cigarette; the hard light of her bedside lamp reveals every line in her wistful face.

Brenda's friends were shocked by the cruel exaggeration of her physical appearance. Arbus, Brenda's friends believed, had turned Brenda into a freak. Actually, Arbus's camera had exposed the freak in Brenda and, in so doing, brilliantly captured her essence.

CHAPTER SIXTEEN

T HE CLINICAL DIAGNOSIS of Brenda's mental condition was "borderline personality"—that is, she straddled the line that separates the sane from the insane. Psychoanalysis was, in some practical ways, a logical choice of treatment for her. Brenda could easily afford its cost—about fifty dollars an hour in the 1960s—and the demands on her time—three to five hours a week. But many analysts would have refused to treat Brenda. Traditionally, classical Freudian analysis has been meant for "healthy neurotics." People with problems like Brenda's—alcoholism, drug dependency, narcissistic conditions—have long been considered by most of the Freudian community as too sick to be analyzed. What is more, orthodox analysis required that the patient possess a degree of maturity, and Brenda was still little more than a child. Yet there have always been analysts willing to take on borderline patients. Freud's colleague Sandor Ferenczi, for example, believed that what these patients needed was to partake of "the advantages of a normal nursery," for the first time in their lives.

It was this kind of "nursery care" that Brenda's psychiatrist provided. He was a distinguished Freudian analyst with a thriving practice, and was associated at various times with several Boston-area universities. He treated Brenda until the end of her life, visiting her at home and in the hospital when she was too sick to go to this office. He had a profound effect on her life. "He kept my mother alive," says Victoria. "He kept her going. And he gave her self-confidence. He was someone she could talk to.'' Adds another of the psychiatrist's patients, an engineer, ''[The psychiatrist] has a reputation for not going by the book. But he was a very pragmatic physician. He more than kept [Brenda] alive. He added a dimension to her life that she wouldn't [otherwise] have had. It's because of him that she started painting and writing.''

''From day one, [Brenda knew] I cared enough to see her, to work with her, no matter how inconvenient or difficult it was,'' says her psychiatrist. ''Brenda knew she could count on me twenty-four hours a day. Brenda would call me and call me. Each time I made it a more vital goal for her not to call me—to internalize me. To know I'm there and I'm ready for her call, but that I'm joyous that she's able not to call. It's the beginning of self-sufficiency. But it took years [for the calls] to stop.

''Brenda used to come two hours late! How could I carry on a practice? I'd give up my lunchtime for her. Finally I'd schedule her for eleven o'clock, but I would know the earliest she'd get here would be eleven-thirty, so I'd plan for the previous patient to stay here until eleven-thirty. If she came early, she'd wait five minutes. Later she came on time, quite on time, quite often. But it took her many, many years.

''I became her most important mother. She had to relive her entire childhood and build a new self-concept. That had to be built up slowly and painfully in therapy. For the first time in her life she had to trust somebody.''

For Brenda this psychiatric nursery was irresistible. She didn't want to leave it, so she used it, like the hospital, as a home away from home. After her hour-long session, Brenda would sometimes stay in the psychiatrist's waiting room all afternoon. With one or two of her maids at her side, she would draw on a sketch pad and eat a picnic lunch of sandwiches and coffee. Then she would lie down on the sofa and fall asleep. One day the psychiatrist was about to lock up the office at seven in the evening, and Brenda was still asleep on the couch. He tried unsuccessfully to wake her. Finally he left to teach a college seminar. When he returned at eleven, Brenda hadn't moved.

In her relationship to the psychiatrist, Brenda played the child. He was caring and fatherly, but he was also autocratic.

He stripped her value system to its core and tried to help her rebuild it. Brenda was still a person searching for herself. Just as she had adopted the identity imposed on her by her family and the press, now she was adopting an identity chosen by her psychiatrist. "He was very much against my mother's life before she met him," says Victoria.

Soon Brenda started to focus on her coming-out party as one of the primary sources of her problems. The psychiatrist wanted her to see the superficiality of her life, the hollowness of her fame. "She had no self-image," says Victoria. "Something went wrong in the way we were brought up. The best part of you isn't brought out. If everything is based on looks, even if you know you're pretty, it doesn't help you. And anyway, it disappears. When you're looking in the mirror, fine. But when you walk away from the mirror, you have nothing. That's what [the psychiatrist] tried to do: give her some goals so she would think of herself as more of a person."

Brenda knew that her fame was hollow, but it pleased her to think about it and talk about it. She still regarded herself as a star. One reason the analysis never completely worked with Brenda was because its goals—growth and maturity—could not compete with the memory of her dazzling fame.

The psychiatrist was more successful in getting Brenda interested in serious subjects, mostly subjects that interested him. Her main preoccupation was with psychiatry itself. Brenda looked for psychological explanations for everyone's behavior, and she encouraged everyone around her to go into therapy. On her bed she kept notebooks and legal pads in which she would jot down her ideas, her notes from books she read on psychiatry, and her dreams. During a period when she was talking in her sleep a great deal, Brenda asked one of her lady's maids to sit by her bed while she slept and write down everything she said. Brenda took these notes to her psychiatrist.

"She seemed to be involved in a search for depth and normalcy," says one of her secretaries, Donald Chase. "She looked for depth, even when there was none to be found. In the most simple and ordinary behaviors she tried to find some great significance, some clue to character."

Being normal meant following current events. Brenda subscribed to *The Wall Street Journal* and *I. F. Stone's Weekly* and faithfully watched the evening television news. Normalcy also meant managing her finances, keeping track of what was spent, checking all receipts against bills, and making phone calls to protest overbilling. She set up an office with file cabinets, a photocopying machine, and a secretary.

Brenda's psychiatrist was interested in education, and she became interested in education. She even established a scholarship in her name at a progressive school attended by his children. She took painting lessons from a Massachusetts artist who was a childhood friend of the psychiatrist. (The psychiatrist called her previous teacher a ''French phony. He had her copy things [instead of painting from] live models.'') Although Brenda had been a Republican all her life, after she'd been in analysis for a while she became a Democrat, joining the party of her psychiatrist. She had a picture of Ship playing gold with Richard Nixon. During the 1972 presidential election, she crossed out Nixon's picture and wrote over it ''VOTE FOR McGOVERN.''

The psychiatrist violated the rules of classic analysis. He let Brenda meet some of his other patients, for example. Brenda became close friends with a man who had the appointment after hers. They had a playful, joking relationship, and several days a week they would spend fifteen minutes chatting in the waiting room, sometimes with Brenda sitting on the man's lap. It was a kind of debriefing for Brenda after her session. The psychiatrist also became involved in Brenda's life outside the office. When he took a holiday to Paris with his son, Brenda went to Paris with her stepson. It was the first time she had been to Europe since her marriage to Ship. ''We prearranged that at a certain time she would call me,'' the psychiatrist says. ''I'd wait for her call. I never saw her. We talked. There was nothing to [the conversation]. It was 'Hello, glad you're here, I hope you're enjoying yourself, etc.' ''

In one of his greatest departures from the orthodox Freudian approach, Brenda's psychiatrist reached outside the analyst's office and far back into Brenda's past to interview her friends, relatives, husbands, and servants. He talked to her baby nurse, Nanny Bishop, and former employees such as Gerald Kelly. Kelly hadn't worked for Brenda in many years, but he flew from his home in Pennsylvania to Boston, where one of Brenda's servants picked him up and took him to the psychiatrist's office. According to Kelly's recollection of the meeting, the psychiatrist tried to probe the nature of his relationship with Brenda. The meeting ended after three minutes, when Kelly, who refused to answer what he considered the psychiatrist's unsuitable questions, walked out.

Servants who threatened to quit would sometimes be summoned by the psychiatrist. (The doctor never called the servants himself. He sent a message through Brenda that he wanted to see them.) He talked to the Drozells once when they were not getting along with Brenda and urged them not to leave her. "You're like a father and mother to her," the couple remember his saying. When Patricia Walsh Chadwick, who had taken a temporary job as Brenda's chauffeur in 1974, prepared to quit at the end of the summer to pursue a real career, the psychiatrist asked her to stay on, and even live with Brenda. "You're the only person whom Brenda Frazier loves at this point in her life. She cares about you more than anyone else around her," Chadwick says the psychiatrist told her. She refused.

The psychiatrist even interviewed the reporters who interviewed Brenda. Bernard Weinraub said that before he wrote his story about Brenda for *Esquire*, she insisted he meet her psychiatrist. "I wasn't used to a shrink questioning me about a subject," recalls Weinraub. "Brenda took me up to his office. So I sat there for a while, and I couldn't quite get what his point was. He wanted to know what I was about. I got the feeling he just wanted to see me to make sure that I was on the level."

The psychiatrist also interviewed some of Brenda's prospective employees. In one of the stranger incidents, he talked to Donald Chase, whom Brenda had hired as a secretary in 1965. On the day of the interview Chase was wearing a suit that he had not worn since his college graduation a few weeks before, and it still had a Phi Beta Kappa key in the lapel. Chase recalls the psychiatrist pointing to the gold symbol and asking, "Why are you wearing that? Are you compensating for an undersized penis?"

The psychiatrist tried to explore Chase's motives for taking the job. He mentioned that Brenda had had a troubled life and that she consumed more liquor and pills than she should have. Chase recalls, "He said he would appreciate my monitoring her liquor and pill intake, and he asked me if I would try to discourage these habits to the extent I could without becoming abrasive and jeopardizing my position." Then the psychiatrist asked Chase what he would do if Brenda made a pass at him. "He wanted to know how would I handle it? And how did I react to his bringing up the possibility? It was assumed that Brenda and I would be alone in the house at night, and he wanted to know if this was something I had already thought about. He presented it as a real and present danger."

Although some of Brenda's friends and relatives were appalled at her psychiatrist's techniques, many analysts today say that borderlines like Brenda need a type of structuring, nurturing therapy—they need doctors like Brenda's who are more active than those practicing traditional Freudian analysis.

In Brenda's relationship as child to her psychiatrist-father, the real child in her household, Victoria, suffered. "He certainly didn't help my life," she says. "He made my life miserable because his first thought was her." Because of the psychiatrist's influence on her mother, says Victoria, "at sixteen my whole outlook on life was supposed to change." Victoria says she "was supposed to start living like his kids," that is, attending a progressive school, earning top grades, and eventually going to a good college.

"My mother didn't want me to go back to Miss Hewitt's, which I desperately wanted to do," she adds. "I loved Miss Hewitt's. My years there when I was younger were probably my happiest years. She wanted me to go to the [same school the psychiatrist's] children went [to]. But I didn't think it was a good idea to send someone who's been used to traditional school to an innovative school in the twelfth grade. Luckily, the headmaster there was really super and when I told him, 'Look, I don't want to come here,' he said, 'Well, Victoria, we don't want people who don't want to come here.' So he wouldn't accept me. So with Daddy's help I got back to Miss Hewitt's and I boarded there."

Under the psychiatrist's influence, Brenda decided that what she really wanted was to be a mother. The object of this sudden maternal attention, of course, was Victoria. "I wasn't used to dealing with a mother," says Victoria. "I wasn't even dealing with a person I knew.

"Everything [the psychiatrist] was trying to do was right. And he is brilliant. But you just can't change someone like my mother. She went from one way to another. And it didn't make any sense. Suddenly she was not just the debutante. She was going to do something worthwhile with her life. She was going to be a mother now."

The problem was exacerbated by Brenda's jealous feelings toward Victoria. "Her mother dearly loved her in her own way. But I will say Brenda was a poor mother," says Frances Griffin. "She was jealous of Victoria: of her youth, of her beauty, of her wit. Victoria never had the kind of clothes that you'd expect a millionaire's daughter to have. Brenda wouldn't give her any money. Then, when she did give her money, she expected it to last forever. Yet she wanted Victoria to have a very high life.

"Brenda certainly wasn't interested in Victoria as a teenager. She paid no attention to her. She acted sometimes like she just couldn't stand Victoria." One night about 4 A.M. Victoria was studying in her bedroom on the third floor. Suddenly Brenda's low, sexy voice wafted up the stairs: "Pookie!" Brenda was in her bedroom on the floor below with Frances Griffin. "I wonder if Pookie is up?" Brenda said. "What do you want?" Griffin said. "A spoon," answered Brenda. "Well, you know Victoria is studying. I'll get you the spoon," offered Griffin. "No!" Brenda insisted. "Pookie will get it."

"Brenda was determined to get that kid to go from her room on the third floor all the way down to the kitchen," recalls Griffin. She rang Victoria's phone and made her go downstairs to get the spoon.

Brenda could not tolerate seeing Victoria as the center of attention. Once her mother and some of the servants planned a birthday party for Victoria in the hospital where Victoria was recuperating following kidney surgery. Several of the girl's friends had gathered in her room to talk and eat birthday cake. In the middle of the party Brenda turned to Dorothy Caverno and said, "Why don't we go in the other room so you can do my nails?"

By the spring of 1963 it had been almost a decade since Brenda's affair with Pietro, and since then she'd lived in relative obscurity. But suddenly her name exploded into the headlines again. The attention was sparked by Brenda's announcement that eighteen-year-old Victoria would not be coming out.

Anyone reading the papers or newsmagazines got the idea that Brenda's decision was the result of a strong moral stand against frivolity and a deep commitment to Victoria's intellectual development. "Brenda intends to guide her daughter into a purposeful life," wrote the Boston *Traveler*. "That's something she feels publicity cheated her out of and something which she only now—in her 40s—is beginning to acquire. College education, Brenda thinks, will give Victoria 'the right outlook.' Does that mean Victoria will come out later? 'No,' said her mother. 'You don't put it off.' . . . How does the non-debutante herself feel about it? 'She feels I know best,' said the former glamour deb."

In another interview in the Boston *Traveler,* Brenda proposed that other debs follow Victoria's example. Instead of coming out, she suggested that each deb "adopt a needy child." This "would give the young people a sense of responsibility and provide a personal contact," Brenda told a reporter.

The national press soon picked up the story about Brenda and her non-debuting daughter. *Newsweek* ran an item under the headline "Mother Knows Best." "Last week, at 41, Medfield, Mass., matron Brenda Frazier Kelly Chatfield-Taylor vetoed a coming-out party for . . . Brenda Victoria Kelly, daughter of the eternal deb's first marriage to ex-football star Shipwreck Kelly. Mother Brenda said: 'I don't think Victoria is ready for it. I don't think I was ready for it either. The publicity got out of control, wouldn't you say? Really, publicity belongs to people who achieve something, and I don't consider being a debutante an achievement.' "

Time ran a picture of Ship, Brenda, and Victoria talking at the Stork Club. A caption read: " 'Too many people see the debut as a goal,' declares Brenda, 'but perspective is more important. I want my daughter to have a full life.' Recently ill, the former glamour girl admits that her own perspective was improved by two years of psychoanalysis. 'I'm very happy now—and looking forward, not backward.' ''

In fact, though, Brenda's surprising moral stand had come quite suddenly—and with more than a bit of expediency. Despite the hours she'd spent with her psychiatrist discussing the frivolity of her debut, despite her new insistence that debuts were wasteful, Brenda had been planning a debut for her daughter, even reserving the roof of the St. Regis Hotel in New York for the occasion. (Victoria ended up giving the reservation to her best friend.) The reason Victoria didn't come out had nothing to do with her mother's new value system. Victoria didn't have a debut because she and her mother had had a fight.

Brenda wanted Victoria to go to Wellesley. But the girl wanted to go to Sarah Lawrence, partly because she wanted to be away from her mother, and partly because she wanted to be in New York. Victoria refused to apply to Wellesley, "So my mother said, 'That's it. No coming-out party,' '' recalls Victoria.

"The only thing I had been brought up to think about was having a coming-out party, getting married, and living happily ever after. I was brought up to be rich, pretty, and marry someone. No one ever said that to me, but that was the message. Then they changed the goals on me at the last minute, and really I was left with nothing.

"I was so aggravated when all these stories came out afterward that [my mother] didn't want me to have the debut because it wasn't good for me, and all that garbage. Everybody who knew her used to read those articles and say, 'Yuk.' Not having a debut was embarrassing. Actually, it probably got more publicity than it would have if I'd come out: 'The deb that didn't come out.' But I went to everybody else's parties. People thought, 'If they're so against coming-out parties, why is it that Victoria is at every single coming-out party that year?' It didn't make much sense.''

That summer *Life* magazine got in touch with Brenda. The magazine was interested in doing a story about her and her non-debuting daughter. Carroll Clancy, who at the time was a young writer in the magazine's "Modern Living" section, recalls visiting Brenda in Medfield on a humid July day. "It was very hot, but Brenda was immaculately turned out, in a

silk dress and pearls, and her hair was beautifully coiffed,"
says Clancy. "She was drinking champagne all day long even
though she was having trouble with her liver." Despite Clancy's attempts to steer the conversation to Victoria, Brenda
refused to talk about anything but herself. "She focused everything on herself, her illness, and her husbands," says
Clancy. "She was very bitter about her second husband. She
said that he had spent so much of her money that she almost
had to dip into her trusts." Clancy went back to New York
thinking, she says, "that Brenda wasn't much of a story, unless you wanted to write a piece about the destruction of a
woman."

But, perhaps sensing Clancy's lack of interest, Brenda wrote
a long letter to Henry Luce, bitterly complaining about the
young woman. Brenda's account of the interview completely
misstated the facts, and her whining tone was out of propor-
tion to the casual nature of Clancy's visit. Brenda complained
in her letter that although Clancy worked for a publication of
"national importance," she had not been as "intuitive . . .
and empathic" as a society editor who had recently interviewed her for a Boston newspaper. What she had wished
was an opportunity to express her views about the role and
responsibility of mothers as the cornerstone of the family
structure, but instead, she wrote, "Miss [Clancy] seemed
most impressed with factual minutiae and with tangential observations, all of which she noted down with avidity; . . . she
seemed little interested in any attempt on my part to discuss
what I felt was the important core of what I had to say. . . .
I cannot hope that the results of the interview will turn out
to be satisfactory either to your purpose or to my intention."

A copy of the letter—or perhaps an early draft—was with
Brenda's papers when she died. It is not clear whether she
sent the letter, but in any case *Life* decided to go ahead with
the story. Under an arrangement worked out with Brenda, the
story would be ghost-written by a professional writer, but
would appear under Brenda's by-line. She would have final
approval of the manuscript and be paid a fee of $10,000. The
point of the story would be that Brenda Frazier, the world's
most famous deb, was denouncing the entire debutante culture. Her psychiatrist encouraged her to cooperate with the
magazine. He was trying to get her interested, if not in a true

career—it was certainly too late for that—then in a serious avocation. He thought that an article that appeared under her own name would give her a sense of achievement and perhaps spark an interest in doing some writing of her own.

In October, a *Life* ghost-writer arrived at Brenda's home for what would turn out to be one of the most harrowing weeks of his career. The writer was meeting the former glamour girl for the first time and was shocked at her appearance. Brenda looked sick and old, with an emaciated body and a drawn, lined face. Yet she was always primping. She struck the writer as "a damn difficult woman. It was a strain to be around her for even five minutes."

She insisted that all the interviews be conducted from her bedroom. As the writer perched in a chintz-covered chair taking notes, Brenda sat up in bed, sipping champagne and talking. It was painful for her to discuss her family and her past, and it was difficult for her to stick to the subject. She rambled continually.

Everywhere was evidence of her sessions with her psychiatrist. She interpreted everyone's behavior in light of the little knowledge she had picked up from him. Brenda regarded her whole family background and her years as a debutante as painful incidents. Recalling her past was unpleasant. So she'd talk for a little while about it, then she'd digress, and the writer would have to steer her back. It took hours and hours to get information for the article out of her.

Brenda was only interested in discussing events that illuminated either her psyche or the writer's. Once, while reading a funny book in front of Brenda, the writer laughed so hard that he cried. "That's a sign of depression," Brenda said.

Another night, as Brenda, Victoria, and the writer were finishing dinner, there was a knock at the door—it was one of Brenda's neighbors, collecting money for a charity. Brenda invited him up to her bedroom to talk. Hours later, the man came downstairs and asked to use the phone to call his wife. The writer overheard him complain that he'd be late because Brenda had kept him there. "There was no way I could get away from her," the man said. After the neighbor left, the writer went upstairs to Brenda's bedroom to resume work. "I just couldn't get rid of that fellow," Brenda said. "He's obviously madly in love with me."

Brenda, however, was in love with the writer, an attractive, gentle man whose rapt attention to her every word was, for Brenda, irresistible. But the writer was a happily married man, and he made it clear he had no romantic interest in her. Nevertheless, "she chased him mercilessly," says Victoria Kelly. When the writer failed to respond to Brenda's advances, she instructed the maids to spray his pillow with her perfume. "Brenda thought that was exciting," says Dorothy Caverno.

During his visit the writer and Brenda went out together only twice. Once on a car ride they passed a roadside tavern, and Brenda decided to stop for a bottle of champagne. It was a cheap, dirty café, and the writer was surprised it sold champagne at all. Brenda wanted her usual brut. The waiter opened a bottle and poured it. Brenda took a sip and said, "This isn't brut. We'll have to send it back."

The ghost-written Brenda Frazier story appeared in *Life*'s December 6, 1963, issue, which went to press a week after President Kennedy's assassination and contained a twenty-page cover story about the slain President's funeral. Brenda was convinced that her story had been bumped off the cover by Kennedy's death, but in fact it had always been scheduled as an inside piece.

The story appeared on page 133 under the headline "MY DEBUT—A HORROR; the most famous deb of all denounces the life she lived."

It began with a scene from one of Brenda's suicide attempts and flashed back through her sad childhood, the misery behind her glittering celebrity, her two failed marriages, and her redemption through psychoanalysis. There was no mention of her alcoholism, her drug addiction, or her anorexia.

The story was generally accurate about the major events of Brenda's life and accurately reflected the ideas she held when it was written. But it contained several exaggerations designed to make the reader believe that Brenda was now a mature, self-confident woman, a woman who had a thriving, happy relationship with her daughter, a woman who was in control of her life:

I have the strength now to view my friends and acquaintances realistically, and to choose deliberately those whom

I like dearly and whom I want to like me very deeply. My feet no longer swell. This may seem like a minor sign of progress, but you have no idea how much it means to me; it means, in a symbolic way, that at last I have the courage to stand on my own two feet. I am a person, an individual, an adult; I can make my own decisions and stand by them, right or wrong. I no longer suffer the fear of nameless mistakes that once was a part of my childhood nightmares.

I am at last becoming a real mother to my daughter; I am free now to give her both love and the guidance that teenagers require and desperately want. (Our first step was to agree that she would not have a coming-out party, a decision in which she takes great pride. She has not been pushed into the first irrevocable circle of a meaningless social whirl and is free to choose her own kind of future.) Indeed, it has been one of my constant joys to watch, each day that I become more mature and self-sufficient as a person, how Victoria also matures and thrives as an individual. This is one of the happy side effects of psychoanalysis: not only the patient but the patient's loved ones profit from it, as the old barriers preventing a free flow of affection and communication are broken down.

I am starting to paint again and may do it seriously. Mostly I want to write, or perhaps lecture, and in so doing tell the world how sad it is, and how unnecessary, that so many of us should never learn to live at all—and, worse, never give our children their birthright, their own chance to live.

Despite the inaccuracies about her physical and emotional health and her relationship with her daughter, the overall tone of the story was authentic, and it revealed that Brenda had indeed acquired some degree of self-knowledge through her analysis. The piece had a powerful effect on *Life*'s readers. Brenda received about two hundred letters from people who were moved both by the tragedy underpinning her fame and by her courage in publicly revealing it. The letters poured in from housewives, evangelical Christians, and inmates on death row; from psychiatrists, long-lost relatives, friends from Brenda's debut days, and former servants. She received a letter from one of the lawyers who represented her mother during the custody battle. "After reading your story in *Life*, I understand now some things which years ago puzzled and saddened me," he wrote. Yale Law School requested permission to reprint excerpts of the article in a book about law and psychiatry. The conservative publisher William Loeb even wrote an editorial about it in his newspaper, the Manchester, New Hampshire, *Union Leader*. Under the headline "BROKEN CHAMPAGNE BUBBLES," Loeb used Brenda's confession as a basis for sermonizing on the evils of inherited wealth and the class of idle snobs it created. Those complaints then segued into a screed on the dangers of excessive publicity:

> The end result is that more attention is paid to the so-called image, created in the minds of the public, than to the intrinsic value of the professional services rendered, the product manufactured, or the painting created, or the political service given. The idea has developed that if you just publicize the third- or fourth-rate enough you can put it across.

With characteristic lack of understatement, Loeb summed up in a paragraph published in all capital letters:

> OF COURSE THIS IS NOT ONLY THE WAY TO LOWER THE QUALITY OF AMERICAN LIFE AND TO DESTROY REAL HAPPINESS; IT IS ALSO THE WAY TO THE RUINATION OF THE NATION ITSELF.

The *Life* article greatly boosted Brenda's self-confidence. She loved the publicity surrounding it. For the first time in all the years of her celebrity, she believed she was getting attention that was well deserved. As she wrote in a letter after the article appeared:

> Publicity today is a totally different subject than it was at the time at which I made my debut. At that time I saw no necessity for publicity as I did not feel that it has any part in the lives of those who have accomplished nothing in life, except to fill space where there happens to be no news item at that time in newspapers. . . . I was unable to live a private life and was, nevertheless, a private citizen you might

*also say! This was taken away from me, because my every
move was recorded and misinterpreted, on many an occasion. . . . It was not an easy article to write, and I was well
aware at the time that it would engender a great deal of
feeling among a certain sphere which I had traveled in, and
in which, I naturally included myself. My satisfaction has
been in the wonderful feeling one has in the knowledge of
having achieved something of value.*

In the aftermath of the *Life* story, Brenda became a kind
of spokeswoman for the abolition of the debut. By then the
custom had already started eroding in the country's growing
mood of liberalism. In the Northeast, in particular, lavish
coming-out parties were increasingly regarded as relics from
an outdated social order. Deb apologists had not been helped
when a ball for Philadelphia debutante Fernanda Wanamaker
Wetherill turned into a wrecking party. Fernanda's friends
demolished several thousand dollars' worth of property at a
Southampton, Long Island, house her stepfather had rented
for the occasion. Apparently there was a great deal of cavorting. Several boys were tried and acquitted of vandalism;
and one boy was turned down for Air Force officers' training
because of the incident.

Brenda appeared on several television talk shows, including David Susskind's "Open End," vigorously arguing her
case. In the end, though, it was probably her physical ravagement, more than anything she said, that made the most
powerful statement against the debut. One man wrote to his
daughter after watching Susskind's show: "What I gather is
that the debutante party is here to stay as long as: 1) the
money holds out, 2) people with money continue to have
daughters and, 3) the daughters don't take a look at [Brenda]
Frazier and suddenly think: 'There I am in 35 years,' and
begin to run as fast as they can."

All this time Brenda was still privately cherishing her memories of debut balls where girls wore "lovely dresses that
flared like flowers when you were dancing and you could look
around the ballroom and everyone looked so nice." She was
always interested in the details of debut parties attended by
her acquaintances. Donald Chase recalls being worried about
telling Brenda that he had attended a few debut balls in New

York. "I thought there might be a diatribe along the lines of 'Why are you wasting your time?' " he says. "But Brenda's reaction was perfectly level. She asked, 'Oh, did you have a good time? Were the girls pretty?' "

In many ways Brenda still thought of herself as Deb of the Year. Her need to be irresistible to men was so strong that it led her to make the most grandiose, unrealistic statements about various suitors who were in love with her. Actually, she didn't seem to have any friends of either sex. One night she admitted to the *Life* writer that no one except Charles Banino called her regularly on the phone.

"Sometimes when I got home after I'd been with her all day, Brenda would call me and say, 'Please, can you come back?' " says Ruth McCarthy. One New Year's Eve she called McCarthy nearly in tears. "I just can't stand being alone. Are you doing anything, dear?" Brenda asked. Occasionally Brenda had dates—her escorts included a married car salesman, a local lawyer, an innkeeper. She was still terrified of social functions. Even a casual dinner date with a man brought out all the anxiety of her debut, and she would avoid going out until absolutely the last moment. Sometimes after waiting for several hours her date would leave. Even if Brenda was bathed and dressed when her date arrived, she would often dawdle for hours in her room, cleaning out a drawer or talking on the phone. Sometimes she wouldn't be ready to go out until midnight or later, long after most restaurants had closed. Celia Mohr's son, Jack, who worked for Brenda while he was in high school, said he sometimes called restaurants in Boston at Brenda's request and offered to pay them whatever it cost to stay open until Brenda arrived. After a while, the men stopped calling, and Brenda spent most evenings alone.

In 1968, at age forty-seven, Brenda decided to leave Medfield. Her large old house was too expensive and too isolating. After considering and finally rejecting a rental on Memorial Drive, she found a ten-room apartment in an elegant old building at 81 Beacon Street, overlooking Boston's Public Gardens. Beacon Street, "the sunny street that holds the sifted few," as Oliver Wendell Holmes described it, has been for two centuries the seat of Boston's social elite.

Although Brenda never became the social climber that Lady

Jane and Big Brenda raised her to be, underneath her new seriousness a part of her yearned to join society. In moving to Beacon Street, she placed herself in a socially advantageous position in one of the few American cities where society still mattered.

Brenda had visions of planning charity balls in Back Bay parlors, strolling through the Boston Common at dusk, and playing bridge at the Chilton Club under the watchful gaze of Victorian socialites preserved in oil on the wall.

Instead, she moved to Boston and went back to bed.

CHAPTER SEVENTEEN

In its mixture of elegance and shabbiness, Brenda's second-floor apartment reflected not only her isolation but also, in a way, her madness. At first glance the rooms appeared opulent, although impossibly cluttered. As visitors entered the foyer, they were met by a large Venetian glass mirror. The fragrance of fresh flowers mingled with an exotic scent (imported from a London florist) that was held in a heated brass tray on a marble table. The living room was crowded with furniture, including two three-tiered tables filled with photographs from Brenda's debut days. Other tables were covered by porcelain figures, pillboxes, lamps, and bowls of fresh flowers. A larger-than-life portrait of Lady Jane by the English portrait artist Simon Elwes hung over an antique desk. But a closer look around the apartment showed that neglect had set in. The chintz upholstery on the chairs was stained and ripped. The paint was peeling and cracked. The entire apartment was a blending of the expensive and the tacky. In the dining room, for example, there was an elaborate crystal chandelier. But the built-in shelves were covered with cheap green Formica.

Brenda spent most of her time in her bedroom at the back of the apartment. The focal point of the room was the bed. It had a high quilted headboard covered in a rose-patterned chintz. On top of the bed were clouds of lacy pillows and flowered cotton sheets, which Brenda always covered with plastic before eating or slitting her wrists. On one side of the bed stood a menagerie of fluffy toy animals. On a table at the foot of the bed were stacks of books, magazines, letters, and notebooks. Frequently Brenda entertained from her bed, seating her guests at collapsible wooden trays set up around her. Other times she simply lay there and wrote letters or talked endlessly on the phone to friends, sipping vodka and smoking cigarettes that she stubbed out in bullet shells. She once sent a friend a picture of herself sitting in bed, smoking a cigarette, surrounded by her pillows and stuffed animals. Underneath the picture she wrote: "Each one has their own fortress and I'm in mine."

Among the bedroom's expensive antiques and gold and silver objects was a collection of kitsch: a scallop fountain on the wall and two framed "moving" pictures—one of the Circle Line trip around Manhattan, the other of the Cape Cod coast. Brenda had a sentimental attachment to presents. A maid she once befriended at Cape Cod Hospital used to send her gifts from wherever she vacationed. Once the maid gave Brenda a plastic ashtray from a resort in New Jersey. For years Brenda kept it on her night table next to a $5,000 gold frame. She also had a collection of novelty clocks, including one that projected the time on the ceiling, and another that announced the time in a man's voice.

The clocks were an ironic touch, considering that time meant nothing to Brenda. She continued her pattern of reversing night and day, and she was usually two hours late for most appointments, including her own parties. Sometimes she never showed up at all. She never made it, for example, to the twenty-first birthday party she had planned for Victoria at the Ritz.

When she first moved to Boston, Brenda made an effort to go out, for a time appearing regularly at charity balls and dinner dances. Yet she was never accepted by the Back Bay Brahmins, just as her mother and grandmother were never accepted by New York's Old Guard. She belonged to no society, except the false community that unites celebrities. Even her stepson, who was only eleven when he met Brenda, sensed immediately that she was an arriviste. "A lot of my feeling was that the Chatfield-Taylors were authentic, and Brenda wasn't," he says. "The Chatfield-Taylors were a family with a lot of pride. Brenda was a kind of newcomer."

But to ordinary Bostonians she was a star. She was interviewed by the local society reporters and asked to model clothes and judge beauty contests. People asked her for autographs, and photographers snapped her picture. "Boston sort of held her in awe," says Bill Fripp, who wrote a society column for the Boston *Globe*. "People would see her and say to themselves, 'That's Brenda Frazier. I remember when she was on the cover of *Life*.' "

Through her forays into Boston's social world, Brenda made many new friends. She met the Canadian writer W. E. D. Ross, who patterned the main character in his pulp novel *Sable in the Rain* after Brenda. She became close to Howard Gotlieb, a director of the Mugar Memorial Library at Boston University. Gotlieb called her every day and invited her to all the library functions. Sometimes Brenda took straw hampers filled with champagne and food to Gotlieb's office, and they would picnic on the carpet. At a party one night she met Alexander MacLeod, a hairdresser and amateur historian. Tall and dignified, with gray hair and blue eyes, MacLeod fulfilled the role Vava Adlerberg had once played in Brenda's life. He dined with Brenda every Wednesday night, escorted her to parties, gave her dozens of books, and sent her flowers every week.

Not all her social forays were successful, and sometimes her ravaged, freakish appearance led to cruel moments. After hearing a famous lesbian poet speak at Boston University, Brenda found herself seated next to the woman at dinner. In the middle of the meal the poet turned to Howard Gotlieb, who had arranged the evening. "Howard, you know I only like to be near *beautiful* women," he recalled her saying.

She was a wispy shell of her former self, yet Brenda was still devoted to preserving her glamour image. Once she showed up to go sailing with a friend wearing a mink-lined raincoat and golf shoes. Throughout her life she preserved the grooming and etiquette rituals of her childhood. "My mother thought your handbag, gloves, and shoes should match," says Victoria. "It was no small thing for her to change her handbag. For most people changing their handbag means putting their wallet, comb, cigarettes, and compact into another one. For my mother it meant taking out thirty things, all solid gold, from one handbag and squeezing them into another.''

As her life grew tawdrier, her gestures grew grander. Instead of sending her local letters through the mail, she had her chauffeur deliver them by hand. Once, when Brenda and MacLeod went to the movies in suburban Boston, her chauffeur followed the couple into the theater, carrying a tray full of hors d'oeuvres and a bottle of champagne. For years Brenda ordered her clothes over the phone from Selma Craft, a saleswoman at Saks whom she had never met. One day Brenda's chauffeur walked up to Mrs. Craft in the store and said that Brenda Frazier was waiting outside in her Mercedes. As Mrs. Craft approached the car, she saw Brenda, dressed in a fur coat and jewels, sitting in the back seat, drinking champagne. Brenda offered Craft a glass, and the two women sat together for a few minutes chatting and sipping their drinks.

Around the house Brenda acted like a queen. Her grandlady posturing was so outrageous that some of her friends started calling her Marie Antoinette. Brenda was incapable of performing many of the most basic tasks for herself. A maid had to draw her bath for her and even prepare her toilet paper. Brenda demanded that four sheets from the roll be folded and placed on a table next to the toilet or the side of the tub. Once when a servant accidentally tore off five sheets, Brenda exploded, "Are you trying to plug up my loo?"

Perhaps because as a child she had often been abandoned during holidays in the care of servants, Brenda put a lot of effort into celebrating Christmas. Every year she embarked on a frenzy of activity to send out three hundred cards and presents, some to people she hadn't seen in thirty years. Dozens of people received Christmas cards saying that her present to them was a donation in their name to her psychiatrist's children's school. She would also send plants, boxes of gourmet food, silver toothpicks, cigarette lighters, walking sticks, briefcases. Everything was done at the last minute, and during the last few days before Christmas the entire staff would be up all night wrapping presents.

On Christmas Day itself, Brenda wanted to be surrounded by people. In 1972 she invited sixty-five people for dinner. Charles Banino was supposed to cook the holiday feast, but he was unable to come. Brenda sent a taxi from Boston to his weekend home in New Hampshire to pick up the pies he had made for the occasion. The party began at seven in the evening. Cocktails and eggnog were served in the living room. A buffet supper of turkey stuffed with smoked oysters and Virginia ham with brandied peaches was served in the dining room. Both Shipwreck Kelly and Robert Chatfield-Taylor were there; so were Bob Jr., Victoria, Brenda's step-brother James Watriss, and an assortment of people from Boston's entertainment, fashion, and sports world. Even Dominic DiMaggio—Joe's brother, and the centerfielder for the 1946 pennant-winning Red Sox—came.

The guests drank, ate, and entertained themselves for several hours, but Brenda never appeared. She spent most of the evening puttering in her bedroom, emerging only at the end of the party to greet friends. At another soiree, when Brenda didn't show up, Alex MacLeod went to her bedroom to talk to her. She had been drinking all day long and now she was drunk. As MacLeod escorted her out of the bedroom, she stumbled. "All right, straighten yourself up, Brenda ol' girl," she said to herself. Moments later she greeted her guests in the living room, standing tall and seemingly sober.

Sometimes when Brenda appeared drunk, drugs may have been more to blame for her behavior. She consumed such large quantities of pills and drank so steadily throughout the day that often it was difficult to know what was affecting her more—liquor or drugs. Throughout the 1970s Brenda's drinking and pill-taking remained a problem. When she was under the slightest stress, when she entertained, or went to the dentist, or attended a charity committee meeting, she often got drunk. Once she showed up intoxicated to judge a Miss Massachusetts beauty contest. During the pageant Brenda kept misplacing her scorecard and forgetting to record her scores. Bill Fripp, who was sitting beside her, let her copy his scorecard. They ended up rating every contestant exactly the same.

At times Brenda seemed to have a need to display her weaknesses. At a dinner at the Ritz she arrived carrying an evening bag with a plastic container inside. Throughout the dinner she kept taking out the container and vomiting into it. Brenda's companions stoically endured her behavior, but the diners at the surrounding tables fled the room. Following the incident, Brenda wrote one of her friends an apologetic note: "I feel very badly that I was sick as it was certainly not pleasant for any of you—although I thought I did it rather gracefully. . . ."

One day Brenda got a fan letter from a man who would become the last love of her life. His name was Stanley Stanwick, and he worked as an accountant for the commonwealth of Massachusetts. In his letter, Stanwick wrote that he had read about Brenda in the local papers and that he remembered her from her debut days. He said he'd like to meet her. Stanwick sounded interesting, and Brenda was deeply flattered by the attention. When he followed up the letter with a call to invite her out, Brenda "was as excited as an adolescent," says Celia Mohr. After consulting with her psychiatrist, Brenda agreed to go out with him.

At about five-thirty on a rainy February afternoon, Stanwick arrived at Brenda's apartment. He was served hors d'oeuvres while waiting for Brenda, who emerged from her bedroom with, for her, remarkable promptness, only fifteen minutes late. Joe Drozell drove the couple to Delmonico's, a restaurant in Boston's Lenox Hotel. "Brenda was lovely that night," recalls Stanwick. "She was brilliant, witty, and charming, and she ate her dinner."

After dinner the couple sat at the bar, sipping drinks and chatting as Gladys Troupin played the piano. At around 11:30 P.M. Drozell picked them up and drove them back to 81 Beacon. " 'Somehow I found myself in Brenda's bed that night," says Stanwick. "I remember waking up there the next morning."

Brenda's relationship with Stanwick was her first serious romance in nearly fifteen years, since her marriage to Robert Chatfield-Taylor.

Of course, there had been a few brief encounters, attempts to prove to herself and others that she was still attractive to men. After the Boston production of *Adaptation* and *Next*, Brenda brought some members of the cast back to her house for a party and ended up going to bed with one of the young actors. Another time, when three priests were visiting 81 Beacon, Brenda took one of them to her bedroom and seduced him. Says Victoria, "It shows that toward the end she wanted to prove that she could sleep with just about anybody. A priest, at least in people's minds, is a challenge.''

Brenda desperately wanted to believe that men still thought her beautiful. She had her face lifted, but her skin was so severely wrinkled from chronic vomiting (the stretching of facial muscles during vomiting caused deep rows of wrinkles on the sides of her mouth) that the surgery did not significantly improve her appearance.

Once she lured a man to her bed, however, she was not much interested in what went on there. She and Stanwick slept together occasionally when they first started going out. The servants always knew when it was about to happen, because Brenda would ask them to remove the stuffed animals, the books, the magazines, and the papers from her bed. Not surprisingly, given Brenda's horrid health, the physical relationship did not last long. Stanwick sought romance elsewhere. At the Cape one time, Joe Drozell saw Stanwick kissing one of Brenda's nurses in the pantry next to the kitchen. When Drozell told Brenda what was going on, she jumped out of bed and ran to the pantry, which she probably hadn't seen in years. She saw the couple embracing, and then "turned around and left," says Stanwick. "It was bad taste, I shouldn't have done it," he adds. "If I wanted to fool around with [the nurse] I should have done it on the outside. There wasn't much warmth in Brenda's bed, to make a long story short. At that point she had no interest in sex.''

Nonetheless, Stanwick remained devoted to Brenda. He kept his own apartment, but spent most nights in one of the guest rooms at 81 Beacon. He often made breakfast for Brenda before he left for work in the morning, and then returned at noon to make her lunch. If her chauffeur was off, Stanwick would leave his job in the afternoon to drive Brenda to her appointment with her psychiatrist.

"At first we were very suspicious of Stan," says Victoria. "[Brenda's financial manager] had him checked out thoroughly when he first started seeing my mother. It didn't turn up anything. Stan was a very good-looking man. He would have no trouble getting girlfriends. Normally, someone who was interested in Brenda Frazier would want to be seen with her, would want to go to parties with her and get the publicity. You couldn't drag Stan to parties. I think he only went to one with her the whole time he was with her. He wasn't getting any money for this. He wasn't having any fun. He took an incredible amount of abuse and got very little out of the relationship. They used to fight like cats and dogs. But he stayed. Why? I guess he really loved her.''

Stanwick did not tolerate Brenda's lateness or her tantrums, and his refusal to be another sycophant seems to have had a healthy influence on Brenda. In the first seven years of their relationship she was not hospitalized once, after being in and out of the hospital repeatedly in the previous seven years.

In addition to getting involved with Stanwick, Brenda was making other attempts, in the early seventies, to open up her life. She tried for the first time to develop her interest in art. One day a week for several years she took private lessons with Philip Hicken, an artist who was a good friend of her psychiatrist. Brenda's chauffeur drove her to Hicken's studio in Watertown, Massachusetts, and occasionally Brenda rented a plane to fly to his Nantucket studio. (She usually arrived an hour late and sometimes asked Hicken for a glass of vodka during the lesson.) Under Hicken's instruction, Brenda completed about nine paintings—mostly landscapes of Cape Cod. ''Her drawings weren't much. But her paintings were [good]. She had definite talent,'' Hicken recalls. ''I harped on her all the time to do more work. But she was very socially involved, and she had physical problems.''

Around this time Brenda also renewed her interest in writing her memoirs, and approached Bill Fripp about being her coauthor. ''I really feel psychologically that I need to do this book,'' she told him. Fripp was willing to take on the project. He called her every few months to remind her, but Brenda would always say, ''Not now, I'm going through a bad period.'' Finally, Fripp realized that Brenda was too chronically distracted ever to sit down and do it.

Perhaps because she had felt so unhappy and frustrated during her own youth, Brenda was very sympathetic to the student movement of the late sixties and early seventies. Through her living room window she watched the students protesting the Vietnam War in the Public Gardens. Once, after a charity benefit, Brenda and Alex MacLeod were standing on a street corner in formal dress at one in the morning, looking for a taxi. Suddenly a van filled with bedraggled, long-haired young people pulled up and stopped. MacLeod offered to pay them for a ride back to 81 Beacon, and the hippies agreed. Much to MacLeod's surprise, Brenda then invited the young people up to her apartment. For an hour they drank champagne and listened as Brenda regaled them with stories of her debut days.

Another time, Brenda invited a troubled young woman whom she had met in her psychiatrist's office to live with her for a few months. The neighbors were appalled by her appearance—cut-off blue jeans, T-shirts, and bare feet. When the doorman demanded that she put on shoes before she entered the building, the girl drew a pair of sandals on her feet with a Magic Marker.

Despite these occasional efforts to expand the scope of her life, Brenda, basically, remained obsessed with herself. She continued to be anorexic, and much of her day revolved around thoughts about food and weight. Lunch was the only meal she regularly ate, and even then she usually ate only half a sandwich, and perhaps a bowl of soup. She picked at her dinner. Still, every night her servants prepared her a full meal, starting with fancy, old-fashioned hors d'oeuvres. If company was expected for dinner, Brenda's instructions for meal preparation grew impossibly elaborate; she wrote out long explanations of how the food was to be prepared, and even drew diagrams showing exactly how the food was to be arranged on the plate.

For a weekday dinner with Alex MacLeod, she wrote out this typical instruction:

MENU
February 2, 1978
appetizers: 7 p.m. to 7:30 p.m.

I like appetizers on a nice appetizer dish, and I have a great many dishes, but the round, crystal platters are the prettiest. Tonight, these appetizers are basically for one person, and Mr. Alexander usually eats them all.

I don't like tiny little appetizers ever.

Most go on white toast and need to be sauteed in a skillet with oil or Mazola or butter. I can help you on what to make and there are probably 80 books that have them in it.

The appetizers should be ready from 7 to 7:30 and kept warm, if there is a wait.

There are all kinds of things over the kitchen sink, from caviar to herring to heaven knows what. However, check with me beforehand.

Also, chopped chicken is good with a little curry and Major Gray's Chutney on top (one or two pieces). The chicken can be minced with soured cream or a little mayonnaise and paprika sprinkled on the top (for looks). And they are easy to do. You just take a rolling pin for the bread or even a plate will do it. (The idea is similar to an English tea sandwich. The bread must be very thin and has to be flattened as above, but they are easy—

The simple things are the nicest and there are many which I can tell you about that you can have at any time—cream cheese done like butterballs and rolled in chives are nice and easy on a toothpick. People love asparagus stalks rolled in white bread. You wrap an asparagus stalk in bread and leave a little of the asparagus showing; but naturally cut off what is not needed. Watercress, the same.

Thin, thin cucumber sandwiches with butter are heaven, and all you need is a little salt, and make the bread as thin as possible and cut finger length wise V's. . . .

Pitted prunes with a blanched and toasted almond inserted where the pit has been removed and wrapped with a piece of bacon around the outside and then heated on a toothpick. People go wild over it, and they're my idea of extra special appetizers. If you made two dozen, I assure you there wouldn't be one left. . . .

February 2, 1978
dinner for Mr. Alexander
8:30 p.m.

Get two croissants from DiLucca's (they come in fresh from Paris)
1. Soup: Put one large tablespoon of orange juice in soup cup, pour in hot consomme and add 1 tablespoon of sherry and powdered herbs—very few. Float whipped, plain (not sweetened) cream on top (never sour cream), and use some

chopped finely ground parsley (we have a parsley chopper) lightly over cream and serve.

2. Chicken in marinade of orange juice.

3. Peas with thyme and ground rosemary. When they are hot put a dab of butter on top of them. Just before serving add chopped parsley.

4. Potatoes Ana: In Charles Banino's cookbook. They are sliced and browned with butter between layers and a serving is just taken out with a spoon and put on same plate with chicken and peas. I suggest putting large helping as Mr. Alexander eats more than most people. Also put a brandied peach on the same plate. Always put a bunch of parsley or watercress on plate. . . .

After dinner,

6. Baked apple in pastry with custard sauce for dessert in a glass bowl. . . .

8. Sanka coffee later on silver tray with cream and lump of small sugar cubes in silver sugar bowl. Use a Silver coffee pot and cup, which I can pick out with you. It should be a teacup sized cup and saucer.

On Wednesday nights, the nights he came to dinner, MacLeod always sat on a chair next to Brenda's bed and ate off a tray at a little table. Although Brenda just picked at her food, afterward she would inevitably get out of bed, go into her bathroom and force herself to throw up into her white porcelain toilet. While Brenda was bent over the toilet gagging, the maids straightened out her sheets. Then she would get back in bed and resume the conversation as if nothing had happened.

She would always throw up when she came in at night from having been out. Says Celia Mohr, "Whether it was food, or just alcohol, she'd have to get rid of it." Her excuse to Celia and the other servants was that her stomach was bothering her and she was in pain. She'd say, "I have to get rid of this so I'll feel better." One time at the Cape, after Brenda had already thrown up once, Dorothy Caverno caught her trying to do it again. "That's enough!" shouted Caverno. "No," said Brenda. "Let me do it one more time."

The servants suspected that Brenda occasionally took ipe-
cac syrup, a foul-smelling, bad-tasting over-the-counter drug
that is used to induce vomiting in poison victims. More often,
she would simply stick her index and third fingers down her
throat. Sometimes Brenda asked Celia Mohr to hold her head
over the toiler while she was vomiting. In the last years of
her life she could will herself to get sick. By then she was
usually too ill to get up, so Mohr brought a basin to Brenda's
bedside and held it under her head while she threw up.

Sometimes Brenda would go on eating binges, usually in
the afternoon, after lunch. She'd eat canned chili, baked
beans, pasta, ham hash. Even in periods when she was starving herself, Brenda always ate enough to stay alive. "Anorexics will let themselves die. But she ate enough to live, even
when people were worried about her," says Victoria. "She
lived on candy. She'd eat a little bit before she'd go to sleep
at night. She had boxes full of jelly [candy]. She loved jellies.
That much sugar is certainly enough to keep you going."

Before he died in 1975, Charles Banino used to do what he
could to see that Brenda got some nutrition. He would cook
up soups in the Ritz kitchen and include puréed steak and
other sources of protein. "Charlie's food kept Brenda from
getting all kinds of recurring illnesses and infections that
might have wiped her away," says Brenda's psychiatrist.

Still, Brenda had symptoms of illness over every part of
her body. Because she took laxatives every night, she frequently had diarrhea. Her hands shook; her abdomen con-
vulsed with cramps; her toenails became infected and fell off.
For a time her hair fell out from psoriasis, leaving her scalp
looking like a shrub garden after a fire: all spiky dark tufts,
which she constantly scratched with a comb.

Partly because she was so physically uncomfortable, Brenda's drinking and pill-taking escalated. She drank less champagne and more vodka. In addition to her regular range of
pills (Librium, Dexedrine, Ritalin, Seconal, antinausea pills,
anti-itching pills) she took large doses of codeine. "In the
last few years it was codeine, codeine, codeine," says Frances Griffin. "In Brenda's mind, if one pill was good, five
were better," adds Dorothy Caverno. "If a [pill] didn't work
right away, she'd take another. She had no patience." Even
the pharmacist who filled her prescriptions was appalled at

the amount of drugs Brenda took. "He used to say, 'She must be overmedicated,' recalls Stanwick. "I used to be embarrassed [because the prescriptions were for such large amounts], so I'd go to another drugstore."

Brenda continued to deny her addictions. She would always refuse to admit she was an alcoholic, even as she was asking the maid to get her a vodka and water. Nor did she think she had a drug problem—drugs were things taken only by wild-eyed misfits. Once when a relative suggested she smoke marijuana to improve her appetite, she screamed, "It's a drug. Those hippies are all drug addicts." Says Alex MacLeod, "In Brenda's mind, if a pill was prescribed, it wasn't a drug, it was medicine. Once at the Cape I was in the guest room. She was in her room and we were talking on the phone. I suggested that she not take so many pills. She started crying. She said, 'I have to take them. I'm sick; they're prescribed.' "

Yet Brenda still maintained an illusion of strength and sobriety. Says Stanwick, "Brenda was either lucid or in a semi-coma. When she talked, she made sense; or she was in a stupor. But she could always pull herself together. She could be dead one moment and the next she was a brilliant conversationalist."

Word of Brenda's condition reached some of her friends in New York. Worried that Brenda's physical deterioration was escalating, Esme O'Brien Hammond traveled to the Cape to visit her old friend. They hadn't seen each other much in the past twenty years, although they talked frequently on the phone. Brenda refused to let Esme and her husband, John, stay at Why Not, so they rented a room at the Wequasset Inn next door. No doubt Brenda was embarrassed by her physical state. She had all the shades in the house drawn, and all the doors were locked. She drank steadily. "I don't want to know if it's day or night. I don't want to know what year it is," she told Esme.

Esme was deeply troubled by Brenda's physical ravagement. One night she insisted that Brenda go to the hospital. Brenda agreed only if she could travel there in a fire engine. While Esme called the fire department, Brenda sat at her dressing table and put on a full array of cosmetics. When the firemen arrived, Brenda was dressed as if to go out on the town. With sirens blaring and red lights flashing, the truck rushed her to Cape Cod Hospital. "Brenda loved it," recalls Esme. "It made her feel important."

If Brenda wasn't arguing with the servants (sometimes she would scream at them all night about something as trivial as an overcooked piece of meat), they were fighting among themselves. At the heart of these disputes was the servants' competition over who was closest to Brenda. They accused each other of stealing, of sabotaging each other's cooking, even of poisoning Brenda's food. Once an employee made an okra and tomato casserole without olive oil, because Brenda regarded olive oil as fattening; later another employee poured olive oil over it and served it to Brenda. Another time the cook refused to prepare some chopped sirloin because she was convinced another servant had poisoned it. Brenda went through a number of secretaries. One of them kept accusing the other employees of hiding her papers. She also claimed that when she was helping out in the kitchen, the other servants would bang the cabinets around her head so she couldn't concentrate. For their part, the other servants accused the secretary of spying on them and reporting alleged cases of indolence and incompetence to Brenda.

In 1977 Brenda decided to spend the winter in Nassau, which she hadn't visited in many years. She eagerly anticipated the trip. Nassau was the scene of some of her happiest moments, and both Ship and Victoria were living there.

Celia Mohr spent a week before the trip at Brenda's apartment, helping her pack. The preparations were excruciating. Brenda demanded that everything be wrapped in tissue and folded exactly so. If she didn't like the way Mohr had packed an item, she would make her redo it. The situation got more tense and frantic as the departure date neared. Brenda and Mohr didn't even go to bed the night before the flight. The next morning Brenda missed her plane. She made a reservation for the following day, but almost missed that one, too. When Mohr and Brenda arrived at the airport, the plane was about to take off. Mohr, carrying Brenda's jewelry and her medicine case, ran ahead and reached the plane just as the door was closing. She asked the steward if he'd wait a few minutes, and he agreed. Then she got a wheelchair and ran back into the terminal, where Brenda was creeping along on invalid legs. "She slumped into the wheelchair and off we went," recalls Mohr. "I was huffing and puffing. But we made the plane."

Brenda rented an apartment at the Islands Club in Nassau. The first month she went out to dinner almost every night, seeing Ship, Victoria, and old friends such as Carl and "Bubbles" Holmes. But in the second month things went downhill rapidly. Frances Griffin, who replaced Celia Mohr after a week, says that Brenda was constantly drunk. She was also taking large amounts of drugs. At one point Brenda sent Griffin back to Boston to replenish the supply. Griffin flew to Boston, retrieved the pills, and flew back to Nassau in one day. "I was told where they'd be," she recalls. "They were in a box on top of a shoe box in a closet. They weren't there when we left." Apparently Brenda had arranged to have someone leave a new supply in exactly that spot.

On August 21, 1978, more than a year after she returned from Nassau, Brenda tripped on her nightgown getting out of bed and broke her arm. She was taken to Mount Vernon Hospital and then transferred later that night to Newton Wellesley, where she stayed almost a year. "She wasn't that sick. She could have been home. But she wanted to be in the hospital," says Shirley Craft, one of four private nurses who cared for Brenda around the clock. "Anybody else in her condition would have been discharged in two weeks, because she had no acute crisis."

Brenda had a room on 6 West, which was known as the country club ward because the patients were served gourmet meals and cocktails every evening before dinner. Brenda's hospital bedroom was as cluttered as her bedroom at home. The tables next to her bed were littered with cards, cosmetics, and Brenda's painting supplies (which she never used). She kept every present that anyone ever sent her, sometimes hanging the ribbon from the wrapping on the bar over her bed. The windowsill was lined with grapes, cheese, and fruit; fresh flowers were everywhere.

When she was first hospitalized, Brenda's stepson, Bob Jr., told her doctors what pills she had been taking at home. Brenda always had denied her drug problem, and she considered Bob Jr.'s meddling a betrayal. "Brenda was so dependent on drugs, to her it was like life and death. Yet she didn't want to think of herself as a drug addict," says Stanley Stanwick. "She was ticked off and hurt that Bobby got involved, that he talked about her case behind her back." A year later, Brenda was still angry. She decided not to leave Bob Jr. her Cape Cod home, as she had promised him, and she wrote a new will, cutting him out.

In the hospital, Brenda continued to take a variety of drugs, according to the nurses who cared for her. As the weeks and months passed, and the summer drifted into the fall and winter, Brenda lay in bed, often too groggy even to read or write letters. She caught pneumonia. She developed bedsores on the end of her spine. The television was on twenty-four hours a day, a background buzz of voices that mingled with the conversation of Brenda's visitors. Many people came to see her. Robert Chatfield-Taylor brought her ground sirloin, which the nurses made into steak tartare. Alex MacLeod came for dinner once a week. Brenda would order him a meal from the hospital menu, careful to choose things he liked. About once a week her psychiatrist showed up. He would sit by her bed and talk to her for an hour or so.

On many nights Brenda stayed up late watching old movies on TV. She loved regaling her nurse with stories about various actors she'd known. She'd point to the screen whenever Mickey Rooney, say, or Errol Flynn, or Desi Arnaz, or Franchot Tone, or Cary Grant appeared, and announce proudly, "I went out with him."

Brenda's doctors allowed her two cocktails every day. Usually she drank vodka. Sometimes she would have cravings for a brandy Alexander or some other mixed drink, which her nurses would make in the blender in the kitchen. Brenda persuaded her visitors to bring her more liquor, which some of them sneaked into her room in witch hazel bottles and flower vases. "I didn't mind bringing her watered-down vodka," says Stanwick, who had dinner with Brenda in the hospital on Saturday nights. "Sometimes she complained that it tasted watered down, and I'd say, 'Gee, you must be getting stronger if you feel that the booze is getting weaker.' I'd bring her about six ounces of watered-down vodka. She'd say, 'Why don't you bring me the bottle?' "

Brenda's nurses say she drank all day long. She'd send her

nurse out of the room to get her something, and while the nurse was gone, she'd have a servant pour her a drink from one of the bottles where she stashed her liquor. When the doctors finally realized what was going on, they banned all of Brenda's visitors for two weeks. When the ban was lifted, Brenda resumed sneaking drinks.

Brenda's nurses also worried about her intake of drugs. She took codeine every three hours, Compazine for nausea, large numbers of laxatives, and sleeping pills. "She was addicted to codeine," says Jacqueline Mackey, who was Brenda's nurse on the three-to-eleven shift. "We were all aghast at the amount of drugs this woman was given, and still lived. She weighed about eighty pounds."

"We were always trying to reduce the orders," adds Shirley Craft, who worked the eleven-to-seven shift. Sometimes Brenda would ask for a pill before she was scheduled to get it. When the nurse refused to give it to her, Brenda would scream for a doctor. Sometimes, under a doctor's direction, the nurse would give Brenda a placebo. She's remove the contents of, say, one of Brenda's sleeping capsules, and replace it with powdered milk.

The drugs exacerbated the difficult side of Brenda's personality, and she frequently threw tantrums. Unhappy with the food a nurse brought her, Brenda threw the plate on the floor and started wildly kicking her legs. "I can't eat this garbage," she yelled.

Despite the nurses' agreement about Brenda's drug intake, the doctor in charge of her treatment says, "Drugs were a minor aspect of Brenda's care. In fact, her drug bill went from several hundred dollars a month to virtually nothing. She was practically medication-free in the last couple years of her life." When asked to explain the disparity between his and the nurses' picture of Brenda's treatment, the doctor said, "The nurses were jealous and in a way totally lacking in understanding of the way this woman had lived and been brought up and her cultural background. They were always seeing phantoms."

Brenda passed her fifty-ninth birthday in the hospital; her servants arranged a large party for her. She showed up in a wheelchair with her arm in a sling. Although the fracture had healed months before, she told Alex MacLeod that she wore the sling so she would not have to shake hands with people. Jacqueline Mackey insists that the sling was a prop, designed to bolster her image of infirmity. "Brenda wanted to stay in the hospital," she says, "so she had to put up a good front."

Nevertheless, on July 31, 1979, Brenda finally went home. The shabbiness of her apartment mirrored her ravaged condition. Mice scurried about on dirty rugs, leaving their droppings in the bathtub. Brenda's health continued to deteriorate, and she became more and more dependent on her servants. Some of her friends thought she was being manipulated by them. Several women became worried when they repeatedly called Brenda and were told by an employee that she was unable to speak on the phone or receive visitors. They perceived Brenda as a victim, lying semiconscious in bed, while the servants controlled her household. But actually the servants were acting on Brenda's orders, turning away callers and visitors because Brenda *wanted* to be left alone.

Still, some people did try to take advantage of her. Once, while Brenda was in the hospital, a visitor came to 81 Beacon to talk to Victoria, who was in town from Florida. While they were chatting in Brenda's bedroom, the visitor, who was someone Victoria trusted, grabbed a small gold clock, worth about $10,000, from a table, and put it in his pocket. He said Brenda had asked him to have it repaired for her. Then, as the visitor was leaving the apartment, Victoria heard his pockets jingling. After he left, she noticed that some jade coasters and a gold ashtray were missing from her mother's room. Brenda later denied that she had asked the man to have the clock repaired.

In 1980 Brenda has a premonition that she would die of cancer. She believed her death wish to be so intense and deeply laid that her body would develop a malignancy. "She predicted that her body wouldn't kill the cancer cells, which fortuitously could develop in any of the organs at any time and probably do," says her psychiatrist. "We all have cancer every day and our bodies and resources come to our rescue and devour those [cancers] and prevent their growth. But if you want to die very much, you allow yourself to die with a cancer growth."

Brenda became severely depressed. After trying to kill herself dozens of times, after insisting that her life was meaningless, after virtually living in bed for twenty years, when the end was near, she decided she wanted to live.

By June 1980, Brenda was back in the hospital—in the intensive care unit at St. Elizabeth's. The problem this time was a severe respiratory infection. Ship and Victoria, who was now the wife of Nassau's harbor master and pregnant with her first child, flew to Boston to be at Brenda's bedside. A priest administered last rites. "I walked into the room and I thought she was already dead," says Frances Griffin. "And to this day I can't believe that she wasn't. Her hand was ice-cold and hard as a rock. They had her eyes taped shut. They had gauze pads over her eyes, and I thought, 'Oh, she's gone.' " Alex MacLeod used to call Brenda "the Phoenix," because like the legendary bird she always recovered. This time was no different. After recuperating at Newton Wellesley for three months, Brenda went home on October 3, 1980.

She spent most of the next year at Why Not on the Cape. "She was in agony that last year at home," says Victoria. "Her hip hurt her. The circulation in her toes started to go. The only things that [numbed the pain] were a pill and a drink. Anybody else in that situation would have said, 'Get me to a doctor, I'm in terrible pain. Find out what's wrong with me.' But my mother was so scared they were going to put her in the hospital and take away the drinks and the pills she was taking every day that she never said a word."

In February 1982, Brenda did go back to the hospital. She was now in the worst pain of her life. She couldn't sleep even with sleeping pills, and she couldn't eat. Her weight had dropped to sixty-five pounds, and she was being fed through a nasal gastric tube. "She'd been complaining about pain for twenty years. So when it came and it was real, she couldn't even explain it," says Shirley Craft. "I know when I touched her it was like [giving her an electric shock]. Every touch [hurt her]. She had me raising the bed up and down, down and up, all night long. She thought the rocking of the bed would make her pain go away, when it was just making it worse."

A body scan revealed that Brenda had inoperable bone cancer. The disease was so advanced that it had conquered almost every part of her body.

Now it was just a question of making Brenda comfortable

and waiting for her to die. She was put on large doses of morphine to relieve her agony. Despite her pain, Brenda was still obsessed with her weight. If she couldn't get her thumb and index finger around her upper arm, she'd get upset, imagining that she was growing fat, and she'd angrily yank the feeding tube out of her nose.

Most of the time she lay in bed, barely conscious. Occasionally she talked of her past in near-delirium. She told her nurses, for example, that she didn't marry Howard Hughes "because he was a faggot." Sometimes she'd forget altogether that she was in the hospital. Her mind would drift back to a happier time, and she would start planning a party. "Tell Joe to set the coat racks up," she'd tell Dorothy Caverno, as the lady's maid sat by Brenda's bedside.

As the end drew near, Brenda became terrified of dying. Her psychiatrist asked her doctors and nurses not to tell her that she was terminally ill. "It was a futile illusion she clung to until the last moment," he says. 'And it was the most important thing I did for her in those last few weeks—making the determination that she didn't want to know she was about to die. It was the most peace she ever had in her life, this curtain of illusion. And even I couldn't predict that this would be what she wanted."

Brenda was also comforted by the fact that she had not been abandoned by the press. Throughout the previous five years society reporters in Boston and New York had solemnly reported her comings and goings from the hospital. Brenda had been employing Burrelle's clipping service since her debut days, and she collected the stories as obsessively as she charted her publicity in 1938. She was still Glamour Girl No. 1, and, indeed, even as she lay dying, vestiges of her celebrated beauty were still evident. Her white complexion was still smooth and fine-pored. Her nails, which Dorothy Caverno manicured regularly, were long and tapered and polished a bright red. Her hair remained dark brown; it had never turned gray.

On the night of May 3, it was clear to Shirley Craft that Brenda was dying. She was weak and dehydrated; her breathing was labored. "Brenda was very sweet that night," recalls Craft. "Not like when she was lying up there [in 1979], when she was snappy and rude, drinking and watching movies on television all night long and always talking about how unhappy she was.''

The ward was quiet, and Brenda's room was dark. Ship and Victoria had been there earlier in the evening, but they had gone home to get some sleep. Occasionally Brenda asked Craft to turn her or wet her mouth. "Don't leave me," she begged the nurse. Finally, at 4 A.M., as Craft held Brenda's hand, she stopped breathing. Brenda's luminous brown eyes, which her friend Bill Fripp called "the most beautiful, lustrous pools I'd ever seen," opened wide and froze in death's stare.

Shirley Craft stayed with the body until seven-thirty. Later that day Brenda's remains were sent to the Waterman Funeral Home, where she was cremated without a memorial service. Victoria had intended to arrange one, but she was too distraught at the time and too overwhelmed with the details of settling her mother's estate.

Brenda's death—a month before her sixty-first birthday—ended her suffering but not the myth that had built up around her. Tormented as she was by fears that her life was meaningless, she would have been comforted by the respectful newspaper obituaries, which acknowledged that she had been an important symbol of beauty and glamour.

CHAPTER EIGHTEEN

OVER THE YEARS, Brenda had promised countless people—friends, relatives, servants—that she would remember them in her will. It had been one of her ways of manipulating, a device for asserting power. But when the will was read, shortly after her death, the bequests were actually few. She left $10,000 to Shipwreck Kelly and $5,000 each to Joe Drozell, Helen Drozell, and a cousin, the Reverend John Morden. She also left $5,000 to Stan Stanwick and $10,000 to her stepson, Dr. Robert Chatfield-Taylor, Jr. Everything else—her apartment at 81 Beacon, her Cape Cod home, her furniture, her jewelry, and most of her cash—went to her daughter, Victoria. According to Stan Stanwick, who had helped Brenda manage her money, the total value of the estate was about $4 million. Victoria also inherited another $4 million from the Frazier trusts, which ended at Brenda's death.

Not everyone was happy with the bequests. Brenda had once promised Stanwick $50,000. He asked her estate for more money and got it. Bob Jr. went further. On July 21, 1983, more than a year after Brenda died, he filed a lawsuit challenging Brenda's will on the grounds that when she signed it on September 6, 1979, she had not been of sound mind. Bob Jr.'s lawsuit sought to reinstate an earlier will in which he was bequeathed Brenda's Cape Cod home. He also sought to tap Brenda's estate to pay for his daughter's education, claiming that Brenda had promised to set up a trust fund for the little girl. He based his lawsuit on claims that at the time

Brenda changed her will she was a paranoid and irrational drug addict and the manipulated victim of her servants, her daughter, and her financial manager.

The lawsuit never went to trial. On October 29, 1984, a Suffolk County judge granted the defendant's motion for summary judgment. In her seven-page opinion, Justice Mary Beatty Muse wrote that she found no basis for Bob Jr.'s charges.

After her mother's death, Victoria cleared out Brenda's apartment and the house on Cape Cod. Some of Brenda's furniture, china, and silver were sold at a Sotheby's auction; the rest was put in storage. Lonely and depressed, Victoria rushed into a second marriage—to Don MacKenzie, a dance teacher whom she had met years before with her mother on a Caribbean cruise. The couple lived together for only a few months before they were divorced. Victoria now lives most of the year in Florida with her young son, Jeremy.

For many of Brenda's servants and friends, even those who observed the course of her dramatic deterioration, she remained a symbol of glamour. Death, in fact, seemed to enhance the power of her image. Some friends, such as Vava Adlerberg, surrounded themselves with pictures of her, as if her photograph was some kind of talisman warding off ugliness and drabness. Billy Livingston still keeps a scrapbook filled with clippings about Brenda. For the past thirty-four years Tom Bennett, one of Brenda's admirers from the thirties, has kept a gold four-leaf clover that Brenda gave him. He wears it every day on a chain around his neck. Howard Gotlieb keeps the tip of one Brenda's bright red fingernails in a box in his desk. She had broken it off opening a champagne bottle when they were eating lunch in his office.

Pietro Mele, who never saw Brenda after steaming back to Italy on the *Queen Mary* in 1954, resides in a house littered with mementos of her. Separated from the French businesswoman he married in the sixties, Pietro lives alone in Rome, in a cottage attached to his family's mansion. He gave up drinking years ago. Now, at sixty-four, he eats compulsively—fistfuls of peanuts, bowls of chocolate gelate, plates of pasta. Some of Brenda's gifts to him—a leather-bound copy of Rudyard Kipling verses, a Cartier clock, a jeweled cock and hen from Tiffany's—are scattered about the house. The focal point of the mansion's enormous drawing room is a marble bust of Brenda, which sits on a pedestal in front of glass doors opening out onto a beautiful terrazza. She posed for it while vacationing with Pietro at the Villa d'Este in the early 1950s. She did not bother to fix her hair for the artist; he sculpted her as he saw her, in her just-off-the-beach pigtails tied with little bows.

Pietro says he has preserved these reminders of Brenda because "I was always full of hope. When you love a woman, what can you do? I thought I was the man for her, and when she came to Italy she understood that I was the man for her. If Brenda had married me, Victoria would some day have all my belongings, and I'm the richest man in town. But Brenda didn't have the courage to leave America."

At the time of Brenda's death, Shipwreck Kelly was living in a Gatsbyesque mansion that sits at the end of a wooden pier jutting out into Long Island Sound. The building was actually an enormous aquatic garage where Jock Whitney, one of America's richest men, once kept his seaplane. During the Jazz Age, Whitney used the house as his private yacht club. Dressed in black tie and tails, he would drive from his nearby estate, hop in the seaplane, and minutes later, after landing at an East Side dock in Manhattan, arrive at the "21" Club for dinner. In the fifties, Whitney turned the house over to Kelly, his best friend, who lived there, rent-free, until Whitney died in 1982 and left it to him in his will.

The second floor of the stone house was an enormous room, and, over the years, Ship had turned it into a sort of museum piece, a spot frozen in time. On one side a wall of dusty glass doors facing the Sound opened onto a deck large enough to hold a small dance band and a bar. The other walls were covered with animal heads, elephant tails, and ivory tusks, most of them trophies from Kelly's hunting expeditions. Old books and fragile glassware lined the bookshelves. Leopard skins were scattered over slightly shabby furniture, and a polar bear skin rug lay in front of the fireplace. Years ago, after one of Kelly's girlfriends suggested that she could be seduced on such a rug, Kelly had sent a servant to buy one while the couple were at dinner.

Photographs of Ship with dozens of figures from the thirties were displayed on tables in heavy silver and gold frames: Ship on a bird shoot with Ernest Hemingway; Ship playing golf with the Duke of Windsor; Ship watching a bullfight with Picasso. In one photograph, snapped aboard the yacht *Christina,* Kelly was chatting with Ari Onassis, J. Paul Getty, and Maria Callas; in another picture he was dancing with Fred Astaire. There were pictures of William Paley on a golf course, aviator Eddie Rickenbacker standing in front of his airplane, and Walter Winchell holding court at the Stork Club.

But the pictures of Kelly and the other celebrities were almost incidental to the room. The most arresting image was a life-size oil painting of a glamorous young girl. Tall and willowy, with a cloud of dark hair swirling about her alabaster face, she looked down from beside the mantel with sparkling brown eyes. Her small mouth was set in a serene half-moon; her soft white hands were cupped together in a flirtatious pose. The girl was dressed in a white satin ball gown with a sash of frothy ostrich feathers cascading from her tiny waist. The painting was dreamy, otherworldly—the portrait of an enchanted princess in a child's book of fairy tales.

The tables overflowed with pictures of the glamorous young girl: lunching at the Stork Club with Joan Crawford; visiting movie director Howard Hawks in Florida; dancing at El Morocco. Dozens of photographs of her in ball gowns, bathing suits, and day dresses were scattered about the room, and portraits of her ancestors hung in the hallway outside.

Ship had not lived with Brenda in thirty years, but the room was a shrine to her memory.

Several years ago, Victoria bought the mansion from her father and started renovating it as a second home for herself and her son. Ship moved into the caretaker's cottage next door.

At seventy-five, the former football hero has a massive chest and full head of graying brown hair. But his blue eyes are cloudy and his misshapen nose (broken four times playing ball) is red and bulbous, the result of a lifetime of drinking. He gave up liquor after his heart bypass operation in 1981. But his health is frail, and he spends his days in bed, propped up against a white wicker headboard. There Ship reads and watches sports on TV, while a housekeeper prepares his meals and medications. At night he listens to the water lapping against the pier, thinking back to the bright lights of New York, to the magical time when he was loved by the world's most glamorous girl.

Notes

The major sources of quoted material are the transcript of Brenda's parents' custody battle over her, and interviews conducted by the author. Some statements taken from Brenda Frazier's personal papers have not been annotated. Whenever possible, the date and place of each interview have been supplied, although for some of the telephone interviews there is no record of the exact date of the conversation.

page	4	"the phantom air"	Dickens, *Great Expectations*, Penguin ed., p. 415.

PART ONE—CHILD

Chapter One

page	7	"born sophisticated"	*World-Telegram*, Aug. 24, 1940.
	8	"unbroken run of successes"	Montreal *Sunday Herald*, Nov. 24, 1913.
	9	"loud and vulgar"	Court transcript.
		"You annoy me"	Court transcript.
		"She was fearsome"	Interview, James Watriss, NYC, Feb. 8, 1983.
		"To my grandmother, my mother"	*Life*, Dec. 6, 1963.
	10	"seized his wife's greatest"	*The Canadian Gazette*, May 31, 1927.
	11	"a great pearl of a man"	Ibid.
		"three small white feathers"	Wecter, *The Saga of American Society*, p. 423.

11	Americans "are everywhere"	Ibid., p. 426.
	"The Americans who forced"	Wharton, *A Backward Glance*, p. 62.
12	"delectable land"	*Canadian Courier,* updated clip.
	"with all the best people"	Court transcript.
	"She was so proud"	Interview, Winston Thomas, Southampton, N.Y., July 24, 1983.
	"She got as far"	Telephone interview, Victoria Kelly.
13	"He left us a plain gentleman"	Montreal *Sunday Herald,* Nov. 23, 1913.
14	"Only by intimate"	*The Canadian Gazette,* May 31, 1927.
	"Sarah wants you"	Ibid.
15	"so quiet, so inconspicuous" and ff.	Court transcript.
17	"My God, I think"	Interview, Rudy Stanish, NYC, Oct. 25, 1983.
18	"Our tastes differed so entirely"	Court transcript.
	"was almost always totally drunk"	Court transcript.
	"men who were better dressed"	Mitford, *Zelda,* p. 19.
	"was hotter than hell"	Brenda Watriss's scrapbook.
19	"no home life at all" and ff.	Court transcript.
21	"Come quick" and ff.	Court transcript.

Chapter Two

| page | 23 | "You are a dear little boy"* | Undated note found in Brenda's papers after her death. |
| | 26 | "Can you live comfortably" | Court transcript. |

---

*Fred Watriss thinks that his father and Big Brenda had previously met, and that they had arranged to be on the boat together.

27 "I found it   Ibid.
     impossible"

   "Are you a home-   Ibid.
     loving person?"

   "I want to be fair"   Ibid.

28 "I felt rejected"   *Life*, Dec. 6, 1963.

   "vague but terrible"   Ibid.

   "right from the   Interview, James Watriss, NYC,
     start" and ff.   Feb. 8, 1983.

29 "I had never seen   *Life*, Dec. 6, 1963.
     this woman"

   "she looked like   *Time*, July 7, 1967.
     Churchill"

   "one of the most   Court transcript.
     well adjusted"

30 " 'Mommy, Brenda   Barrymore, *Too Much, Too
     Frazier' " and ff.   Soon*, p. 52.

   "She was content just   Interview, Gertrude Folmsbee,
     to be" and ff.   Brooklyn, N.Y., Nov. 3,
                                   1983.

   "I remember those   Interview, Winston Thomas,
     card parties"   Southampton, N.Y., July 24,
                                   1983.

31 "But not with the   Interview, Gertrude Folmsbee,
     vehemence"   Brooklyn, N.Y., Nov. 3,
                                   1983.

   "Never hug and   Watson, *Psychological Care of
     kiss"   Infant and Child*, p. 81.

   "Oh, Mother is in   Interview, Gertrude Folmsbee,
     town"   Brooklyn, N.Y., Nov. 3,
                                   1983.

32 "self-centered,   Interview, psychiatrist, Boston,
     infantile"   Mass., Aug. 1–2, 1983.

   "Christmases were   *Life*, Dec. 6, 1963.
     the worst"

   "Unless I placed   Ibid.
     first"

   "If I felt the urge to   Ibid.
     cough"

33 "tough meat"   Court transcript.

   "mental stimulation"   Ibid.

   "risqué, dirty"   Ibid.

	34	"he had nothing to do"	Interview, psychiatrist, Boston, Mass., Aug. 1–2, 1983.
		"when Diana is around"	Court transcript.
	35	"Take no notice"	Ibid.
	37	the only bad investment	*Life,* Dec. 6, 1963.

Chapter Three

page	38	"moral influence" and ff.	Court transcript.
	41	"the little girl came out" and ff.	Telephone interview, W. A. Paisley.
	42	"I think [Frazier] supports" and ff.	Court transcript.
	44	"I think this gentleman" and ff.	Ibid.
	47	"The defendant respectfully represents"	Ibid.
	49	"It is the feeling" and ff.	Ibid.
51–52		"Brenda was a little mannequin"	Interview, psychiatrist, Boston, Mass., Aug. 1–2, 1983.
	52	"no useful purpose would be served"	Court transcript.
		"practically every vestige" and ff.	Ibid.
	53	"The visits, on which"	*Life,* Dec. 6, 1963.
	54	"storm-tossed courtroom existence"	*Daily Mirror,* Sept. 7, 1933.
	55	"Yale is a lovely institution"	Ibid.

Chapter Four

| *page* | 56 | "In those days that was unheard of" | Telephone interview, James Watriss. |
| | | "I had a little talent for music" | *Life,* Dec. 6, 1963. |

57 "my favorite   Diary, Oct. 9, 1937.
    occupation"

"absolutely   Ibid.
    pregnant"

"Overeating agrees   Ibid.
    with me"

"Brenda had a   Interview, Esme O'Brien
    wonderful   Hammond, NYC, March 6,
    personality"   1983.

"Brenda's mother   Telephone interview, Jane Will
    was really evil"   Smith, April 26, 1983.

"Brenda's mother   Interview, psychiatrist, Boston,
    was too self-   Mass., Aug. 1–2, 1983.
    involved"

"I think Brenda had a   Interview, Gertrude Folmsbee,
    lot more"   Brooklyn, N.Y., Nov. 3,
                      1983.

58 "Big Brenda was   Interview, Fred Watriss,
    really quite a   Concord, Mass., May 23,
    nice"   1984.

"Big Brenda pushed   Interview, James Watriss, NYC,
    Brenda"   Feb. 8, 1983.

"everyone raves   Diary, Jan. 14, 1938.
    about Brenda's
    beauty"

"The only way *I* can   Telephone interview, Jerry
    leave"   Pendleton Clark, Sept. 5,
                      1985.

"destined—doomed"   *Life*, Dec. 6, 1963.

59 "was anxiety-   Interview, psychiatrist, Boston,
    provoking" and ff.   Mass., Aug. 1–2, 1983.

"Once we were   Telephone interview, Cobina
    playing a card   Wright Beaudette, May 16,
    game"   1983.

60 "Brenda never got   Interview, Patricia Walsh
    over it"   Chadwick, NYC, May 8,
                      1984.

"The only way I   *Life*, Dec. 6, 1963.
    could gain"

61 "This question of   Diary, Nov. 5, 1934.
    rows"

"We all lunched at   Diary, April 30, 1935.
    the Ritz"

62 "Had a heavenly   Diary, May 8, 1935.
      day"
64 "HEIRESS, 12, GETS   Journal-American, Sept. 8,
      $2 WEEKLY"   1934.
   "Brenda wasn't   Interview, Fred Watriss,
      really beautiful"   Concord, Mass., May 23,
                               1984.
65 "Miss Frazier, a   Undated Daily Mail clip found
      slim"   in Brenda's scrapbook.
   "looked like two old   Interview, anonymous source,
      harlots"   Stonington, Conn., March 6,
                               1985.
   "Look at what Lady   Telephone interview, Victoria
      Jane got"   Kelly, Aug. 31, 1984.
66 "When she was six   Interview, psychiatrist, Boston,
      or seven years"   Mass., Aug. 1–2, 1983.
   "How big was his   Ibid.
      cock?"
67 "a grade A milk   Time, May 4, 1962.
      herd"
   "They were   Telephone interview, Nancy
      sensitive"   Perkins.
   "Girls who wanted to   Interview, Anne Cox Chambers,
      go to college"   NYC, Feb. 15, 1983.
   "If you could keep   Telephone interview, Jane Will
      breathing"   Smith, April 26, 1983.
68 "a little fat"   Interview, Jane Will Smith,
                               NYC, July 14, 1983.
   "She was absolutely   Interview, Anne Cox Chambers,
      beautiful"   NYC, Feb. 15, 1983.
   "It wasn't just piano   Ibid.
      legs"
   "She had some of the   Telephone interview, Dr. Robert
      finest"   Hanned, April 3, 1984.
69 "It was a simple   Interview, psychiatrist, Boston,
      symptomatic"   Mass., Aug. 1–2, 1983.
   "I was not only   Life, Dec. 6, 1963.
      plain"
70 "I remember seeing   Interview, Audrey Gray Chapin,
      her"   Locust Valley, N.Y., April
                               10, 1983.
   "shocked and   Interview, Anne Cox Chambers,
      admiring"   NYC, Feb. 15, 1983.

70	"It was a mechanical problem"	Telephone interview, Dr. John C. McCauley, Jr., April 29, 1983.
	"I didn't see any scientific" and ff.	Interview, psychiatrist, Boston, Mass., Aug. 1–2, 1983.
71	"Brenda has no other thought"	Diary.
	"He is a darling" and ff.	Diary.
	"She was so excited" and ff.	Interview, Jane Will Smith, NYC, July 14, 1983.
72	"It was a modest little school"	*Life*, Dec. 6, 1963.
	"Munich was a new kind of life"	Ibid.
	"was always talking about Hitler"	Pryce-Jones, *Unity Mitford*, p. 104.
73	"Day after obsessive day"	Ibid., pp. 102–3.
	"Unity slept next door to me"	Ibid., p. 98.
74	"We used to see all the funny SS men"	Interview, Audrey Gray Chapin, Locust Valley, N.Y., April 10, 1983.
	"There was a monument"	Telephone interview, Milo Gray, April 12, 1983.
	"They looked like the three Marx brothers"	Interview, Audrey Gray Chapin, Locust Valley, N.Y., April 10, 1983.
75	"One night during dinner"	Telephone interview, Alexander MacLeod.
76	"My grandmother and mother"	*Life*, Dec. 6, 1963.
	"You'll be very sorry if you don't"	Ibid.

PART TWO—DEBUTANTE

Chapter Five

page 80	"It suddenly occurred to me"	*Life*, Dec. 6, 1963.

80	"was an expression used with jouer"	Amory, *Who Killed Society?*, p. 166.
81	"the pomp and the purple"	Wecter, *The Saga of American Society*, p. 242.
82	"the study of heraldry"	Ibid., p. 212.
	"If you go outside that number"	New York *Herald Tribune*, March 25, 1888.
	"was a point of no return"	Amory, *Who Killed Society?*, p. 167.
85	"From the society into which"	*Fortune*, Dec. 1938.
	"Miss Cutting would like to have"	Ibid.
86	"One cannot live in this"	Ibid.
87	"Well, they better"	Boston *Herald*, April 1, 1949.
	"totally out of control" and ff.	Moats, *No Nice Girl Swears*, p. 81 ff.
88	"attempting to seize"	Wecter, *The Saga of American Society*, p. 109.
	"folded in upon itself" and ff.	*The New York Times*, Aug. 1, 1937.
	"Society isn't staying home"	Brown, *Champagne Cholly*, p. 278.
	"café mad"	Ibid., p. 255.
	"see the manner in which" and ff.	Ibid., p. 285.
	"were four or five hundred"	New York City *Pic*, April 1, 1941.
90	"brought to his job"	Walker, *The Night Club Era.*, p. 131.
91	"Edna St. Vincent Millay"	*Time*, March 6, 1972.
92	"fragile, slim youths"	Brown, *Champagne Cholly*, p. 22.
	"No woman is beautiful"	Ibid., p. 29.
	"Maury had a wonderful gift"	Interview, Julian Gerard, West Redding, Conn., Aug. 13, 1983.
93	"from the vulgarity of burlesque"	Fussell, *Mabel*, p. 106.

94	"thousands and thousands"	Undated *Journal-American* clip in Brenda's scrapbook.
	"Republican Glamour Boy No. 1"	Allen, *Since Yesterday*, p. 274.
	"Among those in the Ritz's"	*Journal-American*, June 14, 1936.

Chapter Six

page 96	"Who is that lovely girl?"	Interview, Julian Gerard, West Redding, Conn., Aug. 13, 1983.
	"The properties of glamour"	*The New Yorker*, June 8, 1939.
97	"There is no more rational"	Ibid.
98	"I remember Brenda one day"	Interview, Betty Blake, NYC, July 13, 1983.
99	"You sat around"	Barrymore, *Too Much, Too Soon*, p. 119.
	"I have always thought"	*Life*, Dec. 6, 1963.
	"Being a debutante"	Ibid.
101	"I was furious about Brenda's photo"	Diary, Nov. 17, 1938.
	"It was chic to be written about"	Telephone interview, Victoria Kelly, Aug. 31, 1984.
	"Ewee had about ten young men"	Diary, Dec. 3, 1938.
	"Brenda certainly likes being"	*Daily News*, Feb. 5, 1939.
102	"Brenda's mother forced her"	Interview, Esme O'Brien Hammond, NYC, March 6, 1983.
	"Miss Frazier's secretary" and ff.	Interview, Jane Will Smith, NYC, July 14, 1983.
	"I saw Mrs. Watriss"	Interview, Jerome Zerbe, NYC, March 25, 1983.
103	"I was a fad that year"	*Life*, Dec. 6, 1963.
	"It is the way they get out"	Interview, Lady Keith, NYC, Jan. 7, 1985.

103 "My mother always loved publicity" — Telephone interviews, Victoria Kelly, Oct. 29, 1983, Aug. 31, 1984.

"I had met Brenda" — Telephone interview, Grace Davidson, March 23, 1984.

"I've often noticed" — *Journal-American*, Nov. 16, 1938.

104 "Driving my Studebaker" — Undated, unidentified ad pasted in Brenda's scrapbook.

105 "The problem was we were" — Interview, Esme O'Brien Hammond, NYC, Feb. 5, 1985.

"$8 Million Glamour Girl" — New York *Daily Worker*, Nov. 23, 1938.

"Who says you have to put" and ff. — Niles, Michigan, *Star*, Nov. 17, 1938.

106 "It's tough being New York's" — Milwaukee, Wisconsin, *Sentinel*, Nov. 23, 1938.

"contrived to snub anyone" — *Vanity Fair*, Sept. 1983.

107 "ablaze with ALL her diamonds" — *Journal-American*, Nov. 22, 1938.

"Here she comes, boys" — New York *Post*, Nov. 22, 1938.

"Please remember that" and ff. — *Daily Mirror*, Nov. 22, 1938.

108 "I just can't keep her name out" — *The New Yorker*, June 8, 1939.

"This is the shot that made" and ff. — *Journal-American*, Feb. 14, 1942.

"In thumbing back through" — *Journal-American*, Nov. 28, 1938.

Chapter Seven

page 111 "It's just a cold and ff. — *Life*, Dec. 6, 1963.

"could not possibly" — Ibid.

112 "I remember people talking" — Interview, Harry Cushing, Rome, Sept. 1983.

113 "I don't know how I'm going" — Telephone interview, Charlotte Johnson, March 12, 1984.

115	"I fear Brenda's being spoiled"	*World-Telegram*, Dec. 28, 1938.
	"Three pints a person"	Ibid.
116	"No, you can't take my picture"	Ibid.
117	"O.K." and ff.	Interview, Edythe Friedman Shephard, NYC, July 8, 1983.
	"Didn't Brenda look" and ff.	Brooklyn *Vanguard*, Jan. 6, 1939.
118	"Brenda was still dancing"	*World-Telegram*, Dec. 30, 1938.
	"Doug said I was shivering"	*Life*, Dec. 6, 1963.
	"Miss Brenda Diana Duff Frazier"	*The New York Times*, Dec. 28, 1938.
119	"Diamonds sparkled, champagne corks"	*Journal-American*, Dec. 28, 1938.
120	"In evening dress and slippers"	Brooklyn *Vanguard*, Jan. 6, 1939.
	"It's a trifle tiresome"	*Daily News*, Dec. 30, 1938.
121	"It was a great success"	Diary, Dec. 27, 1938.
	"I hated every minute"	*Life*, Dec. 6, 1963.
	"Unless I married well"	Ibid.

PART THREE—SYMBOL

Chapter Eight

page 125	"the crowd parted"	Telephone interview, Gerald Groesbeck.
	"fresh as a daisy"	King Syndicate, Feb. 4, 1939.
125–26	"I have my own ideas on economy"	Ibid.
126	"Brenda's no flop" and ff.	*Daily News*, Feb. 5, 1939.

126 "I'm just going down   *World-Telegram*, Feb. 6, 1939.
        for my"
     "It was all done by   Telephone interview, Douglas
        indirection"   Fairbanks, Jr.
127 "To the Queen of   *World-Telegram*, Aug. 24, 1940.
        Nassau"
     "accepting the   Ibid.
        compliment"
128 "I got it at lunch one   Ibid.
        day"
     "It made very little   *Life*, Dec. 6, 1963.
        difference"
     "Lady Jane was   Telephone interview, Valeria
        always"   Moss.
     "See, they are   *World-Telegram*, Aug. 24, 1940.
        frozen"
129 "I felt so sorry for   Telephone interview, Mrs.
        little"   Robert Holt.
     "It now appears   *Journal-American*, Feb. 20,
        that"   1939.
130 "Everyone knew that   Telephone interview, Gerald
        Hughes"   Groesbeck, Jan. 30, 1985.
     "when standing, he   Henry F. Pringle, quoted in
        inclines"   *Empire: The Life, Legend and
                                       Madness of Howard Hughes*,
                                       p. 69.
131 "Then a rival   *Daily Mirror*, March 16, 1939.
        company wired"
     "There's no doubt   *Journal-American*, March 30,
        that she"   1939.
     "Frankly, I've always   *Journal-American*, April 3,
        been"   1939.
     "She was so   Interview, Nancy, Lady Keith,
        starstruck"   NYC, Jan. 7, 1985.
     "She was very upset   Interview, James Watriss, NYC,
        because"   Feb. 8, 1983.
132 "Howard came to   Interview, Billy Livingston,
        dinner"   NYC, April 2, 1983.
     "Brenda opened the   Interview, Esme O'Brien
        box"   Hammond, NYC, March 6,
                                       1983.
     "he was a little too   *Life*, Dec. 6, 1963.
        mysterious"

132	"I think Howard proposed"	Interview, psychiatrist, Boston, Mass., Aug. 1–2, 1983.
133	"At no time in the history"	*The New York Times,* Feb. 23, 1969.
134	"Brenda was not passionate"	Interview, Audrey Gray Chapin, Locust Valley, N.Y., April 10, 1983.
	"Brenda loved derring-do stuff"	Interview, psychiatrist, Boston, Mass., Aug. 1–2, 1983.
	"She was so naïve sexually"	Telephone interview, Victoria Kelly, Aug. 31, 1984.
	"She probably liked the emotional"	Ibid.
	"She loved Peter Arno"	Interview, psychiatrist, Boston, Mass., Aug. 1–2, 1983.
135	"It was a good time in New York"	Interview, Angelo Zuccotti, NYC, Oct. 30, 1985.
	"it mattered as much"	Interview, Rudy Stanish, NYC, Oct. 25, 1983.
	"If you were at the Stork"	*New York City Pic,* April 1, 1941.
	"Now Sherman"	*Cosmopolitan,* May 1947.
136	"I should have thought up"	*Daily News,* Jan. 21, 1968.
	"We used to go to the Stork"	Interview, Billy Livingston, NYC, April 2, 1983.
	"As he passes through the Stork"	*Cosmopolitan,* May 1947.
138	"candelit and schmaltzy"	*Esquire,* March 1950.
	"It was speakeasy days"	*Daily News,* Jan. 21, 1968.
	"ate $5 bills"	*Time,* Dec. 26, 1960.
	"I refuse to sit in Siberia"	New York *Herald Tribune,* June 11, 1961.
139	"A hubbub of chatter spreads"	Thompson, *Trousers Will Be Worn,* pp. 67–68.
140	"It was really funny"	Interview, Andy Gillespie, NYC, March 1983.
	"I've just got to look at you"	Telephone interview, Jane Will Smith.
	"There's Brenda Frazier!"	*Journal-American,* April 10, 1939.

140 "yelping women clawed each" *Daily News,* April 10, 1939.

"Brenda epitomized the way" Telephone interview, Letitia Baldrige, April 30, 1984.

"Most of us retain, in most" Schickel, *Intimate Strangers,* p. 4.

142 "on which to hang everything" *The New Yorker,* June 8, 1939, pp. 27–28.

"Everyone there knew who she was" Interview, Gus Ober, NYC, Aug. 14, 1985.

"Brenda Frazier, the over-ballyhooed" Erie, Pennsylvania, *Times,* April 13, 1939.

143 "We're becoming rather bored" Chariton, Iowa, *Herald Patriot,* Feb. 23, 1939.

144 "Brenda had this idea" Interview, Gertrude Folmsbee, Brooklyn, N.Y., Nov. 3, 1983.

"felt that she had to buy" Interview, psychiatrist, Boston, Mass., Aug. 1–2, 1983.

"I'm not a celebrity" Amory and Blackwell, *Celebrity Register,* p. 269.

Chapter Nine

page 145 "Watch me, I think I'll have" and ff. Interview, John Kelly, Manhasset, N.Y., Sept. 9, 1984.

146 "a national figure, in a way" Fitzgerald, *The Great Gatsby,* p. 6.

"Now you know why" Interview, Jerome Zerbe, NYC, May 25, 1983.

"Shipwreck always seemed" Telephone interview, Mrs. Leon Simms, Oct. 14, 1986.

147 "were bigshots, if farmers" Interview, John Kelly, Manhasset, N.Y., Sept. 9, 1984.

"Only one person in this class" Telephone interview, John Kelly, Oct. 4, 1983.

"A good many upperclassmen" New York *Herald Tribune,* June 29, 1941.

148 "possibly the fleetest grid star" *The Kentuckian,* date unknown.

148	"It was difficult even for him"	Interview, John Kelly, Manhasset, N.Y., Sept. 9, 1984.
	"Duke's old man would come"	Interview, John Kelly, Manhasset, N.Y., Oct. 1983.
	"I didn't do anything"	Interview, John Kelly, Manhasset, N.Y., Sept. 9, 1984.
149	"There was something about Brenda"	Ibid., and Oct. 1983.
	"It looks like the real thing"	Brooklyn *Citizen*, Jan. 31, 1940.
150	"She wanted Brenda to marry"	Interview, John Kelly, Manhasset, N.Y., Sept. 9, 1984.
	"To me, Brenda's mother"	Interview, John Kelly, Manhasset, N.Y., Oct. 1982, Oct. 1983, and Sept. 9, 1984.
	"and his Irish charm had"	*Life*, Dec. 6, 1963.
	"It was a very quick and immediate"	Interview, psychiatrist, Boston, Mass., Aug. 1–2, 1983.
151	"She was so young"	Interview, Frances Griffin, Cape Cod, Mass., May 26, 1984.
	"The mother [implied] that otherwise" and ff.	Telephone interview, Jane Teagle Smith, July 17, 1985.
152	"I never asked Brenda"	Interview, John Kelly, Manhasset, N.Y., Oct. 1983.
	"You could see when they were"	Interview, Jerome Doyle, Osterville, Mass., Dec. 18, 1984.
	"Maury was completely sincere" and ff.	Brown, *Champagne Cholly*, p. 123.
	"The U.S.A.'s No. 1 'Glamour Girl' "	*Journal-American*, June 18, 1941.
153	"I felt as I had the night"	*Life*, Dec. 6, 1963.
154–55	"Hadn't Brenda been the most"	*Daily News*, July 1, 1941.

155	"A nice smile, Mrs. Kelly" and ff.	*World-Telegram*, July 1, 1941.
	Miss Frazier, are you happy?" and ff.	*Life*, Dec. 6, 1963.
156	"When the next elevator stopped"	*Daily News*, July 1, 1941.
	"Don't be foolish enough"	*New York City Sun*, July 1, 1941.
157	"had done nothing more strenuous"	*The New Yorker*, date unknown.
	"It would seem that glamour girl"	*Newsday*, July 31, 1942.

PART FOUR—WIFE

Chapter Ten

page 161	"she enjoyed"	Interview, John Kelly, Manhasset, N.Y., Sept. 9, 1984.
	"No more nightclubs for me"	*Daily News*, Aug. 14, 1941.
162	"This kind of life" and ff.	New York *Post*, Feb. 25, 1942.
	"The whole thing was handled" and ff.	Telephone interview, Jane Will Smith, July 17, 1985.
163	"He treated her like she was" and ff.	Interview, Lady Keith, NYC, Jan. 7, 1985.
164	"I was a lonely little private"	Interview, Billy Livingston, NYC, April 2, 1983.
	"I could have just sat"	Interview, John Kelly, Manhasset, N.Y., Oct. 1983.
165	"She was much more voluptuous" and ff.	Interview, Jerome Doyle, Osterville, Mass., Dec. 18, 1984.
166	"more man than diplomat"	*Life*, May 25, 1946.
	"We used to go to the bars"	Telephone interview, Richard O'Connell, April 1, 1985.
167	"She was very pretty"	Telephone interview, Jane Joyce.

167	"I don't think my mother was"	Interview, Harry Cushing, Rome, Sept. 1983.
168	"The idea"	Interview, Jerome Doyle, Osterville, Mass., Dec. 18, 1984.
	"Kelly was no great spy"	Ibid.
	"was a forceful man, yes"	*Esquire,* July 1965.
169	"by the force of Ernest's personality"	Baker, *Ernest Hemingway,* p. 473.
	"that they were scientists"	Ibid., p. 474.
170	"a member of the Gestapo"	Reference made in a letter dated Oct. 8, 1942, in FBI file on Hemingway.
	"This goddamn stupid business"	Interview, Jerome Doyle, Osterville, Mass., Dec. 18, 1984.
	"Ship isn't given credit for it"	Inteview, Jerome Doyle, Dec. 18, 1984.
	"these inescapable FBI men"	Hemingway, *Islands in the Stream,* p. 215.
171	"I don't think Brenda's mother"	Telephone interview, Jane Will Smith, Sept. 26, 1983.
171–72	"as if Brenda was the mother"	Interview, Jerome Doyle, Osterville, Mass., Dec. 18, 1984.
172	"too nice"	Interview, Esme O'Brien Hammond, NYC, March 6, 1983.
	"The grandmother was behind"	Interview, Gertrude Folmsbee, NYC, Nov. 3, 1983.
	"Set Brenda up in a big house"	*Life,* Dec. 6, 1963.
	"Nobody bothered to consult me"	Ibid.

Chapter Eleven

page 175   "Brenda seemed to do everything"   Telephone interview, Mary Sanford, Aug. 2, 1985.

"It was Harold Christie!" and ff.   Interview, Jane Will Smith, NYC, July 14, 1983.

"He used to get drunk"   Brenda to Alexander MacLeod in a tape-recorded conversation.

176   "Brenda *was* older than her age"   Interview, Vasilli Adlerberg, NYC, May 24, 1983.

"She got very, very nervous"   Telephone interview, Lucienne Piro, April 12, 1984.

"They would invite the Argentine"   Interview, Gertrude Folmsbee, Brooklyn, N.Y., Jan 24, 1985.

"My mother would have bad"   Telephone interview, Victoria Kelly, Aug. 31, 1984.

"She was drinking too much"   Interview, John Kelly, Manhasset, N.Y., Oct. 1982.

177   "She went down and worked"   Ibid.

She used to say"   Telephone interview, Gerald Kelly, Jan. 16, 1985.

"Ship wasn't the type to be tied"   Interview, Gertrude Folmsbee, Brooklyn, N.Y., Jan. 24, 1985.

"didn't want anything to do"   Interview, Jerome Doyle, Osterville, Mass., Dec. 18, 1984.

178   "Would you mind cleaning the car" and ff.   Interview, Gerald Kelly, Sinking Springs, Pa., Jan. 12, 1984.

"Brenda's mother had always"   Telephone interview, Jane Will Smith, July 17, 1985.

"like it was an endless pit"   Interview, Gerald Kelly, Sinking Springs, Pa., Jan. 12, 1984.

180   "My mother never had anything to do"   Telephone interview, Victoria Kelly, Oct. 1983.

"Brenda loved baby talk"   Interview, psychiatrist, Boston, Mass., Aug. 1–2, 1983.

180	"For my mother I feel"	*Life*, Dec. 6, 1963.
181	"And he'd holler and scream"	Interview, Gerald Kelly, Sinking Springs, Pa., Jan. 24, 1984.
	"no two people"	Interview, John Kelly, Manhasset, N.Y., Oct. 1982.
	"She told me once"	Interview, Frances Griffin, Cape Cod, Mass., May 26, 1984.
	"With the marriage" and ff.	Interview, psychiatrist, Boston, Mass., Aug. 1–2, 1983.
182	"Well, Ship, I think"	Interview, John Kelly, Manhasset, N.Y., Oct. 1983.
183	"As a rest cure"	Brenda's undated writing, found in her papers after she died.
	"took all the play"	Interview, Jane Will Smith, NYC, July 14, 1983.
184	"At night she would leave"	Ibid.
	"and she probably got"	Telephone interview, Lucienne Piro, April 12, 1984.
	"It faded gradually"	Interview, Vasilli Adlerberg, NYC, May 24, 1983.
	"The picture of Joanne Connelley"	*Newsday*, Jan. 17, 1949.
	"It can't be anybody"	*The Mirror*, Dec. 31, 1950.
185	"that glamour bullshit"	Interview, John Kelly, Manhasset, N.Y., Oct. 1982.
	"Brenda said that she had"	Interview, Frances Griffin, Cape Cod, Mass., May 26, 1984.
	"She was afraid of sex"	Interview, psychiatrist, Boston, Mass., Aug. 1–2, 1983.
	"Lots of girls were mad about"	Interview, Jane Will Smith, NYC, July 14, 1983.
186	"She had a bed"	Ibid.
	"On the way in we had"	Interview, John Kelly, Manhasset, N.Y., Oct. 1982.
	"got back into that whole life"	Interview, John Kelly, Manhasset, N.Y., Oct. 1982.
	"I was so broken up"	Ibid.
187	"When Brenda was first"	Telephone interview, Lucienne Piro, April 12, 1984.

187	"When Brenda married Kelly"	Interview, Vasilli Adlerberg, NYC, May 24, 1983.
	"Brenda told me that Ship"	Interview, Frances Griffin, Cape Cod, Mass., May 26, 1984.
	"I didn't think Ship was"	Interview, Betty Blake, NYC, July 13, 1983.
	"I don't think she ever"	Telephone interview, Victoria Kelly, Oct. 1983.
188	"I have never known the true meaning"	*Life*, Dec. 6, 1983.

PART FIVE—SHADOW

Chapter Twelve

page 191	"I'm not sure of the exact figure" and ff.	Telephone interview, Victoria Kelly, Oct. 1983.
192	"She was spending more"	Interview, financial manager, Purchase, N.Y., June 25, 1985.
	"she had to borrow money"	Telephone interview, Victoria Kelly, Oct. 1983.
	"Things really started to go"	Ibid.
	"I would arrive and Brenda"	Interview, Anne Slater, NYC.
193	"Brenda would call me"	Telephone interview, Diana Vreeland, April 18, 1986.
	"I did a lot of shopping for her"	Interview, Gerald Kelly, Sinking Springs, Pa., Jan 12, 1984.
	"She ate strange foods"	Interview, Constantin Alajalov, NYC, Feb. 4, 1985.
194	"I invented it"	Interview, Helen Drozell, East Harwich, Mass. *The New York Times,* May 11, 1978.
	"can do something nobody"	
	"I was writing a column"	Telephone interview, Doris Lilly.
195	"Her mother was having all these"	Telephone interview, Jane Will Smith, April 26, 1983.

195	"I never got the statistics"	Interview, psychiatrist, Boston, Mass., Aug. 1–2, 1983.
	"I had to take care of her"	Interview, Gerald Kelly, Sinking Springs, Pa., Jan. 12, 1984.
196	"I think so many men"	Interview, Constantin Alajalov, NYC, Feb. 4, 1985.
198	"He was terrifically charming"	Telephone interview, Diana Vreeland, April 18, 1986.
	"I take it for granted"	*Journal-American*, Sept. 11, 1961.
	"jealously watching"	Telephone interview, Constantin Alajalov, March 25, 1986.
199	"I used to run into him"	Telephone interview, Diana Vreeland, April 18, 1986.
	"this was how one should"	Interview, Constantin Alajalov, NYC, April 22, 1986.
	"Brenda was very susceptible"	Interview, Constantin Alajalov, NYC, Feb. 4, 1985.
	"Every single one of her handbags"	Telephone interview, Victoria Kelly, Oct. 29, 1983.
200	"She loved her jewelry"	Ibid.
	"Sometimes she'd want her pearls"	Interview, Gerald Kelly, Sinking Springs, Pa., Jan. 12, 1984.

Chapter Thirteen

page 201	"I hear you are the most"	Interview, Pietro Mele, NYC, April 5, 1986.
202	"Fighting is Pietro's peculiarity"	Interview, Harry Cushing, Rome, Sept. 1983.
	"Today men don't do anymore"	Interview, Pietro Mele, Rome, Sept. 1983.
203	"He was dancing"	Ibid.
	"elegance and personality"	Ibid.
	"He was very domineering"	Interview, Jane Will Smith, NYC, July 14, 1983.
	"He'd disappear for a few hours"	Interview, Gerald Kelly, Sinking Springs, Pa., Jan. 12, 1984.
	"[Pietro] was a sadistic bully"	Interview, psychiatrist, Boston, Mass., Aug. 1–2, 1983.

203–04	"You should never hit a woman"	Interview, Pietro Mele, Rome, Sept. 1983.
204	"thirty hours a day"	*Daily Mirror*, Jan. 22, 1954.
	"My mother was always surrounded"	Telephone interview, Victoria Kelly, Oct. 1983.
	"It was too much"	Interview, Pietro Mele, Rome, Sept. 1983.
	"It was unbelievable" and ff.	Telephone interviews, Victoria Kelly, Oct. 1983; Aug. 15, 1983.
	"Pietro took all his brand-new"	Telephone interview, Victoria Kelly, Aug. 15, 1983.
205	"That night Pietro was really"	Interview, Harry Cushing, Rome, Sept. 1983.
	"With me she was very happy"	Interview, Pietro Mele, Rome, Sept. 1983.
206	"Amore mio"	Papers of Pietro Mele.
	"He was a very kind"	Telephone interview, Victoria Kelly, Oct. 1983.
	"I think that was enough" and ff.	Interview, Pietro Mele, Rome, Sept. 1983.
	"She wanted Pietro to marry Brenda"	Telephone interview, Lucienne Piro, April 12, 1984.
207	"I can get the luggage off" and ff.	Interview, Gerald Kelly, Sinking Springs, Pa., Jan. 12, 1984.
	"See what liquor does"	Interview, Pietro Mele, Rome, Sept. 1983.
	"Let's go"	Interview, Gerald Kelly, Sinking Springs, Pa., Jan. 12, 1984.
	"If I don't go up"	*Daily News*, March 11, 1954.
208	"he was slippery as an eel"	*Journal-American*, Nov. 10, 1953.
	"placed his feet up against"	*Daily News*, March 11, 1954.
	"the cops went after him"	*Journal-American*, Nov. 15, 1953.
	"I wouldn't do a thing"	*Journal-American*, Nov. 10, 1953.
	"You ask Brenda" and ff.	Ibid.

209 "dazed condition"   *Daily News,* Nov. 18, 1953.
    and ff.

    "Who turned on the   Ibid.
    switch"

    "an Italian globe-   New York *Post,* Nov. 10, 1953.
    trotter"

    "be kind to Pietro"   Interview, Igor Cassini, NYC,
                               July 1, 1983.

    "He's a poor,   *Daily News,* Nov. 12, 1953.
    unfortunate"

210 "Brenda could never   Interview, Esme O'Brien
    let"   Hammond.

    "He's desperate to   Interview, Jerome Doyle,
    see me"   Osterville, Mass., Dec. 18,
                               1984.

    "Crocodiles have   *Daily News,* Jan. 22, 1954.
    more charm"

212 "I loved her voice"   Interview, Jerome Doyle,
    and ff.   Osterville, Mass., Dec. 18,
                               1984.

    "Brenda can't go   Ibid.
    on"

    "I remember that   Telephone interview, Gerald
    day"   Kelly, March 13, 1985.

213 "They weren't going   Interview, Jerome Doyle,
    to let"   Osterville, Mass., Dec. 18,
                               1984.

    "You saw him fall"   *Daily News,* March 12, 1954.
    and ff.

214 "I am very happy"   Ibid.

    "At the time"   *World-Telegram,* March 16,
                               1954.

Chapter Fourteen

page 215 "a severe nervous   *Daily News,* March 20, 1954.
       breakdown"
       and ff.

       "She was hysterical"   Telephone interview,
                                 Gerald Kelly, March 13,
                                 1985.

       "hollow-eyed and   Time Inc. file, Oct. 11, 1960.
       heartsick"

216 "Suicide was taken almost" — Interview, Victoria Kelly, Manhasset, N.Y., Nov. 2, 1983.

"The glamour girl had had it" — *Life*, Dec. 6, 1963.

"I'd say she wanted to die" — Interview, psychiatrist, Boston, Mass., Aug. 1–2, 1983.

"I'm going to kill myself" — Interview, Dorothy Caverno, Yarmouth, Mass., Sept. 25, 1985.

216–17 "Wear my pearls" and ff. — Interview, Victoria Kelly, Manhasset, NY, Nov. 2, 1983.

217 "to make someone" and ff. — Ibid.

"I'm guessing, but I'd say" — Ibid.

"Sometimes she asked" — Interview, Dick Gott, Boston, Mass., Dec. 17, 1984.

"Different people" — Telephone interview, Victoria Kelly, Aug. 31, 1984.

218 "She had symptoms" — Interview, psychiatrist, Boston, Mass., Aug. 1–2, 1983.

"I know how many pills" — Telephone interview, Dorothy Caverno, April 17, 1986.

219 "When he found out" — Telephone interview, Dr. William Heisey, April 24, 1984.

"He was such a good shot" — Telephone interview, Bob Morrow, Aug. 12, 1985.

220 "Chatfield-Taylor was very" — Interview, Jerome Doyle, Osterville, Mass., Dec. 18, 1984.

"Brenda could talk for hours" — Interview, Dr. Robert Chatfield-Taylor, Jr., Boston, Mass., May 8, 1983.

221 "defined his life" — Ibid.
"her being the baby" — Interview, Esme O'Brien Hammond, NYC, March 6, 1983.

"Joan, you must be awfully" — Interview, John Kelly, Manhasset, N.Y., Sept. 30, 1984.

222 "Well, I had been sick" and ff. — Court papers from Kelly divorce.

223 "on his personal   Elinor Chatfield-Taylor's
     living expenses"   affidavit in the Chatfield-
     and ff.   Taylors' divorce case.

224 "extreme cruelty"   Court papers from Chatfield-
                       Taylor divorce.

     "she didn't want"   Interview, Dorothy Caverno,
                       Yarmouth, Mass., Sept. 25,
                       1985.

     "that I thought"   Interview, Helen Drozell, East
                       Harwich, Mass.

     "I'm leaving" and ff. Interview, Victoria Kelly,
                       Manhasset, N.Y., Nov. 2,
                       1983.

225 "It was just a place" Interview, Joe Drozell, East
                       Harwich, Mass.

     "for a long time"   Interview, Dr. Robert Chatfield-
                       Taylor, Jr., Boston, Mass.,
                       May 8, 1983.

226 "she was someone" Ibid.

     "She talked to me a Interview, Dr. Robert Chatfield-
     lot"   Taylor, Jr., Boston, Mass.,
                       May 8, 1983.

     "I had a nanny"   Telephone interview, Victoria
                       Kelly, Oct. 1983.

     "My mother just   Interview, Victoria Kelly,
     loved to keep me"   Manhasset, N.Y., Nov. 2,
                       1983.

227 "Once I had a roast Tape-recorded conversation with
     chicken" and ff.   Alexander MacLeod.

229 "If Brenda had a   Interview, Helen Drozell, East
     party"   Harwich, Mass.

     "Brenda had maybe Interview, Dr. Robert Charfield-
     150"   Taylor, Jr., Boston, Mass.,
                       May 8, 1983.

230 "But somehow we   Ibid.
     wound up"

     "She knew   Interview, Dick Gott, Boston,
     instinctively"   Mass., Dec. 17, 1984.

     "We had people   Tape-recorded conversation with
     coming to dinner"   Alexander MacLeod.*

---

*In reference to the story about her falling into the Christmas tree, Joan
Chatfield-Taylor says, "That story is absurd. There may have been some
accident with the Christmas tree. But it was a very minor incident."

231	"Tell the cook" and ff.	Telephone interview, Peggy Eldridge, Sept. 15, 1984.
	"One of the maids"	Ibid.
232	"Why don't you get it" and ff.	Interview, Frances Griffin, Boston, Mass., May 25, 1984.
	"By and large, the people"	Interview, Dick Gott, Boston, Mass., Dec. 17, 1984.
232–33	"She would sleep for days"	Interview Joe Drozell, East Harwich, Mass.

Chapter Fifteen

page 235	"He'd heard of her reputation"	Telephone interview, Grace Davidson, March 23, 1984.
	"Whenever Mr. Wyner"	Telephone interview, Eleanor O'Neill, April 12, 1984.
	"Why?" and ff.	Telephone interview, Grace Davidson, March 23, 1984.
236	"What else could he say?"	Ibid.
	"The maids were always"	Telephone interview, Eleanor O'Neill, March 23, 1984.
	"I was standing in the hall"	Telephone interview, Ruth Trader, March 18, 1985.
	"about what a travesty"	*Life,* Dec. 6, 1963.
237	"She's a fascinating woman"	Interview, psychiatrist, Boston, Mass., Aug. 1–2, 1983.
	"I understood almost nothing" and ff.	Ibid.
238	"Even then"	Ibid.
239	"In the hospital"	Interview, Victoria Kelly, Manhasset, N.Y., Nov. 2, 1983.
	"Darling, you just can't stay here"	Telephone interview, Dorothy Caverno, April 17, 1986.
	"I thought my father"	Interview, Dr. Robert Chatfield-Taylor, Jr., Boston, Mass., May 8, 1983.

240 "He took other
      women"   Ibid.
    "My eyes wouldn't   Interview, Celia Mohr,
      stay open"   Medomak, Me., Nov. 17,
                               1984.
    "no one wanted to be   Interview, Victoria Kelly,
      the last one"   Manhasset, N.Y., Nov. 2,
                               1983.
242 "You couldn't take"   Telephone interview, Victoria
                               Kelly, Aug. 31, 1984.
    "She'd have a drink"   Interview, Dr. Murray Gavel,
      and ff.   Boston, Mass., May 24,
                               1984.
243 "She could make you   Telephone interview, Ruth
      think"   McCarthy, Sept. 7, 1984.
    "She looked   Interview, Bernard Weinraub,
      ghastly"   Washington, D.C., Feb. 8,
                               1985.

Chapter Sixteen

page 245 "the advantages of a   Sandor Ferenczi, quoted in
           normal nursery"   Malcolm, *Psychoanalysis,* p.
                                    133.
       "He kept my mother   Telephone interviews, Victoria
         alive"   Kelly, Oct. 1983; Aug. 31,
                                 1984.
246 "[The psychiatrist]   Telephone interview, anonymous
      has a"   source, June 27, 1985.
    "From day one"   Interview, psychiatrist, Boston,
                               Mass., Aug. 1–2, 1983.
247 "He was very much   Telephone interview, Victoria
      against"   Kelly, Aug. 15, 1983.
    "She had no self-   Ibid.
      image"
    "She seemed to be   Interview, Donald Chase, NYC,
      involved"   April 11, 1985.
248 "French phony   Interview, psychiatrist, Boston,
                               Mass., Aug. 1–2, 1983.
    "We prearranged   Ibid.
      that"
249 "You're like a father   Interview, Helen and Joe
      and mother"   Drozell, East Harwich, Mass.

249 "You're the only   Interview, Patricia Walsh
     person"   Chadwick, NYC, May 8,
                                   1984.

     "I wasn't used to a   Interview, Bernard Weinraub,
     shrink"   Washington, D.C., Feb. 8,
                                   1985.

     "Why are you   Interview, Donald Chase, NYC,
     wearing that?"   April 11, 1985.

250 "He said he would   Ibid.
     appreciate" and ff.

     "He certainly didn't   Telephone interview,
     help my life"   Victoria Kelly, Aug. 31,
                                   1984.

     "at sixteen my whole   Telephone interview, Victoria
     outlook"   Kelly, Aug. 15, 1983.

     "My mother didn't   Telephone interviews, Victoria
     want"   Kelly, Oct. 29, 1983; Aug.
                                   15, 1983.

251 "I wasn't used to   Telephone interview, Victoria
     dealing"   Kelly, Oct. 1983.

     "Everything [the   Ibid.
     psychiatrist]"

     "Her mother dearly   Interviews, Frances Griffin,
     loved her"   Cape Cod, Mass., March 27,
                                   1984; May 25–26, 1984.

     "Brenda certainly   Interview, Frances Griffin, Cape
     wasn't" and ff.   Cod, Mass., May 26, 1984.

     "Why don't we go   Interview, Dorothy Caverno,
     in"   Yarmouth, Mass., Sept. 25,
                                   1985.

252 "Brenda intends to   Boston *Traveler,* Aug. 7, 1963.
     guide"

     "adopt a needy   Boston *Traveler,* Dec. 9, 1963.
     child" and ff.

     "Last week, at 41"   *Newsweek,* April 15, 1963.

     " 'Too many people   *Time,* June 14, 1963.
     see' "

253 "So my mother said"   Telephone interview, Victoria
                                   Kelly, Oct. 29, 1983.

     "The only thing I   Telephone interview, Victoria
     had"   Kelly, Oct. 1983.

     "I was so   Telephone interview, Victoria
     aggravated"   Kelly, Oct. 29, 1983.

253	"It was very hot" and ff.	Telephone interview, Carroll Clancy, April 29, 1985.
255	"a damn difficult woman"	Interview, anonymous source, Glen Rock, N.J.
	"That's a sign of"	Ibid.
	"There was no way" and ff.	Ibid.
256	"she chased him"	Telephone interview, Victoria Kelly, Oct. 29, 1983.
	"Brenda thought that"	Interview, Dorothy Caverno, Yarmouth, Mass., Sept. 25, 1985.
	"This isn't brut"	Interview, anonymous source, Glen Rock, N.J.
	"I have the strength now"	*Life,* Dec. 6, 1963.
258	"The end result" and ff.	Manchester, New Hampshire, *Union Leader,* Dec. 13, 1963.
259	"What I gather is that"	Letter to Mollie McKaughan, Feb. 10, 1964.
	"lovely dresses that"	Boston *Herald,* Aug. 22, 1976.
260	"I thought there might"	Interview, Donald Chase, NYC, April 11, 1985.
	"Sometimes when I got home" and ff.	Telephone interview, Ruth McCarthy, Sept. 7, 1984.

Chapter Seventeen

page 263	"A lot of my feeling"	Interview, Dr. Robert Chatfield-Taylor, Jr., Boston, Mass., May 8, 1983.
264	"Boston sort of held"	Interview, Bill Fripp, Boston, Mass., May 25, 1984.
	"Howard, you know I only"	Interview, Howard Gotlieb, Boston, Mass., May 27, 1983.
	"My mother thought your"	Telephone interview, Victoria Kelly, Aug. 15, 1983.
265	"Are you trying to plug up"	Telephone interview, Ruth McCarthy.
266	"All right, straighten"	Telephone interview, Alexander MacLeod, Nov. 7, 1984.

Notes

267 "was as excited as" — Telephone interview, Celia Mohr, Dec. 11, 1985.

"Brenda was lovely" — Telephone interview, Stanley Stanwick, July 4, 1985.

"It shows that toward" — Interview, Victoria Kelly, Manhasset, N.Y., Nov. 2, 1983.

268 "turned around" — Interview, Stanley Stanwick, Boston, Mass., May 2, 1985.

"At first we were" — Telephone interview, Victoria Kelly, Aug. 15, 1983; Aug. 31, 1984.

269 "Her drawings weren't" — Telephone interview, Philip Hicken, Oct. 1983.

"I really feel psychologically" — Interview, Bill Fripp, Boston, Mass., May 25, 1984.

272 "Whether it was food" — Telephone interview, Celia Mohr, April 9, 1985.

"I have to get rid" — Ibid.

"That's enough!" — Interview, Dorothy Caverno, Yarmouth, Mass., Sept. 25, 1985.

273 Anorexics will let themselves" — Telephone interview, Victoria Kelly, Aug. 31, 1984.

"Charlie's food kept Brenda" — Interview, psychiatrist, Boston, Mass., Aug. 1–2, 1983.

"In the last few years" — Interview, Frances Griffin, May 25, 1984.

"In Brenda's mind" — Interview, Dorothy Caverno, Yarmouth, Mass., Sept. 25, 1985.

274 "He used to say" — Interview, Stanley Stanwick, Boston, Mass., May 2, 1985.

"It's a drug" and ff. — Telephone interview, Alexander MacLeod, April 8, 1985.

"Brenda was either lucid" — Interview, Stanley Stanwick, Boston, Mass., May 2, 1985.

"I don't want to know" — Interview, Esme O'Brien Hammond, NYC, March 6, 1983.

275 "Brenda loved it" — Ibid.

318

276 "She slumped into the"   Interview, Celia Mohr, Medomak, Me., Nov. 16, 1984.

"I was told"   Interview, Frances Griffin, Boston, Mass., May 25, 1984.

"She wasn't that sick"   Interview, Shirley Craft, Sharon, Mass., May 1, 1985.

276–77 "Brenda was so dependent"   Telephone interview, Stanley Stanwick, July 4, 1985.

277 "I went out with him"   Telephone interview, Shirley Craft, Dec. 9, 1985.

"I didn't mind"   Interview, Stanley Stanwick, Boston, Mass., May 2, 1985.

278 "She was addicted to codeine"   Interview, Jacqueline Mackey, Wellesley, Mass., May 2, 1985.

"We were always trying"   Interview, Shirley Craft, Sharon, Mass., May 1, 1985.

"I can't eat this"   Telephone interview, Ann Bradley, July 3, 1985.

279 "Brenda wanted to stay"   Interview, Jacqueline Mackey, Wellesley, Mass., May 2, 1985.

"didn't upset her"   Interview, Stanley Stanwick, Boston, Mass., May 2, 1985.

"She predicted that"   Interview, psychiatrist, Boston, Mass., Aug. 1–2, 1983.

280 "I walked into the room"   Interview, Frances Griffin, Cape Cod, Mass., May 25, 1984.

"She was in agony"   Interview, Victoria Kelly, Manhasset, N.Y., Nov. 2, 1983.

She'd been complaining"   Interview, Shirley Craft, Sharon, Mass., May 1, 1985.

281 "because he was a faggot"   Telephone interview, Shirley Craft, April 3, 1985.

"Tell Joe to set"   Interview, Dorothy Caverno, Yarmouth, Mass., Sept. 25, 1985.

"It was a futile illusion"   Interview, psychiatrist, Boston, Mass., Aug. 1–2, 1983.

281 "Brenda was very sweet" Interview, Shirley Craft, Sharon, Mass., May 1, 1985.

282 "Don't leave me" Telephone interview, Shirley Craft, Dec. 9, 1985.

"the most beautiful" Interview, Bill Fripp, Boston, Mass., May 25, 1984.

Chapter Eighteen

page 285 "I was always" Interview, Pietro Mele, Rome, Sept. 1983.

Selected Bibliography

Allen, Frederick Lewis. *Since Yesterday*. New York: Harper & Row, Perennial Library edition, 1968.

Amory, Cleveland. *The Last Resorts*. New York: Harper & Brothers, 1952.

———. *Who Killed Society?* New York: Harper & Row, 1960.

———, and Blackwell, Earl. *Celebrity Register*. New York: Harper & Row, 1963.

Baker, Carlos. *Ernest Hemingway: A Life Story*. New York: Charles Scribner's Sons, 1968.

Baldwin, Billy, with Michael Gardine. *Billy Baldwin: An Autobiography*. Boston: Little, Brown & Company, 1985.

Barrymore, Diana. *Too Much, Too Soon*. New York: Holt, Rinehart & Winston, 1957.

Bartlett, Donald L., and Steele, James B. *Empire: The Life, Legend and Madness of Howard Hughes*. New York: Norton, 1979.

Bender, Marilyn. *The Beautiful People*. New York: Coward-McCann, 1967.

Bessie, Simon Michael. *Jazz Journalism: The Story of the Tabloid Newspapers*. New York: Russell & Russell, 1969.

Birmingham, Stephen. *Duchess: The Story of Wallis Warfield Windsor*. Boston: Little, Brown and Company, 1981.

Brinnin, John Malcolm. *The Sway of the Grand Saloon: A Social History of the North Atlantic*. New York: Delacorte Press, 1971.

Brown, Anthony Cave. *The Last Hero: Wild Bill Donovan*. New York: Times Books, 1982.

Brown, Eve. *Champagne Cholly: The Life and Times of Maury Paul*. New York: E. P. Dutton & Company, 1947.

Churchill, Allen. *The Upper Crust: An Informal History of New

York's Highest Society. Englewood Cliffs, N.J.: Prentice-Hall, 1970.

Curtis, Charlotte. *The Rich and Other Atrocities*. New York: Harper & Row, 1976.

Dickens, Charles. *Great Expectations*. London: Chapman & Hall, 1861.

Dolmetsch, Carl R. *The Smart Set*. New York: Dial Press, 1966.

Erenberg, Lewis A. *Steppin' Out: New York Nightlife and the Transformation of American Culture, 1890–1930*. Connecticut: Greenwood Press, 1981.

Fahnestock, Beatrice B. *Look Back With Joy*. Washington, D.C.: Andromeda Books, 1975.

Fitzgerald, F. Scott. *The Great Gatsby*. New York: Charles Scribner's Sons, 1925.

Fontaine, Joan. *No Bed of Roses*. New York: Morrow, 1978.

Fowler, Gene. *Beau James*. New York: Viking Press, 1949.

Fussell, Betty Harper. *Mabel*. New Haven and New York: Ticknor & Fields, 1982.

Gill, Brendan. *Here at The New Yorker*. New York: Random House, 1975.

Goldsmith, Barbara. *Little Gloria . . . Happy at Last*. New York: Alfred A. Knopf, 1980.

Hemingway, Ernest. *Islands in the Stream*. New York: Charles Scribner's Sons, 1970.

Hoffman, Frederick J. *The 20's*. London: Collier-Macmillan, 1949.

Israel, Lee. *Kilgallen*. New York: Delacorte Press, 1979.

Kahn, E. J., Jr. *Jock: The Life and Times of John Hay Whitney*. Garden City, N.Y.: Doubleday & Company, 1981.

Lawrenson, Helen. *Whistling Girl*. Garden City, N.Y.: Doubleday & Company, 1978.

Leighton, Isabel, ed. *The Aspirin Age: 1919–1941*. New York: Simon & Schuster, 1949.

Levenkron, Steven. *Treating and Overcoming Anorexia Nervosa*. New York: Charles Scribner's Sons, 1982.

Malcolm, Janet. *Psychoanalysis: The Impossible Profession*. New York: Alfred A. Knopf, 1981.

Mann, Marty. *Marty Mann Answers Your Questions About Drinking and Alcoholism*. New York: Holt, Rinehart and Winston, 1970.

Maxwell, Elsa. *The Celebrity Circus*. New York: Appleton-Century, 1963.

McAllister, Ward. *Society As I Have Found It*. New York: Cassell, 1890.

Milford, Nancy. *Zelda*. New York: Harper & Row, 1970.

Moats, Alice-Leone. *No Nice Girl Swears*. New York: St. Martin's/ Marek, 1983 ed.

Pryce-Jones, David. *Unity Mitford: An Inquiry into Her Life and the Frivolity of Evil*. New York: Dial Press, 1977.

Schickel, Richard. *Intimate Strangers: The Culture of Celebrity*. Garden City, N.Y.: Doubleday & Company, 1985.

Schlesinger, Arthur M., Jr. *The Age of Roosevelt: The Politics of Upheaval*. Boston: Houghton Mifflin Company, 1960.

Shirer, William L. *The Rise and Fall of the Third Reich: A History of Nazi Germany*. New York: Simon & Schuster, 1960.

Silverstein, Dr. Alvin and Virginia. *Alcoholism*. Philadelphia and New York: J. B. Lippincott Company, 1975.

Tanner, Louise. *Here Today*. New York: Thomas Crown, 1960.

Thompson, C. V. R. *Trousers Will Be Worn*. New York: G. P. Putnam's Sons, 1941.

Turner, William W. *Hoover's F.B.I.: The Men and the Myth*. Los Angeles: Sherbourne Press, Inc., 1970.

Ungar, Sanford J. *F.B.I.* Boston: Atlantic Monthly Press, 1975.

Walker, Stanley. *The Night Club Era*. New York: Frederick A. Stokes Company, 1933.

Watson, J. B. *Psychological Care of Infant and Child*. New York: W. W. Norton & Co., 1928.

Wecter, Dixon. *The Age of the Great Depression: 1929–1941*. New York: Macmillan Company, 1948.

———. *The Saga of American Society: A Record of Social Aspiration*. New York: Charles Scribner's Sons, 1937.

Wharton, Edith. *A Backward Glance*. New York: D. Appleton Century Company, 1934.

Wilson, Earl. *I Am Gazing into My 8-Ball*. Garden City, N.Y.: Country Life Press, 1945.

Worden, Helen. *The Real New York*. Indianapolis: Bobbs-Merrill Company, 1932.

Acknowledgments

This book could not have been written without the kindness and intelligence of many people. First of all, I would like to thank Victoria Kelly for making available to me her mother's scrapbooks, photograph albums, and appointment books, and her grandmother's diary. This material helped me piece together a detailed chronology of Brenda's life, gave me a cast of characters with whom to work, and provided a blueprint for the intensive interviewing that followed. I am also indebted to the late John "Shipwreck" Kelly, who, in our many meetings over three years, gave me a rich and vivid picture of his life with Brenda.

More than three hundred people were interviewed for this book. I would like to thank everyone mentioned in the footnotes. Also, I am especially grateful to Constantin Alajalov, Dorothy Caverno, Joe and Helen Drozell, Gerald Kelly, Alexander MacLeod, Pietro Mele, Celia Mohr, Jane Will Smith, James Watriss, the late Gertie Bennett Folmsbee, and the late Esme O'Brien Hammond for their sharp memories, astute observations, and endless patience in answering questions.

My agent, Rhoda Weyr, believed in the project from the start, as did my editor, Vicky Wilson, whose guidance helped me realize my vision of the book.

My husband, Richard Babcock, spent many hours over the past few years discussing the material with me and reading drafts of the manuscript. At every stage he provided wisdom, wit, and an all-enabling love.

G.D.

Index

Adlerberg, Count Vasilli ("Vava"), 176, 184, 187, 196–98, 205, 210, 264, 284

Affleck, Marjorie, *see* Frazier, Marjorie Affleck

Alajalov, Constantin, 193, 196, 198, 199

Alcoholics Anonymous, 243

Alexander, Helen, 154

Alexander II, Czar of Russia, 197

Alexandra, Queen, 11–12

Altman's (New York store), 45

Ambassador Hotel (New York), 198

American Museum of Natural History, 169

American Presbyterian Church (Montreal), 28

Amory, Cleveland, 80–82

"Anatomy of a Debutante, The" (*Harvard Crimson* article), 142

Anderson, Robert H., 44

Arbus, Diane, 244

Armstrong, Alice, 9

Armstrong, Isabel, 33, 45–46

Arnaz, Desi, 277

Arno, Peter (*né* Curtis Arnoux Peters), 100, 115, 118, 133–35, 143, 149

Arostegui, Cathleen Vanderbilt, 165, 167

Arostegni, Martin, 165

Arrivabene, Madina, 211–12

Associated Press, 106

Astaire, Fred, 286

Astley, Hon. Edward (now Lord Hastings), 129–30

Astley, Sir Thomas, 129

Astor, Lord, 129

Astor, Alice, *see* Obolensky, Alice Astor

Astor, Caroline, 82, 88

Astor, John Jacob, 197

Astor, Mrs. Vincent, 99, 162

Atwell, Edwina, 185

Atwell, George, 185–86, 196

Aubert, Marian, 19

Author's Club (London), 66

Autumn Ball (Tuxedo Park), 83

Baard, Wilma, 143

Bachelor's Cotillion (Baltimore debutante ball), 83, 105

Bahamian Club (Nassau), 130

Baker, Carlos, 169

Baker, Mrs. George F., 174

Baker, Gloria ("Mimi"), 94

Baldrige, Letitia, 141

Baltimore *Sun*, 97

Banino, Charles, 235–36, 238, 260, 265, 272, 273

Bank of Montreal, 7–9, 13, 43
Bankhead, Tallulah, 145
Bar Association Building (New York City), 44
Barrymore, Diana, 29, 99
Barrymore, John, 29
Bartlett-Frazier Company, 15
Bath Club (New York), 139
Batista, Fulgencio, 166
Baum, Eva Marie, 72
Baylor College of Medicine, 194
Beaver Country Day School (Boston), 83
Beebe, Lucius, 88, 138, 143
Beekman, Barclay, 108, 131
Bel Air Hotel (Hollywood), 146
Belmont racetrack, 97
Bendel's (New York store), 96, 111
Benítez, Gen. Manuel, 166
Bennett, Tom, 284
Bentz, Eddie, 177
Bergdorf Goodman (New York store), 141
Berkeley, Busby, 94
Berlin, Ellin, 182
Berlin, Irving, 139, 172, 182
Bernhardt, Sarah, 14
Billingsley, Fred, 135, 136
Billingsley, Sherman, 99, 135–37, 145
Bishop, Mabel, 24, 28, 179, 221, 242, 248
Blackford, Mrs. Thomas A., 86
Blake, Betty, 98, 187
Bloomingdale's (New York store), 60
Blue, Ben, 144
Blythe, Diana, 30
Bob Hope Radio Hour, 142
Boeing School of Aeronautics, 131

Bogart, Humphrey, 202
Boleyn, Anne, 10
Booth, Willis, 60
Boston Globe, 264
Boston Red Sox, 266
Boston Traveler, 252, 254
Boston University, 264
Boynton, Antoinette, 35
Braden, Spruille, 166–70
Braden, Mrs. Spruille, 167
Braun, Eva, 73
Braun, Julius, 38–40, 49
Breakers Hotel (Palm Beach), 17
Brisbane, Arthur, 92
Brissette, Harry, 24
British Colonial Hotel (Nassau), 130
British Union of Fascists, 73
Brooklyn Dodgers, 146, 148, 168
Brown, Eve, 91, 92, 152
Bruch, Hilde, 194
Buckingham Palace (London), 11
Buford, Just. (Florida Supreme Court), 52–53
Bulgari of Rome (jewelers), 210
Burrelle's clipping service, 281
Butterfield, Paul, 229, 230
Butterfield, Mrs. Paul, 230
Butterfield, Wally, 120

Cabot, Bruce, 106, 204
Cagle, Chris, 148
Callas, Maria, 286
Canada Club (London), 13
Cape Cod Hospital, 224, 263, 275
Capote, Truman, 221
Carlton House (New York), 97, 101, 110, 114, 126, 132, 134, 141, 149, 153, 155, 162, 180, 234

Carlton Tea Rooms (Munich), 74
Caruso, Enrico, 29
Caruso, Gloria, 29
Cassini, Igor, 209
Catholic Charities of the Archdiocese of New York, 62
Caverno, Dorothy, 176, 218, 224, 236, 251, 266, 272, 273, 281
Cecil, Amanda, 68
Chadwick, Patricia Walsh, 60, 243, 249
Chambers, Anne Cox, 67–70
Chapin, Audrey Gray, 70, 74–75, 134
Chariton (Iowa) *Herald Patriot*, 142–43
Chase, Donald, 191, 247, 249–50
Chase Securities Corporation, 198
Chatfield-Taylor, Adelaide, 239
Chatfield-Taylor, Elinor, 220, 223–24, 226
Chatfield-Taylor, Joan, 223, 230
Chatfield-Taylor, Robert, Jr., 229–30, 236, 239–40, 248, 266
  on Brenda, 220–21, 225–26, 263
  Brenda's relationship with, 221, 226, 239–40, 276–77, 283
Chatfield-Taylor, Robert, Sr., 219–21, 228, 230–31, 266, 267, 277
  background and personality of, 219–20
  Brenda's relationship with, 220–21, 223–25, 236, 239–40, 254

divorce from Elinor, 223–24
  marries Brenda, 224
Chemical Bank and Trust Company, 148
Chesapeake and Ohio Railway Company, 16
Chesterton, G. K., 10
Chesterton, Mrs. G. K., 10
Child, Julia, 230
Children's Welfare League, 140
Chillingworth, Curtis E. ("Chick"), 26–27, 42, 45, 48, 49, 50, 51
Chillingworth, Marjorie, 42
Chilton Club (Boston), 261
"Cholly Knickerbocker" newspaper column, 101, 104, 209
Christ Church Cathedral (Montreal), 8
Christie, Duncan, 208, 213–14
Christie, Harold, 175, 183
Christina (yacht), 221, 286
Christmas, Fredrick J., 35–39
Clancy, Carroll, 253–54
Coe, Natalie, 84, 112
Coe, William Robertson, 84
Coe, Mrs. William Robertson, 84
Coleman, Emil, 114–15, 118
Colette, 64
Colonial Hotel (Nassau), 19
Colony Restaurant (New York), 69
Columbia University, 142
Communist Party U.S.A., 105
Connelley, Joanne, 184
Conrad, Peter, 106
Constitution (steamship), 210
Cope, Denzil, 17
Corrigan family, 88
Cosmopolitan magazine, 136
Coty (cosmetics manufacturer), 157
Court of St. James's, 64

Covent Garden Opera (London), 10
Craft, Selma, 265
Craft, Shirley, 276–78, 280, 281–82
Crawford, Joan, 106, 139, 286
Crichton, Sir George, 48
Crosby, Bing, 137, 174, 179
Cunard, Lady, 12
Currie (chauffeur), 24
Cushing, Harry, Jr., 112, 167, 202, 205
Cushing, Harry, Sr., 205
Cutting, Juliana, 84–87, 111, 116
Cutting, Robert Livingston, 85

Daily Mail (London), 65, 119
Daily Mail (New York), 91
Daily News (New York), 89, 102, 116, 119–21, 126, 141, 156, 210
Daily Newsense (newsletter), 90
Daily Worker, 105
Davidson, Grace, 103, 235, 236
Davies, Marion, 92
Davis, Bette, 3
De Vries, John, 38–40, 49
Delmonico's restaurant (Boston), 267
Delmonico's restaurant (New York), 82
Democratic Party, 248
Dempsey, Jack, 139, 173, 202
Denkmal monument (Munich), 74
Dewey, Thomas E., 94
di Cicco, Pat, 131
Diario de la Marina (Cuban newspaper), 166
Dickens, Charles, 4
Dietrich, Marlene, 64, 138
DiMaggio, Dominic, 266

Disney, Walt, 94
Doctors Hospital (New York), 172, 180, 215
Doherty, Helen Lee Eames, 84
Doherty, Henry L., 84
Donnelly, Ruth, 35
Douglas, Rachel Peabody, 17, 30
Doyle, Jerome, 152, 164–65, 168, 170, 177, 192, 196, 210–13, 220, 224
Doyle, Mrs. Jerome, 177
Drozell, Helen, 219, 224, 229, 231, 232, 249, 283
Drozell, Joe, 219, 225, 231, 232–33, 249, 268, 283
Duchemin, Hippolyte, 25, 41, 43–44
Duchemin, Marcel, 25, 41, 43–44
Ducolomb, Mlle. (governess), 32, 47, 48, 49, 56, 61
Duke, Angier Biddle, 198
Duke, Doris, 93, 115, 136–37, 156
Duke, Washington, 198
Duran, Gustavo, 167

Edward VII, King of England, 7, 11–12
Edward VIII, King of England, see Windsor, Duke of
El Morocco (New York nightclub), 89, 102, 125, 135, 137–39, 149, 172, 184, 202, 221, 286
El Morocco No News (newspaper), 138
Eldridge, Peggy, 231
Elizabeth II, Queen of England, 81, 200
Elsner, Maximilian, Jr., 156
Elwes, Simon, 128, 262
Embassy Club (Hollywood), 133

Emerald Beach Club (Nassau),
127, 130, 150
Empress of Scotland
(steamship), 48
Englischer Garten (Munich),
73
Erie (Pennsylvania) *Times,* 142
Esquire magazine, 243, 249
Essex House Hotel (New
York), 210
Everglades Hotel (Palm
Springs), 20

Fairbanks, Douglas, Jr., 110,
115, 118, 126
Falange (Spanish fascist party),
166
Fanjul, Alfonso, 167
Fanjul, Mrs. Alfonso, 167
Farmer, Chick, 96, 108, 137
Farmington (Conn.) finishing
school, 67–68, 71
Farwell, Charles B., 220
Faulkner Hospital (Jamaica
Plains), 237, 238
Fayrer, Sir Joseph, 7
Federal Bureau of Investigation
(FBI), 90, 164–65, 166,
168–71
Federal Home Loan Bank of
New York, 61
Ferenczi, Sandor, 245
Field, Marshall, 220
Field, Marshall, IV, 71
Firpo, Luis, 139
"First Mrs. Frazier, The"
(play), 30
Fitzgerald, F. Scott, 18, 88,
146
Fitzgerald, Zelda Sayre, 18
Flair (magazine), 199
Flannelly, Rev. Joseph, 154
Flato, Paul, 153
Fleitmann, Alice, 112
Flynn, Errol, 106, 185, 277

Foley, James Aloysius, 62–64,
111, 153
Folmsbee, Gertrude Bennett,
30, 31, 57, 98, 144, 152,
153, 172, 176, 177
Fontaine, Joan, 146, 221
Ford, Henry, II, 198
Fortune magazine, 84, 99
42nd Street (Broadway show),
94
Four Seasons restaurant
(Munich), 74
Foy, Cynthia, 184
Frazier, Brenda Diana Duff
Alex MacLeod and, 264
in Bahamas (1939), 125–31
birth of, 20
birth of Victoria to, 172
at Boston Ritz-Carlton
(1960–61), 234–37, 239–
40
on Cape Cod (1955–60),
218–19, 224–33
Charles Banino and, 235–36,
238, 260, 265, 272, 273
Chatfield-Taylor Sr.'s
relationship with, 219–21,
223–25, 236, 239–40,
254
and Cobina Wright junior,
29–30, 58–59, 142
and daughter Victoria, 179–
80, 192, 194–95, 216–22,
226–27, 236–37, 250–53,
257
death of, 281–82
debut of, 1, 4, 76, 79, 80,
110–21, 157
divorce from Ship Kelly, 188,
221–23
drug and alcohol dependence
of, 2, 176, 186, 192, 194,
196, 205–07, 215, 217–18,
224, 225, 241–45, 266,
273–74, 277–78, 280

Frazier, Brenda (*continued*)
eating disorders of, 103–04,
193–94, 215, 226–27, 230,
241, 266, 270–73
education of, 29, 32, 56, 64,
67–68, 71–76
Edward Astley and, 129–30
in England (1930), 48
and father, 22, 27–28, 34–
36, 49–53, 132, 152, 181–
82, 219
first pregnancy and abortion,
151, 163
Frazier trusts and, 36–37,
54–55, 62–64, 111, 162,
171, 192
George Atwell and, 185–86,
196
grandfather Williams-Taylor
and, 41, 46–47, 51
grandmother Williams-Taylor
and, 4, 30, 41, 48, 51,
64–66, 76, 128, 152, 157,
172–73, 176, 182, 262,
263
Harry Wilson and, 125, 126
in Havana (1942–43), 165–70
hospitalizations of, 215, 224,
237–39, 274–82
Howard Hughes and, 32,
134, 239, 281
at Ida Krebs School (1976),
1–4
last days of, in Boston, 2–4,
266–81
in Latin America (1943), 171
leg and foot problems of,
68–70, 212–13
Life memoir of, 99, 103,
121, 188, 253–60
Long Island life of, 172–80,
186–87
loses fourth baby, 183
marriage to Ship Kelly, 151–
88, 191, 192

marries Chatfield-Taylor Sr.,
224
in Medfield (1961–68), 239–
60
meets Ship Kelly, 145–46,
149
and mother, 4, 21–22, 27–
28, 31–33, 36, 45–46, 49–
52, 56, 57, 58, 59–62,
65–66, 75–76, 97–98,
129, 171–72, 176, 180–81,
192, 226, 260–61
in Munich (1937–38), 71–75
in Nassau (1977), 275
parents' custody battle for,
38–53
parents' divorce and, 24–28
at Park Avenue duplex (1950–
55), 186, 192–200, 218
Peter Arno and, 118, 133–35,
149
Pietro Mele's affair with,
201–14, 218, 221, 224,
236, 252, 284–85
post-debut celebrity in New
York, 140–44
precocious sexual activity of,
65–67
precocious social activity of,
56, 58–60
pre-debut life as debutante,
96–109
psychiatric drug and shock
therapy for, 194–95, 212
psychoanalyst's views on, 36,
51–52, 57, 59, 66, 69, 70,
132, 135, 181–82, 194,
195, 242–51
psychoanalytic treatment of,
181, 237–39, 245–51, 276–
77, 279, 281
second pregnancy and
miscarriage, 162
servants' treatment by, 227–29,
231–32, 240–41, 265, 275

Ship Kelly's relationship
with, 149–51, 151–52,
163–64, 181–82, 187–88,
203, 285–86
as small child, 23–30
social success in England
(1935), 64–65
Stanley Stanwick and, 267–69
and stepbrother Jimmy
Watriss, 23–24, 28, 33,
36, 220
and stepfather Watriss, 58
stepson Chatfield-Taylor Jr.
and, 220–21, 226, 239,
276–77, 283
suicide attempts of, 215–18,
236–37, 279
and Tommy Weldon, 66–67,
69–71
"Vava" Adlerberg and, 197–
99, 205, 210, 264, 284
wedding of Ship Kelly and,
152–57
will of, 283–84
Frazier, Brenda Germaine
Williams-Taylor, see
Watriss, Brenda Germaine
Williams-Taylor
Frazier, Clara Duff, 14, 15, 17,
18, 20, 23, 26, 27, 36–38,
43
Frazier, Franklin Duff, 15–29,
34–54, 62, 115, 130, 219
and battle for custody of
daughter, 38–53
Big Brenda's marriage to,
17–26, 57
birth of, 15
daughter Brenda's
relationship with, 21–22,
27–28, 34–36, 49–53,
132, 152, 181, 219
death of, 53–54
divorced from Big Brenda,
26–28

family history of, 15–17
first marriage of, 17, 30
Frederick Williams-Taylor
and, 20, 41, 46–47
Jane Williams-Taylor and,
41–43, 51
marriage to Marjorie Affleck,
48
mother's will and, 36–37, 54
personality of, 15–19, 19–20,
35–38
in World War I, 18–19
Frazier, Franklin Pierce
("Skip"), 15–16, 17, 18–
21, 37
Frazier, Marjorie Affleck, 48–
51, 54
Frazier, Rachel Peabody, see
Douglas, Rachel Peabody
French (butler), 175
Freud, Sigmund, 238, 245
Friedman, Edythe, 113, 117,
119–20
Fripp, Bill, 264, 266, 269, 282
Fruitful Vine, The (Hichens),
11
Fussell, Betty, 93

Gable, Clark, 139, 203
Gallagher, Ed, 227
Gamble, Catherine, 112
Gandhi, Mahatma, 202
Garbo, Greta, 64
Garland, Judy, 173
Gavel, Murray, 243
Gaynor, Dr. William, 183, 209
Gellhorn, Martha, see
Hemingway, Martha
Gellhorn
George V, King of England, 48
George VI, King of England,
48, 71
Gerard, Julian, 92, 96
Getty, J. Paul, 286
Gillespie, Andy, 140

Goebbels, Joseph Paul, 74
Goelet family, 88
Goering, Hermann, 74
Goldbloom, Alton, 33
Gotlieb, Howard, 264, 284
Gott, Dick, 217, 224, 230, 232
Gough, Lord, 48
Gould, Edith, 101
Grand Hotel (Rome), 203
Grant, Cary, 139, 198, 277
Gray, Milo, 74
Great Expectations (Dickens), 4
Great Gatsby, The (Fitzgerald), 146
Green, Gov. (of Illinois), 137
Green Carnation, The (Hichens), 11
Greenaway, Kate, 154
Greentree Fair (Manhasset, L.I.), 97
Griffin, Frances, 151, 181, 185, 187, 232, 251, 273, 276, 280
Griffiths (chauffeur), 48, 61, 68, 98, 110, 126
Groesbeck, Gerald, 125, 130
Guest, Winston, 167

Haas, Alexander, 116
Hahn, Fred, 136–37
Hammond, Esme O'Brien, 57, 102, 105, 132, 152, 172, 210, 221, 274
Hammond, John, 274
Hammond, Ogden, 126
Hannagan, Steve, 172
Hanned, Robert, 68
Hannon, Catherine, *see* Kelly, Catherine Hannon
Harrach, Countess, 74
Harvard Business School, 235
Harvard Crimson, 142

Harvard University, 23, 24, 85, 235
Hastings, Lord, *see* Astley, Hon. Edward
Hausman, Louis, 195, 212
Havana Country Club, 167
Hawks, Howard, 103, 163, 286
Hawks, Mrs. Howard, *see* Keith, Lady Nancy
Hayward, Leland, 103, 135
Hearst, William Randolph, 90, 92
Hearst, Mrs. William Randolph, 110
Heisey, Dr. William, 219
Hellzapoppin (Braodway show), 119
Hemingway, Ernest, 135, 164–71, 286
Hemingway, Martha Gellhorn, 166, 169
Henderson, Leon, 137
Henie, Sonja, 144
Henry VIII, King of England, 10, 48
Henshaw, Jane Fayrer, *see* Williams-Taylor Jane Fayrer Henshaw
Henshaw, Joshua, 7
Hepburn, Katherine, 130
Hewitt, Caroline Danella, 29
see also Miss Hewitt's Classes
Hichens, Robert Smythe, 11
Hicken, Philip, 269
Hitler, Adolf, 73–75, 91, 128
Holmes, "Bubbles," 276
Holmes, Carl, 276
Holmes, Oliver Wendell, 260
Holmes, Ralph, 115
Holt, Mrs. Robert, 129
Home Insurance Company, 149, 161, 168
Hoover, J. Edgar, 90, 164–65, 168, 169, 170

Hopkins, Henry H., 229
Horst (photographer), 140
Hôtel du Grand Cerf (Evreux), 25, 44
Hôtel La Perouse (Paris), 25
Hôtel Mirabeau (Aix-les-Bains), 25
Hôtel Mirabeau (Paris), 36
Hotel Pierre (New York), 140
Hôtel San Regis (Paris), 36
How to Marry a Millionaire (Lilly), 194
Hughes, Howard, 130–32, 134, 239, 281
Hutton, Barbara, 54, 84, 93, 112
Hutton, Marjorie Post, 85

I. F. Stone's Weekly, 248
Ida Krebs School (Lexington, Mass.), 1–4
International Flower Show (1939), 140
Intimate Strangers: The Culture of Celebrity (Schickel), 141
Irish Guards, 48
Islands Club (Nassau), 276

Jackson, John, 44, 50
James, I, King of England, 81
Jeanet, Adolph, 115
Jelke, Frazier, 102, 107
Jessel, George, 162
Johnson, Charlotte, 105, 110, 113
Johnson, Owen, 59
Johnson, Parks, 120
Johnston, "Duke," 148
Johnston, Percy, 148
Jones, Ethel, 19
Jones, Lewis, 33
Joyce, Jane, 167
Joyce, Peggy Hopkins, 138
Joyce, Robert, 167
Jungle Club (Nassau), 129, 130

Junior Assembly (New York dances), 83, 105
Junior League, 105

Kahn, E. J., Jr., 96, 157
Kara, Beta, 29
Kavanaugh, Mrs. George, 107
Keith, Lord, 103
Keith, Nancy, Lady, 103, 131, 163
Kelly, Catherine Hannon, 223
Kelly, Brenda Victoria, 150, 163, 173, 182, 183, 184, 206, 229, 239, 263, 266, 276, 279–84, 286
  on Big Brenda, 101
  birth of, 172
  on Brenda, 103, 134, 187–88, 191–92, 199–200, 216–17, 242, 256, 264, 268–69, 273
  on Brenda's psychoanalyst, 245–46, 247, 250–51
  Brenda's relationship with, 179–80, 192, 195, 216–17, 226–27, 237, 250–53, 257
  on Brenda's relationship with Chatfield-Taylor, Sr., 224–25
  on Lady Jane, 12, 65–66
  marriages of, 280, 284
  on Pietro Mele, 204–06
  Ship and Brenda's divorce and, 222–23
  on Stanley Stanwick, 268–69
Kelly, Gerald, 174, 177–79, 181, 182, 184, 193, 195, 200, 203, 206–07, 210, 213, 248–49
Kelly, John Simms ("Shipwreck"), 71, 196, 217, 229, 240, 248, 250, 252, 266, 275, 283

Kelly, John Simms
     ("Shipwreck"),
     (*continued*)
  Big Brenda's view of, 149–
     50, 151–52
  Brenda's relationship with,
     149–51, 152, 164, 181–82,
     186–88, 203, 286
  business career of, 148–49,
     161, 168, 177
  divorce from Brenda, 188,
     221–23
  at dying Brenda's bedside, 282
  education of, 147–48
  family background of, 146–47
  as FBI operative, 165–71
  football career of, 146–48
  Lady Jane and, 150, 152, 172
  marriage to Brenda, 150–88,
     191, 192
  marries Catherine Hannon, 223
  meets Brenda, 145–46, 149
  in old age, 285–87
  personality of, 146, 147–48,
     149, 187
  screenplay of, 177
  separation from Brenda, 183–
     87, 221–22
  Sir Frederick and, 150
  wedding of Brenda and, 151–57
Kelly, Richard, 146–47
Kelly, Victoria, *see* Kelly,
     Brenda Victoria
Kennedy, John F., 202, 256
Kentuckian, The (yearbook), 147
Kentucky, University of, 146–
     48
King, Archibald Gracie, 82
King, Martin Luther, Jr., 202
Kipling, Rudyard, 284
Krida, Arthur, 69

Laroche, Baroness, 72, 75
Le Coq Rouge (New York
     club), 207

Leddy, Raymond, 168, 170
Leigh, Mary Gerard, 73
Lenox Hotel (Boston), 267
LeRoy Sanitarium (New York),
     69, 163
Life magazine, 79, 94, 99–101,
     103, 118, 121, 184, 188,
     253–60, 264
Lilly, Doris, 194
Lindbergh kidnapping, 59
Livingston, Billy, 126, 129,
     132, 136, 164, 284
Lockhart, Miss (numerologist),
     60
Loeb, William, 258
Lombard, Carole, 130
London *Daily Mail*, 65, 119
Louis, Joe, 202
Luce, Henry, 101, 110, 254
Lupino, Ida, 130
Lyons, Leonard, 138

MacDonald, George, 61–62,
     153
MacGonigle, Miss (Frank
     Frazier's mistress), 35–36
Mackenzie, Don, 284
Mackey, Jacqueline, 278, 279
MacLeod, Alexander, 75, 225,
     227, 230, 264–66, 269–
     74, 277, 278
Madame Tussaud's wax
     museum (London), 48
Mailer, Fritz, 60
Majestic Hotel (Paris), 25
Malm, Clara, 39
Manchester (N.H.) *Union
     Leader*, 258
Marcello, Countess, Ida, 201,
     206, 211
Marlborough, Duchess of, 203
Maroger, Jacques, 229
Matarazzo family, 201
Maxwell, Elsa, 114, 119, 140,
     175

Mayflower Hotel (Washington, D.C.), 84
McAllister, Ward, 81–82
McCarthy, Ruth, 243, 260
McCauley, John C., Jr., 70
McGovern, George, 248
Mele, Pietro Francesco, 201–14, 218, 221, 224, 236, 252, 284–85
Mellon, Paul, 135
Men at War (ed. Hemingway), 169
Metropolitan Dancing Club (New York), 84
Metropolitan Opera (New York), 83, 106–07
Mexican Seaboard Oil Company, 23
Meyers, Jeffrey, 170
MGM (Metro-Goldwyn-Mayer), 130–31
Michael's (New York hairdresser), 60
Millay, Edna St. Vincent, 91
Milton (Pa.) *Evening Standard*, 97
Miss Chapin's Classes (New York), 83
Miss Hewitt's Classes (New York), 29, 64, 83, 226, 250
Miss May's School (Boston), 83
Miss Porter's, *see* Farmington finishing school
Mitford, Unity, 72–73
Moats, Alice-Leone, 87
Moffett, Cleveland, 14
Mohr, Celia, 240, 260, 267, 273, 275
Mohr, Jack, 260
Mongeles, Anna, 74
Monte Carlo (New York club), 89

Montreal Maternity Hospital, 20
Montreal *Sunday Herald*, 13
Moorcock, Eva, 205, 206, 226
Morden, Rev. John, 8–9, 283
Morden, Margaret, 9
Mosley, Sir Oswald, 73
Moss, Valeria, 128
Mount Vernon Hospital, 276
Mountbatten, Iris, 73
Mugar Memorial Library (Boston University), 264
Munargo (steamship), 125–26, 128
Murphy, Frank, 94
Murray, William, 208
Muse, Mary Beatty, 284
Museum of Modern Art (New York), 202

Nast, Condé, 115
National Enquirer (newspaper), 101
Navy Relief, 161, 162
Nazis, 72–75, 91, 166, 169
New York County Surrogate's Court, 62–64, 162
  see also Foley, James Aloysius
New York *Daily Mail*, 91
New York *Daily News*, 89, 102, 116, 120–21, 126, 141, 156, 210
New York *Evening Graphic*, 90
New York *Evening Journal*, 92
New York *Evening Mail*, 92
New York *Evening Post*, 91, 92
New York Giants, 146, 148
New York *Herald Tribune*, 90, 139, 147
New York Hospital, 184
New York Infirmary, 100
New York *Journal-American*, 64, 84, 92, 94, 108, 119, 152–53

New York *Mirror*, 55, 90, 108, 131

New York *Post*, 161, 194, 209

New York Times, 82, 88, 93, 118

New York University School of Medicine, 195

New York *World-Telegram*, 84, 119, 214

New Yorker, The, magazine, 91, 96, 100, 133, 193

Newsweek magazine, 252

Newton Wellesley Hospital, 276–79, 280–81

Night Club Era, The (Walker), 90

Nixon, Richard M., 248

No Bed of Roses (Fontaine), 146

No Nice Girl Swears (Moats), 87

Notre Dame University, 147

Oakes, Sir Harry, 127, 175

Ober, Gus, 142

Obolensky, Alice Astor, 197, 198

Obolensky, Catherine Bariatinska, 197

Obolensky, Serge, 197–98

O'Connell, Richard, 166

Office of Special Intelligence Services (SIS), 164, 177
  see also Federal Bureau of Investigation

Office of Strategic Services (OSS), 164

O'Higgins, Patrick, 196, 198

Olin Corporation, 220

Olympic (steamship), 13

Onassis, Aristotle, 221, 286

O'Neill, Eleanor, 235

"Open End" (television show), 259

Ostergren, Anders, 150

Osteria Bavaria (Munich), 73, 74

Otello (Verdi), 106–07

Pacaya (documentary film), 202

Page, Walter Hines, 11

Paisley, W.A., 41

Paley, Babe, 221

Paley, William, 221, 286

Palm Beach County Circuit Court, 26–28, 40–52, 54, 63

Palm Beach School for Girls, 29

Parkinnen, Rosa, 40

Paul, James, 82

Paul, Maury, 84, 88, 91–95, 99, 106–09, 116, 119, 129, 138, 152–53, 209
  see also "Cholly Knickerbocker" newspaper column

Peabody, Rachel, *see* Douglas, Rachel, Peabody

Peckham, Ted, 87

Pendleton, Jerry, 58

Perkins, Nancy, 67

Perón, Evita, 171

Perón, Juan, 171

Perona, John, 138–39, 172

Perry, Henry Pierrepont, 171

Peters, Curtis Arnoux, *see* Arno, Peter

Philadelphia Assembly (debutante ball), 83

Phyfe, Hal, 110, 154

Physician's Desk Reference, 2, 218

Picasso, Pablo, 286

Pilar (fishing boat), 169

Pion, Georges, 40

Piro, Lucinne, 176, 184, 187, 206

Piux X, Pope, 11

Plaza Hotel (New York), 171, 198
Pocahontas, 81
Pompadour, Madame de, 200
Porcupine Club (Hog Island, Bahamas), 19, 127
Porter, Mrs., 33
Porter, Cole, 116, 145, 180
Porter, Mary, 83
Porter, Sarah, 67
Portner, Irwin, 235–37
Post, Emily, 105
Princeton Tiger, The (magazine), 142
Princeton University, 142
Pryce-Jones, David, 72, 73
Pudukkotai, Ranee of, 127
Pulitzer, Herbert, 130
Pulitzer, Joseph, 130

Queen Mary (steamship), 214, 284
Quo Vadis restaurant (New York), 180

Redesdale, Lord and Lady, 73
Reilly, Katherine, 34, 42
Republican Party, 248
Reuben's restaurant (New York), 135, 229
Reynolds, Robert, 213
Rich, Helen, 129
Rickenbacker, Eddie, 286
Ritz Cookbook, The (Banino), 235
Ritz-Carlton Hotel (Boston), 132, 224, 234–37, 240, 263, 266
Ritz-Carlton Hotel (New York), 1, 21, 31, 61, 84, 94, 97, 108, 111–12, 155–57
Ritz Hotel (London), 10
River Club (New York), 112
Robbins, Richard P., 54, 63
Rogers, Millicent, 93

Rolfe, John, 81
Rooney, Mickey, 106, 277
Roosevelt, Eleanor, 118
Roosevelt, Franklin, D., 118, 164
Roosevelt, Theodore, 10
Rose, Irving, 156
Ross, Harold, 91
Ross, W. E. D., 264
Rothschild, Baron, Guy de, 221
Rothschild family, 199
Royal Society of Arts (Canada), 8
Rubinstein, Helena, 143, 196, 199
Rubirosa, Porfirio, 202–03
Runyon, Damon, 136–37
Rurik (Viking sea lord), 197

Sable in the Rain (Ross), 264
Sackville, Lady, 12
Saginaw (Mich.), *News*, 97
St. Bartholomew's Church (New York), 184
St. Cecilia's (Charleston debutante ball), 83
St. Elizabeth's Hospital, 280
St. Mark's prep school (Southboro, Mass.), 226
St. Mary's school (St. Mary's, Ky.), 147
St. Nicholas Hotel (New York), 19
St. Patrick's Cathedral (New York), 62, 110, 154
St. Regis Hotel (New York), 104, 107, 112, 194, 198, 253
St. Thomas Church (New York), 141, 180
Salm, Count Ludwig, 93
San Domenico Hotel (Taormina, Sicily), 11
San Francisco *Chronicle*, 118

Sanford, Mary, 175
Sarah Lawrence College, 253
Sarong perfume, 81, 104
Sassoon, Sir, Victor, 129
Sattler's hairdressing salon
  (New York), 105, 110
Savoy Restaurant (London), 13
Schickel, Richard, 141–42
Sea View Golf Club (New
  Jersey), 62
Selznick, David, Jr., 196
Shearer, Norma, 146
Sherry Netherland Hotel (New
  York), 112, 197, 198
Shipman, Bshp. Herbert, 19
Shor, Toots, 172
Shoreham Hotel (Washington,
  D.C.), 165
Simms, John ("Dude"), 146–
  47
Simms, Mrs. Leon, 146
Simms, Prudence, 146–47
Slater, Anne, 192–93
Smith, Jane Will, 57, 68, 71,
  102, 151, 162, 171, 178,
  183–86, 195, 203
Sobel, Lou, 138
Social Register, 114, 235
Sotheby's auction house, 284
Southampton (L.I.) Hospital,
  183
Southern Cross (yacht), 130
Spear, Ida, 115
Spellman, Francis Joseph
  Cardinal, 172, 206
Springfield, Ky., 147
Spry, Constance, 112
Stacey, George, 173
Stanish, Rudy, 135
Stanwick, Stanley, 267–69,
  274, 277, 283
State Department, U.S., 164
Steel, Drexel Biddle, 133
Stevens, George, 14, 16–17
Stevens, Helen, 16

Stewart, James, 198
Stork Club (New York), 79,
  89, 91, 96, 97, 99, 102,
  103, 125, 135–37, 139,
  145, 149, 165, 172, 173,
  177, 184, 252, 286
Sunset Lodge (Lakewood,
  N.J.), 40
Supreme Court of Florida, 52–
  53
Surrogate's Court, New York
  County, 62–64, 162
Susskind, David, 259
Sutherland, Duke of, 129

Tailer, Tommy, 154, 155
Tappe, Herman Patrick, 153
Tappin, Mrs. Huntington, 84
Tew, Mrs. William H., 84
Thackeray, William,
  Makepeace, 82
Theodore's Restaurant (New
  York), 210
Thomas, Winston, 12
Thompson, C. V. R., 139
Thompson, Dorothy, 130
Thompson, Wilson, 44
Tiffany, Charles, 153
Tiffany's (jeweler's), 153, 284
Tighe, Dixie, 116
Time magazine, 118, 138, 252
Tone, Franchot, 277
Topping, Dan, 148
Tower of London, 48
Trader, Ruth, 236
Troupin, Gladys, 267
Tunney, Capt. (detective), 41
"21" Club (New York), 285

U.S. Army, 164, 166
U.S. Navy, 164
Usher, Harry A., 41

Vallee, Rudy, 84, 133
Valz, Fred, 43–45

Vanderbilt, Cathleen, *see*
    Arostegni, Cathleen
    Vanderbilt
Vanderbilt, Cornelius, 114
Vanderbilt, Mrs. Cornelius,
    89, 107, 114, 119, 133,
    156, 228
Vanderbilt, Cornelius, Jr.,
    133
Vanderbilt, Mrs. Frederick,
    106
Vanderbilt, Gloria, 59, 65, 112,
    165
Vanderbilt, Reginald, 165
Vanguard (Brooklyn College
    newspaper), 113, 120
Vaudeville News, 90
Velvet Ball (New York), 100
Venice Film Festival (1949),
    201
Verdi, Giuseppe, 106
Vicaji, Dorothy, 140
Victoria Hotel (Nassau), 129
Vile Bodies (Waugh), 73
"Vox Pops" (radio program),
    120
Vreeland, Diana, 193, 198, 199

Wagner, Richard, 75, 154
Waldorf-Astoria Hotel (New
    York), 59, 112, 161
Walker, Stanley, 90
Wall Street Journal, 248
Warburton, Rosemarie, 107
Ward, Mrs., 19
Warren family, 88
Washington, George, 83
Waterman Funeral Home,
    282
Watriss, Brenda Germaine
    Williams-Taylor ("Big
    Brenda"), 13, 14, 67, 68–
    71, 95, 125, 126, 129,
    131, 133, 134, 141, 162,
    234

affair with Fred Watriss, 23–
    27
battles Frazier for custody of
    Brenda, 38–53
birth of, 8
and Brenda's anorexia, 194
and Brenda's debut, 76, 98–
    105, 107–14, 116, 117, 121
and Brenda's marriage to
    Ship Kelly, 149–50, 151–
    57
Brenda's relationship with, 4,
    21–22, 27–28, 31–33, 36,
    45–46, 49–52, 56, 57, 58,
    59–61, 65–66, 75–76, 97–
    98, 129, 171–73, 175, 178,
    180–81, 192, 226, 260–61
death of, 180–82
divorced from Frazier, 25–28
family background of, 7–8
and father, 17
and Frazier trusts, 36–38,
    54–55, 62–64, 111, 162
marriage to Frank Frazier,
    17–26, 57–58
marriage to Fred Watriss, 28,
    31, 32–34, 40–42, 57–58,
    62, 75, 162
marriage to Henry Perry, 171
and mother, 9, 11–12, 31,
    56, 57, 58, 172
personality of, 11, 17, 20–21,
    32–34, 56–60
presented to English royalty,
    10–11
Watriss, Frederic, Jr., 24, 25,
    28, 47, 48, 57–58, 114,
    224, 237
Watriss, Frederic, Sr., 55, 57,
    62, 64, 69, 97, 150
affair with Big Brenda, 23–27
and Brenda, 58
and custody battle for
    Brenda, 38–39, 40–44, 45,
    46, 48, 49

Watriss, Frederick, Sr.,
(*continued*)
death of, 75
marriage to Big Brenda, 28,
30–31, 33, 40, 57–58, 62,
162
meets Big Brenda, 23–24
Watriss, James, 9, 23–24, 28,
33, 36, 48, 58, 62, 131,
220, 224, 237, 266
Watson, John B., 31
Watt, Dr., 162
Waugh, Evelyn, 73
Weaver, Mrs. John, 72
Webb, G. Creighton, 156
Wecter, Dixon, 81, 88
Weinraub, Bernard, 243,
249
Weldon, Tommy, 66–67, 69–
71
Wellesley, College, 253
Westbury Hotel (New York),
178, 193
Wetherill, Fernanda
Wanamaker, 259
Wharton, Edith, 11
Whitney, Jock, 186, 221, 285
Whitney, Mrs. Payne, 97
Who Killed Society? (Amory),
80–81
Who's Who, 235
Wideman, Frank, 26–27
Widener family, 88
Wilde, Oscar, 11
Williams, Francis, 183, 186
Williams-Taylor, Brenda
Germaine, *see* Watriss,
Brenda Germaine
Williams-Taylor
Williams-Taylor, Sir Frederick,
7–14, 20, 24–25, 43, 61,
64, 71, 127, 128, 153
in Bahamas, 127–28
banking career of, 7–9, 13
death of, 182

and Frank Frazier, 18–19,
40–41, 46–47
and granddaughter Brenda,
40–41, 46–47, 51
knighted, 12
personality of, 7–8, 128
relationship with Lady Jane,
8–9, 16, 24
and Ship Kelly, 150
Williams-Taylor, Lady Jane Fayrer
Henshaw, 7–14, 15–16, 20,
24, 25, 30, 46–47, 71, 111,
115, 153–54, 182
affair with George Stevens,
14, 16–17
Bahamian social life of, 127–
28
birth of children of, 8
and daughter Brenda's
divorce from Frank
Frazier, 41–43, 51
death of, 192
drug use by, 176
family history of, 7
and George MacDonald, 61–
62
and granddaughter Brenda,
4, 31–32, 41, 50, 51, 64–
66, 76, 129, 152, 157,
172–73, 175, 176, 182–83,
260
marries Sir Frederick, 8
personality of, 7–12, 12–14,
50, 57–66
pre-World World I social life,
9–14
relationship with daughter
Brenda, 9, 11–12, 31–32,
57, 58, 172
relationship with Sir
Frederick, 8–9, 16, 24
and Ship Kelly, 150, 152,
172
Williams-Taylor, Travers
("Felix"), 8, 14, 182

Wilson, Earl, 161–62
Wilson, Fritz, 66
Wilson, Harry, 125, 126
Wilson, Woodrow, 11
Winburn, Jay Te, 116, 119
Winchell, Walter, 90–93, 99,
    135, 137, 138, 145, 286
Windsor, Duchess of, 112, 164,
    174, 175
Windsor, Duke of, 112, 139,
    164, 174, 221, 286
  as Prince of Wales, 48, 85,
    89
Windsor Castle (England), 10,
    48, 75
Windsor School (Boston), 83
Winston, Harry, 197, 210
Woodward, Ann, 174

Woodward, William, 174
Wright, Cobina, junior, 29–30,
    59–60, 142
Wright, Cobina, senior (Elaine
    Cobb), 29–30, 59
Wright, William May, 59
Wyner, Edward, 235

Yale Law School, 165, 258
Yale University, 15, 24, 34,
    54–55, 56, 96, 125, 133,
    219
Young, Eleanor, ("Cookie"),
    93, 157
Young, Robert R., 93

Zerbe, Jerome, 102, 138, 146
Zuccotti, Angelo, 135